The Endless Text

SUNY Series,
The Margins of Literature

Mihai I. Spariosu, editor

The
Endless
Text

**Don Quixote
and the
Hermeneutics of Romance**

Edward Dudley

STATE UNIVERSITY OF NEW YORK PRESS

The triple spiral on the front cover and interior design is a
rubbing from the passage grave at New Grange,
County Meath, Ireland.

Production by Ruth Fisher
Marketing by Patrick Durocher

Published by
State University of New York Press, Albany

For information, address the State University of New York Press,
State University Plaza, Albany, NY 12246

Library of Congress Cataloging-in-Publication Data
Dudley, Edward J.
    The endless text : Don Quixote and the hermeneutics of romance /
Edward Dudley.
        p.   cm.—(SUNY series, the margins of literature)
    Includes bibliographical references and index.
    ISBN 0-7914-3525-3 (HC : alk. paper).—ISBN 0-7914-3526-1 (PB :
alk. paper)
    1. Literature, Medieval—History and criticism.   2. Romances—
History and criticism.   3. Cervantes Saavedra, Miguel de,
1547–1616.   Don Quixote.   I. Title.   II. Series.
PN671.D83   1997
809.3'9355—dc21   96-52143
                                                             CIP

10 9 8 7 6 5 4 3 2 1

For my wife

CONTENTS

Acknowledgments

Karen Blixen once said that she could not have lived without Shakespeare. Anyone who speaks, thinks, or studies in Spanish could say the same thing about Cervantes. He simply made language and existence a different arrangement of possibilities for the people of Spain, Europe, and the Americas. In the very minor case of the present study I can only say he taught me that the shape of our inner lives is vastly different from the actualities of daily life. Thus in the question of gratitude due to all the friends, colleagues, and students in Spanish and Comparative Literature who have contributed to this book there would be another endless text. Nevertheless a few pressing contributions come to mind: a course from Enrique Andersen-Imbert on what is now called "metatheater" (probably any class from Andersen would be a type of metatheater in itself); a special focus on Cervantes' use of the interpolated tales in a course from Karl-Ludwig Selig (and life in itself is an interpolation); the presence and teachings of Krausismo from Walter Pattison, a maestro who lived what he taught. Thanks and apologies to all my colleagues and students at my various academic incarnations including UCLA, the University of Pittsburgh and SUNY at Buffalo.

Nothing can cover my endless debt to readings of all kinds, especially in the world of Cervantismo. Particular occasions also helped formulate this study. There was first a long and supportive talk with Javier Herrero. Then, a special session at the University of Cincinnati Conference a few years ago and a small postperformance luncheon with Ruth El Saffar, Diana de Armas Wilson, and Frederick de Armas. It was there over a magical bottle of Verdicchio that I made an initial presentation of the hermeneutics of Romance. The occasion was memorable for me at the time, and it became even more so only a few years later when we could

no longer consult with Ruth. An important opportunity to read the segment "The Story of the Name and the Name of the Story" in a graduate
seminar of Ciriaco Moron Arroyo at Cornell University provided much
needed input on the topic. An impressive resonance was generated by a
public lecture presented to an amazing audience at Trinity College in the
University of Dublin, an encounter made possible by Victor Dixon. Again
it provided a chance to test out some Celtic interpretations on the home
turf so to speak. Both Doris Vidaver and Howard Wescott have been
friends of the heart as well as the text from its inception.

Thanks also to the people at SUNY Press, including James Peltz and
Carol Newhouse. Special mention is due to Production Editor Ruth Fisher
for the care and insight so freely dispensed.

In the immediate environment I have found that my sons, John and
David Dudley, have ushered me into the twenty-first century of com-
puter mysteries, as well as into other aspects of current phenomenologi-
cal concerns. Ultimately, however, my wife, Patricia, has inspired,
sustained, and helped shape whatever is of value in this study.

A Prolegomenon for Romance

In the Beginning
There Was Trouble with the Word

I n the ninth-century fragment "How the *Táin Bó Cuailnge* Was Found Again" a narrator sets forth what comes to be the fundamental storytelling situation of Romance.[1] This anecdotal shard, rescued from oblivion by scribal chance, ritually delineates an archaic spectrum of narrational and linguistic anxieties that precedes the tale. With this brief particle, the unknown narrator has already articulated the curiously disjunctive components of what we now recognize as the discourse of Romance.

The features of this storytelling arrangement are found in tales of Romance even to our own day: the story to be told is more ancient than human memory can reach, and its recovery is itself an Otherworld adventure for the storyteller. Rather than an epic invocation of the muse, the storywriting task is presented as an encounter, not without peril, with the Indo-Celtic idea of Truth as the ordering force of the universe (Dillon 103). This primal energy, the most supreme of all powers, can be tapped only by the shamanistic rituals of the Druid/poet, whose role is to recover and reveal the most important of all stories. The value of this story is that it underwrites the entire meaning of human life and society. We find here an example of the belief that the function of sacred narrative is, not to *explain*, as it would have in later cultural configurations, but to *perform* this Truth. In this kind of narrative act the storyteller accomplishes a necessary spiritual benefit for society as a whole. Likewise, to hear the story, like the later *oír misa* (hearing Mass) of the Spanish, was equally beneficial to the listeners and allowed them to participate in a power that sustained the universe and all life within it.

We might look at this performance today as an effort of early humans to create the possibility of meaning in a universe that operated according to unfathomable patterns. The desire to understand such a mysterious cosmos seems not to have been an important part of the game. Rather, the function of the story can be seen as a way of coming to terms with the unknowable, capricious, and often threatening forces encountered in human experience. In this sense, the story strikes a profound accord with the similar experiential situation that confronts us today after the collapse of

---

1. In capitalizing Romance I am establishing a term that refers to an entire discourse and not just to the various genres of romance, such as chivalric, pastoral, Greek. In addition, it is important to recognize that Romance in this sense refers to an informing force that underlies many kinds of stories whether in drama, poetry, opera, film, television or other visual arts. It represents a view of life that provides or attempts to provide a sense of meaning to the shape of human events. Explication of the full nature of such a discourse is the basic purpose of this book.

the logocentric, humanistic aspirations that have motivated the Western world since the twelfth century. The fragment even seems to anticipate a Heideggerian postmodernism in which the possibility of language, however unstable, is our only means of confronting an un-understandable external reality. This language does not seek to reflect that reality but rather to create a useful story that allows the individual to cope.

Such a story reveals what we find to be one of the most enduring features of later Romance: the attempted recovery of forgotten modes of knowing and systems of signification. For us this kind of phenomenon is removed to the category of aesthetic experience, but for earlier writers and listeners it belonged to the realm of a hierological participation in an un-understandable power, and something of that occult force still haunts the passageways of Romance today.

Since this cultural incipit is brief, it can stand here as a guidepost for our own study of Romance. We should consider this story as a locus where the "possibility of meaning" takes place, or as a narrative ritual that performs the all important function of authorizing a language, however fallible, that makes life a sustainable experience:

> The poets of Ireland one day were gathered around Senchan Torpeist, to see if they could recall the "Táin Bó Cuailnge" in its entirety. But they all said they knew only parts of it. Senchan asked which of his pupils, in return for his blessing, would travel to the land of Letha to learn the version of the Táin that a certain sage took eastward with him in exchange for the book Cuilmenn. Emine, Ninene's grandson, set out for the east with Senchan's son Muirgen. It happened that the grave of Fergus mac Roich was on their way. They came upon the gravestone at Enloch in Connacht. Muirgen sat down at Fergus's gravestone, and the others left him for a while and went looking for a house for the night. Muirgen chanted a poem to the gravestone as though it were Fergus himself. He said to it:

> > "If this your royal rock
> > were your own self mac Roich
> > halted here with sages
> > searching for a roof
> > 'Cuailnge' we'd recover,
> > plain and perfect Fergus."

A great mist suddenly formed around him—for the space of three days and nights he could not be found. And the figure of Fergus approached him in fierce majesty, with a head of brown hair, in a green cloak and a red-embroidered hooded tunic, with gold-hilted sword and bronze blunt sandals. Fergus recited him the whole Táin, and how everything had happened, from start to finish. Then they went back to Senchan with their story, and he rejoiced over it.

However, there are some who say that the story was told to Senchan himself after he had gone on a fast to certain saints of the seed of Fergus. This seems reasonable. (Kinsella 1–2)

Even for the modern reader this passage has an evocative force, recalling a forgotten but still powerful emblematic energy. At the same time it is suggestive of later masters of Romance, like Chrétien and Cervantes, who prefaced their tales with similar prolegomena. In this context a few hermeneutic comments will help orient the reader to anticipate the course of the present study.

First we must recognize that the prestige of Druid poets in Celtic society cannot be overestimated. Their word preceded that of kings, and their function was precisely to perform these enabling stories, narratives that sustained the universe and Celtic societal structures. The *Táin* story is obviously phyletic and crucial to this culture. The sage who returned to the east, where the Celts themselves came from, perhaps as far east as the Indo-Aryans of India, is a figure who still inhabits the originary navel of the world. The exchange of the *Táin* for the book Cuilmenn (the *Etymologies* of Isidore of Seville) suggests a fatal error in trading divine knowledge for mere human information, however prestigious. This detail reveals the narrator's rejection of a mundane knowledge for a wisdom now in danger of being lost. This same attitude survives in Chrétien's prologue to *Yvain* where the narrator champions the "old wisdom" over the new. More surprisingly, a coincident ethos can be uncovered beneath Don Quixote's chivalric vision.

Senchan's blessing is of course the beneficent power of language, as opposed to a curse, the most feared of all linguistic acts in Celtic culture. Muirgen's name contains the Gaelic etymon *muir* meaning sea, a locus for hidden knowledge that reappears in the fish and pearl imagery of the grail and in the ritual meal Don Quixote has at the first inn (1: 2). The

gravestone as the substitution for the persona of the hero and narrator
Fergus is an instance of the virtue of sacred stones, such as those found
in numerous stone circles along the Atlantic littoral from Ireland to Spain.
A residual belief in the curative powers of the megaliths at Stonehenge,
for instance, still survives. In the scribal fragment, the poem recited at the
gravestone is the linguistic key of access to the desired knowledge. The
Otherworld mist, that survives in Chrétien's Joy of the Court episode in
Erec and Eneid, is an Otherworld sign for the scribe's recovery of the lost
manuscript, part of what Northrop Frye calls the "descent to knowledge." Mists are scarce in Don Quixote's Spain, but other features (such
as the knight's cave of Montesinos adventure, which plays off Aeneas's
descent to the underworld) can perform this same function. Likewise the
strange darkness surrounding the watermill in chapter 20 of part 1 is an
emblematic signal announcing the hero's confrontation with an Otherworld force.

Muirgen's absence for three days is a clear another sign of his visit to
the Otherworld, and the Druid's three day absence may predate the
scriptural account of Jesus's descent into hell. Fergus's "fierce majesty"
and green and red tunic mark him as some sort of deity armed with all
his powers and thus a suitable source of divine knowledge.

Finally the narrator's subversive editorial commentary about another
recovery story being equally valid forestalls the possibility of any privileged logocentrism. There can never be a definitive text. We are not even
told whether the version recovered by Muirgen is identical to the version
carried off to the land of Letha by a mysterious sage. This lack of a
definitive or originating text for the story is an important feature that
Cide Hamete plays with at several points in his editorial practices, most
notably in his account of the knight's paradigmatic Otherworld *aventura*
with the windmill. In both the *Táin* and the *Quixote* the narrator's citing
of the existence of a variant account precludes the eventuality of closure.

Most important of all this is what can be termed the narrator's encounter with the story as his own Otherworld *aventura*, one that empowers him
with the same majesty that surrounds his hero, whether that be CuChulainn,
Perceval, or Don Quixote. This equation of the majesty of language with
that of arms energizes the boasting of the narrator in the prologue to *Li
Contes del Graal* where Chrétien promises to tell the best of all tales for the
best of all patrons in the best of all courts. The competition between hero
and narrator also survives in the arms and letters debates of the *Quixote*
as well as in Cide Hamete's self-promotion at the end of part 2.

As prolegomenon, the story of the recovery of the *Táin* situates the narrator as the transcriber of a pre-told tale whose value pre-empts all earthly discourse. This kind of language is the necessary precondition for the possibility of Romance, and the storytellers must come to terms with the imperative in their own ways. A telling sign of a Romance is the narrator coming upon a forgotten story, often related in a sacred language no longer accessible to mere mortals. His re-inscription of the text often includes editorial commentary about the validity of "other" versions. In one instance, the *Táin* narrator includes two versions of the same episode. This narrative arrangement of authorial incompetence becomes a literary convention in both Chrétien and Cervantes where the narrator, like Muirgen, doesn't quite understand the inherited story. As a result of this authorizing insecurity, Chrétien's narrator generally exhibits a logocentric hubris about the story's meaning, while Cide Hamete is deceptively ironic.

In various ways this same linguistic feature survives throughout the history of Romance. In Hawthorne's *Scarlet Letter*, for instance, it is Hester's offending letter itself that functions as an Otherworld hieroglyph empowering both narrator and heroine. The narrator's discovery of the lost story in the attic of the Custom House and his subsequent encounter with the dead Surveyor Pue offers a remarkably close parallel to Muirgen's meeting with the dead Fergus. In both instances the ghost narrator "authorizes" the scattered fragments of the story but the actual narrator does not fully understand the meaning of the text. This uneven authorial insecurity persists in various way in twentieth century texts. A narrator like Conrad's Marlow, whose authority is delimited by the comments of another narrator in both *Lord Jim* and *Heart of Darkness,* nevertheless has strange access to parts of the story he himself does not witness. Other more complex narrative arrangements can be found in current Spanish American novels like García Márquez's *One Hundred Years of Solitude,* where the narrator cites ancestral sources for the story.

In film literature this feature may simply be the unexplained presence of the camera itself as an all-powerful signifier or as the similarly unexplained insertion of the written intertitles in silent film. Intertitles even survive into talking films, as in *Gone With The Wind,* but are more often transformed into the voice-over or, more obviously, into the traditional storyteller, as in *Lost Horizon* or in the confessional voice of the film noir detective in *The Maltese Falcon* or *Double Indemnity.* Frequently this feature may also appear at the end of a film, where it takes the form of the final fade-out of the hero walking away from the camera, as in *Casablanca*. These Romance gestures remind the viewer that he or she has been privileged to participate in a story of singular power.

In this way the hermeneutics of Romance reach us today as a kind of rhetorical residue surviving from a more empowered discourse that still lies hidden in the stories from Chrétien to Cervantes to Conrad and García Márquez. The present study will concentrate on revealing how the traditional rhetoric of Romance functions in the *Quixote* to provide the text with its multiple and unending appeal.

One

The Endless Text

In this connection there is a story from the Wichita . . . which is full of significance. It tells of a contest between Coyote and an opponent as to which knew most, i.e., which knew more stories. The contest takes place at night, and the two opponents, sitting beside the fire, tell each a story in turn. Coyote's opponent begins to show signs of fatigue, and is slower and slower at finding a new tale . . . At last the opponent owns himself beaten, and is killed.

Raffaelle Pettazzoni, *Sacred Narrative*

"I Read; Therefore I Am": The Romance Discourse of Celtic Storytellers, Chrétien de Troyes and Cervantes

"- ¿No han leído vuestras mercedes—respondió don Quijote—los anales e historias de Ingalaterra donde se tratan las famosas fazañas del rey Arturo . . . ?" (1.13). " 'Haven't you *read*,' responded Don Quixote, 'the annals and histories of England where the famous deeds of King Arthur are recounted . . . ?' " This response of Don Quixote to a question about what being a knight errant meant is quite appropriately framed within the problematics of reading. And what is *Don Quixote* about but the problem of reading and in a larger sense about a history of reading?

1

For both the general reader and the academic specialist, Don Quixote's question about reading Romances grounds the ontological challenge of how-to-be and the epistemological problem of how-to-know within the parameters of the language of Romance. These considerations constitute the paradigm of Romance as the metaphor for all narrative and for any problem of reading. By extension *Don Quixote* becomes the story of stories, the supreme metatext of the Renaissance, in which a dismaying plethora of questions about the nature of language and the nature of knowing are narratized. Don Quixote himself becomes the *figura* of the dilemma of how-to-be in a world in which new modes of knowing have subverted the traditional epistemological arrangements. The emergence of the novel as a new kind of story can be seen therefore as an answer to a specific challenge, and *Don Quixote* becomes a response to the questions that the new science posed about the possibilities of knowing, a conundrum narratized by the story of the "Curioso impertinente."

In the same way, for Don Quixote to begin a disquisition about reading the stories of King Arthur, the knights of the Round Table, and the loves of Lanzarote del lago with a question is also an appropriate rhetorical strategy when addressing the topic of Romance. The aptness of Don Quixote's question about reading can be discovered within the chivalric Romances themselves. As a literary kind, Romance presents more questions about the reader's ability to interpret than what is found in other modes of writing, and the problem of how the reader reads the story is part and parcel of the storytelling process. Reading is thus inscribed within the rhetoric of the text itself. Therefore we find that in both the multiple grail Romances themselves, as well as in the modern scholarly studies, the problem of interpreting the grail has been a central concern. This has created two kinds of discourse directed at solving a single problem. In this way both ancient fictions and modern critical studies, each with its own mode of analysis, search for the meaning of the grail. From its origins, Romance has been a discourse capable of self-reflection and self-criticism, a factor which partially accounts for its newfound vogue among both postmodern writers and the posthumanistic critical establishment.

For the contemporary reader the particular challenge of reading Romance is even more difficult, since for us the reader's ability to "read" Romance has been conditioned by a long tradition of privileging realistic stories over earlier forms of fiction. One disturbing result of this critical tradition has been the tendency of modern critics to consider Romance as a "primitive" narrative form that was rendered obsolete by the development of the realistic novel, just as myth is now viewed as an imperfect form of science. Thus Romance seems to belong to the prerationalistic view of the world that was left behind by the seventeenth-century formulation of the scientific method.

The subversive strength of this kind of negative hermeneutic can already been seen at work in the *Quixote* where it inhabits the problem of viewing the hero as mad. In fact if the old chivalric Romances are not found as the critics claimed to be "false and deceiving" rather than "true," then the belief that the hero is crazy is itself in peril. It is suitable that the *Quixote* appear in the opening years of the seventeenth century precisely because its publication coincides with the development of the belief that the new scientific methodologies were the only reliable measure of an external reality. As a result Romance is seen as a kind of writing that is deceptive and dangerous. Such an attitude is reinforced for us today by the unquestioned belief that Romance seems to survive only in a "degraded and deprivileged discourse" found on the women's reading shelves of the drugstore. As in the twelfth century, Romance is relegated to a separate and unequal world of women and therefore is beneath the consideration of the (masculine) critical establishment. Now, as then, Romance is not seen as "serious" writing in part because it belongs to a deliberately distorted view of women.

Furthermore, it is a commonplace of this serious masculine critical enterprise that in fact Cervantes replaced the fashion for Romance with the fashion for the realistic novel. That this change was a broader revolution in ways of reading is not so commonly recognized, even though this hermeneutic phenomenon is fictionalized for the reader by the *Quixote* itself. There, the source of narrative action, the cause of the hero's adventures, always finds its origin in the problem of how to read. At first sight we seem to have a story about a protagonist who doesn't know how to interpret the old books of chivalry, and the hero's madness is presented as a hermeneutic dislocation. However, the failure to see that the narrator's interpretation of the hero's madness is also part of the fiction produced by the text, and not a valid external view that the reader must accept, has been a common critical error. This misconception has led to a lengthy debate about the validity of the old *libros de caballería* as well as to the confusion about the question of whether Don Quixote is a hero of a Romance. The time has come, however, to recognize that these debates are already inscribed within the fiction of the text itself. Therefore scholarly disputes about such matters are merely continuations of fictions within the story. They are not issues external to the text.

This kind of confusion can be clarified if we recognize that the problems of hermeneutic viability are not restricted to the question of the hidalgo's "madness" but rather that they find their true genesis in the writing strategies of the narrator. Since his storytelling procedure, the scene of writing within the text, is presented as dependent upon his interpreting an undefined collection of source documents, the narrator's first action is also the first hermeneutic event. In such an arrangement we realize that the narrator's act of reading the source documents precedes his writing effort and thereby deprivileges the objectivity of his storytelling agenda. It is the problematics of this kind of narrative authority that calls for an examination of the hermeneutics of Romance, whether in Celtic tales, in the medieval Matter of Britain, or in *Don Quixote*.

Arthurian and "Other" Stories

When in the fourteenth century Charles VI, the young king of France, was advised about his reading habits he was told to pay much attention to the Romances concerning his ancestor Charlemagne but to avoid spending too much time reading about Arthur because the stories contained excessive amounts of "empty fables." At an even earlier date, in the closing years of the twelfth century, the author of the *Chanson des Saisnes*, divided up the current literary materials of Romance into three categories: "de France, de Bretagne et de Rome le grant" (Keen 114). Of these he recommended the stories about Charlemagne and the Romans because of their veracity and instructive value but observed that the matter of Britain was mostly "vain and pleasing." Thus from a very early time we have evidence that some readers clearly distinguished a fundamental difference that separated the "matter of Britain" from the competing matters of Charlemagne and Rome.

One distinction was certainly implicit in the advice to the young king: as a ruler of men he must give special attention to "serious" topics. Vain and pleasing fables might be all right for women, since they had no power and legally did not exist, but such matters were subversive to the roles of kings and leaders of men. In spite of the advice, however, it is likely that Charles VI ignored the warning, and it is obvious that most everyone else did too, since today the stories of Arthur and Guinevere and Lancelot survive in the popular culture of novels, film, musical comedy, television, and comic strips, while the other two "matters" are seldom found outside the domain of graduate studies.

However, the two comments cited above are instructive of a basic truth that was very important for the culture of the late Middle Ages. The matters of Charlemagne and of "Rome le grant" did for the most part deal with historical events, whatever amount of legendary material they carried along. In fact it was their weakness in the area of their "historicity" that finally undid their popularity, since later research quickly revealed their faulty knowledge of the subject matter. The fact that no such problem beset the Arthurian tales, however, is not just a question of the status of historical studies then or now. The more fundamental difference is that the Arthurian tales for the most part do not deal with history at all. Thus we have to look elsewhere for the enduring power of the Arthurian matter. We know now that in their origins the narratives derived from a large store of Celtic tales, both Irish and Welsh, that became available in the twelfth century to writers of French, such as Chrétien de Troyes and Marie de France. Of particular importance to the Arthurian romancers were two specific genres of Celtic tales, the *echtrai* (adventures) and the *immrama* (voyages) (Dillon and Chadwick 240–241, Lida de Malkiel 265 ff). More than other Gaelic tales these genres deal with situations in which the heroes and heroines have encounters with figures of the Otherworld. They are stories in which the special ontology of the protagonist is due to a fated encounter with the gods and goddesses, involvements from which the protagonist in some way or other cannot return to his or her original identity. The meeting in this sense is both fated and fatal, and the everyday world for the hero is forever changed and inaccessible. We recognize that this basic focus carries with it an essential feeling of adventure and loss that we associate with Romance. The linguistic link to this is found in the word *echtra*, the Gaelic word that Myles Dillon has shown to be the ultimate source for the romance term *aventure* with its Otherworld connotations, (Dillon and Chadwick 145) a meaning that survives in Chrétien and later writers, including Cervantes.

So it has been noted that Arthur, in the stories that have gathered around his name, spends very little time fighting historical forces or figures. Rather he and most of his knights are engaged with individual struggles involving forces of the Otherworld, whether they be giants or enemy enchanters. The Romance knight is the high hero of Western individualism; he is not a member of an organized fighting troop. In fact, many of the knights of the Round Table are in themselves disguised deities who take the form of euhumerized heroes like Lancelot and Galahad (Darrah 38–46, 75). It is worth recalling that Lancelot originally had nothing to do with Arthur or his court. He was the hero of another cycle of stories, just as Tristan was, and only later did these stories come to rest within the more powerful orbit of Arthurian tales. The fact that Lancelot, unlike Arthur, was originally a god also tells us something about Don Quixote's choice of role model, a problem to which we will return.

In addition to noting the distinction between history and fable that these early commentaries point up, we can suspect that two other problematic attitudes were also involved. They are the high valorization role of reason as a cultural artifact and the marginalized role of women within the hierarchal workings of a society of clerics and warriors. Since these two groups, both exclusively male, shared and competed for the direction of the society as a whole, certain attitudes came to the fore which inevitably effected the channels in which gender roles were segregated. Both of these topics are addressed by R. W. Southern's book *The Making of the Middle Ages* in such a way as to clarify the symbiotic workings of ideas about women and reason. In discussing the role of law in the formation of the idea of liberty Southern makes the following point concerning both women and reason:

Liberty is a creation of law, and *law is reason in action*; it is *reason which makes men ends in themselves.* Tyranny, whether of King John or of the Devil, is a manifestation of the absence of law. The man who lives outside the law, whether under the rule of his own will or that of another, is bound by the iron chains of servitude. The gossiping Franciscan chronicler of the thirteenth century, Salimbene, distinguished five kinds of rule by which a man was disgraced: *the rule of women*, of serfs, *of fools*, of boys and of enemies. The common feature of all these forms of tyranny was lack of law; *they were destructive of the rational order.* The inclusion of women in this list deserves notice, because it emphasizes the point *that rule over free men should be rational.* In practice of course women often exercised rule, and sometimes with conspicuous success. But equally in the theological and chivalric conceptions of the time, woman stood for that which was either below or above reason: woman, in the person of Eve, was the agent by which sin came into the world, and, in the person of the Virgin, the agent by which Salvation came; in courtly literature, women stood at once for that which was below reason—*caprice*—and for a higher principle than reason—*love*. But liberty, at least in this world's affairs, was a product of *the masculine quality of reason*, as expressed in law. (109, emphasis added)

Much of this has now passed into the common fund of feminist analysis but it remains freshly relevant to the matter of the status of Romance as a literary kind. For instance, we now can detect a component of anti-feminism in the advice given to the young Charles VI. A king must not be under the rule of women or of fable, for in both these categories he is not a *rational* man, and by implication not a man at all in the legal structure of the society he hopes to rule. Thus, Arthurian romance, like women, is disenfranchised, while the history with its concern for the affairs of this world is not. Hence both fiction and women are of little concern in the affairs of men. This belief that Arthurian stories are contaminated with matters of women and the Otherworld is to have serious consequences for the status of literature in a society increasingly committed to privileging the rational male order. By the time of Cervantes the issue of the role of women and fiction reaches a second stage of conflictive intensity. The new science that challenges the old order, with its civilizing rules of chivalry, is even more fiercely "masculine" and rational. Only "rational" men are functionally men at all, and mad, aging knights belong to the vanishing order of the Arthurian world and the Old Wisdom with its concern for irrational love and dealings with enchantment. The division between this inner world of feeling and intuition projected onto the image of woman and the "serious" affairs of a male society is final. Such a distinction is already clear for the author of the *Chanson de Saisnes*, who affirms that his writings are more important because they do not concern "vain and pleasing" matters, which for him signify fictions already relegated to the world of women. Thus by the seventeenth century it is not surprising that the tone of suspicion toward fiction is even stronger in many of the comments of Cide Hamete. At the same time Don Quixote is clearly mad because his valorizations of literary genres does not conform with those his narrator professes nor with those of the age in which he sees himself imprisoned.

The total effect of these early commentaries, however, provides us with four significant characteristics that constituted Arthurian literature:

1. it concerns a hero or heroine in conflict with the forces of the Otherworld,

2. it is constituted as fiction or fable not history,

3. it displays a suspect attitude toward the value of reason,

4. it places women in roles which subvert the authority of a male society of clerics and warriors.

All of these points deserve fuller analysis but their importance here is that they receive precisely that kind of attention in the text of *Don Quixote*. For the moment, however, we will concentrate on the importance of the textual problems inherent in the transmission of this Arthurian material from its Celtic origins to the time of Cervantes, because the manner of transmission becomes a feature of Romance as a literary discourse.

The Trouble with Texts
and the Blindness of Institutional Readings

The advice to the young monarch cited above reveals another attitude which has an even broader importance for a study of *Don Quixote*. We note that the problem of the valorization of Arthurian narratives was not that the historicity of Arthur himself was doubted but that other material, nonhistorical in nature, had been added to the texts. Empty fables had corrupted the stories, matters that concerned giants and enchantments clearly did not belong to the world of the reasonable men who ran the affairs of state. Such things were purely "vain and pleasing" tales, fit for women and idle, suspect men, men not seriously concerned with practical matters. Cide Hamete, although he too has a subversive side to him, displays similar attitudes, and in fact on the surface of it Don Quixote himself also argues that the *libros de caballería* are important because they deal with history and not fiction. Initially, however, the narrator and the hero seem to disagree only on the matter of hermeneutics. What is also at issue is the condition of the texts themselves. Already, from the point of view of the fourteenth century, they are clearly corrupted. "Alien" material has been added which renders them suspect. This problem of course was not confined to Arthurian texts alone but was a genuine concern to both clerics and rulers who sought the lessons of history.

By the time of Cervantes both textual and hermeneutic problems were in a major state of cultural crisis. The concern of Renaissance humanism with accurate texts had inflamed the question of the status of biblical accounts, and tremendous institutional resources, both Catholic and Protestant, were poured into the effort to recover a reliable biblical text. The indefatigable Cardinal Cisneros, Isabel the Catholic's confessor, initiated the tremendous project of the Complutensian Polyglot Bible, published from 1514 to 1517. Given the death and life issue of textual purity, every bit as lethal a challenge as the issue of purity of the blood, it is curious that the Inquisition showed no particular sensitivity to the subversive challenge that *Don Quixote* presents to the problem of textual reliability and authority. No doubt this threat was not perceived because of the apparent generic orientation of *Don Quixote* as a work of comic fiction. This horizon of expectations constricted the hermeneutic foreknowledge with which readers approached the task of reading of the story (Gadamer 235–67). This kind of hermeneutic blindness must have obtained even though it could be argued very reasonably that the task of Cide Hamete, as it is constituted in the work, is a parody of the humanistic editorial practices of the era as they influenced the editing of both secular and canonical texts. Actually the Protestant north should have been even more upset, but, to my knowledge, no one at the time noted any connection. The popularity of the book was unhampered by any of these considerations, and the inquisitorial *aprobación* of part 2 goes so far as to recommend the reading of the book as a healthy pastime. So much for the insights of institutional reading when confronted with the power of genre. If Cervantes himself wrote the *aprobación* he was skillfully protecting himself by placing his work safely outside the hermeneutic anxieties of the Inquisition.

Yet in spite of this blindness, both the prevailing institutional specialists and the general reading public were highly sensitized to the problems of reading corrupted texts. Medieval manuscript traditions had undoubtedly been more reliable than those of the new printing establishments, but everyone knew that all written materials contained a vast range of errors. On a more sophisticated level both church and state authorities were obsessed with the problem of how religious texts were read. People were put to death for what was considered a "misreading" of the Old Testament, the New Testament, or even of St. Augustine, St. Thomas, or other sensitive texts. Sir Thomas More stands as the paradigmatic victim of what price was to be paid for "deviant" hermeneutic practices, practices clearly narratized in *Don Quixote*. One can also assume that hidden beneath the book's meteoric rise to popularity was the fact that the comic power of the work functioned to release deep reserves of reading anxieties. In any case, the work illustrates a persistent concern with reliable and unreliable texts and with the matter of how written texts should he interpreted. The two questions of textual purity and hermeneutic differences stand as the basic issues motivating the entire story of the hidalgo.

The history of the rise of institutional hermeneutics has been traced by Hans-Georg Gadamer in *Truth and Method*, a work that itself helps institutionalize the co-opting of hermeneutics by the philosophical establishment (153–234). The consequences of this heady mix of interpretation and philosophy are already inscribed on the reading problems narratized within *Don Quixote* and can be seen in an overview of the stormy history of the book's reception both inside and outside the academy. Both Anthony Close and Robert Flores have documented key aspects of the work's interpretive history.

To begin, however, it will be useful to look at some recent analyses of the interpretive problematics of other texts with long histories of manuscript corruption and hermeneutic disputes as well as at more modern texts that in some way replicate these issues. A study that addresses these concerns in regard to both sacred and secular narrative is Frank Kermode's *Genesis of Secrecy: On the Interpretation of Narrative*. Kermode's analysis has the advantage of considering the same problems of interpretation as they apply to two texts, both of which bear important similarities to *Don Quixote:* the Gospel of Mark and James Joyce's *Ulysses*.

The affinities found in these three works are all fortuitous, or at least I will treat them as fortuitous. This approach is safest in spite of the fact that it can be argued that Cervantes certainly knew, if only from childhood attendance at mass, the Gospel of Mark, and I suppose at some time Joyce read at least part of *Don Quixote,* or, if he didn't, the culture of the modern narrative was too deeply steeped with Cervantine problematics for him to have been innocent of them. In fact the Mark text is already embedded in many hermeneutic and narrative features that reach forward in time to both Cervantes and Joyce. This view assumes the generalized existence of a continuum containing specific narrative strategies found within a very long but unbroken storytelling tradition. What is important here is how these similarities pose similar interpretative problems in all three texts. In my discussion I am conflating questions addressed both by Kermode and other critics who have dealt with the problems of the Arthurian narratives. In the latter group, which includes Hispanists like Maria Rosa Lida de Malkiel, Luis Murillo, and Martin de Riquer, I specifically need to cite Jessie Weston, Roger Sherman Loomis, Myles Dillon, D. D. R. Owen, Pronsias MacCana, Venceslas Kruta, Alwyn and Brinley Rees, John Darrah, and Miranda Green among many other Celticists. This conflation of two scholarly traditions is particularly relevant to Cervantine studies both because of the Arthurian content in his works and because of the replication, more or less deliberate, that Cervantes presents of the textual/reading problems found in Arthurian texts as part of his own text. At the same time these questions also replicate problems found in biblical studies.

Therefore, I am not positing or discussing a question of influence. Nor do I mean to suggest that as a work of narrative fiction the *Quixote* concerns only these issues. But it is reasonable to assume that, given the content of the story and the fictionalized narrative practices of Cide Hamete, that the work itself assumes a general awareness on the part of readers of the textual anxieties of Renaissance humanism and Reformation hermeneutics, specifically the problems of garbled texts and the interpretative strategies used to extrapolate a variety of meanings. In this way we recognize that both the questions of textual purity and conflicting hermeneutics strategies were prominently inscribed within the *Quixote*.

On an even broader basis of assumption, all the Mark, Cervantes, and Joyce texts present historically significant narratives that deal with problems of narrativity. In the case of the *Quixote* these same problems are themselves narratized from the very first paragraph of the work. But much the same can be said for the Mark text in its straightforward opening assertion: "The beginning of the gospel of Jesus Christ, the Son of God." We are already in the presence of a self-conscious narrative strategy and a clearly stated hermeneutic goal. As for Joyce, he is the heir to all these narrative riches. It should be emphasized also that I am approaching all of these works as secular texts, whatever their institutional backing may be. *Don Quixote* has proverbially been called "the Spanish Bible," and certainly has often been approached as at least a semi-divine text, an attitude that may have some historical basis as we will see.

Nevertheless, the matter of textual veracity is not the concern of my own approach, and therefore I make no claims for or against the accuracy of the external referentiality of the Mark text. As John P. Meier, the general editor of the *Catholic Bible Quarterly*, has observed, there is a "hermeneutics of belief" and a "hermeneutics of unbelief" when approaching biblical texts, a distinction which reminds us that all strategies of hermeneutics operate according to their own agendas *(NYT)*. In current critical studies there is also the term "hermeneutics of suspicion" applied to all texts. It is in this same spirit that my own study focuses on certain problems of reading in the *Quixote*. The sacred provenance of its ontology is not at issue, and, for purposes of this discussion, the Marcan and Joycean texts will be granted the same privilege.

The Hermeneutics of Unbelief

In Kermode's discussion of Mark's gospel and Joyce's novel a number of issues are foregrounded in a way relevant to general problems of interpretation. Other difficulties concern what happens to very old texts, texts that have been transmitted in written form by multiple unknown scribes, editors, and other savants, each with problematic agendas of their own. Things may be inserted into a text by anonymous hands either by error or by intent. In the same way other passages may be omitted. Maybe entire episodes have been inserted from other sources, or the position of these episodes may reveal that they were moved there by the scribe even though they were originally placed elsewhere. Cervantists will recognize that many of these questions have been raised about the *Quixote*. One thinks readily of the problem of the location or even inclusion of the interpolated stories in part 1 (Stagg). More important to the issues at hand, however, is the fact that these kinds of problems are already narratized within Cervantes' text as part of its fiction. The example of the location of the episodes or sequencing of the episodes, as raised by the narrator in chapter 2, clearly illustrates this. A similar problem is also found in *The Táin*.

At the same time the reader is brought into this process as he or she reads. For instance, the question of the validity or historicity of the source materials that Cide Hamete claims to have at hand is a matter of hermeneutic choice for the reader. The fact that most readers have accepted this as a fictional device rather than a statement of historical truth merely reminds us of the always present function of interpretation in the act of reading. In exactly the same way, but with the opposite results, many biblical scholars assume that Mark did have written sources at hand when he redacted the version we now read. There is even a component of biblical specialists that assumes there was another version of Mark's text that was later suppressed because of theological considerations about its interpretation.

This same kind of concern is clearly, on a secular level, at issue in chapter 20 when Don Quixote himself calls for the suppression of the entire chapter. If the text had been considered institutionally sacred at the time, heads would have rolled over how it was to be read. Yet the Inquisition's reader considers the work healthful, thereby implying that other kinds of reading are dangerous to the reader's health, whether in London, Geneva, Rome, or Madrid. This merely illustrates that many texts show concern for how they could or should be read, and in this sense Mark's, Cervantes' and Joyce's masterworks are typical. What is also typical is that all three texts have generated an immense quantity of interpretative studies, many of which have produced noticeable heat.

There are other kinds of problems shared by the three works. For instance the advantage of Mark over the other gospels is that it begins its account of Jesus' life with the hero already in operation as a full-blown hero. Mark spends no time on birth or Jesus' childhood events, a deficiency taken up by the other gospel authors. In *Don Quixote*'s case we particularly note the absence of this kind of opening information, an ingredient one would expect to find in the story of a Romance hero. Such items are standard genre-linked features of the *libros de caballerías* starting with the *Amadís*, but they are missing in *Don Quixote*. Thus both Mark and Cervantes's works concentrate on what Cide Hamete calls the *caso*, or case of the hero, a matter specifically presented to the reader as a problem calling for interpretation. In this way, the interpretative act becomes a self-conscious genre-linked feature of Romance, one that goes all the way back to Chrétien and to the Irish tales.

It can be argued that in one way or another the act of interpretation is always present even if the narrator makes no note of it. Curiously or not, the Joyce text does not self-consciously inscribe interpretative responses in the opening paragraphs. That absence can be read as either more deceptive or less deceptive on the part of Joyce. Perhaps by the twentieth century the narrative voice was merely embarrassed to include a component that could be confused with the "dear reader" approach popular in nineteenth-century novels. Wayne Booth has accused Joyce and other moderns of this kind of deliberate maneuver, but however the author presents the text the question of interpretation cannot be excluded as a feature of Romance.

Another element of commonality between the biblical text and *Don Quixote* is the fact that the two figures Jesus Christ and Don Quixote have become powerful cultural symbols in society as a whole. Certainly no other figure from secular literature has exceeded Don Quixote in this kind of significance. Most people, readers or not, have some idea who he is and what he has come to stand for. Don Quixote, Hamlet, Faust, Ulysses, Don Juan stand as imposing emblems in Western thought, and I suspect Don Quixote would win out over the others in a scientifically posed opinion poll on name recognition, even in the United States, a nation of nonreaders. Thus we become aware that we are dealing with texts of unusual power and diffusion through time and space.

The word mythic comes to mind in all these cases, but it is worth noting that in its origins Don Quixote as a figure is the only one of this group of five heroes that is an original creation of an individual imagination. What is important to keep in mind, therefore, is that his mythic status is produced entirely by the operations of the text itself and not by an overt calling upon a previously known figure such as the Messiah or Ulysses. There are other considerations to be dealt with, but from these items it is apparent that comparative analogies between or among the Gospel of Mark, *Don Quixote,* and *Ulysses* possess validity. To this list we must add the Arthurian texts which, in their drift from Ireland and Wales to Flanders, reveal the same transmission problems that haunt Mark's account. The only difference is that no single institutionally sanitized and canonically approved version of the Celtic narrative material has been formulated. Unlike the gospels, the Arthurian stories were in most ways left free to infiltrate Western culture in their own subversive way.

The interpretive gestures that emerge from Kermode's study are in any case moveable, since the texts he utilizes are arbitrarily chosen (50–73). His basic concern is to explore possible hermeneutic functions for certain items that somehow stand out from the overall texture of the work. He cites in Mark the young man in a linen shirt who attempts to follow Christ after his arrest but then is stripped of his clothing and flees naked. The figure is particularly enigmatic since he doesn't appear in the passion narratives of the other gospels. In such a heavily studied text as Mark's there have been numerous attempts to explain what the function or meaning of this figure is. Apparently none of the interpretive resolutions has carried the day, and Kermode suggests that maybe, like Joyce's man in the macintosh at Paddy Dignam's funeral, no claim to a definitive meaning can be found for the figure (50). At this point the logocentric agenda of the theologians has stalled. Suffice to say that every kind of explanation has been dredged up from a simple scribal error to the possibility that he was an impassioned lover.

Nevertheless in a general way we find that the following explanatory procedures have been utilized in biblical hermeneutics:

1. the passage has been erroneously inserted from another text

2. there was more to the passage, but it has been suppressed

3. it is a deliberate enigma

4. there actually was such a young man, and Mark is merely presenting a transparent account of what happened

5. the young man represents all the figures that abandoned Christ when he was arrested, and hence it is an intertextual reference to another text

6. there is a linguistic link between the term used to denote the young man and the word used to describe the angel figure found by the women at the tomb of Christ

7. the figure is emblematic and represents a genre-linked feature of an unknown genre (i.e. the meaning cannot be recovered)

8. the figure is an early attempt at realism, a fortuitous episode presented in order to create the illusion of what happens in everyday events

While I have not reproduced the exact order of Kermode's exposition, I have come up with a broad list of possible interpretive maneuvers. All these explanations fall within the spectrum of two conflicting views:

1. the figure has no "meaning" and we shouldn't attempt to impose closure on all items in a text

2. the figure of the young man points to the possibility of a lost or occult meaning suggesting the existence of a hidden text within the manifest one

In other terms we recognize that the hermeneutic challenge is situated at the center of all logocentric expectations, and therefore all textual "meaning" is uncontrollable. In this way the story is like the "Cheshire style" forms in Celtic manuscript art depicting scrolls turning into faces or faces turning into scrolls so that the interpretation of the direction of this temporal process is left to the viewer (Kruta 94).

Kermode's analysis of the Joyce text is not quite so suggestive for our purposes, but he finds that the figure known as the man in the macintosh has produced a similar hermeneutic aporia. One explanation, however, relates him to the figure of Theoclymenos in Homer, with the suggestion that both in Homer and Joyce the enigmatic figure is a Hermes-type apparition, the god of tricky texts and thieves. In all these characteristics he resembles the fat innkeeper in part 1, chapter 2, The Hermes *figura* also introduces the problem of borders and border crossings within a literary text and brings to the surface the question of the precarious ontology of certain kinds of heroes. This in turn questions the genre definition of the text being read. Such problems suggest Don Quixote himself, a figure who lives on the edge of many kinds of borders, including those of literary genres. The dilemma is further narratized in the troubled chapter 23 of part 1, where, as we will see, two figures, Ginés and Cardenio, seem to signal a shift in the generic orientation of Don Quixote's adventures. This kind of reading is an example of the hermeneutic use of both typology and intertextuality.

In the case of the *Quixote*, however, one further possibility can be considered. The argument can be made that Cervantes, either deliberately or inadvertently, reproduced "errors" or enigmatic contradictions of the types found in the vast accumulation of Romance literature that he had read. Kermode cites Joyce himself as claiming to have purposely inserted enigmas in *Ulysses* in order to confound his readers (64). But in the *Quixote* the situation is somewhat different, since the case can be made that such "unreadable" items themselves constitute a recognized convention of Romance. The parodic import of the *Quixote* could even have exaggerated these items for comic purposes. Exactly such an example of generic exaggeration is in fact introduced by the narrator himself at the opening of chapter 2 when he considers the problem of the chronology of the hidalgo's adventures, whether Don Quixote came first to the windmills, to Puerto Lapice, or to the inn. Similar editorial problems are also narratized in the *Táin*.

A different example of enigmatic material can be found in the "errors" inserted by Dorotea in her Micomicona story. How are these mistakes to be read? Does she make the geographic and other errors as a deliberate way of presenting herself as a harassed romance heroine and therefore intend the errors to be a parody of the genre-linked features of Byzantine romances? Or is she really flustered and needs the priest's corrections? Or, on a different level of import, are her errors and omissions a signal to the reader that her original story to the priest, her account of her own adventures with Fernando, is also unreliable? As in other aspects of Dorotea's behavior her words and actions are difficult to read. In fact it seems that the function of her role, like those of Celtic heroines, is to escape logocentric closure. Further consideration of these and other "unreadable" enigmas will be examined later, but it is obvious that this overview of biblical and secular hermeneutic strategies suggests the possibility that the *Quixote*, a text constituted out of other texts, deliberately, and in imitation of the problems found in Arthurian Romance, creates its own hermeneutic quandaries.

Therefore I have chosen the term *hermeneutics of unbelief*, borrowed from biblical studies, as indicative of my own bias. This places my approach within the range of the two opposing interpretive options: Any item may be without significance, or it may signify an occult or suppressed meaning. The fact that these interpretations are in some ways contradictory may not be so lamentable when analyzing a Cervantine text since, as already noted, this condition is part and parcel of the tradition of Arthurian romance, a factor to be more fully explored below. At the same time, the eventuality that the lack of closure for all parts of a text exists enriches its interpretive horizons. A recalcitrant passage in any work may avoid notice or, contrariwise, may have attracted immense attention. Any nondescript phrase or word may abruptly emerge as meaningful once placed within the structure of an unsuspected pattern, while the nonclosure of meaning may signify an occult meaning. Thus these reading strategies exist as binary opposites, each taking meaning from the existence of the other possibility.

What I am proposing is an approach to the *Quixote* in which all these procedures will be considered. As a result we will recognize that certain kinds of hermeneutic clashes are seen to be literary conventions. In this way the "unreadable" items come to be read as a narrative strategy inherited from Romance. At the same time it must be kept in mind that this situation is not just a result of a parodic design within the *Quixote*. Instead, this textual condition becomes an inevitable product of the narrator's agenda. Without being aware of the power of his subtext, Cide Hamete himself is carried along by the force of his own story. Like the Celtic storytellers and like Chrétien before him, he includes an encounter between the teller of the tale and the tale, an event that constitutes an *aventura* in the Celtic sense of that word, a fateful meeting between a hero and an Otherworld force. In this case the Otherworld force of the Celtic cosmogony becomes the equally mysterious power of language itself. As does the formulation of Celtic art as an artifact that asks for interpretation, language, even when reduced to its smallest signifying components, presents the same question (Jameson 17).

In this way something else emerges that presents a much more radical face, and we are confronted with a configuration of textual energy, an energy of ruthless power and unknowable limits. No other explanation accounts for either the shifting shape of the *Quixote* as a story or for the conflictive history of its interpretation. I will argue also that such a history is part of the ultimate adventure envisioned by the disturbing force of the old Gaelic stories, stories of heroes turned to ashes when they try to return from their Otherworld encounters. Perceval is the best known of this kind of hero, and we have to recognize that medieval attempts at a spiritual transcendence for such a figure were based on the unstable foundation of a fragile Christian logocentrism. In the same way the *Quixote* as a text demonstrates that this effort to control or delimit meaning was an enterprise·to which Cervantes did not belong.

Why Real Men Don't Read Romance

One process we have traced in the history of biblical texts has led to the realization that, in the act of reading, the reader may find that a particular item presents itself as a puzzle or enigma. This same item may in effect have no meaning or, in opposition to that conclusion, may signal the existence of a hidden or forgotten meaning, a condition we have termed an "occult" text. The latter may be the result of some deliberate omission, due to ignorance or the failure to recognize the importance of the item, or it may be the result of deliberate suppression, an institutional cover-up by a group that has a reason to want to remove a meaning not in accord with the prevailing mode of thought. But whatever the cause, the result leaves an incomplete meaning buried but still resonating within the text, a meaning that tantalizes later readers.

What is more surprising, however, is that while this may happen as a historical event in the process of transmission, it is also a process that occurs in the writing of a text by a single author and is, therefore, a condition found in all texts. It is part of their ontology and part of the way in which they come to be. This same phenomenon of suppression occurs, it would seem, in the creation of any text. The process of writing itself contains similar procedures in which the writer, faced with decisions of what to include and what to exclude, introduces what can be considered a certain amount of "corruption" of the intended discourse. Any work, no matter how seamless it may at first appear, is the result of authorial decisions of this kind, and longer texts, like *Don Quixote* or *Ulysses*, are more prone to show the fissures that mark a turn in the way the tale is told. Kermode's study of Joyce's man-in-the-macintosh figure is one example of such a phenomenon. Hermes figures function as self-referential signs indicating that the text itself has stirred, that some partially hidden force has surfaced and created what we can call a "fissure in the textuality" of the discourse. We will see that Ginés de Pasamonte is such a Hermes figure in the *Quixote*. Through the confrontation between him and Cardenio, the reader becomes aware that the text is taking an abrupt turn, one which signals an interruption we can term a "Ginés point." The fact that he is also a thief accords with his Hermes-like interpretation of his own story, and at the same time this Herm function also marks a boundary in the Cide Hamete text itself. The rupture occurs when the picaresque possibilities of Ginés's story are abruptly suspended, clearing the way for the arrival of the Cardenio and the problematics of love. This in turn precipitates Don Quixote's recognition that it is in the field of love not war that he will excel Amadís. This change in the nature of the knight's adventures is marked by Rocinante's choice of the road, a feature inherited from the Celtic tales, and presages the onset of a prolonged series of interwoven love stories. This interpolative sequence should be seen as a Romance condition that comes to underwrite Don Quixote's own story.

The question of why these narrative fault lines appear is sometimes studied by means of a psychological analysis of the author's mind. This can be fairly hazardous. Missing information about the author's life can easily lead to a "mis-reading" and the results rendered problematic. Since we have very little information about Cervantes's inner life, such an approach would be a great risk, even though it could produce challenging speculations. As an alternative route, the methodologies of biblical hermeneutics offer a safer road, one that is based on the self-presenting strategies of the text itself, and one with the promise of a richer yield. Within this broad approach, however, there is one strategy that demands further consideration, and that is the question of *translation,* a term important both within the history of Romance as a literary discourse and within the hermeneutics of Hans-Georg Gadamer (345ff.).

At first sight this problem may seem not relevant to a study of the *Quixote,* where we have the text in the author's original language. But at another level of interpretation the idea of translation has been adapted by Gadamer as the most appropriate metaphor for the hermeneutic process itself (349). When we read, according to Gadamer, we in essence "translate" the text into our own terms, into the specific meanings we personally attach to the many aspects of language. I have found for instance that native speakers of Spanish often discover a certain meaning in the text that reveals an orientation in their own particular linguistic heritage. One perceptive student I recall termed the experience of reading Golden Age texts the learning of a new language. On the simplest level this may be due to changed meanings of words. An example of such vagaries of individual language heritage occurred just a few years ago with a phrase that Pedro the rustic shepherd uses in his story of Marcela and Grisostomo (1: 12). In describing the beauty of Marcela's mother, Pedro adds: "No parece sino que ahora la veo, con aquella cara que del *un cabo tenía el sol y del otro la luna*" [It seems that I see her now, with that face that had the moon on one side and the sun on the other.] (my translation). The origins of the phrase seems to have had something to do with an alchemical completion symbol. However, in many years of teaching I have encountered only one native speaker who had ever heard the phrase as an item of current usage, and this student was from Puerto Rico. Curiously or not the peninsular students seem never to have heard the comparison, probably because most of them come from urban backgrounds, while the young woman from Puerto Rico was not. Obviously the reader already familiar with the phrase will "read" it with a different hermeneutic resonance than one who has not. Compounding the matter of familiarity, however, is the problem of what the term may mean in certain contexts and not in others, and this kind of difference in language recognition points up the question of survival of linguistic terms and, even more problematically, the survival of particular meanings attached to the terms. So we all realize that it is not easy to be certain of what such a term might have meant in the Madrid of 1605.

A classic study by Eric Auerbach on the term *figura* provides an opening into the infinite complexity of loss of meaning suffered by a single term in its migration from ancient Greece through Rome to Medieval Europe and on up to its inclusion in the lexicon of rhetoric and philosophy in our own time (11ff.). Specifically Auerbach shows how in the process of translation a word loses the power of its original etymon and subsequently exists with only an impoverished and denuded signification. It is this kind of phenomenon of translation that Gadamer compares to the individual reader's personal interpretation of a text. Thus, each reader's "translation" alters, often very slightly, the earlier thrust of the language. In a long literary text this slight drift may amount to a significant current of new meaning.

But this type of translation problem is a very limited example of what Gadamer is suggesting. Every reader brings certain personal associations with words or terms that modify the meaning the text has for him or for her. Only very recently has feminist criticism shown the woman as reader is a force in critical studies. An even more radical interpretation of this kind has been taken by other critics, and the idea that the text is different for the same reader each time it is read has been made. But the question of the woman as reader has particular relevance for the study of the *Quixote* because of its relations to Romance as a kind of writing, since certain strains of Romance were dedicated to women and to women readers. Chrétien's dedication of the Lancelot story to Marie de Champagne is the most famous historical instance, but in Spanish we recall Diego de San Pedro's dedication of his *Tractado de amores de Arnalte y Lucenda* to the "damas de la reina" as well as the fact that he claims that his *Sermón ordenado* was requested of him by certain "señoras."

It is this historical development that is at the base of the anti-feminism found in the advice to Charles VI. It stems from the recognition that the Matter of Britain, as opposed to other Romance formulations, did not deal with the affairs of men. Real men don't read Romance, at least certain kinds of Romance. Similarly, the division of Romances dealing with battles from Romances dealing with love is inherent in this kind of differentiation. Menéndez y Pelayo long ago made the clear distinction between what he called the *novelas sentimentales* of the fifteenth century and the *libros de caballería* along these same dividing lines of love and war. Don Quixote himself at the beginning of his adventures in the Sierra Morena (the literary landscape of San Pedro's *Cárcel de Amor*) recognizes that his truest imitation of the perfect knight can best be achieved in matters of love, not arms:

Amadís fue el norte, el lucero, el sol de los valientes y enamorados caballeros, a quien debemos de imitar a todos aquellos que debajos de la bandera de amor y de la caballería militamos ... Y una de las cosas en que más este caballero mostró su prudencia, valor, valentía, sufrimiento, firmeza y amor fue cuando se retiró ... a hacer penitencia en la Peña pobre ... Así, que me es a mí más fácil imitarle en esto que no en hender gigantes, descabezar serpientes, matar endriagos, desbaratar ejércitos, fracasar armadas y deshacer encantamentos. (1: xxv)

[Amadís was the pole star, day star, sun of valiant and devoted (enamored) knights, whom all we who fight under the banner of love and chivalry are bound to imitate ... Now one of the instances in which this knight most conspicuously showed his prudence, worth, valor, endurance, fortitude and love, was when he withdrew ... to do penance upon Wretched Rock ... So, as it is easier for me to imitate him in this than in cleaving giants asunder, cutting off serpents' heads, slaying dragons, routing armies, destroying fleets, and breaking enchantments.]

As a signal, such a statement indicates that a new hermeneutic fix is being called up, an indication that the reader will need to consider in "translating" the text. This passage is in fact a sign that a type of fissure has occurred in the text. Don Quixote's half-awareness of the change in his fictive situation is coupled with his new involvement in a series of interpolated tales that fundamentally alter the overall formulation of the 1605 *Quixote*. The reader is warned, however delicately, that new kinds of translations are to be required.

In considering Gadamer's use of translation as metaphor for reading, it is useful to look also at Heidegger's examination of the grammatical functions of language and the nature of the meanings it makes possible. In *An Introduction to Metaphysics* Heidegger presents an *excursus* on the role of language in his search for the early Greek meaning of the idea of being (52ff.). He specifically examines two instances of loss of meaning that occurred with the translation into Latin of the idea of the verbal infinitive form of the term for being (being as in the sense of Spanish *ser*) and of the concept of case in the sense of grammatical form. The latter term of *casus* survives in both the Spanish and English concept of case forms that make up the entire range of inflected forms a word may display. Heidegger then traces the term to its Greek roots and finds that the terms *ptosis* and *enklisis* mean "falling, tipping, inclining," from which we get our sense of declension. He also finds that before the idea of a noun was clearly distinguished from that of a verb, that the same term was used in Greek to designate the inflection of both parts of speech. Hence *casus* in its broadest signification included the idea of all variations in word forms, in the sense of the "inclining or tipping" they suffered in its acts of self-presentation.

Heidegger's agenda in this linguistic commentary is concerned with the problem of being, and his incursion into language is one stage of that examination. Nevertheless his analysis provides a basis for considering the operations of language as in themselves a means of signification and, therefore, the dependence of meaning on the power of these operations. We thus recognize that such a shapeshifting of the word has a life of its own and may therefore posit the possibility that the meaning of a case change points back to the process of language change itself rather than to an external referent. This sets up the phenomenon of word inflections as a self-reflecting process, as a mode of self-presentation that forms part of the broader ontology of language and of literary language in particular.

This possibility is of course a factor in wordplay of all sorts and is often co-opted in literary titles, where it has a hermeneutic function. Such a simple instance as the title of Galdos's *Fortunata y Jacinta* is a well-known example of a title that suggests something of the hidden problematics of fate and the roles it plays in the lives and characters of the two women. On a more complex level, a title like Baroja's *Camino de perfección* is a reference back to St. Teresa's title and at the same time an ironic commentary on itself. This procedure is utilized in an even more radical manner by Borges in "El evangelio según Marco" (The Gospel of Mark), where the title is an open hermeneutic challenge and at the same time a clue to the denouement of the story. In mystery or spy stories, genres always close to Borges's productions, such wordplay is a commonplace aspect of the title. Agatha Christie's *And Then There Were None* picks up on a children's word game, while John le Carre's more deceptive *Tinker, Tailor, Soldier, Spy* brings the wordplay back to the idea of a conjugation of nouns, the meaning of which is not at all clear. This is an operation that we will also find in the title *Don Quixote,* where Cervantes places his language in a position of punning the hero's name on a piece of armor. The fact that *quixote* refers to a piece of armor covering the thigh may or may not suggest the wounds of the grail king. We will return to this topic in examining the status of the language of fiction that Cervantes establishes for his text, but it should also be noted that word-play forms part of the challenge faced by a Romance hero, who often has to read a warning or prophecy presented in the form of a riddle. This feature as a title of detective stories reminds us that this genre is closely related to Romance as a literary form, particularly so in the works of Poe, Conan Doyle, and Borges.

What remains for us to consider is that all these operations of textual change, suppression, corruption, and linguistic metamorphoses are factors that both enrich and distort the hermeneutic possibilities available to the reader of Romance.

What Happened to Romance: Transformation as Literary Form

After his misadventure with the two herds of sheep (pt. 1, ch. 18), Don Quixote tells Sancho to watch the sheep as they withdraw: "verás como, en alejándose de aquí algún poco, se vuelven en su ser primero, y dejando de ser carneros, son hombres hechos y derechos, como yo te los pinté primero" [You will see that when they have gone some little distance, they will return to their original shape. Ceasing to be sheep, they will become men exactly as I described them to you]. (My translation.) The phenomenon to which Don Quixote refers, shapeshifting, is a common occurrence in Celtic tales, and it survived as a genre-linked feature of Romance. It can be seen in a peculiarly pristine formulation in the descriptions of Urganda la desconocida in *Amadís*, where as the hero's familiar she abruptly changes from an old hag to a young girl and back again before the protagonist's eyes. The feature itself is frequently invoked by Don Quixote to disguise his many apparent failures. He first uses it in explaining to Sancho the problem of the windmills. In that instance he adds the following commentary: "Calla, amigo Sancho . . . que las cosas de la guerra, más que otras, están sujetas a continua mudanza" (pt.1, ch. 8). [Silence friend Sancho, . . . The fortunes of war more than any other are liable to frequent fluctuations]. (My translation.) Thus the term "mudanza" (change or transformation) enters Don Quixote's lexicon and recurs later as a phenomenon even more closely linked to "things of love" during the adventures of Dorotea at the inn in part 1 and with the enchantment of Dulcinea in part 2. In fact both these heroines seem to transform themselves before the amazed eyes of the men who pursue them.

In its Celtic origins this type of transformation can be seen in love stories such as "The Wooing of Etain." Here the heroine suffers repeated transformations into many forms: a pool, a worm, a brilliantly colored fly, and so on. Other common types of metamorphoses include the famous swan incarnations of both lovers, an image that survives in the figure of the swan knight or heroines described by poets as having breasts as white as swans. In a similar manner other knights are sometimes accompanied by their transformational identity in a kind of doubling, as in Chrétien's *Yvain*, the knight of the lion. This *nom de guerre* even survives in *Don Quixote* when the hero re-names himself after his encounter with the lion in part 2.

The survival of these features from their Celtic origins to their medieval usages are in themselves a type of transformation, as though the phenomenon of shapeshifting comes to inhabit the literary formulations of the stories themselves. The factor of transformation of literary forms as they accommodate themselves to cultural change is common to all literary history (Fowler 170–212), but in the case of Romance the shapeshifting energy seems to afflict the very forms of the stories. Perhaps because of their oral formulations, the shapeshifting became not just a motif but a feature of its literary form, where the same story is often repeated with slight variations as a second or third story. This tendency can be seen in the *Quixote*, part 1, where the intertwined love stories replicate themselves with considerable vigor. In fact it may be this repeated quality of the stories that drew the critical attention to them that Sanson Carrasco speaks of (pt. 2, ch. 3). The underlying basis for this is simply that the fashion for Romance was waning by the beginning of the seventeenth century, and Cervantes had to find another narrative format for part 2.

In tracing this problem of literary history we will have to look directly at some instances of early formulations of Celtic tales, formulations that set Romance as a literary kind on its road to adventure. These examinations of the Celtic ur-romances and of Chrétien's fully developed Romance tales do not claim, however, that Cervantes read these specific works. By the sixteenth century he would not have had to do a source study, he merely had to deal with the commonalities of Romance as they had survived into his own era. Alan Deyermond, for instance, has shown how the matter of Romance, even the Lancelot story, had so penetrated

Spanish society by the fifteenth century that it could serve as material for sermons to illiterate congregations. Cervantes himself took his Romance orientation from a broad spectrum of sources, not only the *libros de caballería*, but also the ballads, the Italian *Orlando*s, other Romance forms such as Heliodorus's Byzantine romance, the *novelas pastoriles*, and endless other kinds of writing such as the chronicles that were steeped in chivalric ideals.

It should also be stressed that Cervantes' overall literary trajectory from the *Galatea* through the *Quixote*s and on to the *Persiles* (Wilson) never abandoned his commitment to Romance, but rather modulated this attachment to serve changing literary needs. His hopes for the success of the *Persiles* seem based on the belief that Romance could be adapted as a literary form suitable for the literary valorizations of humanism. The fact the no later critic has felt that the *Persiles* could be considered his greatest work can be seen as a misunderstanding of Cervantes' view of Romance.

In examining the earliest examples of the Celtic tales that we possess, the modern reader is immediately impressed by the presence of an alien and disturbing strangeness. The tales strike us as products of a reality unknown to us. I stress the term *alien* because it is recognized that these stories in the primitive forms were no longer acceptable to the medieval world of the twelfth century. This was the society that was creating its own cultural synthesis precisely in the time of Chrétien. Thus it is Chrétien's adaptation of these tales that provides the most powerful formulation of medieval Romance as a literary kind. In this sense the Celtic tales are not yet fully Romances. Rather it is in the process of disguising the Celts' disturbing view of an alien reality that the new form of Romance comes-to-be. In fact it is often in examining the suppression of certain Celtic "barbaric" items, head hunting, cannibalism, transmigration of souls, that we come to understand both medieval Romance and its Celtic origins.

In other words, the nature of the violent "translation" suffered by the Celtic tales into Romance became written into the new literary form. It is rooted in an anxiety of interpretation which results in repeated attempts of later narrators to "explain" the meaning of the stories, precisely because they were no longer understandable. The old hermeneutic power of the pagan society had eroded to such an extent that the stories now appeared mysterious and incomprehensible, but at the same time something of the old meaning still inhabited the "marvellous" adventures of the heroes. This appeal exercised its numinous power on later readers and later writers. In particular the grail scene of Chrétien's *Li Contes del Graal* stands as the paradigm of this phenomenon of mysterious attraction. And it is from this troubled formulation of Romance as a literary discourse that Cervantes discovered the essential elements of his own agenda. His many adaptations of Romance as a basic narrative formula, rather than merely his concern with parody—a feature already inscribed within Romance—provided him with the language needed for the *Quixote*.

How this occurred is the focus of this analysis.

Two

The Celtic Reserve

The Celtic artist does not describe the world around him, he reproduces it in his own way, on the basis of an inner projection that shatters appearances.

Venceslas Kruta

Ireland, Wales, and France

Much of the work of Celtic Studies has concerned itself with problems of transmission. The question of how the Celtic stories found their way to Chrétien and to his successors is often the focus of the discipline. These problems are valid in themselves, but younger Celticists have complained that in the study of sources the scholars have often failed to examine the works in themselves (Adams et al. 78). This is certainly true to some extent, but the scholarly questions have their own hermeneutic posture as well. What emerges from their efforts is a vast compilation of studies that replicate in many ways what Kermode found in biblical hermeneutics, in that the Celtic Studies institutional establishment has also concerned itself with problems of the meaning of the tales as well as with problems of how they changed during their transmission, and often the two are intertwined. It is in this process that the problems of "translation" from Gaelic to Welsh to French that the

29

question of literary form is foregrounded. In this sense we can approach the matter as a question of genre, that is, as a question of a series of specific hermeneutic fixes that became written into the text itself. Chrétien and his fellow romancers were, much like Cervantes long after them, readers of tales. Their re-formulations of the narratives tell us how they read the earlier forms of the stories. What emerges from all this study of transformations is essentially a history of hermeneutics. Each reader/writer finds in the tales what is useful to his or her own agenda. Each gives us a new reading as the story becomes transformed in its re-telling. What these transformations tell us is how the tales have been read at various times.

Even more fundamental to the question of the *Quixote* as a literary kind, however, is the problem of how Don Quixote's reading is articulated by the narrational strategies of the work as a whole. What the study of this articulation tells us is quite another story. The hero's madness is presented as hermeneutic in its origins, and as we read we become aware that all the action of the novel is the result of his reading practices. I don't mean to clinically examine the validity of the claim that Don Quixote is insane. Rather I will seek to explain how the text presents that problem. This critical procedure inevitably becomes an examination of how the problem of Romance as a literary presence functions within the text. That question is much more radical than the question of how Don Quixote reads: it leads instead to an examination of how the narrator's reading/re-writing of Romance constitutes the ontology of Cervantes' text.

In order to approach that problem we will have to take a look at how earlier writers, both Celtic and Christian, address the same dilemma. This question therefore looks at Romance as a hermeneutic enigma. In this kind of approach Romance itself becomes an unstable sign. It becomes a genre that asks for interpretation.

In this way the problematics of understanding Romance becomes in many ways its most powerful genre-linked feature, and this factor is one it inherited from Celtic art. This feature of "asking for interpretation" (Kruta 83ff.) radically differentiates the Celtic worldview from the classical ideal of Greek and Roman art. Furthermore the way the interpretive problem is formulated in Celtic tales is what passed into the narrative strategies of medieval storytellers. What must be recognized here is the centrality of this phenomenon in the ontology of the new medieval genre of Romance. It is one of the distinctions by which the genre separated itself from other literary forms. From this it is only one step to the recognition that Cervantes' utilized this feature in a highly sophisticated way in his own re-formulation of chivalric Romance in the *Quixote*.

The source of this feature is found in the expression of Celtic art and its preoccupation with what can be termed "unreadable items." Celtic craftsmen created plastic images which, instead of proclaiming the validity of their ontology, asked rather what was their ontology. Their art projected questions about the nature of reality rather than attempted to define reality in logocentric terms. It inscribed the marvelous as the essential feature of a reality in which images changed disturbingly back and forth between contrasting presentations of their ontology. Venceslas Kruta has examined the problematics of this in his study *The Celts of the West*.

> Plastic metamorphosis means that the artist has chosen the precise moment at which, in the transition from one form—vegetal, human, animal, abstract—to another, the balance is not yet disrupted and none of these forms is allowed to predominate. Unlike certain representations of metamorphosis in classical art, there is nothing here to suggest the direction of the transformation and its irreversible character. For Celtic artists, each form contains the embryos of other forms and the prevalence of one form over the others can never be more than temporary and incomplete. . . . this plastic invention, which is remarkable originality, shows clearly the interest felt by the Celts in the change from one form to another, thus confirming and enriching what we know from written documents, in which metempsychosis emerges as an essential element in Druidic doctrine. To a greater extent than any other, perhaps, this aspect of early Celtic art at its height reflects a view of the universe in which, by perpetual movement, the boundaries between the natural and the supernatural become blurred, in which the marvellous is regarded as a fundamental and omnipresent element of everyday reality. (94–95)

Thus, in "The Wooing of Etain," is the heroine a pool, a worm, a scarlet fly, or a woman? In the same way, are her relations to the various men adulterous, incestuous, perfidious, or merely evanescent? There is no authorial valorization of her multiple appearances. One form is just as true as another. The result is indeed a world of "mudanzas" as Don Quixote explains. And like the true hero he is, Don Quixote possesses powers of perception that allow him to see a reality denied to non-heroes. For this

reason, like CuChulainn, like Perceval, like Lancelot, and like all protagonists of Romance, he has a funny way of seeing things and will be scorned
and laughed at. Heinrich Heine was right; such is the fate of true heroes
(Murillo 49–50).

The first point to be made in this approach is that the Celtic tales, an
alien product, lost their primitive hermeneutic fix in the process of cultural
translation from Ireland to Wales to France (Owen, *Evolution*). They survived as tales, but the audience for which they were created had vanished.
Residual clues as to the original nature of this audience do remain of
course. We can infer meanings that seem to be asked for, but the brutal
facts are that we cannot with confidence establish how that long vanished
audience "read" the stories. It is much more possible to reconstruct the
hermeneutic fix of the first audience of the gospels than it is to project the
interpretive strategies of early Ireland. If, as Pronsias MacCana speculates,
the medieval monks deliberately didn't translate the hermeneutic texts of
the early Celts, their ploy was successful (O'Driscoll 148). Much of Celtic
reader-response capabilities remains inaccessible to us.

What is especially important is the fact that the most radical break
occurred when Chrétien first adapted the stories for the world of Marie
de Champagne and Philip of Flanders. The lords and ladies of the courts
of northern France in the twelfth century had no interest in Celtic studies. Like all self-centered audiences they cared not at all for the original
forms or purposes of the stories. For them the tales had to reflect their
own values and concerns so that they could read their affective needs
into these events of long ago and far away, and the stories had to achieve
this reflection without breaking the mirror, so to speak. They had to
fascinate their audience but not openly challenge their logocentric view
of reality. This process of adaption was abrupt and brutal, because the
world of Chrétien at that particular junction was one seeking to create its
own identity and define its own problems. It was a situation similar to
the era in which modernism emerged in our own century. The new establishment was impatient of the old order and self-consciously sought
to impose its own. Therefore Chrétien inevitably suppressed or ignored
any content that didn't meet the requirements of the moment. We are
thus presented with some extraordinary tales, tales to be re-told and re-
read by later generations, but *tales in which a significant epistemological
break became a recognizable feature of the genre.*

The mysteries of the grail, as the most paradigmatic example of this
feature, beg for an explanation in Chrétien's formulation of the tale. The
problem is then exacerbated by Chrétien's death. In this instance the

death of the teller of the tale shifts from being a problem of history and becomes instead a problem of the story itself. The question of how he would have ended his grail romance in effect becomes part of the story and a recognizable feature of the genre. The challenge of the unknown ending is narratized within the story when the second narrator takes up the task of how to conclude the tale. The ancient problem of authorial intent is transformed into a hermeneutic question posited by the story to the reader. In a schematic way this same problem is narratized by Cervantes in Sancho's tale in chapter 20 of part 1. There the question of authorial intent is problematized by the form in which the story is told. The narrative structure is so constituted so that the tale cannot be concluded. It is literally a "cuento de nunca acabar," (a never ending tale) to use Rodríguez Marín's terminology. In its own way the story narratizes the death of the narrator, which in effect kills the original meaning of the story. In the same way the happenstance that Chrétien left the Perceval tale without an ending becomes a feature of the story. The grail mystery foregrounds the problem of reading in such a way that it becomes the paradigmatic feature of Romance as a genre. The search for an answer subsequently became the goal of narrators re-telling the tale from the time of Eschenbach's *Parzifal* to contemporary scholars who seek to "explain" what is going on in the story.

Logocentrism versus Romance

That all this occurred at a moment in history when allegorical reading was the dominant hermeneutic mode provided later writers and readers with the means to incorporate the results of that hermeneutic conundrum into the story itself. The problematics of this enigma came to constitute the fundamental question of the ontology of Romance as a genre, and this in turn lead to the subsequent devalorization of Romance by moralists and literary *preceptistas* alike. Reverberations of the problem reach into the Renaissance with its urgent anxieties about the ontology of fiction. From this perspective we can see that the *Quixote* as a work of fiction sets forth the most complex response to the dilemma of fiction and truth. It is this achievement, more than anything else, that leads to the future development of the modern novel.

The question is still with us and has emerged in a new form in the modernist and postmodernist, structuralist and poststructuralist movements that have dominated our own time. This helps explain the curious resonances of Romance found in writers such as James, Kafka, and Borges as well as in the current postmodernist writers as science and realism have lost their hold on the contemporary imagination. That we live in an age of a crisis in the question of the ontology of reading makes the *Quixote* again, and as usual, a focus of debate.

At question in all this ferment is the ontology of Romance as it emerged in the form of a literary genre in the twelfth century and the role it came to play in the literary and social culture of the time. To a great extent Romance was defined in both its form and function by the curious position it enjoyed in the courts of the northern French and the Anglo-Normans. Their attitudes toward it are in many ways a clear anticipation of what is found in the *Quixote*. In this sense the particular hermeneutic fix found in Cervantes replicates hermeneutic attitudes already built into Romance by Chrétien. These attitudes take their form precisely along the fissure lines that separate the world of the alien Celts from the world of a new logocentric concept of reality then emerging in the culture of the West. The consequences of Chrétien's success, however, left a glimpse of an ancient and now forbidden vision of a disturbing Otherworld reality.

This rip in the curtain of a rationally "explainable" universe exercised an almost irresistible numinous attraction for the new audience because it articulated precisely what their culture sought to deny: the inevitable limits of reason's power to explain.

Friederich Heer in his *The Medieval World* (26–27) makes a point that further sharpens the observation already cited of Southern about the newly forming identity of Western culture. In speaking of the twelfth century Heer comments that in this era the dominant concerns of the new civilization took their basic form in an interaction between France and England, in the flow of ideas and prejudices that unified the French and Anglo-Norman world of kingdoms, universities, and church. He adds that as a result all other formulations, even those as closely related as the culture of western Germany and Italy achieved the status of the alien. Needless to say, more removed articulations of European societies such as the Slavs or the Iberians were that much more alien. Heer also maintains that these attitudes have persisted unchanged into our own time. England and France between them define the core of Western civilization. All else is marginal, off center, alien. This point must be stressed in order to recognize the innate alienness of Celtic culture to the new Anglo-French synthesis.

These tales present a world very foreign to the one celebrated in the mainstream of European representations of reality. Auerbach's *Mimesis* analyzes the history of this synthesis in his study of how Western culture has represented this "reality" since antiquity. Heer on the other hand is concerned only with what has happened since the twelfth century. His study is relevant because it was in that time that Romance as a genre came-to-be, came to present itself within the larger spectrum of the culture. It cannot be irrelevant that Romance as a genre defines how that new culture came to terms with a much "wilder" view of reality, that of the ancient Celts. This culture was under extreme pressure from the Anglo-Normans in Wales and was suffering a similar crisis from the French in Brittany. The Irish were also under siege from the Normans in the area of Dublin, and those parts of Irish identity that survived were considered "beyond the pale," that is, beyond the control of the new invaders' view of reality. In many ways the next seven centuries in Ireland chronicle the continuation of that struggle between a "primitive" wild indigenous culture and the growing power of a new Anglo-Norman identity. Thus when we observe that the ancient Gaelic tales lost their original hermeneutic fix, what we are saying is that their audience was losing its culture, its means of reading the tales. And this ultimately happened in Ireland and Wales much in the same manner that it had happened in Champagne. The Welsh themselves by the end of the twelfth century were translating back into Welsh Chrétien's versions of their own tales, and in the next century French vulgate versions of the entire repertoire of Arthurian romance were being translated into Welsh for audiences in Wales. Studies of these translations provide us with a fairly exact picture of what was happening to the stories themselves, changes that help define Romance as a genre (Lloyd-Morgan 78 ff.). That the Welsh translations dropped what they considered alien in the French tales helps define what was being lost and what was being gained in all this ferment. The result helps clarify the perimeters of the Celtic contribution as it was absorbed by the new masters of Western civilization. Among the more prominent of these concerns are attitudes toward reason and reasonableness, very much in the way Southern has defined it. Even more profound is the new concern for the operations of cause and effect. If such an operation is lacking in a particular story, of course, it presents a threat to the supremacy of reason, the cardinal virtue of the new society and its masculine masters. It was the preoccupation with cause and effect that seems most to have concerned Chrétien in his adaptations (Owen). What he achieved made his stories acceptable to women but not to the magnates of the new dispensation. Thus the role of women is also carefully marginalized outside the pale of reason, only ceding to them the lesser kingdoms of caprice and love. Certainly Chrétien's "definitive" Guinevere in his *Lancelot* admirably fulfills these expectations.

The clash between love and power seems to have been particularly vivid in the courts of Marie de Champagne and her more famous mother, Eleanor of Aquitaine. However, with both Chrétien and Andreas Capellanus in tow, Marie was the intellectually more central figure, and while it is possible to read a subversive text into both the *Lancelot* and the *Arts of Love*, the net result of the dominant hermeneutics left women marginalized from the central concerns of power and knowledge—that is, from the institutions of government, education, and church. From that time forward women had no direct access to any of these centers. They did continue to play a role in the development of literature, both as an audience and as producers of tales, but we find much of this activity confined within the same topics left to them by the culture as a whole, the area of love and the irrational. Perhaps the first woman writer to significantly transgress these boundaries did so within the church. Santa Teresa of Avila wrote of church doctrine and was declared the first woman doctor (teacher) of the Church. That she did so within the lifetime of Cervantes is not irrelevant to what he was about in the matter of the power of Romance.

The essential items in this view of the alien survive in the matters of the Celtic tales as they were adapted by Chrétien and his followers for a new audience, and in what they found acceptable and what they tried to suppress. In these two categories we will discover the purposeful functioning of Romance as it came to be articulated in Western culture. It should be stressed that in the material they pushed underground we can see what constituted a threat to the new cultural identity of the era, but at the same time we will also find that the suppressed material didn't truly vanish from the scene. It continued its life underground, beneath the surface of the genre, much as the old Celtic gods were believed to dwell in their underground palaces along the Boyne river in Ireland. In this sense the forces they epitomized did not vanish, they assumed disguises and remained a potential threat to the well-ordered reality of the new male-dominant culture of court, church, and university. Inevitably these same forces found their refuge in the culture of women, and in the literature written for and by them. Romance was the most powerful of these articulations, and it continued to suffer the ostracization that Charles VI's councilor assigned to it. Thus the primary locus of the suppressed energies was to be found in Romance, as the other forms of storytelling became co-opted by humanism and history.

In this long struggle of the marginalization of Romance, *Don Quixote* as a book and Don Quixote as a hero played a crucial role in its survival. Cervantes' achievement redefined the battle lines and provided the world of the fading chivalric (Arthurian) vision with a life closer to the mainstream of the dominant culture. *Don Quixote* as the source of the novel as a new literary kind made these concerns again central to our culture. By establishing the modern novel on the ruins of Romance, Cervantes created a powerful new discourse that made possible the articulation of the fundamental issues of the power of love, intuition, and human relations. What is equally important the *Quixote* constitutes this genre as both free from and yet "acceptable" to the mainstream male concerns of this culture. Cervantes' later contemporary Pascal put it very clearly: The heart has its reasons which reason knows not. Such a statement re-establishes the heart as a powerful force within the assumed dominance of logic.

Don Quixote as a story addresses the same challenge. It achieves this success by inscribing the question of interpretation into the operations of the novel as a literary formulation. Within this kind of formulation it becomes impossible to set forth any project which can claim a single privileged agenda. The novel as a literary kind comes to be with the necessary spaces for subversive subtexts. Such subtexts can occur in the interpretation of all literary forms, but in the novel after the *Quixote*, the question of interpretation is a necessary component of its discourse.

Celtic Narrative as Knowledge

> Myths belong to the world of symbols, and one's apprehension of them is a matter of insight. . . . The full "content" of a myth can never be adequately expressed "in other words." There can be no definitive exegesis.
>
> Alwyn Rees and Brinley Rees

The Hidden Text in Romance: Ontological and Epistemological Arrangements for Heroes, Heroines, and Narrators

The contention that the alien world of the Celtic narrative tradition is embedded within the form of medieval Romance itself contains a double agenda. The alien force is both contained/imprisoned within the later narrative form and at the same time exists there as a hidden configuration with its own signifying capabilities and contradictions. This condition is in its essential features replicated in the 1605 *Quixote* where, among other functions, it serves as a reserve force of Romance power for the 1615 continuation. In focusing on the 1605 articulation of the confrontation between an alien and disturbing source of epistemological energy and its outward re-formulation within a Renaissance narrative structure, the basic epistemological break narratized in Cervantes' text is revealed.

Cervantes' problems with Romance underlie not only the *Quixote* but also the *Galatea* and the *Persiles,* where he sought and partially found other solutions for dealing with them. At issue in the entire spectrum of his work was the question of how to come to terms with a condition of fiction that was not effectively addressed within the poetics of his era. The general condemnation of Romance by both the moral and critical establishments of the Renaissance set up a dichotomy that Cervantes' work sought to undermine. The matter was further exacerbated by the general crisis in epistemology that led up to Descartes's canonization of a division in kinds of knowledge, a division still exercising a powerful influence on Western thought. In this sense, Cervantes' work addressed the same problem but achieved a different resolution, in that he posits a more radical revision to the problem of knowing in literature than Descartes does in philosophy. As we shall see Cervantes allowed a more diversified role for the operations of the instinctive and irrational as modes of knowing. The belief that the heart has its reasons, for Cervantes, meant creating a narrative space for this energy to play itself out within a hostile cultural dispensation that sought to locate the irrational and intuitive outside the dominant discourses. From a practical viewpoint Cervantes' space was a literary genre that became known as the modern novel. The nature of this achievement would not have been possible without the medieval genre of Romance and its inscription of a disruptive Celtic epistemological arrangement. It is there that the story begins.

In the Irish tale known as "The Wooing of Etain" the modern reader finds a poetically powerful articulation of the alien world of Celtic narration. The version we possess may contain language going back to the eighth century, but it presents a mythological world of a much earlier time (Gantz, *Mabinogion* 20). For us the problem of reading the story is complicated by the fact that what we have is a written version of what was originally an oral story, so at best we have a single version of a narrative that circulated in several various guises. The problem is worsened by the fact that the late transcription already incorporates modifications that show some adaptation to the new culture of the Christian middle ages, and as a result certain aspects of the story already have accommodated themselves to the loss of the hermeneutic fix of the original audience. Beyond any normal loss of meaning, clerical transcriptions of tales would show deliberate suppression of pagan material not acceptable to the new religion. In any situation of this kind the well-known process of euhemerization of gods into heroes would be accelerated, even though heroes generally still have access to Otherworld powers.

In this story, for instance, the figure of the Dagda is still recognizably a major deity. One interpretation of his name, "lord of perfect knowledge" (Owen, *Evolution* 5), identifies him as a figure that addresses the problem of what possibilities of knowing existed. The power of this kind of knowledge is obviously not organized around a twelve-century principle of reason. In the same way the Dagda does not represent a category of knowledge that will find a place within the curriculum of the medieval university. In short he represents a kind of knowing that has already been marginalized by Western civilization. He is, however, a figure who will find various incarnations in the later genre of Romance. Merlin is not a direct descendent of the Dagda, but he occupies certain spaces that originally belonged to the Dagda's larger domain. Thus a wizard figure or a powerful enchanter in a romance will survive to play a significant role in the *libros de caballería*. Through the medium of popular Romance from Chrétien onwards, the enchanter survives, although in a trivialized or demonized role. Old gods go underground and inhabit the world of popular legends, tale, superstitions, and so forth. But in the genre of Romance Chrétien created a literature flexible enough to accommodate the survival of an un-understandable power. In the *Amadís* Urganda la desconocida and Arcalaus present figures that seem to divide between them the positive and negative forces of fate and chance, even though the demonization of Arcalaus is still not a completed process.

But even in this very early Irish tale the Dagda's behavior is problematic for an all-powerful god, which may indicate that he has already suffered some diminution of his status. He resorts to all sorts of tricks to achieve his goals. He therefore has to "enchant" the husband of a woman he wants to possess sexually. He does this in such a way that he deceives the husband but not the woman. This is different from the Uther Pendragon/Igraine situation in the begetting of Arthur, where the woman is also deceived. At this earlier time, it would seem that women did not have to disguise their sexual motives to themselves in the same way that we find in later stories. The manner in which the Irish story narrates this duplicity and lack of duplicity is quite straightforward and shows no Christian scruples:

> The Dagdae wanted to sleep with Boand, and she would have allowed him, but she feared Elcmar [her husband] and the extent of his power. The Dagdae sent Elcmar away, then, on a journey to Bress son of Elatha at Magninis; and as Elcmar was leaving, the Dagdae cast great spells upon him, so that he would not return quickly, so that he would not perceive the darkness of night, so that he would feel neither hunger nor thirst. The Dagdae charged Elcmar with great commissions, so that nine months passed like a single day, for Elcmar had said that he would return before night-fall. The Dagdae slept with Elcmar's wife, then, and she bore him a son, who was named Oengus; and by the time of Elcmar's return, she had so recovered that he had no inkling of her having slept with the Dagdae. (Gantz, *Mabinogion* 39)

From this beginning follows a long story in which after numerous transformations, the Dagdae, also known as Echu, falls in love and lives with his own daughter. It is during the course of these events that the girl, Etain, is at a certain stage turned into (1) a pool of water that (2) turns into a worm that (3) turns into a fly that (4) is swallowed by a queen who bears her as (5) a daughter, also named Etain. During this series of transmogrifications she is loved and sought after by Oengus; by his stepfather, Mider; and finally by Echu, his original father. While numerous features of this kind of story survive as recognizable components of Romance, the re-incarnational elements are generally suppressed or disguised, probably due to Christian scruples.

Today Celticists relate this feature to similar re-incarnational beliefs in India where early Indo-European beliefs received a different development (Dillon; Rees and Rees 230f.). Only occasionally in certain rapid displacements of heroes in Romance do we find similar situations in later fiction, and these became precisely the features of Romance that were made the object of comic scorn. Don Quixote, for instance, tells Sancho that a hero can go to sleep and be transported to the ends of the earth in the winking of an eye. We also can just barely recognize the trajectory of the juxtaposing realities in Ariosto and in the machinations of Angelica something that seems to originate in another kind of reality than the one we are accustomed to. In the *Amadís*, however, Urganda la desconocida still shows instances of a very primitive transformational capability. In a more disguised format we can see a distant similarity in the shifting incarnations of Dorotea/Micomicona at the inn, particularly as she is perceived first by Sancho and then by Don Quixote. However long the tradition, Dorotea and Angelica both descend from Etain. The most radical difference between them, however, is that woman's "changeableness" is later valorized as a profound defect by Christian anti-feminism. The illusion of male logocentrism has projected its inner anxieties onto the other sex in order to localize a threat in an external other.

There is another genre of Irish tales that also has a bearing on the heroic achievements of all chivalric heroes, including Don Quixote. This grouping, called "boyhood deeds," casts a long shadow over the world of Romance. Some of the Welsh stories collected under the title *Mabinogion*, including the story of *Peredur*, belong to this literary kind. One of the meanings associated with term Mabinogi in fact is boyhood deeds. The French term *enfances* and the Spanish *mocedades* are part of the same tradition. In the narrative form in which these stories come to us the genre is characterized by a series individual events in the youth of the hero strung loosely together. This serial aspect of the story is to enjoy a long and productive history in its tendency to relate an unending series of adventures in the *libros de caballería*. In one sense both parts of *Don Quixote* are prolonged versions of the hero's youthful exploits with the matter of the hero's age reversed. Sequels are inevitable in this genre, since new adventures can easily be added and the hero's adventures become "inacabable" "unendable" as both Cide Hamete and Don Quixote observe.

An examination of some of the narrative features of this genre provides an insight into how the hero's adventures were organized. Given their episodic nature, we will observe how certain aspects of the Irish articulation of this reality were lost or suppressed in their translation from the "primitive" Celtic tales to their later, more "reasonably" ordered Romance format. At the same time we will also note how other narrative features survived into Chrétien's tales and thence into later fictional formulations including *Don Quixote*.

In the cycle of stories gathered around the figure of CuChulainn we find the usual mysteries surrounding his birth, the expected confusions concerning his parentage, and then a series of boyhood deeds. These features mark his as a major hero complete with divine ancestry and Otherworld powers. He is in fact the son of Lug, a major god associated, among other attributes, with thunderbolts, roads, chess, and crafts and was identified with Hermes by Julius Caesar (Rees and Rees 143). In the confusing galaxy of Celtic deities, Lug's name is one of the few to have a wide geographic distribution, and the etymon of his name is found in numerous towns such as Lyon, Leiden, and Liegnitz. While Roman approximations of Celtic deities are never adequate, the association with Hermes is of interest. The Irish tale states clearly enough that Lug is the hero's father, though he is also known as the son of his mother's mortal husband. All this provides the necessary nexus for the mystery of the hero's identity. The latter point is further complicated by the fact that he is born with one name but later acquires another, a factor associated with many heroes including Lancelot and Don Quixote. However the name confusion is rather prominent in the Irish tale, and there is even discussion by the hero and his mother as to which is the best name for him. In fact the name mystery is left unresolved, since the narrator continues to disregard the hero's preferences and call him CuChulainn, just as Cide Hamete continues to call Don Quijote by his *nom de guerre* after the hero says he prefers Alonso Quijano. Another item of enduring importance in this kind of tale is that his mother, or sometimes other women, rear him in the absence of a father. This seems to be important in what follows since, in spite of his mother's objections, he chooses to go through a second education in order to become a warrior. In one sense this constitutes his rejection of a world of women for a world of men, and it may reflect the historical shift from a pastoral culture to a warrior culture of horses and chariots. Whatever the origins, this factor also has something to do with the hero's search for his true identity, which was obscured by his ignorance of his divine father. Perceval is the most famous of these heroes because of Chrétien's much later re-articulation of this story in *Li Contes del Graal*. Even in *Don Quixote* the hero rejects his feminine household and goes in search of his new male identity, and at the same time his true parents are never mentioned, so that Cervantes' "new" story accords with arrangements found in the early tales. In this sense one reads the CuChulainn story with heroes like Perceval and Don Quixote in mind.

CuChulainn, however, is closer to his divine ancestry than later warriors, and his empowerment as a warrior simply descends upon him as his "riastarthae" or battle fury. Something of this kind of empowerment survives in modern comic strip heroes like Popeye (whose name inscribes another attribute of Celtic heroes), Spider Man and even Superman. In this arrangement the teaching/learning process is much abbreviated and does not show the gradual evolution of a perfect courtly hero found in Chrétien. In fact the courtly element is entirely missing in the Irish tale, since gods are perfect in their nature and do not need or want human tutoring. The problem of human tutoring is precisely what creates the story in the later development of the tale. Likewise CuChulainn spends little time acquiring fame as the greatest warrior, since he achieves this glory while still a child. Another narrative feature is that the story is told with parodic humor, even though this aspect of the story is not particularly apparent to the modern reader (Gantz, *Mabinogion* 25]. As Eisenberg has noted with the *Quixote*, its humor was more pronounced for the original audience than it is for modern readers (*A Study*).

This general outline of the tale, sometimes categorized as the adventures of the fair unknown or *Le Bel Inconnu*, is very familiar in later European literature, both in Romance and in realistic formats. The earliest Irish version presents us with a kind of reality unknown in the more modern forms. A brief quotation from the beginning of CuChulainn's boyhood deeds will illustrate this gap.

The story opens with the relation of the mysteries of his parentage and his birth. These events include a complex impregnation process of his mother in which a god, a dream, a copper vessel, and a human husband each have a role. In the instance of the copper vessel from which his mother drinks there is already a proto-grail suggestiveness about the cup. "Every time she put the vessel to her mouth, a tiny creature would leap from the liquid toward her lips, yet, when she took the vessel from her mouth, there was nothing to be seen" (Gantz *Early Irish* 132).

The birth sequence is followed by the boyhood-deeds-story proper. Here the reader notes that the narrative act, as in other parts of the CuChulainn cycle, is performed by a chieftian who recalls the boyhood of the hero. The chieftian in this segment is named Fergus, and at the time of the act of narrating he is hostile to the Ulaid, CuChulainn's clan. This factor seems to be used to help verify the validity of the narrator's interpretation, a situation that anticipates the Islamic attitude of Cide Hamete toward a Christian Don Quixote. In spite of the fact that the narrator's hermeneutic is thus circumscribed, the story is told from a viewpoint that is not limited in any way by the narrator's ability to

observe the events. Instead the story often reads as though he is omni-
scient, since he himself is not consistently present.

He relates that, after initially failing to follow the culturally approved
sequence of acts leading to warrior status, CuChulainn is attacked by
several groups of boys who represent the usual schooling process. The
hero's alienation from normal warrior schooling is to be a crucial and
consistent feature of this kind of story, from CuChulainn to Perceval and
Don Quixote. In CuChulainn's case, it is only after foiling the prelimi-
nary assaults of the other boys that he suffers his first seizure of the
"riastarthae," his battle fury. The narrator presents this singular development with considerable rhetorical elaboration:

> Then his riastarthae came upon him. You would have thought
> that every hair was being driven into his head. You would have
> thought that a spark of fire was on every hair. He closed one eye
> until it was no wider than the eye of a needle; he opened the
> other until it was as big as a wooden bowl. He bared his teeth
> from jaw to ear, and he opened his mouth until the gullet was
> visible. The warrior's moon rose from his head. (Gantz, *Early
> Irish* 136)

It is obvious that there is a lot of coded information here, the meaning
of which is not accessible to later readers. In trying to explicate this kind
of passage scholars can suggest anthropological sources for the imagery
or other cultural associations with bowls, warrior's moons, and so forth.
Whatever meanings can be put forward, however, it is clear that we can
only tentatively reconstruct an original hermeneutic fix. We can never
approach the tale with the automatic ease of the original audience armed
with the necessary cultural information for a proper read. In addition,
this version comes to us in a fairly late re-formulation, which means that
some of the language may have been inserted or modified by later tellers
of the tale. It has also been observed that such re-teller's of these tales,
by the time of the middle ages, were themselves no longer certain of
original meanings. The loss of meaning had set in long before Chrétien
took up the material.

In the passage cited we can even find suggestions of this collapsing
hermeneutic fix as the narrator attempts to adjust the material for his
own audience. The phrase "you would have thought that," used to introduce comparisons in both the second and third sentences, not only in-

scribes the reader into the text but in itself sound suspiciously like an attempt to come to terms with some unfamiliar goings on. We seem to be reading a later, perhaps poetic rhetoric found necessary by the re-teller of the tale. Certainly the last image of the warrior's moon has crossed over from its coded anthropological sources into the domain of poetic expression. This means that the language now accommodates a double hermeneutic fix: one a literal statement of a culturally recognized sign and the other a later "poetic" statement of considerable suggestive power.

Chrétien himself seems to be coming to similar rhetorical strategies as he adapted the traditional material for his own audience. A well-known instance would be the case of the flirtatious Lunette's encounter with Gawain in *Perceval*. In this passage the known anthropological associa-tions of the characters of Lunette and Gawain with the moon and the sun still seems to play upon the surface of the language and suggest a par-tially hidden symbiotic attraction between the two which enhances their well-developed erotic individuality. This feature of the double hermeneutic fix of the language of Romance did not commence with Chrétien but finds its source in much earlier formulations of the stories. In all these cases, however, the narrators are already "unreliable," in that there is a gap between their own value system and an earlier value system implicit in the story.

In the next paragraph of the CuChulainn sequence there are other narrative and linguistic devices that reveal additional problems with the narrator's authority, even though the contentual tonality of the action is more modern.

> Cu Chulaind (sic) struck at the boys and overthrew fifty of them before they could reach the doors of Emuin. Nine of them ran over *Conchubur and myself as we were playing fidchell*; Cu Chulaind sprang over the board after them, but Conchubur took his arm and said "Not good your treatment of the boy troop." "Fair play it is," answered Cu Chulaind. "I came from my mother and my father to play with them, and they were not nice to me."

> *"What is your name?"* asked Conchubur. "Sétantae, the son of Sualtaim and of *Deichtine, your sister*. I did not expect such a reception here." "Why did you not secure the boys' protection?" asked Conchubur. "*I did not know* that was necessary," replied Cu

Chulaind. "Accept my protection now, then," said Conchubur.
"That I will," answered Cu Chulaind. (Gantz, *Early Irish* 137
emphasis added)

In this passage we note the appearance of a number of narrative arrangements found in later Romance. First the narrator appears within his own
tale just at the point in which the hero jumps over a chesslike game called
"fidchell." The meeting of narrator and hero over a game of chance may
harken back to the connection of Lug with chess, but it also foreshadows
a persistent appearance and re-appearance of chess imagery in such tales,
often a sign of the struggle of the center against chaos (Rees and Rees
154ff.). Gawain's shield in the Castle of the Ladies episode of Chrétien's *Li
Contes del Graal* is only one instance of the recurrence of such imagery. The
appearance of Conchubur at this point is also of note in that the hero's
trajectory intersects that of his maternal uncle, a point at which his actions
receive a crucial correction of their course. This is a persistent function in
later Romance of tutor-uncles who inform the hero of his ancestry, his
destiny, and other matters. In other terms, both the narrator and the male
relative may signal a fateful energy operative in the text, and the hero is
presented as fulfilling a pre-ordained role. A related item is the "deterio-
rated role" (Gantz, *Mabinogion* 134) of Conchubur. In the birth tale he is the
hero's grandfather; here he is the uncle. This kind of contradiction points
to the problem of garbled texts and a possible conflation of later and
earlier versions of the tale. However this effect of layering of textual versions occurred, it remains as a narrative feature of Romance. Whatever the
"book" was that Chrétien claimed to be his source for his *Perceval* very
likely contained similar instance of textual layering, since such textual
"errors" came to exist as a feature of the genre. Like the Kafka story of the
leopards who came to the temple to drink the blood of the sacrifice, the
account of their repeated appearance eventually becomes part of the ritual.
In this same way the feature of narratival contradictions became part and
parcel of later Romance.

Another problematic here is the matter of the narrator's authority. His
sudden appearance as an actor in the scene is remarkable for various
reasons. How is it, we ask, that the narrator now assumes a minor role
in the action when at other times he narrated *in absentia* with an unquestioned omniscience? The result is a jarring awareness of the fluctuating
presence and non-presence of the narrator, first as an authorial narrational voice-over and then as an actor in a specific instance. It would be

more accurate to say that the narrational voice is a complex of various voices, sometimes speaking with absolute authority and other times assuming a more mediating role, placing himself between the reader and the main action of the story. The effect is that certain narrational mysteries are incorporated into the manner of telling stories which give the voice a character of an Otherworld force. In this way the narrator is not unlike the events narrated in that both the hero and the narrator suffer kinds of transformations that are intrinsic to the ontological force of the tale itself. Certain aspects of this arrangement are found in the status of Cide Hamete and other narrators in the *Quixote*. Don Quixote explains this by observing that narrators in the *libros de caballería* are enchanters who know the most secret thoughts of the hero, even though Cide Hamete generally presents himself as an external historian working from a collection of documents.

Still the arbitrariness of the game of fidchell seems a coded reference to another meaning. The fact that the hero is asked for his name at the moment of a leap across the game board is too specific to be inadvertent. The semiotics of the scene is now getting a bit crowded, and it is necessary to keep the various signs both separate and inter-related. First, we have noted that the appearance of the narrator occurs during a game of chance. Then, the hero crosses over the game board, and at that instant, is asked his name, thus associating the question of his name with the leap over a game of chance. At this point the hero says his name is Sétentae and indicates his relationship to the interlocutor who turns out to be an uncle. But in spite of this exact information about his name the narrator continues to call him by another name, CuChulainn. The birth name *Sétentae* in Gaelic means "knower of roads and ways" (Gantz, *Early Irish* 131), an altogether suitable name for the son of a Mercury-like deity. The name itself, however, also brings up the question of knowing, or of having access to certain kinds of knowledge, which foregrounds the question of the hero's epistemological powers at this juncture. The leap over the board also suggests that the hero can rapidly cross barriers and obstacles, another mercurial capability. His nature seems to incorporate a knowledge of how to overcome or cross over boundaries, and the boundary factor in later versions becomes important. Meanwhile, the maternal uncle is a figure of an older warrior who himself possesses knowledge that the hero lacks. This disparity of knowledge is narratized in the verbal exchange between Conchubur and CuChulainn: "Why did you not secure the boys' protection?" . . . "I did not know that was necessary." Thus the appearance of the game and the players, both here and in later versions, coincides with both chance and the fateful acquisition of necessary knowledge concerning his role, an arrangement that perseveres in both the Welsh tale of "The Dream of Macsin" and in Chrétien's *Perceval*. In the *Quixote* Karl-Ludwig Selig has found a relation between references to the game of chess and the signifying system of the text itself. While he posits no single source for this phenomenon, he notes that multiple emblematic and other referential instances of chess were common in the literature of the era (Selig "chess..."). This association between the signifying power of chess and language is also consistent with Cervantes' use of textual auto-referentiality. This feature, both in the Celtic tale and in the *Quixote*, is therefore one that fictionalizes literary practices so that they become part of the hero's "story."

In the Irish tales this kind of linguistic self-dramatization creates a numinous energy, indicative that there is a hidden meaning buried in the language. Even though we cannot fully "read" what meaning the game and the players may have, we do perceive an association of the narrator with a game of chance and an unknown fateful power. Rees and Rees sees the use of riddles as a sign for crossing borders to the Otherworld (266). Thus, here narrator is not just narrating but presenting his own identity as an Otherworld mover of figures in a game. It is only a short step from this placement to a condition in which the narrator can intervene in the action of not just the game but of the story. This capability survives as a genre-linked feature in the *libros de caballería*, as Don Quixote observes. More than once he attributes this kind of force to the narrator, and in one action the narrator's intervention also relates to the form of the hero's name. In the episode of Don Quixote's encounter with the funeral procession (an icon of the Otherworld) in part 1, chapter 29, we find that Sancho calls Don Quixote the *Caballero de la triste figura*, and the knight immediately attributes that name, which he accepts, as an instance of the narrator intervening in the story.

Covarrubias's *Tesoro de la lengua* includes among the many meanings of *figura* its usage both as a trick in a game of cards and in the devices of astrologers, thus relating Don Quixote's new name to the operations of both chance and game structure. This association picks up the earlier references the wounded mourner has made to his own lack of good fortune. Thus a set of narrative features found in an early Celtic tale are re-assembled in a similar instance in the *Quixote* in which there is the problem of the hero's name. In the case of CuChulainn we find that, when asked, the hero gives his original or birth name, Sétantae, although the narrator, speaking from another perspective, calls him CuChulainn, a name he does not acquire until a later action. In the *Quixote* the narrator calls the hero "the hidalgo" until the point that the hero himself invents his name, but from that point onward he is called Don Quixote even though other names are acquired from time to time. Even at the conclusion of part 2, when the hero is dying and has called himself Alonso Quijano, the narrator still calls him Don Quixote. Thus the gap between the narrator's usage of the name and that of the hero remains as a feature of the Romance narrative repertoire. How Cervantes enhances the problem of the hero's name to establish a fictional language will be examined more fully below.

One other adventure of CuChulainn is significant from the perspective of later Romance and is indicative of the condition of both language and literature within the story itself. The erratic narrative movement in this segment of the story is compatible with the hero's mercurial nature since he is projected as the "knower of roads and ways" in his first chariot ride on a curiously meaningful road. It is often observed that the locations in these tales are Irish or of the Otherworld or a conflation of the two. The scene here partakes of both environments and provides a glimpse of a lost and disturbing reality. The chariot imagery easily dates this episode as pre-Roman. Caesar himself had observed that the Celts still fought with chariots in the manner of the Homeric Greeks. As a people living on the outer boundary of the Indo-European linguistic/cultural group, the Irish preserved patterns of behavior long lost on the continent. In this story the importance of the chariot as a symbol of CuChulainn's empowerment as a warrior clearly signals the value this episode once had.

In this series of adventures CuChulainn, following a Druid's advice, insists on taking up arms for the first time on a specific day since the Druid prophesies that anyone who steps into a chariot that day will be famous forever. In the episodes that follow CuChulainn is inevitably successful against various enemies of the Ulaid and returns to his clan with his victims' heads tied to the chariot. At the very outset of these adventures he is very much the explorer in a new land, and Conchubur's charioteer serves as his servant and to some extent his guide. Again we find that the hero, although uninitiated, has certain kinds of knowledge that have their source in his nature rather than in anything learned from his experience. We are quickly reminded that he is a hero whose birth name identifies him with knowledge of roads and therefore knows something of his own destiny.

The charioteer—Ibor was his name—turned the chariot about, saying " Come out of the chariot, now." But Cu Chulaind replied "The horses are beautiful, and I am beautiful, lad. Take a turn round Emuin [the place of the Ulaid] with us, and I will reward you." After that, Cu Chulaind and Ibor take him to say goodbye to the boys, "so that the boys might bless me." He then entreated the charioteer to return to the road and when they arrived he said "Put the whip to the horses, now." "In what direction?" asked Ibor. "As far as the road leads," Cu Chulaind answered. (Gantz, *Early Irish* 142)

Both in the arrogance and in the poetic tenor of CuChulainn's language we sense the unnerving inner force of his character. Considering that he is only six or seven at this point his precociousness is not merely human. He is a fully grown hero inhabiting a child's being. In the next encounter we learn something about both the nature of the hero and the cultural perceptions of the world he inhabits.

They went on to Sliab Fuait, where they met Conall Cernach. That day it was Conall's turn to protect the province—every Ulaid warrior of worth took a turn at Sliab Fuait, *protecting those who came with poems*, fighting enemies and seeing that no one came to Emuin unannounced. (142, emphasis added)

The location is obviously a border crossing point, another locus of the god Mercury. Two activities apparently occur here, one having to do with the arrival of poems and the other with fighting enemies. Poetry and enemies apparently both arrive from the Otherworld and require in different ways the participation of heroes. The linking but differentiating quality of these two functions is further clarified in what follows:

"May you prosper," said Conall,"and may you be victorious and triumphant." "Return to the fort, Conall, and leave me here to watch in your place," said Cu Chulaind. "Well enough that," said Conall, "for protecting those with poetry, but you are not yet able to fight."

"Perhaps it will not come to that," said Cu Chulaind. "In any case, let us go to look at the sandbar at Loch nEchtrae, for it is customary for young warriors to rest there." "Very well," replied Conall. (142)

It is clear that protecting those who come with poems in the first duty of the hero, but just what constitutes this type of protection is unknown, since it may not require fighting. But because the protection from physical danger is not part of the task, the danger must come from another quarter, perhaps from the Otherworld itself. In either case the status of poetry is established as both powerful and yet somehow vulnerable. Fighting itself, however, is another matter, but the warrior is this cultural nexus is somehow empowered to act in each capacity.

While the world of the Renaissance is still a long way off, we do note that Don Quixote's obsessive concern for the competing but symbiotic values of arms and letters has a long pedigree. Its origins are not quite clear in this passage, but the dangers of each activity are located at the boundary with the unknown. The final exchange between CuChulainn and Conall also brings out the link between the initiation of warriors and the concept of 'echtra,' the Celtic word for a predestined heroic encounter and a predestined fame for the hero. It is particularly significant that CuChulainn is the source of this information, thus linking it with his kind of personal foreknowledge originating in his own divinity. The hero, by definition, clearly knows what is and is not an *echtra,* or adventure, a power repeatedly at risk in Don Quixote's search for fame and his insistence on knowing which adventure is reserved for him alone (Dudley "Ring . . ." 18 ff.).

Thus in summary we find a number of narrative strategies and features that define the condition of both a mythological hero and later chivalric heroes like Perceval or Don Quixote. We note that the hero:

- has a mysterious birth and identity

- has access to certain kinds of knowledge having to do with roads and adventure but lacks knowledge of common social codes information; in other terms, he sometimes has exceptional foreknowledge of his destiny but at the same time is socially incompetent

- leaves a world of women to seek fame in a male warrior society

- is helped by a maternal uncle or some other teaching figure

- achieves both a new heroic identity and a new name

All these kinds of features are indicative of a euhemerized hero with both divine and human epistemological powers.

Even more significant is the fact that the narrator (Fergus/Cide Hamete) is a member of a hostile cultural group, so that the validity of his information is conditioned by this hostility. The narrator is also inserted into the action at a crucial moment of conflict in which the hero's name is at issue. In addition the narrator's actions seem to indicate the existence of another story about a curious game, but we are not told what that story is. The result of all these features and narrative strategies is a sense of mystery relating to the existence of categories of knowledge to which we as readers do not have access, thus placing us in a situation in which our own hermeneutic fix is shown to be inadequate. The question of this type of inadequacy in turn foregrounds the fact that the narrator's authority is not always adequate to his own task of narrating. The condition of the hero in particular is problematic for the narrator. He is seen at certain times to possess more knowledge than the hero (in the question of the name) but at other times does not seem to know everything pertinent to a full understanding what is happening in the story.

This disparity between the hero's sense of his own destiny and the narrator's view of what is happening emerges as type of epistemological rift in the text. The narrator is defined as partially endowed with knowledge of the meaning underlying the action, but his appearance as a character in the action also inscribes him as a learner. He presents himself in a position of seeing how the action will work out as he sits at the playing board. His narrational voice is endowed with other kinds of social knowledge, such as how the hero got the name by which he is usually called, but at the same time he seems unaware of the hero's Otherworld origins. This in turn brings out a crucial element of disagreement between the hero and the narrator concerning the most suitable name for the protagonist, a difference which will determine how the story is to be told. These contradictions puts the hero's knowledge of himself in a curiously constrained epistemological situation. We note, for example, that he suffers his battle fury without questioning its sudden appearance but apparently still doesn't know or use the name by which the narrator calls him.

In an important sense this curious mix of knowledge and ignorance on the part of both the hero and the narrator becomes the topic of the story. The hero, the narrator, and the reader (the "you" is inscribed into the text) are all situated within the tale with different levels of knowledge, and as a result the story itself becomes more a story about how certain kinds of knowledge will be made accessible than a story about what happened to the hero. In this way the nominative actions of the hero achieve a emblematic function that to a great extent undermines the story as a relation of external events. Instead we are presented with events as a sequence of signs whose arrangement has to do with their meaning rather than a reflection of the order in which they may have happened. The "story" is determined by a grammar of meaning rather than by reference to a sequence of external events. This feature survives in the *Quixote* at various points at which the narrator does not seem certain of the ordering of the hero's adventure. Thus we do not get a sense that events in the story happen as the result of other events in the story. It is not a cause-and-effect situation. It is in this sense that the events seem coded to a hidden category of knowledge.

Likewise, that these stories were later to be re-told according to a very different cultural context and re-read with a new hermeneutic fix becomes an essential feature of Romance as a genre. It must be further remembered that an allegorical reading, such as the one attempted for the grail story, is a radically alien hermeneutic. The originating myths were not allegories in the medieval sense. The result is that the "new meaning," Chrétien's *sens*, often does not belong to the narrative pattern as it was originally constituted. Instead, such transformations, inevitably occurring as the original meaning begins to lose its force, become one of the features of Romance as a story. The half-forgotten meaning remains in the language and continues to exist as a "hidden text" operating beneath the surface of new interpretive concerns.

This narrative arrangement constitutes a crucial condition of Romance as a genre. The fact that Romance inscribes the problem of its own shifting hermeneutics as a genre-linked feature marks it as a genre about reading genres. Its self-conscious hermeneutic fix is paradigmatic of what happens to the referential power of stories when the hermeneutic act itself becomes the subject of the story. Thus the controlling factor of the organization of the story has to do with the problematics of narrativity and reading and not with an external sequence of events that happened. This narrative condition, by an accident of history, was to be later passed on to medieval writers of Romance and later reformulated by Cervantes in the *Quixote*. How this became possible will be seen in the next stage of the transformation of tales of mythic beings into tales of Romance knights.

Peredur/Perceval and the Grail Configuration: One Hero Two Ways

> "So tell me who is the purest knight?"
> "That knight is King Arthur."
>
> Wolfram von Eschenbach, *Parzifal*

The transmission of Celtic material from Ireland and Wales to the new centers of culture in northern France remains the subject of important debates. How and why the tales of half-forgotten heroes of a lost insular Celtic world became the most popular topic of a new continental literature in the twelfth century remains a mystery. Reducing the inquiry to the matter of *why* this occurred has certain advantages. The compelling fascination with the matter of Britain in medieval Europe does not, on the face of things, seem an inevitable outgrowth of the social or political concerns of the times. Whatever answers are suggested to such a question will probably fall short of satisfying the need. Nevertheless the "why question" can both enrich and sharpen the nature of the debate about how it happened.

To a great extent the question of how this transmission occurred, how a cultural phenomenon of the fringe areas of Europe moved to center stage in the twelfth century, has obscured the more fundamental question of why this occurred. The French were certainly not under pressure from a rising Celtic power. Rather, the Celtic material represented a fading world, one already on the brink of extinction or absorption into the new ascendent French and Norman hegemony. It would seem therefore that the task for Chrétien and his followers was to rescue the remnants and re-constitute them for a new public. This can be explained as a type of longing for the victim, something like the endeavor of the literature of the New World, both Spanish and English, to come to terms with the culture of the Indians. Writers like Cooper in the United States or López y Fuentes in Mexico fall into the broad category of such a project. Still the success of the matter of Britain is much more spectacular than anything experienced so far for the American Indian. Arthur and his knights did not just become another group of heroes, they became *the* paradigmatic heroes of the new culture, the supreme archetypes incarnating the most privileged virtues of feudalism, chivalry, and courtly love.

The success of this achievement is attested to by the nature of the attacks against it, attacks that persevered into the Renaissance and beyond. The curious phenomenon of *Amadís de Gaula* is an important example of the strength of Europe's fascination with the chivalric vision of a lost Celtic world, even in a country like Spain in which the pre-Roman underpinnings of its identity are much more deeply buried than in France or Britain. Yet it was *Amadís* that became this first popular success of the age of the printing press, not only in Spain but in Europe in general. The power of this development then went on to evoke a work like *Don Quixote*, another international best-seller. Again the question *why* rather than *how* cannot be unimportant. From this context we can approach a study of the role of Romance as it appears in *Li Contes del Graal* and in the *Quixote* as a question with wide cultural implications.

Furthermore, we find specific topics within that broad endeavor that are relevant to the problem of the ontology of Romance itself. And we can stipulate that the importance of the *Quixote* for this project is that it is already a major examination of the same question: Why does reading Romance cause madness? The nominal formulation of the work is ostensibly a critique of the power of Romance. The error has been in taking Cide Hamete's formulation of this question as the purpose of the work. Rather it should be seen that Cide Hamete's articulation of his anti-Romance agenda is part of the question and not part of the answer. The problem is to get outside the arguments for and against Romance put forward by either Cide Hamete or Don Quixote. This can be done by examining how specific narrative and thematic features of Romance were re-articulated by the *Quixote* as a text. In this perspective the work is to be read as the ultimate meta-Romance in which the validity of the topic is examined again and again. The grail question for the *Quixote* is not, Who is served by the grail? as it was in Chrétien but rather, What happens when we read Romances? It must be recognized that *Don Quixote* is the ultimate book about reading as a cultural phenomenon. As such its relevance is more crucial today than it was in 1605.

Reading and Romance

To select specific items for study from the wide history of medieval Romance is difficult but necessary. I have therefore chosen two primary foci for this study. They are first the *figura* of Perceval and then his most paradigmatic adventure, the encounter with the grail procession at the castle of the Fisher King. Reference to many other aspects of Romance will be necessary, but these two topics, the "funny" hero and his grail adventure, will serve as important defining configurations for an illusive literary genre.

The appropriateness of this choice is supported by the continuing power these icons have demonstrated both within subsequent literature and within a broader cultural context. We see this not only in the proliferation of a grail literature in the vulgate and post-vulgate cycles of Romance literature but also in the fact that the grail has become a common item in our cultural lexicon. The image survives not only in the fiction of everything from spy novels to detective stories and films but in advertising, industry, sports, and even politics. We find expressions such as the holy grail of science (the discovery of DNA) or sport (the winning of Wimbledon, the World Cup, the Super Bowl) and in politics where Camelot has come to signify the appeal and contradictions of the Kennedy years in the United States. Because of all these echoes the grail procession scene in *Li Contes del Graal* survives as the most potent and enduring image of medieval literature, comparable in many ways to the windmill scene in *Don Quixote* as far as its broad cultural impact is concerned.

In a sense, much later literature and scholarship, starting with the first grail continuation, are attempts to re-interpret this scene. Both the Celticist D. D. R. Owen and the French scholar Jean Frappier have speculated that part of the scene's power and immortality has been due to the simple fact that Chrétien died before finishing the work and thus left open to speculation whatever closure or lack of closure he had in mind. To some extent this is true, but a closer look at both the Celtic tales and Chrétien's text reveals that the self-reflecting question of interpretation was already written into the general discourse of Romance. In fact, this self-questioning stance is one of the most distinctive features of Romance and of the *Quixote*. Nevertheless Chrétien's terse narratization of the grail scene as the ultimate interpretive challenge provides the necessary climactic intensity to launch this project. The enigmatic procession has become the *figura* of Romance as a literary kind (Lacy et al. 1: 33–56).

The recognition of this development in part addresses the question of why Romance moved to the center stage of medieval literature. Quite simply its numinous appeal must have served an affective need within the culture as a whole. The point is that the question without a single clear answer responded to an unspoken need for those matters that eluded the logocentric agenda of the era. Chrétien effectively created a narrative space where neglected emotional needs of both women and men could find expression. While a full answer to that question is beyond the purpose of this study, it is not surprising that the *Quixote* would intrude itself into the problem, since the work of Cervantes is central to the entire history of Romance, both before and after his time. In this sense the question of why we have Romance at all lies very close to the questioning heart of the *Quixote*, and Don Quixote and Cide Hamete as readers of Romance are, in a specific sense, the most important emblems of reading in the history of literature.

So far we have examined a few episodes in the Irish CuChulainn cycle and have found even at the most primitive stage the reading problem of the double hermeneutic fix. This means that the story, as related, tells of events which carry a significant burden of their original import, of the meaning they must have had for the early Celts, but at the same time these early meanings have begun to blur and new interpretations of them have been written into the stories. A most important consequence of this historical development produces a narrative voice that does not fully understand the various horizons of the meaning of a tale. This authorial uncertainty becomes even more pronounced as the tales begin their move from a Celtic context in Ireland and Wales to the central nexus of the Anglo-Norman-French world of Chrétien and his contemporaries.

It is generally accepted that the first step of the tales' cultural migration occurred in Wales. This is not surprising if we recognize that, since the time of the withdrawal of Roman forces in the fourth century, Wales was under heavy pressure from Irish marauders on one side and the power of the Saxons on the other. By the eleventh century the French speaking Normans had replaced the Saxons as the dominant challenge. At that time they were expanding their power across the expanse of the Christian world from Dublin to Beirut and Jerusalem. In this way Wales became the paradigm of a border culture where the new and the old were at greatest risk. Perhaps that was one reason why the typology of Irish heroes appealed to the Welsh. The heroic image of CuChulainn at the Ulaid border became a most apt icon for their own cultural situation. They needed a border hero, a Marcher Lord, to shore up their own endangered identity. The fact that CuChulainn was also a hero of another kind of border, of a frontier with the Otherworld, may have made this typology even more appealing.

Cultural extinction poses problems and for Celts these concerns were at a breaking point. After a thousand years of being pushed to the western fringes of the Europe they had once dominated, the experience had transformed them into a border people in every sense of the word. In this sense the need for an Arthur figure preceded his emergence into their literature.

His first appearance as a king at whose court others seek help or adventure is in the Welsh story of *Cuhlwch and Olwen*. This story comes to us as one of the ur-Romances in *The Mabinogion*, a collection of early Welsh tales that have survived in medieval formulations. Another tale in that same collection is the story of *Peredur*, whose name and adventures parallel the more famous Perceval of *Li Contes del Graal* (Gantz, *Mabinogion* 217). Many studies of the two works have been made and have sought to clarify the relationship between them. We find no scholarly agreement on this problem. The basic options are a combination of three opinions. First, *Peredur* is the earlier version even though in the form we have it, it seems to date slightly later. Second, *Peredur* is fundamentally a Welsh reworking of Chrétien's tale. Certain linguistic borrowings point this way. Third, the two tales share common source material now lost. None of these views totally excludes aspects of the other, and, from the point of view which I will take here, perhaps it doesn't matter all that much. One thing, however, does matter: both tales are re-readings of earlier narrative formulations. This arrangement of a story as a re-narratization is to be one of the most fundamental features of all later Romance. The Welsh version, whatever its relation to Chrétien, must be seen as affirming its own interpretation of the tale, and this reading or "translation" will reveal something of the importance that tale has within Celtic culture. However imperiled by the Normans, the Welsh would still retain more of the earlier Celtic view of the world than would Chrétien's version, redacted in a non-Celtic language. Each author, the unknown Welshman or the French clerically trained Chrétien, would inevitably adjust the story to his own audience.

A recent study of other French Romances, later translated into Welsh, reveals exactly this point (Adams et al. 78). In this study the Welsh translators are consistently found to drop out material dealing with French notions of chivalry, an idea quite alien to the Celts, and to re-align the knights into the typology of their own heroic traditions. In short, the French knights become Welsh heroes. If that is true at even a latter date we can expect no less of the earlier work. *Peredur* gives us a glimpse of the traditional Celtic hero lacking in Chrétien's *Li Contes del Graal*, even though Chrétien's protagonist is presented as "Perceval li Galois." Chrétien's hero is inevitably a French view of what a Celtic barbarian would be like. This is very much what Cooper produced in *The Last of the Mohicans*: a fictionally interesting but not anthropologically sound view of an alien hero. Thus, whatever its corruptions, the *Peredur* is the most Celtic version that we have, and the difference between the two versions reveal something of what happened to Romance in the period of transition from Celtic culture to French culture. Since the two works are nearly contemporary the contrast is all the more valid. One hero, two ways.

The presentation of Peredur as a Welsh hero provides a powerful view of how the epistemologically disoriented hero, which we first saw in CuChulainn, has moved into a medieval mise en scène. It is in that conflictive borderland that we can discover the outlines of a new and more enigmatic Romance hero.

Gods and Closure: Ritual as Logos in Peredur

Language defines the hermeneutic relation.

Martin Heidegger

In analyzing the Welsh story of Peredur found in *The Mabinogion* the reader is immediately aware that the view of reality it presents is considerably more modern than what we have seen in the CuChulainn stories. At the same time the overall structure of the tale seems to obey no concern for a literary closure in the modern sense of that term. Instead the story strings together a series of episodes and adventures which often show no clear sense of relationship to one another. While the tale is structured on a quest format, the various adventures often display a repetitious similarity, and they do not clearly build to either a climax or denouement. In other words the sequencing of the adventures does not reveal a modern awareness of cause and effect leading to closure. Whatever pattern they follow is not one recognizable to a modern hermeneutic fix. The result is that there is no "meaningful" order—or if there is we cannot read it. As in the case of some of the items found in the Gospel of Mark there is either the double hermeneutic fix of a hidden meaning or no meaning, and the modern reader is left to ponder the cause of the arrangement.

In his study, *The Real Camelot* John Darrah provides a clue to what may be happening here. Darrah, following the lead of Jessie Weston, has suggested that the endless episodic structure of Romance is due to the fact that the adventures are in their origin narratized versions of rituals once practiced by the Celts. He demonstrates that the frequent combat encounters experienced by the knights show considerable similarity to the type of practice studied by James Frazer in his description of the cult at Nemi. In this situation the warrior fights to establish his domination over the ford, grove, well, or fountain and subsequently takes possession of the defender's wife or daughter. Darrah's study posits that the real Camelot was not the medieval court of King Arthur and his knights but rather a cult center of the late Stone Age re-presented as the brilliant citadel of chivalry found in the Romances of Chrétien and his followers.

In *The Mabinogion* a tale such as "Owein; or, The Countess of the Fountain" fits this paradigm. In this kind of narrative the "meaning" or purpose of the story is located entirely within the adventure, and its original narrative purpose, like a primitive mass, was simply to celebrate a ritual practice. We also know that the mere repetition of certain kinds of stories was believed to have a beneficial influence on the listener due to its ritual function (Dillon). It would follow that such a belief would encourage repetition of key episodes and would become a normal practice of storytelling traditions. Something of this fascination seems to have stayed with medieval listeners of Romance who never tired of the endless repetition of the hero's ritual encounters.

This theory for the ritual origin for prose narratives was first developed long ago by Jessie Weston in her justly famous *From Ritual to Romance*, a work that has influenced both scholars and poets. T. S. Eliot's *The Waste Land* is the best known of the many works utilizing her insight. Today, even though no one entirely accepts her Middle Eastern fertility rite origin for the grail procession, her explication of ritual structure for these kinds of stories is still a revelation. However no one to my knowledge has examined the reader-response consequences of her interpretation, which in fact posits an unsuspected but radical hermeneutic situation: the implied reader of such stories is a god, and the purpose of the story is to conjure the god's will. It therefore follows that its narrative grammar has nothing to do with relaying mundane information or explaining the workings of human psychology. Instead the recitation of the story is like a prayer intended to achieve a benefit from a divine source. This interpretation sets up the language of narrative as referential to an external cult practice which provides it with an Otherworld power. Furthermore this power, a kind of secret magic, is specifically lodged within the knight's ontology. He is the master of a special language whose purpose is to influence a divinity capable of "reading" the narratized ritual practice.

Nevertheless, as we have seen, the meaning of the stories would inevitably change as the original cultural nexus eroded. At some point in time the ritual power of the story would fade, and the teller of the story would lose the awareness of the listening god and instead direct the story toward listening humans seeking entertainment. This would also mean that the purpose of the sequential structure of a string of episodes would lose the ritual validity of repetition and force the teller of the tale to seek some other organizing principle. Such a change would favor the linking together of episodes on a cause-and-effect basis, and we can begin to understand Chrétien's intention of seeking a new *sens* in his retelling with these simple "stories of adventure." This in turn would force him to find a meaningful "conjointure" or linking mechanism. Nevertheless the prolonged repetition of such adventures remained as a recognizable genre feature of Romance. Don Quixote's comments about "historias inacabables" are not only accurate, but the fact that he himself sees no fault in this arrangement indicates that he still "reads" the tales with an older horizon of expectations in which something of the power of ritual repetition still held sway. For the same reason the Church's continued disapproval of the old tales seems also to be based on the recognition that the tales retained a pagan challenge to the primacy of Christian beliefs.

There are various hermeneutic consequences of this cultural arrangement which have profound impact on later readers and on the valorization of Romance as a literary genre. First, as we have seen, this helps explain the fact that the tales never seem to tire of repeating similar kinds of events, nor does the narrator show any concern for linking the episodes or for building consistently toward a climax or closure.

We will see how Chrétien attempted to come to terms with this aspect of the stories, but the difficulty remained problematic until well into the Renaissance and became part of the literary debate on the superiority of classical epic over medieval Romance. In fact this same debate is curiously re-articulated in the *Quixote* from the very first chapter. We remember that the hidalgo's original intention, before he went mad, was to write a conclusion to the book of Don Belianis: "Pero con todo, [don Quijote] alababa en su autor aquel *acabar* su libro con la promesa de aquella *inacabable aventura*, y muchas veces le vino deseo de tomar la pluma y dalle fin al pie de la letra, como allí se promete . . ." (pt. 1, ch. 1).

"[He commended, however, the author's way of ending his book, with a promise to go on with that interminable [un-endable] adventure, and many a time he felt the urge to take up his pen and finish it just as its author had promised]." In Spanish the pun on *acabar* (to end) and *inacabable* (un-endable) are the narrator's means of underscoring the impossibility of the protagonist's intention. In fact the same problem comes to the fore again in the task of concluding the *Quixote* itself, where Cide Hamete himself finds himself stymied.

It is also important to recall that Chrétien likewise had difficulty bringing his Romances to closure. He deliberately chose not to complete the *Lancelot*, while in the case of *Li Contes del Graal* the lack of closure may not be due entirely to his death. Even though the first continor of the work tells us that Chrétien died before he completed it, this does not guarantee that he would have done so had he lived longer, since the dilemma in so deeply inscribed in the generic pattern of the tales. D. D. R. Owen's *Evolution of the Grail Legend*, for instance, clearly shows that Chrétien also had difficulty completing his earlier Romances, *Cligés, Yvain*, and *Erec et Enid*. All these texts reveal that a long tale of many distinct adventures performed by one knight creates a literary tension between ritual repetition and the idea of literary closure.

But one suspects that the unknown Welsh author of *Peredur* did not feel that this was a problem. He seems comfortable with the structure he presents, since the cultic "meaning" for him resided within the episode themselves. It is the modern reader, with an entirely different horizon of expectations, who creates the problem. However, Chrétien, no doubt influenced by his clerical training in classic letters, does show an awareness of the repetition as a problem. In addition, as Owen *(Evolution)* suggests, the length of Chrétien's tales may have been determined by the length of time needed for their performed reading at court. His earlier tales all conclude at about eight thousand lines, while *Li Contes del Graal* goes far beyond that length. In this, as well as in other narrative procedures, the nature of the grail Romance was posing new closure problems for him.

One other feature of this sequencing problem relates back to the Irish genre of "youthful exploits." *Peredur*, like the CuChulainn cycle, is a story that narrates the hero's life from his birth to his maturity and includes the kinds of adventures told in an *enfances* or *mocedades* tale. In contrast to the purely episodic format, this genre provides the narrator with a chronological sequence that tips the scales toward a possible closure posited on the victory or the death of the hero. However the possibility of this kind of conclusion is only hinted at in *Peredur*. His last adventure, accomplished with Gwalchmei (Gawain), is the defeat of the hags, and this is an Otherworld adventure foretold by ancient prophecies. But to a great extent the *Peredur* merely ceases, and both Peredur and Gwalchmei remain at the ready for the next adventure. This kind of open-ended formula went on to become a genre-linked feature of Romance. Such stories can always have a sequel or sequels. Historically Romance as a genre usually has a recognizable beginning (the birth of the hero) but leaves the conclusion without a generically determined format.

Other hermeneutic consequences of the cult origin for these tales are not so easy to measure. Various scholars have recognized a close connection between the storytelling powers of the Druids and bards (fili) and the function of the poet or storyteller as priest. This problem is discussed by Myles Dillon in his *Celts and Aryans*. In analyzing the relationship between the prose and verse parts of the tales he notes that both in India and in Ireland that the verse segments of the traditional tales are linguistically much older than the prose, indicating that they are in effect hymns. The prose, an oral improvisation by the teller, functioned to add narrative explanations and to make the meanings of the hymn understandable to the audience. Likewise the tradition that the listener received important benefits in the form of health, reputation, children, wealth, and the like would support this interpretation (93). This belief is the consequence of the idea that the tale was a bearer of the magic power of Truth and could be put to use as magic (74, 88). "An extension of the notion of the power of Truth is the 'sravana-phala' ('reward for hearing') bestowed upon those who listen to a story" (90). Dillon cites several examples of this belief inscribed in Hindu stories, and he finds similar examples in Irish tales. One of them, from the *Táin* "promises that he who hears it recited will enjoy protection for a year." This tradition of linking prayers, charms, and stories as part of a divine or Otherworld knowledge seems to remain attached to Romance and may account for the its demonization by moralists. This prejudice persisted well into the Renaissance and was particularly strong in writers as diverse as Ignatius of Loyola and Sir Philip Sidney. Both scorned the books of chivalry, although they admitted reading them. Martín de Riquer gives an impressive list of "serious" Spanish writers of the sixteenth century who railed against the books of chivalry, a genre he specifically identifies as originating with Chrétien de

Troyes (*Cervantes, Don Quixote*, ed. Jones and Douglas 895). He finds that
the moralists particularly criticized the use of the "marvellous." Although
it was not recognized at the time, nor commented upon by Riquer, this
is certainly a feature linked to the Celtic stories. The moralists also con-
demn the overt eroticism of the stories and their effect on the readers. In
this category Northrop Frye has noted that this anxiety was prompted by
an underlying fear of inciting masturbation (24).

A different kind of concern is expressed by Teresa of Avila in her
autobiography where she confesses to reading books of chivalry as one
of her greatest sins. She relates that her mother was fond of reading such
books but that because of her mother's strong character the damage was
controlled. In herself, however, she allowed the reading of books of chivalry was like an addiction to a forbidden practice that distracted her from
her more important religious considerations. "Era tan estremo lo que
esto me embebia que, si no tenia libro nuevo, no me parece tener contento"
(*Libro de su vida*, 5). [So extreme was my absorption (enchantment) with
this that, if I didn't have a new book, I didn't seem to have contentment]
(my translation). Even granted that the genre of pious autobiography
tends to exaggerate the sins of pleasure, this is still a revealing statement.
Being a saint she overcomes the fault, but the situation is not different
from what is found in the opening paragraphs of *Don Quixote*, where the
protagonist succumbs to the pleasure of reading and as a result goes
mad. Thus the aura of forbidden magic hovers over the tales, an appeal
that Chrétien, as we shall see, did nothing to lessen.

If the tale, like a prayer, is addressed to a divinity, this means that it
posits its ideal reader as a god. On a practical level this arrangement
would indicate that while the divinity figure would understand the
"meaning" of what is going on, the assumed "empowerment" of the
reader is the result of acquiring manipulative capabilities in the area of
Otherworld knowledge. After all, only a god can perfectly "read" such
a story which confirms the existence of a hidden meaning. This strange
endowment accounts for the curious pleasure that Romance provides the
reader. The access to forbidden Otherworld pleasure enjoyed by the reader
is almost irresistible. Less resistant readers like Don Quixote reveal a
moral and psychological danger inherent in the vice. The hidalgo loses
his original identity and becomes a strangely different person. Don
Quixote openly speaks of the power of this seductive pleasure in his
debate with the canon of Toledo over the value of the *libros de caballería*
(pt. 1, ch. 1). The key moment of the debate occurs when Don Quixote,

tired of arguing in the terms of abstract aesthetic principles, seeks to clinch his case by telling such a story and describing curious pleasure it provides. He concludes his story in way which addresses both the episodic nature of the stories and the endlessly prolonged pleasure they purvey: "No quiero alargarme más en esto, pues dello se puede colegir que *caulquiera parte que se lea de cualquiera historia* de caballero andante ha de causar *gusto y maravilla a cualquiera que se leyere*" (pt. 1, ch. 1, emphasis added). [I will not expatiate any further upon this, as it may be gathered from it that whatever part of whatever history of a knight-errant one reads, it will fill the reader, whoever he be, with delight and wonder.] The recognition that the original reader of a Celtic prose narrative was an alien god empowered with strange epistemological and hermeneutic abilities reveals something of the undissolved pagan power that underlies the genre. A half-suppressed awareness of this uncomfortable Otherworld content would be particularly distressing to a sacramentally focused Church and to a culture intent on discovering truth by means of reasoned discourse.

Peredur: The Bifurcated Epistemological Powers of the Hero

If thou be'st born to strange sights,
things invisible to see . . .

John Donne

Returning to the Welsh tale, however, we can see that it presents a very different world than the one found in the CuChulainn cycle. Now, the hero is presented as entirely human, born of a noble warrior and an intelligent and sensitive woman. The euhemerization has therefore clouded his divine ancestry, but a curious linkage with the supernatural does emerge as he acquires uncles and cousins who claim descent from the Fisher King, a cloudy figure with an unclear ontology. His later Christian incarnation as a descendent of Joseph of Arimathea only hints at semidivine origin. A supernatural aura also hovers over the image of the blood dripping from the spear. The fact that later writers saw this as Christ's blood and the spear as that of the legendary Longinus reveals that an Otherworld force was present in the spear and ready for adaptation. The images of the grail and the spear, however, were not Christian in their origin. They merely succumbed to the allegorical hermeneutics of the Christian Middle Ages. The Welsh author of the *Peredur* shows no concern for such goings on.

Another genre-linked feature that finds its origins in *Peredur,* however, was to have lasting impact on the development of the Romance hero. Peredur loses his father and apparently knowledge of who he is when he is taken away in his infancy to a remote place where he is reared by his mother. The latter is determined to hide from him not only his identity but also any knowledge of the world of war or arms or horses. The boy has a horse but has no awareness of horses as part of the world of warriors. This suppression is particularly important, considering the divine status horses had in Celtic religion. The Celts in fact worshiped a horse deity, named Epona, who was associated with the valorization of war and warriors. In the case of CuChulainn, he is born at the same time as a colt, a feature found in other heroes as well. Thus the essential characteristic of Peredur is that he knows neither his parentage nor the social importance of warriors.

Furthermore, he takes his interpretation of reality entirely from his mother's teachings. This epistemological dislocation is partially gender oriented and suggests a lost matriarchal tradition. The conflict between matriarchal and patriarchal teachings may in its origins be the import of this kind of story. This development explains how the impact of the suppressed patriarchal knowledge accounts for the powerful sense of recognition that hits the boy when he first sees a warrior. The situation is not unlike that of the ugly duckling the first time it sees a swan. This recognition effectively overwhelms the child's ego consciousness and radically alters his personality. In Chrétien the impact of the recognition is more intense and more personal than in the Welsh tale and causes one of the knights to characterize Perceval as "fol." But it is the way in which Chrétien portrays this transformation that becomes in fact a dominant feature of the new genre and the new hero.

In the *Quixote* this personality alteration is called "madness," but the nature of the change in the hero is the same in that the hidalgo is compelled psychologically to follow his inner yearnings. However, in the Welsh version the effect is more muted since the narrator is closer to his Celtic sources and not interested in the psychological development of the hero. Nevertheless, the scene is presented so that the child's epistemological disorientation is more apparent than in the case of CuChulainn:

> Every day Peredur would go to the forest of tall trees to play and
> to throw holly darts, and one day he saw there a herd of his
> mother's goats, along with two hinds who were standing nearby,
> and he marvelled to see these two without horns when all the
> others had them, for he supposed that they were all goats and
> that these two had lost their horns. (Gantz, *Mabinogion* 218)

This failure to see what others see is to be the key to the new Peredur/
Perceval personality. He sees strangely, and this capacity is both a weakness and a strength. At first it cripples him and makes him an object of
humor, but ultimately it is tied to his seeing the grail procession, an
adventure reserved for him alone.

Thus his ability to see things as no one else sees them was in fact a
sign of the hero's divine origins, but here it is presented as a humorous
childish error. What is important is that this hermeneutic disorientation
has replaced the earlier "divinity sign" that was an overt display of
Otherworld power observed in the CuChulainn story. Now the hero is
on the surface entirely human, and his Otherworld power is disguised as
an hermeneutic aberration which is the result of a hidden epistemological power. The process of euhemerization has reduced the hero's divinity
to the level of the comic, but what is not at first recognized are the
narrative potentials of this character trait for a hero in search of the grail.
Taken as a purely human child, Peredur has a "funny" perception disorder that can be read as a psychological defect.

What has happened is that a new hermeneutic possibility has begun
overlay the original one. The double hermeneutic fix has emerged. For
the original reader Peredur is marked as semi-divine; for the later reader
he is psychologically disturbed. Although this character disorder is an
apparently mild one, important cultural consequences are to come as the
genre develops. The goat/hind episode does not appear in Chrétien's
version of the tale, but this kind of epistemological disorientation becomes even more severe and more comic in his hero. He prepares the
way for the *figura* of the mad knight in *Don Quixote*, where the hero's
epistemological powers are an overt challenge to reasoned discourse.

This problem is not immediately exploited by the Welsh narrator since
he introduces here two other genre-linked capabilities of the Romance
hero. While at one level this is merely a continuation of the hind/goat
episode, it is also a presentation of the hero's other capabilities before he
reaches the grail castle:

> By speed and strength he drove the hinds along with the goats
> into the house for the goats at one end of the forest, and then he
> returned home and said, "Mother, what a strange thing I have
> seen near by: two of your goats have been running wild, and
> after roaming the forest for so long they have lost their horns. No
> man has ever had a more difficult task than I had in driving
> them inside." Everyone rose to go and look, and when they saw
> the hinds they marvelled that anyone should have the speed and
> strength to overtake such animals. (218)

Two fundamental traits of the hero are revealed in this event. He is
shown to be a supposedly "normal" child with only hints of his hidden
strengths. First, having initially made the error of taking the hinds for
goats, he then develops a fully explicated but persistently erroneous
explanation for his actions. Peredur, like Don Quixote, is a (mis-)reader
of situations who comes up with surprisingly lucid explanations of what
he had done. Once having made the error, he is capable of acting on his
interpretation in such a way that he displays a more than human capability in the matter of strength and speed. In the case of CuChulainn this
speed was frequently shown by his ability to catch his own spear casts
or to drive the chariot at the speed of the spear. Peredur is not so clearly
set apart from the purely human but he does display unusual but not
quite supernatural capabilities. This feature persists today in many comic
book heroes such as Superman, who is "faster than a speeding bullet."

In addition, Peredur's capture of the deer is related to his control over
animals, which represents another aspect of his divine nature. Like the
Celtic Lord of the Beast or a folkloric wild man, Peredur has a special
power over animals and nature. This feature can also be presented simply as great success in hunting, or, in another articulation, he may possess a mysterious ability to communicate with them. The romance of
Yvain and the lion is an example of the latter. In this arrangement an
animal companion operates in the story as an alternative epiphany of the
hero or what is sometimes called an "external soul." Many wild child
tales, including the one of Tarzan, utilize this feature.

While the deer/goat episode shows that the Welsh author had sources
for his story that Chrétien chose not to use, it also indicates that the Welsh
version as a genre tends to be inclusive. The narrator may simply have
utilized all the stories relevant to the hero. In contrast Chrétien is much
more discriminating. He selects and places his episodes with concern for

a temporal extension of the action, leading the hero from a confused childhood to a flourishing maturity. This provides a sense of psychological development that is largely absent in *Peredur*. This contrast between the two versions has often been used by critics to illustrate the so-called primitiveness of the Welsh narrator, but, from the viewpoint of another hermeneutic, the rhetorical intent of the Welsh tale is simply obeying a different principle of organization. It may be that there were in fact more than one narrator of the version we have and that the apparent "contradictions and repetitions" reveal nothing other than an editorial procedure. On the other hand even in that case "organization" can mean different things to different cultures. The Welsh tale gathers, while Chrétien selects. But the Celtic organization does not indicate an inferior culture. Rather it is steadfastly resistant to what we now recognize as a European sense of cause and effect. It must be seen that the material of Britain was not invented and left sitting around just for Chrétien to put it in order. We should view Chrétien's achievement for what it is: a new organization of alien material, one that made it (almost) acceptable to Western civilization. His "translation" of the material can be seen as simply what Gadamer describes as "reading." It is an interpretation that is meaningful to a new system of cultural signs. Chrétien represents an adaptive process by which the Christian Middle Ages could come to terms with what it regarded as a fascinating but "wild" narrative material. That he dropped out or suppressed items not in accord with the values of his audience accounts for the profound success of his effort. But it should not be proclaimed that his achievement is superior; it is merely more acceptable to another culture. This in turn means that there are unacceptable elements in the original material that were not to become part of the mainstream of European culture. In this sense it is important to examine what signification the disturbing and alien omissions possessed.

An importance instance of this hidden material can be found in Peredur's crucial experience of discovering a capability of his own nature. The scene describing this discovery of his true self follows immediately upon the adventure with the hinds and the goats: "One day three knights came down the bridle path alongside the forest: Gwalchmei son of Gwyar, Gweir son of Gwestyl and Owein son of Uryen, the latter bringing up the rear while pursing the knight who had distributed the apples in Arthur's court" (Gantz, *Mabinogion* 219).

As noted, the narrative procedure here is again inclusive rather than sharply focused, as it is in Chrétien. The Welsh scene presents a gathering of knights, and we are presented with considerably more information, some of which we have difficulty evaluating. In contrast to Chrétien, the knights are fully named and provided with geneaological histories. Owein is singled out as bringing up the rear and there is a reference to another story having to do with the distribution of certain apples at Arthur's court. The relevance of this reference is unclear to us. To the Welsh audience it must have been have been well known and probably contained coded information related to the episode at hand. Like the biblical apple of the knowledge of good and evil, the apples may have represented certain forbidden knowledge. We can only note that the apples are not subsequently utilized in the story. Likewise Gweir is not destined to play any particular role in this version of Peredur's adventures. Gwalchmei (Gawain), on the other hand, is a key figure in both the Welsh and French tales, although he does not seem to add anything to the present action. Only in retrospect can it be seen that perhaps Peredur's destiny is somehow interwoven with that of Gwalchmei. Nevertheless one clue does remain that is to be important later. In some versions Gwalchmei, a divine solar knight, is Peredur's father, while in others he will merely function as a tutor to Peredur. On the other hand, Owein, the hero of another tale in *The Mabinogion,* is singled out here because he is the knight that Peredur is going to question. He also is a knight particularly associated with animals and may for this reason have more in common with this wild child who catches deer as though they were goats. All these data are going to be suppressed by Chrétien for various reasons, the most obvious seeming to be that he does not need them. His style is elegant and restrained and achieves the new kind of sequential "lucidity" so admired by his critics. This newfound lucidity, however, is to be achieved at a price, as we will see.

For the purposes of the Welsh tale, the significance seems to have to do with the fact that Peredur has suddenly come upon a company of divine heroes to which, by reason of his birthright, he belongs. Gwalchmei, for instance, is a euhemerized god and will play a crucial role in the drama of the grail. Like the ugly duckling, Peredur has suddenly seen a flock of swans. His reaction is swift, even abrupt: "Peredur asked, 'Mother, what are these? ' 'Angels, my son.' 'I will be an angel and go with them,' said he" (219).

The Otherworld economy of the Welsh narrative is clearly seen here. The story moves with brisk rapidity because the events are coded, and there is no explanation or exploitation of the emotional impact of the conflict between the son and the mother. The emphasis remains on the exploits of Peredur and moves quickly ahead to relate the unfolding of his destiny. The so-called organizational defects refer solely to the linkages between the various adventures the hero has, but within the episodes the story is fresh and rapid. The narrational focus remains on the exploits of a hero who suffers his destiny without question. From an uninitiated youthful enthusiast he quickly matures into the competent man of action, the traditional Welsh hero of a warrior class.

In this brief exchange between mother and son there is little concern for her feelings and his departure is almost immediate. In Chrétien the departure is extended to a matter of a few days as the mother makes new clothes for her son. In both cases she provides advice for him, but in the Welsh version her advice is quickly superceded by that of one of his male tutors, who bluntly tells Peredur to forget what she has told him. In contrast, Chrétien, with his concern for the dictates of chivalry, specifies that her advice remain important, and Perceval's tutor makes him promise to cherish her words, even though they conflict with his chivalric destiny.

However, the brief exchange between Peredur and his mother reveals the fundamental seed of the conflictive situation that is later is to be exploited by the authors of Romance. First we have the element of loss or suppression of meaning already operative in this version. We see that the hero is curiously ignorant of the basic features of the world in which he lives. The depth of this defect is shown not only by his question but by his unquestioning acceptance of his mother's response. Peredur is ready to believe in a literal way exactly what he is told. His own reading of reality has the crucial component of judging what is seen, not by sense perception, but by means of information provided by another text. In this way an important epistemological split is already inscribed in his personality: the hero judges the external world by reference to an internalized "text." Here it is the mother's text, soon to be replaced by the tutor's text. The way is cleared for Don Quixote, who reads external reality by means of the written text of the *libros de caballería*, which replaces the admonitions of the tutor.

In many ways this epistemological break was already present in CuChulainn. We have seen that the Irish hero has a fierce inner agenda that allows him to command established heroes like Conal. His inner "text," suggested by the Druid, merely confirms his divine identity. The Welsh hero, in contrast, is more vulnerable to human teaching. His certainty of his own identity has eroded as his divinity has receded. In this scene he recognizes a sense of kinship with the heroes but is unaware of its source. It is worth noting also that the crucial figure of Gwalchmei is a disguised deity. Gwalchmei (later Gawain) is to a great extent going to assume the role of an older brother who helps the hero adjust to reality. But the hermeneutic signal of Gwalchmei's identity has eroded in such a way that Peredur's response to the sight of the heroes makes him seem psychologically disoriented in a way not seen in earlier tales. CuChulainn never really doubts the power of his own identity, and the role of the tutor uncle is merely a helpful addition in his development. The basic point is that the earlier hero is not vulnerable to what he is told. On the contrary, he repeatedly demonstrates the power of his identity over and against the advice of sensible mortals. This can be seen in the exchange between Conal and CuChulainn in the border episode. The hero knows very well that no contingency will undo his destiny. While this type of confidence is gracefully euhemerized in later heroes who overcome great obstacles by their native wit and resourcefulness, in the case of Peredur we see only a partial shift from the divine hero to a rather awkward human hero.

The textual clue to this transitional state is clearly seen in the nature of the mother's response. Since the original version undoubtedly would have revealed the fact that Gwalchmei and company are gods or divine heroes, it seems likely that at some point a clerical scribe, armed with his own agenda, felt uneasy with the pagan condition of the material. For us the awkward substitution of "angel" for "god" seems a deliberate distortion of crucial information. The term angel substituted what is an acceptable Christian superhuman being for the pagan deity. Seen from the viewpoint of "translation," the reason for the substitution is easily understandable. The textual result, however, opens up new horizons of hermeneutic indeterminacy. While the idea of an angel dressed as a warrior is within the range of possible acceptances of the Christian view of the world, it places the mother in an ambiguous position. She is thus depicted as either deliberately lying or suffering from some perceptual disorder of her own, not too different from her son's. This complicity of the mother renders the tutor's later advice to ignore her wisdom less unjustified. This shift also shows the influence of medieval anti-feminism. From a male point of view she is either lying or disoriented and can't be of any further use to her son. This mitigates the moral fault of his abandoning her. Chrétien, of course, plays it differently and makes the mother a more sympathetic figure. In this way Perceval's moral fault of abandoning her becomes the "cause" of his failure to ask the question in the grail cast. On the other hand *The Mabinogion* version has its own validity.

In either case, what resides in the text is again a double meaning or reading that renders the text mysterious in a way that was not true of the Irish tale. With this development a crucial step from myth to Romance has been taken. The situation is now prepared for the hermeneutic ambiguity of the grail procession. The "meaning" of such a scene is rendered problematic and a hidden significance seems to reside just below the surface of the text. The stage is now set for a series of continuations by other writers, all of whom seek to explain the enigma of the grail.

Evidence for this problem exists in the presentation of the grail scene in both *The Mabinogion* and in Chrétien. That we can not be certain whether or not the Welsh author knew Chrétien's version is intriguing in its own right but not entirely relevant to our analysis. The Welsh text presents certain kinds of information and contradictions that are accessible to analysis regardless of how they got there. What *The Mabinogion* text gives us is a late twelfth century transcription of much older material that shows evidence of a partial adaption to new interpretations.

The progression of the Welsh story takes Peredur, now embarked on a heroic/chivalric career, to two successive castles. In the first he receives instruction from the lord of the castle, who not surprisingly turns out to be an uncle. He abruptly tells him to forget his mother's words and then instructs him in the manly skills of the warrior. Buried in this re-education process is a warning statement, more explicit than what is found in Chrétien, in which the uncle specifically tells Peredur not to ask questions: "From now on follow this advice: though you see what is strange, do not ask about it unless some one is courteous enough to tell you; any rebuke will fall on me rather than on you, as I am your teacher" (Gantz, *Early Irish Myths* 225). With this command the ground is prepared for Peredur's fatal omission to ask the all important spell-breaking question in the grail castle. The hero's error become inevitable because of his human education, which overlays his divine propensity to ask questions. In Chrétien's version the nature of this contradiction will become more disguised.

Peredur leaves this castle and proceeds to another one, where he is again received with honor. This time the host, also an uncle, is described as a "handsome hoary-haired man seated to one side." The adjectival handsome replicates the description of the castle itself. This emphasis on the aesthetic appearance echoes the strange use of beautiful we found in CuChulainn's self-awareness: "the horses are beautiful and I am beautiful." We are reminded that the beautiful is a characteristic of the divine, and we find that Perceval who called "biax fix" by his mother.

Next Peredur is seated at the table and everyone is served. Then another teaching or testing episode follows in which Peredur is instructed to strike a metal column with his sword. He performs this test three times, each time breaking both the column and his sword, and two times he is able to put them together again. A third attempt however results in his not being able to repair the sword. The host then says to him, "Well, lad, go sit down, and God's blessing upon you—you are the best swordsman in the entire kingdom. You have come into two parts of your strength, but the third is still wanting." The coming-into-his-own of the hero is thus still not complete, but this process as stipulated by the uncle is not a human educative process. There is instead a suggestion of Peredur's divine nature revealing itself at its own mysterious pace. In later Chrétien stories, this situation becomes a presentation of a special sword to the hero with the proviso that it will break in only one kind of adventure. In either case the sword episode indicates that the hero has reached a crucial but not complete stage of his development.

In the *Quixote* we find a curious echo of this scene in the episode of the hidalgo testing his helmet in chapter one, where we find a curious linguistic conundrum. The narrator states that the hidalgo strikes two blows to test the helmet but that he destroys it on the first blow. Various editors have sought to explain away the textual ambiguity in different ways (see Rodríguez Marín, 1, 60). In any explanation possible, however, we are still left with the situation that the hero's paradigmatic piece of armor proves defective when tested and that further development of the helmet problem will follow. Hence Don Quixote later replaces the faulty helmet with the barber's basin (pt. 1, ch. 21) which he perceives as the magic helmet of Mambrino.

In *The Mabinogion*, Peredur's grail test follows immediately upon the problem with the sword. It is also noteworthy that the grail procession occurs after they have eaten and not as part of the meal, though what this means is not clear.

> Then Peredur sat to one side of his uncle and they talked. He saw two lads entering the hall and then leaving for a chamber; they carried a spear of incalculable size with three streams of

blood running from the socket to the floor. When everyone saw the lads coming in this way they set up a crying and a lamentation that was not easy for anyone to bear, but the man did not interrupt his conversation with Peredur—he did not explain what this meant, nor did Peredur ask him. After a short silence two girls entered bearing a large platter with a man's head covered with blood on it, and everyone set up a crying and lamentation such that it was not easy to stay in the same house. Then a chamber was prepared for Peredur and he went to bed. (Gantz, *Mabinogion* 225)

Now we find a significant number of variations between this scene and Chrétien's. One can immediately see that the Welsh version does not readily lend itself to a Christian re-interpretation. The author has not sought to suppress the pagan and "barbaric" elements. The scene clearly evokes the head-hunting practice of Celtic culture. The only Christian parallel would have been Salome's equally barbaric request for John's head. Obviously the Welsh scene is too uncomfortable for the self-conscious courtly decorum of the world of Philip of Flanders. Ironically, Cervantes does include a significant decapitation scene in Don Quixote's dream at the second inn. It may also be significant that his dream does occur just before the banquet scene in the inn, and even more significantly the decapitation dream can be read as part of the disenchanting dilemma found in the Dorotea adventure. We will return to this analysis later.

In the case of Peredur we can recall that the decapitation of a giant is a regular procedure in Celtic tales. Evidence for the widespread use of this practice in warfare dates back to classical commentaries such as Caesar's, and some archeological and anthropological findings corroborate this. Even in the Christian Middle Ages we find churches and crucifixes in Ireland with carved decorative patterns made up of severed heads that suggest a cultic background. We know also that heads were collected in cult sites in Roman Gaul. Therefore the French suppression of the severed head in the grail scene does have some bearing on their own cultural history. In CuChulainn's tale we also have found that he cuts off his enemies' heads and ties them to his chariot in preparation for a triumphal return to his own people. There are other severed head episodes of obvious ritual sources in more than one Gawain Romance, some of which, as in *Sir Gawain and the Green Knight*, allow for the return to life of the victim. In all these cases decapitation seems to be a spell-breaking procedure which allows the giant to assume his rightful form, usually that of a handsome young man.

What is important in the Welsh grail procession is that the severed head is also related to spell-breaking procedures. This kind of meaning is encoded in the figure of the severed head, but the hero cannot respond to the sign because of the prohibition against asking questions, and therefore fails to break the spell upon the castle. The nature of this failure is clearly the center of the story, both in the Welsh and French versions, but it must be stressed that neither version succeeds in explaining or de-coding what the hidden meaning is. From this omission, as already noted, has sprung the extraordinary power of the scene and the repeated attempts by other writers of grail romances to provide the missing "meaning."

The absence of the explanation in *Peredur*, however, also suggests that the narrator himself may not know what the figures of the procession meant. As a storyteller and entertainer he is merely manipulating story elements whose original hermeneutic value has already vanished. The result is to be historically significant: The story contains "un-readable" content. There is a gap between what the storyteller knows and the original meaning of the story. This epistemological conundrum is to become one of the most paradigmatic features of Romance as a literary genre. In the grail scene, the teller of the tale, the hero of the tale, and the reader of the tale are united in their perplexity. This failure to understand accounts for the haunting evocation of lost knowledge that marks the secret appeal of Romance. It also reveals the basis for the curious logocentric hostility the genre has always aroused. It is a secret appeal to the irrational and intuitive responses of the reader. As such, it would naturally not find a comfortable niche to a new society attempting to establish its power on the infallible explanatory power of reason. Romance as a genre became a threat to that agenda, and by the seventeenth century the hostility of the new science to anything evoking old superstitions further exacerbated the situation.

Perceval, the Inner Text

Morfran, son of Tegid, was so ugly that he was thought to be an evil demon; therefore he was avoided in Arthur's last battle at Camlan. He was as hairy as a stag. Sandde Angel-Face was also left unharmed at that battle, but for a different reason: he was so beautiful that he was thought to be an angel.

Anonymous Welsh Tale, tenth century

Chrétien opens the Perceval narrative with an elaborate description of the scene in which the youth for the first time in his life encounters knights. This passage is a parallel to the meeting we have already noted in *Peredur*. As in the Welsh version Perceval also mistakes the knights for "angels," but the formulation of this event is radically different in Chrétien. The youth (Li valles) is alone in the forest unaccompanied by his mother. This arrangement means that the mother does not directly tell him they are angels, thereby removing her from immediate responsibility for the error. Instead Chrétien creates a scene in which the hero himself reads the signs according to his own inner text, a text already articulated in the Welsh tale cited above.

To begin with, the youth hears the knights coming through the forest before he sees them. This allows for him to make his first "mistake." The sound made by the passage of the armed mounted men riding through the thick brush and wood is carefully described by the narrator who, unlike the narrator in *Peredur*, never identifies the knights. In Chrétien's version they remain nameless. Thus the youth, like Don Quixote in the adventure of the water mill, reads the sound according to his own hermeneutic:

> Li vallés oit et ne voit pas
> Ciax que vers lui vienent le pas;
> Molt se merveille et dist: "Par m'ame,
> Voir se dist ma mere, ma dame,
> Qui me dist que deable sont
> Les plus laides choses del mont . . ." [111–16]

[The youth heard but did not see (the knights) who were advancing toward him at a good pace. He was much amazed and exclaimed: "By my soul, my mother spoke truly when she told me that devils are the ugliest things in the world . . ."] (my translation)

The error is amusing and highlights the naivete of the youth, but at the same time two very profound traits of his heroic personality are revealed. First, like the Celtic heroes CuChulainn and Peredur, he suffers from a curious kind of epistemological disorder. He does not perceive things the way that other people do, a trait that is to be crucial in his grail adventure. Here, the apparent cause of the error is the youth's limited knowledge of the world beyond the forest. Nevertheless it does not inevitably follow that the sound of men riding through the forest is so remote from his experience (he has lived in the forest all his life) that he would automatically conclude that the sounds mean that devils are coming toward him. His "error" is strange only in that he assumes that the sounds are made by Otherworld creatures. Rather, the boy's recognition that this will be an Otherworld adventure can be read, not as an error, but as a sign that he is the hero of a Romance, a hero given to see strange sights.

This is the Romance signal that Northrop Frye calls the "change of consciousness" suffered by the hero or heroine (102). As here, it usually occurs at the beginning of what begin as a realistic story. In other of Chrétien's tales this sign may appear in Arthur, who either suddenly falls asleep during a banquet in *Yvain* or inexplicably allows a strange knight to barter away possession of Guinevere in *Lancelot*. This feature has persisted with amazing tenacity into modern literature. Alice falls asleep before she sees the rabbit, a trickster figure, run down the hole. Likewise, in the film version of *The Wizard of Oz*, Dorothy's famous metacommentary, "Toto, I don't think we're in Kansas anymore," marks the point in which the Technicolor reality of Oz replaces the black-and-white image of Kansas. Her re-mark indicates that both the heroine and the viewer know they have entered the world of Romance. In the case of Perceval he has recognized that he will be challenged by Otherworld figures so that the hero's "error" can also be considered a genre sign. In its original Celtic articulation this ability to perceive Otherworld phenomena alerts the reader to the fact that the story is an *echtra,* a narrative genre in which the hero will have a meeting with the gods. In this sense the youth knows better than the narrator who the knights are and what is involved in the encounter. He has correctly perceived that what is coming toward him through the wild forest is the beginning of an adventure. The hero's "error" then is the first sign that the youth is capable of perceiving something valid about events, a kind of perception that escapes other people entirely. On the surface his "error" seems funny, but on the level of literary genre he is not wrong: he is going to have an adventure in which Otherworld ontology of the grail castle will have a dominant role.

A second and perhaps even more profound difference between Peredur and Perceval is found in *the manner* in which the unnamed youth makes his error. The importance of this difference is particularly significant and perhaps more "readable" in the light of the personality of Don Quixote. The latter begins his road to madness and adventure by reading books of chivalry and then trying to utilize them as a means of interpreting everyday reality. From that vantage point we note here that the youth perceives that the sounds signify the approach of devils on the basis of what his mother has told him. In other words he "reads" an event of everyday reality with the hermeneutic of an inner text that his mother has articulated for him. In this context the mother's advice is an instance of matriarchal wisdom originating in an older form of the society, one at risk in the world of the youth. This means that now the hero, instead of knowing because he is a god—as CuChulainn knew—knows on the basis of another text. In other words, the epistemological source of knowledge for the hero has suffered a literary transformation: the hero who "misreads" signs that have been introduced also signifies that the genre of his story has moved from myth to Romance. This shift will cast a long shadow for the new kind of protagonist emerging out of a mythic world into the discourse of modern fiction.

It has been noted that Chrétien does not name the knights who are coming through the forest, but in the Welsh tale the first knight was identified as Gwalchmei, an Otherworld ancestry solar knight (Loomis, *Celtic Myth* 35 ff., 252, 356). The process of euhemerization has deprived him of his overt divinity but in the earliest versions of the tale he would undoubtedly be a god. It is in this sense that Perceval's first question, "Are you not God?" is an accurate perception of what has now become a hidden meaning. In other words, Perceval sees a god, the narrator sees a knight. This rupture between the hero's epistemological powers and those of the narrator is an uncanny anticipation of the gap between Don Quixote and Cide Hamete. In both instances what is at issue is a hermeneutic conflict which in effect is the subject of the story. This situation indicates the existence of a hidden text underneath the apparent one. It also introduces the mysterious figure of the unknown knight, a figure with divine blood who can intervene in human affairs for good or evil.

On closer examination, we also find that Chrétien's narrative strategy sends out a double signal which not only suppresses the matter of the knight's identity but also disguises the original ontology of the story. Thus the strange boy seems to be "reading" the event as though it were happening in an earlier narrative formulation in which the knights are gods. However the unstable identity of the knights is manifested by the erratic behavior of the youth. Thus, having made the error of believing that the knights are devils, the youth then reverses himself and decides they are angels. The basis of this reversal is his first sight of the knights, a moment carefully orchestrated by Chrétien:

> Et quant il les vit en apert,
> Que du bois furent descovert,
> Et vit les haubers fremïans
> Et les elmes clers et luisans,
> Et vit le blanc et le vermeil
> Reluire contre le soleil,
> Et l'or et l'azur et l'argent
> Si li fu molt bel et molt gent,
> Et dist: "Ha! sire Diex, merchi!
> Ce sont angle que je voi chi. . . . (127–38)

[And when he saw them (the knights) in the open as they came out of the woods, and he saw their chest armor glistening and their brilliant gleaming helmets, and he saw the white and vermillion reflecting the sun; and the gold and blue and silver were so beautiful and noble to behold, and he said: "Mercy, Lord God! These are angels that I see . . ."] (my translation)

The image of the sun reflecting on the white and gold is the metaphorical remnant of the Gwalchmei's original ontology as a solar deity, just as the swan ontology of a maiden may remain in the text only as the image of her swan-white breast. In Perceval's case he continues to "read" what he encounters on the basis of his internalized text, which now functions as a euhemerized epistemological power for the hero. The emphasis on beauty as a sign of divinity has many sources in Celtic tales, including the one cited in the epigraph. The idea fits comfortably within the scope of a Platonized Christianity and reappears in many medieval Romances. We recall CuChulainn's self-glorifying boast when he wanted the boy warriors to admire the beauty of both his horses and himself: "The horses are beautiful and I am beautiful." In Romance self-praise is forbidden, but the narrator or other characters in it make frequent reference to the outstanding beauty of the hero. Perceval is frequently characterized as *biax frere* (beautiful brother) and *biax fix* (beautiful son) until he eventually discovers his name. This same emphasis is found in von

Eschenbach's *Parzifal*, a work only slightly later than Chrétien's. In *Parzifal* the first knight, exasperated in trying to deal with this strange boy, makes a telling commentary: " 'May God protect you!' said the prince. 'How I wish I had your looks! If only you had some sense in you, God would have left you nothing to wish for.' " (*Parzifal* 74) In Perceval's case his response to the visual beauty of the knights is, in effect, a recognition of his own kinship with these divine creatures. We note also that Chrétien gives tremendous emphasis to the first knight, who is pictured as much more beautiful than his companions. Perceval decides on the basis of this difference in beauty that the first knight is in effect God himself and falls down on the ground and begins to pray in adoration. The knight, believing that the youth is terrified, approaches and tells him not to be afraid:

> Et dist: "Vallet, n'aiez paor."
> - "Non ai je, par le Salveor,
> Fait li vallés, en cui je croi.
> N'iestes vos Diex?" (171–74)

[And he said: "Young man, don't be afraid." "I am not, by our Savior," replied the boy, "in whom I believe. Are you not God?"] (my translation)

Now a question such as "Are you not God?" is not just an ordinary level of confusion for a naive country youth. He is both fundamentally correct and at the same time curiously flawed. His abrupt seizure of knowledge seems to border on madness. Its power is so persistent that in the subsequent conversation with the knight the youth, instead of answering the questions put to him, responds by asking new questions. This questioning characteristic is of course his original ontology, which will empower him to ask the crucial grail question, "Who is served by the grail?" and thus disenchant the castle and heal the Fisher King. But in his immediate context it leads the second knight to observe that it is folly to try to talk with him since the Welsh by nature are "Plus fol que bestes en pasture." ["More stupid than the beasts in the field . . ."] But Perceval's animal-like behavior also suggests folly and madness. Like Yvain and other of Chrétien's heroes the young Perceval appears at times to be psychologically disoriented, a behavior that harkens back to the double identities of other Celtic heroes. Yvain, after his period of disorientation, is accompanied by a totemic-like lion. It is as though the appearance of the lion signifies the externalization of his madness and allows him to proceed in a more "normal" way. In the case of Perceval, where there is no animal companion, the narrator makes him out to be an animal-like barbarian with a tinge of madness. This characteristic is also evident when he first enters Arthur's court:

> Cler et rïant furent li oeil
> En la teste au vallet salvage.
> Nus qui le voit nel tient a sage
> Mais trestot cil que le veoient,
> Por bel et por gent le tenoient. (974–78)

[Clear and laughing were the eyes in the head of the young savage. No one who saw him took him to be very prudent, but everyone watching judged him to be beautiful and noble.] (my translation)

With this combination of madness, beauty, and nobility Chrétien has defined the new Romance hero. He is the young barbarian who has to be civilized into the greatest of knights in Arthur's court. "Madness" now appears in Chrétien as a sign of his exclusion from the world of chivalric virtue. But at the same time something of the original meaning of a divine madness persists in his strange comments about ordinary events. This idea of madness as an ability to perceive hidden meanings reappeared with the Romantics in the nineteenth century and finds noteworthy expression in Coleridge's *Kubla Khan*, where the idea of the mad artist is given a holy and sacred appearance. In Spain this Otherworld quality appears in the demonization of the Don Juan figure in Espronceda's *El estudiante de Salamanca*. According to Anthony Close's study of Cervantes it was the Romantics who popularized the idea of Don Quixote as noble rather than foolish, but as we see this view of such a hero was not new. Rather the change was due to the recovery of the traditional recognition of virtues hidden beneath the "comic" behavior of the divine fool. In this sense the Romantics re-inscribed an older hermeneutic, not a modern one.

What has happened in Chrétien's presentation of the story is that the external world in which the youth lives has become quite ordinary. A new realism has entered in which the supernatural is no longer an ordinary part of every day life as it had been in the Celtic tales. In contrast to Chrétien's translation of the story into a depiction of what appear to be everyday events, the hero himself has retained his divine nature, his unique ability to encounter the supernatural, so that to other people—and to the reader as well—he merely appears mad. The supernatural component of the tale has contracted into the spaces in which this special hero has his encounters, his *echtrai* or adventures, spaces located at magic castles, fountains, wells, crossroads, and the like. The result is that Chrétien's stylistic shift toward a more realistic presentation of the hero's world makes the hero himself appear crazy, until, by means of later developments, he vindicates himself. The divine youth has been transformed into the naive country bumpkin who will put his tormentors, like Kay, to shame and will vindicate himself to the world at large.

At the same time his social incompetence is expressed primarily as an ability to ask questions, a habit that has been socially repressed by the time he reaches the grail castle. This imposition of the dictates of courtly behavior upon the hero is in fact the primary cause of his failure to ask the spell-breaking question at the grail castle. How Chrétien intended the reader to evaluate this failure is complicated by the hermit's insistence that the failure was due to Perceval's moral culpability in abandoning his mother. If that is so, then why is the episode of his tutor's telling him not to talk so much still retained? It would seem that this is an important instance—but only one—of the original order of the tale undermining a stated goal added by Chrétien in an attempt to Christianize the *sens*.

Later in the story this same type of self-absorption occurs when Perceval does in fact meet Gawain at Arthur's court. There, Perceval has to be cajoled out of a trance-like fixation on three drops of blood he observes in the snow. This feature is also an image taken from Irish sources in which the snow, the bird, and the blood awaken Deirdre to the idea of male beauty. So Perceval is transfixed by the same three images into visualizing an image of female beauty. Within a Celtic context this kind of behavior is a recognizable "seizure of knowledge." In this instance it is only Gawain, by means of great courtesy, who is able to "disenchant" Perceval and extract him from his trance. Thus the hero's inner world and his ability to see what is hidden within ordinary events lead him to behave in a strange madlike manner. Only by a long and gradual re-education brought about by acquiring the virtues of "courtiousie" is he able to function more successfully in the medieval world of chivalry. It is also significant here that it is Gawain, an Otherworld knight, who can understand Perceval. He then introduces Perceval into the court of Arthur, the locus where the youth must achieve his full powers as a knight. This would indicate that the intercalation of the Gawain story into *Li Contes del Graal* reveals his kinship with a powerful Otherworld quest.

This narrative arrangement also can be read as a clue as to Chrétien's intended resolution of the tale. The interweaving of the Perceval and Gawain stories as an early instance of *entrelacement* as a genre feature of Romance, is here imperfectly achieved. In the original Celtic formulations, no particularly narrative subtlety would have been called for. The appearance of Gawain would simply be relevant on the basis of his belonging to the grail quest. If the patchwork linking of the two stories seems unsatisfactory to the modern reader, it is nevertheless valid on both narrative and thematic grounds. This kind of *entrelacement* procedure was to remain problematic throughout the Middle Ages and lead to the devalorization of Romance by Renaissance *preceptistas*.

The entire question of Gawain's role in *Li Contes del Graal* may also be tied in with Chrétien's decision not to identify the first knight that Perceval meets as Gawain. Several critical interpretations have suggested that Gawain, as the perfect knight in Arthur's court, functions as a model for Perceval in his education as a knight. But Gawain and Perceval may in the source material have been related in another less chivalric manner. They are in some way kindred, as we have seen, in their possession of divine powers, but there may be another kind of suppressed link in their relationship. We recall the problems concerning the naked young man in the Mark account of Christ's arrest, where there may be suppressed material of an erotic nature. The historical evidence, as we know, reveals that Celtic warriors, like Greek warriors, were homosexual. In the collection of studies entitled *The Celtic Consciousness* the matter is evaluated in the essays of Maire Cruise O'Brien and Hamish Henderson (O'Driscoll 243 ff.) and by Gerhart Herm in *The People Who Came out of Darkness* (57–58). At the very least the warrior class was isolated as a group from the larger society, just as we have seen in the CuChulainn material. However, any overt reference to homosexual content is already suppressed in the manuscripts that survive. It may be that CuChulainn's curious boasting about his own beauty may not be merely a sign of his divinity. Likewise, Chrétien's presentation of Perceval's reaction to the beauty of the knights may indeed contain a hidden text. In spite of the Christian prohibitions, homosexuality was not unknown or even hidden among twelfth century knights and princes. Richard the Lionhearted is the most famous homosexual warrior, but fairly obvious references to it also occur in heraldic coats of arms. Partridges indicated that the bearer of such insignia participated in "unnatural" sexual practices (Keen 130–31). Needless to say no such reference would survive in clerical manuscripts.

The most that can be said at this point is that Chrétien, in his effort to "translate" alien Celtic material into medieval French culture, would also drop out all unacceptable items. Nevertheless, Perceval's first meeting with knights has been orchestrated by Chrétien in such a way that the hero's insistence that the knights are gods or angels makes Perceval seem odder than he appeared in the Welsh version. What is more, Chrétien's careful re-interpretation of the Celtic material re-constitutes the pagan Otherworld content as a hidden reality with which the hero must come to terms. In this sense, Chrétien in an attempt to "explain" the alien material has instead mystified it. What was comfortable and open about the presentation of the supernatural in the Celtic tales has now become secret and enigmatic. In so doing the author has created an occult text and infused Romance with a numinous appeal not found in the Celtic tales themselves. Romance, as a literary kind, has taken on one of its most characteristic genre features.

Other Suppressions of the Grail Castle

The presence of other hidden material is found in subsequent adventures, and it is precisely from this condition that the story's referential meanings become problematic. This arrangement of deliberately excluding material unacceptable to the institutional structures of medieval knowledge accounts for darkly attractive powers of Romance and for the feeling of guilt associated with reading the *matter of Britain*. As for Perceval his entire story can be read as an *aventure* in reading signs, and *Li Contes del Graal* exists as the paradigmatic challenge of a special language.

It is not surprising then that both the medieval continuators of the tale and the modern critical establishment have exercised themselves at length trying to establish a "legitimate" meaning for the tale. Thus the "meanings" attached to the grail procession have ranged from seeing it as a narratized fertility ritual to an agenda for the conversion of the Jews. Between these two poles several other interpretations have flourished, among them a strong case for the influence of Cistercian mysticism (Adams et al. 23ff.). The validity of any of these studies is not what is at issue here. Rather my concern is with the referential volatility of the imagery as a condition of the text.

Certainly no other single scene in literature has suffered or enjoyed quite the same kind of referential instability as Chrétien's grail procession. We have seen that there always exists the possibility of hidden texts, but it should be stressed also that the possibility of fluctuating meanings is an essential genre-linked feature of Romance. We read such literature because of its evocative and equivocating concern with the mystery of life itself, an appeal that hovers just below the surface of our perception, seductive but ultimately elusive.

Something of this condition is perhaps basic to all literature, and certainly to all literature that subsumes the condition of Romance into its ontology. Thus the grail procession functions as a challenge for every reader and comes to exist as a *figura* for the act of reading itself. The images in the grail procession, the bleeding spear and the enigmatic grail platter, pass before all of us as signs. Like Perceval we want to ask what they mean, and like Perceval we cannot. Once the moment has passed, and with it the opportunity to solve the mystery, we feel, as the loathly damsel proclaims, forever bereft. We have come to the threshold of all meaning, only to have it pass irrevocably into the closed room.

Like all truly numinous moments in literature, the grail scene is presented to us in great simplicity. As with Don Quixote's windmill adventure, the profile of an enigma has become engraved on the consciousness of our culture. In both instances it is the unstable referential condition of the imagery that creates the power and allows the scene itself to become the *figura* of its own enigmatic appeal. To read it is to experience something of the lost power of Celtic narrative and the forbidden referential knowledge it codifies. In Chrétien's articulation there are, in addition to these half-hidden Celtic significations, many things that involve other medieval horizons of meaning as well. The result is a scene whose full meaning is forever beyond our ken.

Other problematics of critical readings of the grail scene are due to Chrétien's organization of the story line. Frappier, for instance, finds that the tale is an amalgamation of three basic narremes: (1) an *enfances* organization of Perceval's growth, (2) a discrete *graal* adventure, and (3) the story of Gawain. He sees these components as the *matiére* that Chrétien is trying to interweave in a new *conjointure*. Not everyone agrees with this explanation, but it would be hard to deny that Chrétien is incorporating different narrative strains, whatever else in the way of Celtic, Byzantine, Middle Eastern, or Jewish material he had in mind. Frappier also feels that Chrétien intended to leave some of the mysterious quality of the imagery, and that the situation became exacerbated by the incomplete condition of the text or texts.

What I would suggest, as an interpretive strategy concerning the last item, would be rather to consider it a case of textual conflicts caused by the disappearance of a signifying authority from the scene. It is this phenomenon, a type of death of God, that cuts loose the linguistic signs from a known referential anchor. Whether this disappearance is due to the literal death of Chrétien is another matter altogether. What we as readers are confronted with is instead the premature disappearance of the authorial presence. It is this presence that seemed to offer but did not deliver an explanation of the meaning of the grail procession. Whether such a presence could have provided the longed-for explanation can never be known, since the possibility of referential indeterminacy is already inscribed in the stories as Chrétien presented them.

The exact source material Chrétien possessed for the grail scene is unknown, but there is no reason to believe that Chrétien would be limited by source meanings, since he modified the order and *sen* of other sources he used. The ambitious goals he proclaimed in his prologues would indicate he was about something new. In any case, no one from Chrétien's time to our own has been bashful about reading new meanings into the story, regardless of what importance is assigned to the troubled idea of authorial intent. Still it is useful to look at a few of the Celtic sources, since earlier meanings would have conditioned reader response. D. D. R. Owen, in his careful study of Celtic sources for the grail, points out that numerous cups, bowls, caldrons, and dishes in Celtic tales were associated with the questions of identity (the kingship of Ireland), fertility (the birth of CuChulainn), the healing of the wounded, and so forth. All and any of these meanings might have inhabited Chrétien's source material, although neither his audience nor even Chrétien himself would have been able to fully decode such meanings. What can be argued, therefore, is that not only Perceval but the narrator himself could not fathom the meaning or purpose of the procession.

Whatever answer the Fisher King might have given to the missing question would not necessarily have explained the fundamental mystery underlying the scene. At no point in the story is it indicated that the crucial question would have lead to such an answer. Rather, both Perceval's cousin and the loathly damsel insist only that the question itself would have broken the spell which has befallen the castle and its inhabitants. The question in this sense becomes an end in itself. It is a means of breaking a spell and not necessarily a means of eliciting information, however haunting or desired that information might be. The first clue to this situation has already been noted in the Welsh version of the tale in which the grail holds a severed head, itself a spell-breaking item. The absence of such a severed head in Chrétien's version of the procession might be as significant as its presence. Actually, a redundancy seems to exist in *Peredur* since the story provides for both the presence of the spell-breaking severed head and the absence of the spell-breaking question.

The question in fact seems to replace the more familiar riddle in this kind of story. Frye discusses this means of acquiring a forbidden knowledge in his analysis of themes of descent: "When it is wisdom that is sought in the lower world, it is almost always connected with the anxiety of death in some form or other, along with the desire to know what lies beyond. Such wisdom, however displaced, is usually communicated in some kind of dark saying, and riddles and ciphers and oracular utterances of all kinds proliferate around the end of the descending journey" (122). Frye does not cite the grail scene as an example of this narrative arrangement, but his observations apply once one substitutes the question for the riddle as Loomis has suggested. The other substitution is the kind of narrative where a certain linguistic dark saying produces the desired breaking of the enchantment often in the terms spelled out by the loathly damsel.

An important clue to the cause of this problem can be found in Chrétien's attempts at Christianization of the pagan Celtic material. The prologue states that Count Philip outshines Alexander, the paragon of warriors, precisely because of the Christian virtues he embodies. Likewise, within the tale itself, Chrétien has positioned several of the adventures around the Christian festivals of Pentecost, Ascension Thursday, and Good Friday, holy days for which Celtic roots are not strong. It is also the specific Christian items that loom large in the Holmes-Klencke interpretation of Jewish conversion theme as the key to the grail riddle. While their interpretation may not convince, it is the question of the anti-Semitic content gathered into the Christian agenda that provides a clue as to the nature of the contradictions. If one accepts the proposition that Chrétien himself turns out to be of Jewish descent, the plot merely thickens. In fact, the theory of Jewish identity may result not from any evidence for such a claim but rather from Chrétien's attempt to suppress the Celtic meanings of the material.

Two other important factors of medieval culture contributed to anxiety about the nature of the story: the valorization of literature for women and the problematic status of fiction itself. The question always remained that if fiction does not tell "true" stories, what kind of stories does it tell? To make matters worse this question stirred up fears that the Celtic source material dealt with adventures of the Otherworld, a factor generally demonized by Christianity. Because of the uneasy situation of Arthurian Romance, many writers took special care to adapt a Christian allegorical reading of the material, since this procedure offered a way out of the danger. All of these factors contributed to a need to baptize the material, into a more acceptable twelfth-century Christianity, a Christianity self-consciously moving toward a reasoned theology. God, after all, must be as reasonable as the men who ruled a Christian society, and this tendency was creating a need for Romance. In addition, two pressing political issues also reinforced the anxiety about unreasoned discourse. The Anglo-Norman-French hegemony was confronting the threat of an exotic Islamic world which seemed to deny the "reasoned" proofs of Christianity. The Moslems were consistently seen as devious and passionate in their rejection of reason. At the other end of the Norman sphere of influence was the continuing presence of "wild" Celts on the Welsh and Irish frontiers of their world. It is not surprising that something of these problems should find resonance in the work of the greatest writer of the moment, whose text seemed to create an enclosed generic space for the feminine world of intuition and the irrational. These categories could safely be assigned to women since they were excluded from the operation of the new masculine hegemony of reason and "freedom." Hence Arthurian Romance effectively fulfilled the cultural need of both presenting and containing dangerous and threatening content.

One reason for re-examining the problem of Chrétien's anti-Semitism is the uncomfortable nature of its role within the text. An awareness of this unease is attested to by the many rebuttals and responses elicited by the Urban Holmes thesis. What is really at issue is the unresolved problem of the existence of unacceptable content in the text. One of these is the overt and unsettling instances of anti-Semitic references in Chrétien's version of the story, material clearly not of pre-Christian origin. While it is not unusual, however, for anti-Semitic exhortations to appear in Christian texts of the Middle Ages, it is all the more likely to erupt in a text in which other non-Christian matters are also being suppressed.

Erupt is a good term to describe its appearance in *Li Contes del Graal*, since as a genre Romance is not a form in which social problems are likely to appear in such a blatant manner. Realism, after all, is the genre for those kinds of issues. In fact some critics have felt that the violent language of the Good Friday knight in regard to the Jews may not be by Chrétien but rather was inserted by a later scribe. Again the critical issue is whether a certain item "belongs" to a text. All that can be said is that to a modern reader the anti-Semitism does seem to violate the decorum of the genre, but it is the nature of Romance to suffer such "violations" from time to time. Nevertheless, such an eruption may in fact be the result of too much suppression of other kinds of alien content, and this is what seems to be happening here.

The two key passages in this case are the hostile references to Jews, first the attack by Perceval's mother and then the more violent condemnation by the Good Friday knight. Both outbursts occur as part of an attempt to explain religious matters to Perceval, and hence clearly belong to the project of inserting Christian themes into pagan events. The mother's milder attack comes as she responds to Perceval's question about what is a chapel. She tells him:

> Une maison bele et saintisme
> Ou il a cors sains et tresors,
> Si i sacrefion le cors
> Jhesucrist, le prophete sainte
> Cui juïf fisent honte mainte.
> (578–82)

[It is a beautiful and holy house where there are displayed holy relics and treasures, and where they sacrifice the body of Jesus Christ, the holy prophet whom the Jews treated so badly.] (my translation)

While this reference seems more mild than what is to follow, it does have two specific references to violence. First she emphasizes the act of sacrifice, which we know to have been very bloody among the Celts, and the reference here does have a double use of *cors* which parallels the meaning of sacred relics and the body of the victim. This word play of course is not unusual in Christian terminology. However, the problem of sacrifice and redemption does seem extraneous to this story of a Welsh wild boy but it foreshadows the idea of the grail knight as a sacrificial offering. Secondly she refers to Jhesucrist as *prophete* which links Christ to the succession of Jewish prophets and suggests the Christian idea of the

Jewish Bible as precursor to the Christian. In what follows of her explanation she stresses the sacrifice as necessary to free souls from the fires
of hell. Curiously for a boy who seems never to have heard of a Church,
all the theological subtlety rouses no further questions. This behavior,
which does not seem consistent with his character, may further account
for the impression of an inserted explanatory passage not integrated into
the dramatic action of the scene. For a medieval reader these comments
would have appeared normal, but the fact remains that Chrétien has
failed to present a psychologically coherent picture of Perceval's behavior here, and the Jewish material addresses thematic concerns rather than
presenting a convincing portrayal of the hero's character. Ruth Harwood
Cline in her translation makes the following comment: "The virulent
anti-Semitism of v. 582 and vs. 6292ff. is atypical of Chrétien's works;
Lejeune notes . . . that Chrétien never mentioned the Jews in his previous
romances. These passages may reflect an intensification of the anti-Semitic
spirit of the times. Early in 1180 Philip-August signed the first edicts of
persecution of the Jews at a time when Jews were actually put to death
in the vicinity of Paris" (Chrétien, *Perceval* 19).

The same emphasis on thematics rather than character also marks the
Good Friday episode. Whether Chrétien wrote this episode has been
disputed, but Frappier among others is willing to accept it as Chrétien's.
This question is not as crucial as the recognition that it functions, or
attempts to function, as an explanation of what happened in the grail
scene. The hermit attributes Perceval's failure to ask the question to his
moral sin of abandoning his mother. He thus groups the grail failure
among Perceval's sins of omission. What is most to be noted, however,
is that this explanation is a re-reading of something that happened earlier
in the story. Its function marks it as a hermeneutic sign possibly inserted
to help the reader interpret the story. In that sense it could easily be an
addition by the first continuator of the tale and have little to do with
Chrétien's intended closure. At the same time we also note that Chrétien
himself does include this kind of explanatory gesture in his general narrative procedures, so that this strategy in itself is not alien to the decorum of the story. What is important is the fact that the narrator is
apparently trying to come to terms with meaning, and as we have seen
both Chrétien and later continuators show signs of not understanding
the figures of their own stories. Rather, explanatory gestures do not occur
when meaning is unproblematic. In any case, the appearance of anti-
Semitic content, whether by Chrétien or a scribe, occurs as part of a

thematic agenda that is being imposed rather awkwardly on a much
earlier, pre-Christian story line. In this sense anti-Semitism is not alien to
the Christian thrust of Chrétien's maneuvers nor to the generic fix that
the twelfth century was trying to impose on pagan stories.

   In this context we note that the Good Friday knight's extended condemnation of the Jews occurs in conjunction with exactly the same thematic
point as it did in the mother's discourse: on the question of the sacrificial
death of Christ. The knight, however, gives a fuller theological explanation
since he discusses the role of the Jews within a general discussion on the
dual nature of Jesus as God and as man. It should be emphasized that this
topic is the most fragile of fault lines in Catholic theology. Almost all
heresy, from the Church's point of view, arises along the borders of this
dogma. From the point of view of a Catholic center, heresies tend toward
(over)emphasizing either Christ's humanity, like the Arians's, or, his divinity, like the Monophosytes's. The attempt to express the Catholic balance
is always difficult, and the Good Friday hermit carefully threads his way
through some very arcane and sensitive material. His rhetoric is charged
with paradox as he tries to explain to Perceval, ever the ingenue, the
connection between the Incarnation and the guilt of the Jews:

> "Quls jors, sire? Si nel savez?
> C'est li venredis aorez,
> Li jors que l'en doit aorer
> La crois et ses pechiez plorer,
> Car hui fu cil en crois pendus
> Qui fu trente deniers vendus.
> Cil qui de toz pechiez fu mondes
> Vit les pechiez dont toz li mondes
> Fu enliiez et entechiez,
> Si devint hom por nos pechiez.
> *Voirs est que Diex et hom fu il,*
> Que la Virge enfanta un fil
> Que par Saint Esperit conchut,
> Ou Diex et char et sanc rechut,
> Si fu la deïtez coverte
> En char d'ome, c'est chose certe.
> Et qui issi ne le querra,
> Ja en la face nel verra
> Cil fu nes de la Virge dame
> Et prist d'ome la forme et l'ame

Avec sa sainte deïté,
Qui a tel jor par verité
Come il est hui fu en crois mis
Et traist d'enfer toz ses amis.
Molt par fu sainte cele mors
Ki salva les vis et les mors
Resuscita de mort a vie
Li faus juïf par lor envie,
C'on devroit tüer come chiens,
Firent als mal et nos grans biens,
Quant il en la crois le leverent;
Als perdirent et nos salverent."
(6265–95, emphasis added)

[What day, my lord? You don't know? Today is Good Friday, the day you should adore the cross and lament your sins, for today He was hung on a cross, having been sold for 30 silver pieces. He who was free of all sin saw the entire world enmeshed in filth, and he became a man because of our sins. *He was God and man in one* because the royal Virgin conceived a son by the Holy Spirit so that God took on flesh and blood, and in this way his divinity was concealed. All this is a certainty and he who does not believe it will not see His face. He was born of a Virgin Mother and received the form and soul of a man to cover his holy divinity, and who truly on this day was put upon the cross and freed from hell all his followers. Most holy was that death which saved the living and *restored the dead to life. The false Jews, because of their envy, ought to be killed like dogs. They did evil to themselves and great good to us when they raised Him on the cross, damning themselves and saving us.*] (my translation)

The language here is as highly charged as the topic it addresses. The repeated use of paradox traces the dangerous fluctuation between damned and saved, between deity and human, between rising and falling, between death and life, between sin and innocence, between clean and unclean, between hatred and love, and finally and irrevocably between Christian and Jew. What is drawn is nothing less than a final line that forever divides these opposites.

What is even more disturbing is the fact that the oppositions become the essential element in the constitution of the new faith and the new

salvation. Their meaning would be emptied without the binomial concepts of belief/disbelief and salvation/damnation, Christian/Jew. Such
is the faith of the age of the crusaders, and such would be the condition
of the identity of a new culture defining itself against the threats of
Moslems, Jewish, and Celtic counter-identities. What is also at stake is
the French absorption of the Celtic stories as part of their own self-defi-
nition. All one can say of the other threats confronting the lords of Flanders
and Champagne is that they are ready to incorporate the Celt, while the
Jew, somehow a greater threat, remains alien. The French can neither
come to terms with them nor absorb them. What the text does is clearly
inscribe the Jew outside the border, beyond the pale, to utilize the term
the English developed to refer to the unabsorbed Celts. Thus the rhetoric
in this passage replicates the thematics of inside and outside that constitute the identity of the newly defined space of Christian existence.

    In the same way the identity of Romance as the literary genre at issue
is posited on a similar electric-like current that traces an unstable passage
toward a constituted meaning. Romance as a literary kind comes into
being not as a formed space but as a movement between poles of meaning. It is this gesture which creates the double hermeneutic fix that char-
acterizes its identity. This ontology of signification is, of course, most
appropriate for a work which posits the need for two heroes. Gawain
and Perceval themselves also represent binomial polarities, as do Christ
as man and Christ as God, in this conflation of pagan and Christian
values; neither knight could achieve identity without the other. Perceval
the wild boy could signify only by means of his interaction with Gawain,
the perfect ideal of courtesy. Perceval in that sense is beyond the pale
himself. He will never *be* the perfect knight-redeemer, he will only appear to be so defined, just as for the Monophosytes Christ only appeared
to be human. At heart, *cors*, he also cannot be contained. He is never fully
human and his essence is not fully describable in language or narrative.
He exists precariously on the border of some final Good Friday marking,
the knight of the linguistic fissure that creates the possibility of meaning.
The quest for the meaning of the grail image narratizes an ontology of
meaning. This explains the appeal that lies buried in the heart of his
story. Perhaps at the heart of all stories, but certainly at the heart of
Romance.

    One other image in the hermit's discourse provides the clue for the
condition of its story. In lines 6279–80 we find the phrase "Si fu la deïtez
coverte / en char d'ome." Whether orthodox or not (probably not) he

images the deity as hidden (rhyme word *coverte*) in the body of man. The drama of this image empowers the idea of Christ as a narrative possibility, a necessary condition for the story itself. The idea of hidden/revealed hangs in the referential space and charges the drama being enacted, and re-enacted, on that day. Perceval, like CuChulainn, is at the border and is challenged to determine what shall pass and what shall not pass. This is his moment of highest drama, the moment that comes to him because of his failure in the grail castle. It is the ultimate *echtra* and the spiritual core of the Romance. What it *means*, by its very nature, cannot be defined, and that is the set-point which marks the condition of Romance as a literary kind. It exists as a confrontation with the Otherworld, the final border of human existence. Its flawed signifying power both appeals and forbids, calls and denies.

Chrétien's Perceval: The Knight of the Marche/Border Lord

Outside the Bible, a text of unparalleled institutional authority in Western culture, there are only a few scenes in the secular narrative tradition that have gained universal recognition. Along with the scenes of Adam and Eve and the apple, or the crucifixion or nativity of Christ, perhaps only Don Quixote's attack on the windmill has a comparable profile. If there is another such *imago* it would be the grail as it is articulated in Chrétien's *Li Contes del Graal*. The work as a whole is today less known to the general public, but the grail as an image, separated now from the ritual procession that presented it, has survived as the most famous sign in all medieval literature. What is most curious is that now its popular form rests not on Chrétien's image of a fish platter but on its later re-articulations as a chalice. This transformation, the most successful double hermeneutic fix, itself seems symbolic of the shape-shifting energy of its Celtic ancestry, and remains as a supreme and unique example of an ontology not dependent on a single definitive physical representation. Furthermore, the persistent question of what specifically is known or can be known about that ontology seems to be part of its appeal.

Some of the reasons for this appeal have already been mentioned. The fact that it is a re-working of older mythic paradigms is certainly important, but without the specific articulation given to the scene in *Li Contes del Graal* it would be no more than a cultural footnote. The key to its

powerful hold on the imagination is its ability to suggest half-forgotten
meanings, many of which are disturbing to a cultural nexus based on the
primacy of reason as the only reliable foundation for human knowledge.
The enigma of the grail constitutes nothing less than a major challenge
to that epistemological hierarchy. This means that the true locus of the
scene is on an epistemological border, on that "perilous" frontier between the known and the unknown which constitutes a cultural fault
line for any society. The grail procession signifies in the simplest of terms
a movement from the known to the unknown, from the seen to the
unseen, from the dining hall of the castle to a closed chamber. Whether
that chamber represents the holy of holies or some other repository of
hidden wisdom is not the issue. It matters only that the chamber is
closed off and that the hero cannot see what is in it.

One of the names sometimes given to the testing castles that Romance
knights visit and in which they experience other world adventures is *le
Chastel de la Marche*. One thinks of the Norman designation of Marcher
Lords as the chieftains set to guard the uncomfortable border between
the Norman hegemony and the world of the wild Celt. Noting that *marche*
means border, Darrah has pointed out that such castles also mark the
frontier between this world and the Otherworld (63). This border also
marks one of the margins of the territory of Romance as a literary genre.
As with the *echtra* of Irish tales and CuChulainn's encounters at the
border of Emuin, the Romance knight is the hero at the border, the one
destined from before time to confront the dangers that cross over from
an unknown world into the lives of mortals. The Romance knight, in an
important sense, is the hero of the medieval "everyman" and not just the
culture hero of the national epic like Roland or the Cid. He is the hero
of the ordinary individual confronted with the classless challenges of the
human condition: death, danger, sexuality, unreasoned fears. And as such
he appeals to everyone, women and men and children. He has no invest-
ment in protecting merely the national or ethnic culture of a specific
society. This factor, or something related to this factor, accounts for the
universal and undying appeal of Romance, of the fairy tale, of the
children's story, of the challenge of adventure. It is not irrelevant that it
is this kind of knight that Don Quixote seeks to become and that his ideal
is Amadís de Gaula or the Orlando of Ariosto or the Lanzarote del Lago
of Arthurian provenance and not the historical figures of the Cid or the
Gran Capitán. Remembering also the sounded pronunciation of the final
vowel in old French, it is not uninteresting to hear the verbal and etymo-

logical echo of *chastel de la marche* in the sound of Don Quixote de la
Mancha. La Mancha, as Covarrubias makes clear, means also the territory marked out as a border, as differing from its neighbors. Don Quixote
is also a knight of the frontier between certain kinds of knowledge, both
known and unknown. He is the border lord between the known and
unknown, as he himself boasts in part 1, chapter 20. The humor generated by this condition, just as in the case of Perceval, is the sign of the
hero's divine descent. Dostoyevsky, Cervantes' greatest reader, was right.
It is in this designation of "comic" that the work is the divinest utterance
of the human mind. The parodic effects in the stories of CuChulainn,
Peredur, Perceval, and Don Quixote are part of this Otherworld energy.
This is not surprising if we recall that parody is a genre about borders,
about crossing over from one kind of knowing to another.

The place of Chrétien in the historical process of marking out this
literary space is central. Without him, or someone like him, the genre of
Romance as we know it would not have come to be, not have received
the particular configuration that we know. The grail procession, perhaps
because of its incompleteness, has become the textual *figura* of the genre.
Its referential indeterminacy is indicative of both the way in which he
found the material and the condition in which he left it. His version is
in itself a *gathering* in the Heideggerian sense of the term. It is a coming-
into-being of the grail enigma as a *figura* which haunted the narrative
imagination of the following centuries from *Parzifal* and *The High Book of
the Grail* to Malory and beyond. Don Quixote's brief disquisition on the
unexplainable appeal of this kind of literature (pt. 1, ch. 1) is only a
symptom of its articulation into the *Quixote* as a text. In the same way
when we as readers focus on the problematics of meaning in the grail
image we are attempting to cross the border, to penetrate into the holy
of holies, into the secret chamber that has closed off a forbidden knowledge. This is the meaning of the adventure reserved for the grail knight
as the hero of the human condition. The fact that Perceval fails to gain
full access to this knowledge makes him the perfect image of the frailties
of this same human condition. I would like to think that Chrétien, if he
had lived, would have left Perceval in this imperfect condition: empowered to see the mystery but ultimately resigned to not being able to
reveal its meaning.

Our own cultural identity has been conditioned by the synthesis of
Western culture that took its form in the twelfth century. Hannah Arendt
has spoken of the fact that the Jews in the Middle Ages never became an

effective part of feudalism and therefore remained a caste apart in modern Europe. Their subsequent "classless" condition marked them as not an effective part of the Western society, leaving them outside the cultural borders that Europe drew for its own identity. In the twelfth century, as the new feudal society grew to its perfection in northern France, its idea of inside and outside also marked out the border terms that Friederick Heer has defined. So it is not surprising that the expression of a virulent anti-Semitism found a place within the Perceval romance.

In the same way the existence of the Marcher Lords on the Welsh border confirms the fact that the Celt, like the Jew, did not belong to the new hegemony. It goes without saying that from the point of view of this hegemony the new Spanish kingdoms of the Reconquista were at best Marcher realms themselves. Catalonia was the original Carolingian Marche in Iberia, and later kingdoms of Leon and Castile were merely added to this perspective. Ortega y Gasset in his *España invertebrada* also noted that European feudalism failed to integrate the Peninsula into the world of the new European nation states, thus leaving Spain as an exotic border entity of the medieval world. The French re-discovery of Romantic Spain in the nineteenth century only confirms the border status of Spanish culture. More recently Paul Julian Smith's *Writing in the Margin* examines this topic in relation to current critical concerns. The fact that *Don Quixote* is the only work of Spanish literature to gain full citizenship in the canon of European classics is not unrelated to this situation, but Don Quixote as a literary character has suffered a shifting ontology as either a comic or noble hero. The double profile is partly due to the double hermeneutic fix of his genre and partly to the ambivalent status of Spanish culture itself. Borders are unsettling but they have an appeal that cannot be denied.

In spite of the fact that Chrétien is the product of the new European identity, he too suffers the status of a border lord. In this sense Chrétien achieved the impossible in that he created the literary space for the survival of threatening Celtic ideas, but at the same time his contemporaries assigned a problematic valorization to his work. The "vain and pleasing" matter of Britain was popular, but not granted a label as a "serious" subject for men, who were the only arbiters of power in the society. The literature of Celtic Arthurian matters was allowed because it proved useful as a way of entertaining women. After all the stories of the Celts, as a marginal people, were suitable for women, a marginal segment of the society. But the powers of state, university, and church failed to fully recognize that they had allowed the forbidden within the gates. Chrétien's work provided access to forbidden knowledge, and the grail procession passing before Perceval and vanishing into a closed chamber can be read as the image of what medieval society sought to banish from the main agenda of power: vain stories and capricious women.

If the political roots of the nation state are to be found in the adventuring Norman lords as they marked off the boundaries of France and England, the intellectual ferment of the twelfth century takes its impetus from the new dialectic of Aristotelianism that had penetrated France from Moslem Spain. The twelfth century provided the groundwork for the triumph of Thomistic thought and the spread of scholasticism. The place of Chrétien in this movement is curiously contradictory, because the triumph of reason over intuition seems to sit uneasily in his work. In fact, the scholarly and popular visions of Chrétien's achievement celebrate opposing aspects of his tales. For the general reader he is cherished as the founder of Romance with all its trappings of courtly love, mystery, and chivalry. At the same time the critical and academic community stresses the clearness and lucidity of his language and his classic presentation of character and plot. He has been called the "founder of the modern novel" and the "first master of modern narrative." There can be no doubt that what he did has shaped the ideals of European narrative form, and precisely because of this it can also be said that he shaped the locus of emotional and intuitive literature. This aspect of his achievement is less studied in the history of narrative forms, and it is this component that defines the function of Romance as a literary discourse. From the point of view of *Don Quixote* as a literary phenomenon, the nature of this function is crucial. Re-reading Chrétien from the vantage point of the *Quixote* provides an illumination of what the hidden texts are doing within the gathering form of Romance narrative.

Chrétien and the Art of the Impossible

The question of Chrétien's achievement with the *matiere de Bretagne* should be looked at not only from the perspective of what he included but also from the point of view of what he excluded, or tried to exclude. The question of his ordering of the sequences of adventures that his knights suffered can be seen in all the major texts of the canon: *Cliges, Erec et Enid, Yvain, Le Chevalier de la Charrette,* and finally *Li conte des graal* (Owen,

Evolution 121ff.). Each of these works centers on an episodic string of adventures besetting a particular hero, Cliges, Erec, Yvain, Lancelot, and in the last case two knights Perceval and Gawain. The problem of structuring the adventures are what we have already seen: the story must strive toward some sort of totalization that takes the hero from a problematic beginning to a type of fulfilment or triumph. Two of these deal with the conflicting demands of heroic adventure and marriage. Since marriage as defined by the feudal status of women constituted itself as the only career open to them, there was an inevitable conflict between how men should fulfill their dual roles as husbands and heroes. In *Erec et Enide* the hero neglects his commitment to chivalric adventure; in *Yvain* he neglects his wife. In both a type of compromise is achieved at the end, but the problem itself is not done away with. In the more enigmatic and perhaps more paradigmatic *Knight of the Cart*, Lancelot can rescue Guinevere from the mysterious knight but must betray his king in order to sleep with her and fulfill the demands of her "capricious" nature. This story provides or seems to provide the definitive medieval definition of "woman," a creature whose demands eluded the reasoned analytic of Freud. Finally, attempting to re-locate women in the life of the hero, *Li Contes del Graal* struggles again with the elusive destiny of the knight of the border and his relation to women. It is not surprising that in later formulations of this conundrum, as in Malory, Galahad, the virgin knight, replaces Perceval as the primary seeker of the grail, an adventure denied to the lustful Lancelot.

In considering the dual roles of men, it is significant that Darrah insists that Galahad and Lancelot are two names for the same Celtic hero. He suggests that the two names take their origin from separate ritual "offices" or titles, as does the term *dauphin* in France (44–4). Thus men in the source stories were defined by differing ceremonial roles. As a consequence we find that in Chrétien's world of Romance, men must in effect be two people if they are to meet the demands of both pagan women and the rituals of chivalry. Hence in Chrétien's tales Gawain plays a curiously complimentary role to the primary hero, taking up the slack, so to speak, of the hidden ritualist demands of the stories. So in *Li Contes del Graal* we have both Gawain the philanderer and Perceval the sexual ingenue. If Chrétien had finished the *Lancelot* we would have had some idea of how he might confront the problem of the perfect lover and hero in *Li Contes del Graal*, but a successful resolution seemed to elude him.

As for Cervantes, it is curious that Don Quixote's personal role model is often Lanzarote, a name inscribed into his own, and yet Don Quixote, the idealist in love, never addresses the question of Lancelot and adultery. Perhaps the answer is that for Don Quixote Lancelot's love is purely spiritual, and in this way he would see no sin in Lancelot. But that ideal isn't found in the Lancelot ballad that Don Quixote continually cites or in the figure of the intermediary dona Quintanona that he also calls to our attention. Nor is the answer found in the challenges posited in such stories as the "Curioso" or even the case of Dorotea, the princess of lust, who provides Don Quixote with his heroine in his climactic battle with the giant of lust in the inn. The problem has more horizons that any of these formulations allow, and Don Quixote continues to operate in a world of Romance, where erotic desire is the greatest force in the formation of the knight. The warrior without his lady, he insists, is like a tree without leaves. We can only assume that the curious gap in Don Quixote's valorization of Lancelot's adultery seems to be an inherited feature of Romance, an enigma that brings to mind Celtic heroines such as Maeve or Etain, who flit from one sexual partner to another. These instances seem to signal that adultery as constituted in Romance left everyone, including Chrétien, uneasy. But at its core this conflict is the result of the marginalization of women in Feudal society and the Christian insistence on their sexual fidelity in marriage, two demands not placed on Celtic women.

In the same way, the issue of border wars took its origina from the Celtic source material. The divine provenance of heroes like Lancelot and Gawain was obviously the target of Christian repression. The fact that Don Quixote does not give the pagan sources a thought demonstrates how effectively this task was accomplished. In the age of the Reformation the unease over the revival of paganism within the humanist movement would make the topic highly sensitive. The youthful Cervantes had certainly felt the pull of Greco-Roman paganism in his love affair with the pastoral, and there remains a distinctively pagan vitality in his descriptions of the rituals surrounding the death of the poet in the *Galatea*. The problem surfaces openly in the story of Grisostomo and Marcela in the *Quixote* where we recall that the local "abates" are exercised about Grisostomo's burial in unsanctified ground. The event arouses suspicions of pagan practices according to Pedro, the shepherd narrator. So we are aware that paganism was not a topic that escaped Cervantes' attention. For Chrétien, however, the specifically Celtic formulations of paganism posed a much dicier problem. Everyone, it would seem, wanted to hear stories of Arthur and his court, but how this *matiere* was to be articulated into the mainstream of Christian culture was to be the singular achievement of Chrétien. What he did with the grail procession set the absorption of Celtic imagery onto its path to glory. Even though later writers, like Eschenbach, sought to "correct" Chrétien, his stories marked the boundaries of "acceptable" Romance. Subsequent development of the genre was merely the result of the introduction of new Christian allegorical readings, a hermeneutic that left intact the basic imagery of Chrétien's grail procession. In the same way Lancelot's adultery became part of the canon of courtly love and was included in the list of acceptable, if touchy, topics. The awareness of the pagan origins of the adultery of heroes like Lancelot and Tristan vanished from the consciousness of the cultural mainstream.

This process of euhemerization of pagan material, however, accounts for the problem of unresolved mystery that haunts the grail imagery. The energetic co-opting of its pagan power by Christian allegorical re-readings and re-writings can be seen in the works of later writers. The strategy of devising allegorical readings had developed in early Christian apologetics when it confronted Classical pagan literature that could not be suppressed. The success of that enterprise naturally recommended itself to the domestication of Celtic material, and the allegorization of the stories seemed certain to succeed. The results, however, proved more problematic, since the force of paganism in the Celtic tales was less understood. The transformation process set in motion by Chrétien was to receive a dynamic re-formulation in *Don Quixote*. For in that work it must be seen that the problem of hermeneutics is at the heart of its narrative agenda.

Prologue to the Challenge

As mentioned before, Chrétien's artistry should be measured by measuring the success with which he re-ordered the episodes of the stories, achieving a kind of logocentric organization missing in earlier versions of the same material. As a result we look for and find in Chrétien much greater attention to the psychological motivation of the hero as he moves from episode to episode. What had been a series of discrete narratives of what happened to the hero at various times becomes instead a study of how the hero changes and grows through the course of his adventures. In the new arrangement the question of his motives and reactions, for instance, assumes a totally new role. As Darrah has shown, when the primitive warrior kills the black knight and takes over his castle or fountain it is normally expected that he also takes over his women, whether they be his wife or daughters. The question of the woman's feelings in this kind of tale is not relevant, since what we have is a narratized version of a ritual practice. In Romance, on the other hand, with its new and different valorization of woman, her feelings do become important. The result is that she is then depicted as perhaps a prisoner of the evil black knight and looks upon the new knight as her rescuer, thus motivating her love for him. This kind of change can easily be found in Chrétien's version of *Yvain*. Such modifications merely indicate that the purpose of the story has changed to suit the horizon of expectations of a new audience. Nevertheless the author's *translatio* from one set of hermeneutic expectations to another is never without problems. Something of the original purpose may still persist in the story giving the reader a sense of the presence of another "meaning" buried in the text.

Of all the material adapted from Celtic sources the grail scene is without question the most important example of this condition, and for that reason it came to function as a hermeneutic challenge to later writers. Each writer tried in some way or other to re-interpret the scene for his own purposes. Since everyone knew the story, the new meaning or *sen* provided the motivation for reading the story. This process of re-telling and re-interpreting is thus very near the surface of the story and very much part of the audience's expectations. It is in this sense that we can speak of the grail procession as a *figura* for the condition of the text. The story has become a conundrum containing multiple versions of itself, and these other versions hint at other meanings. To a great extent modern critical studies have merely continued this interpretive process, and yet no amount of explaining seems to eliminate the power of the hidden appeal.

In this process we find the cause of the numinous appeal attributed to Romance as a genre, where the reader gets the feeling that something is going on which is not apparent on the surface of the story. For this reason *Li Contes del Graal* represents a crucial point in the history of the art of narration, one in which the author tries to psychologically motivate the ritual order of events in the tale. His considerable success in this venture results in an overlay of new meaning upon the old, but without completely submerging the original meaning of the signs. In fact this condition is much more pronounced in Romance texts than in biblical ones, because Romance as a genre constitutes itself as a new interpretation of the story. In this way both the original and the later meaning are inscribed as an integral component of the text. While this may occur in any re-telling of a traditional tale, in the case of Romance it is inscribed as a paradigmatic genre-linked feature. The reader recognizes the story as a Romance specifically because it fulfills this expectation .

Chrétien's process of narratizing his story-telling strategies, of telling the reader how he came to write the story, can be seen to some extent in all his writings. As both a moralist and a storyteller Chrétien set about "improving" and "enlightening" his readership by telling them tales in which the true meaning value of love and chivalry was made known. Thus in the prologue to *Yvain* he proposes to tell of love in Arthur's court, because in that place and in that time the true meaning of love was still understood. This creates the expectation in the reader that by reading the tale he or she will be enlightened and will come to know love for what it truly is. This anticipation of enlightenment is particularly emphasized in the prologue to *Li Contes del Graal,* where expectations of an inner spiritual enlightenment is stressed. The reader is alerted to look for a hidden benefit, a secret knowledge thematized in the tale. It is no wonder that argument about just what that secret knowledge is has preoccupied readers of the grail procession ever since.

The prologue to *Li Contes del Graal,* like the prologues to Chrétien's other works, has a story of its own. Critics have questioned what these dedications "mean" in relation to the work. Many scholars have stated that they believe that court flattery is their sole purpose, but this convention in itself would not limit meaning. Chrétien, more inspired than most romancers, also found new uses for this formula, just as he did for the tales he adapted. In the case of the prologue to *Li Contes del Graal* he is at pains to link the worth of his patron to the worth of the tale. Furthermore, now a self-confident "master" of the art of storytelling, Chrétien presents himself also as worthy to tell the tale. His successes in "rationalizing" and ordering the Celtic material in the earlier Romances may have given him a false sense of confidence in approaching the task. In any case the last lines of the prologue can be read as a challenge to the reader, exhorting him or her to expect the best:

> This man is Count Philip of Flanders who is worth much more
> than Alexander, who has been praised so highly. But I will prove

that the Count is of more worth that he surpasses Alexander, who gathered into himself all the faults and vices of which the Count is free and pure . . .

. . . Let the truth be known, that the gifts which the good Count Philip gives are from charity. No one advises him to do this, but rather his generous heart urges him to do good. Is he not of more worth than Alexander, who was devoid of charity and good works? Yes, without any doubt. Chrétien will have well employed his efforts, as he strives, by the count's command, to put into poetry the best story ever told in a royal court. This is *The Story of the Grail* given to him by the Count. Hear now how he performs it. (lines 13–20, 51–68) (my translation)

The tone of high expectations is carefully orchestrated by linking the best of patrons with the best of storytellers and with the best of stories. The sense of worth is intensified in the French by a fortuitous play on the forms and meanings of the word *conte* itself which ties in the count with the tale and the art of telling the tale and with the title of the tale:

. . . Par le comandement le *conte*
A rimoier le meillor *conte*
Qui soit *contez* A cort roial:
Ce est li *CONTES* DEL GRAAL . . . (emphasis added) (64–67)

The rhyme and repetition has thus intertwined both the meanings and forms of *conte* as story and *conte* as man, thus linking the worth of one with the worth of the other. In the same way the repetition of *contez*, referring to the stories generally told, to *Contes*, as the specific story about to be told, alerts the reader to the task of finding a special meaning. In this way Chrétien places himself in the challenge position, and he now has to deliver on his boast.

The question of meaning and specifically the meaning of written language is even more overtly addressed in an earlier segment of the prologue in a way that also anticipates the nature of the verbal challenge to be set before his hero Perceval. In this segment Chrétien makes use of wordplay to emphasize the question of meaning and language. In his disquisition on the count's virtues Chrétien particularly singles out the importance of charity. Then, in another kind of wordplay he equates the

name of the virtue charity and the name of God by means of a reference
to the gospels and to the letters of St. Paul. Thus his appeal to linguistic
meaning is reinforced by an appeal to the highest authority that language could claim in his culture, the authority of God. This in turn brings
into question the authority of his own discourse, where its meaning is
linked to a belief in an ideal presence in language and, by extension, to
an ideal presence in narrative. The ancient value of Celtic tales is thus re-
interpreted by appeal to the value of the Christian Bible. This finely
crafted interweaving of the value of the pagan story at hand with the
value of the Christian story becomes a disquisition on the problem of
meaning in language and in stories. At the same time Chrétien achieves
the graceful flattery of his patron and of himself that is part of the convention of a prologue:

> The count loves true justice, loyalty, and the Holy Church, and
> he despises uncourtly acts. His charity is greater than is known,
> for he gives without hypocrisy or guile and according to the
> Gospel, that says: Don't let your left hand know the good your
> right hand does." Only the recipient knows this, and God, who
> knows all things secret and things hidden in the heart and breast.
> (25–36) (my translation)

Thus far he has set up a heirarchy of values and grounded it to the
highest institutional and textual authority. But a complication is introduced with the idea of hidden intentions as secrets which only God can
read. It follows from this arrangement that there is also a hidden text in
human actions. He then amplifies this condition by explicating the meaning of the biblical text he has cited:

> Why does the gospel say "Hide your good deeds from the left
> hand"? The left hand, according to the story, signified vainglory
> that comes from false hypocrisy. And the right hand, what does
> it signify? Charity which boasts not of its good works, but rather
> covers them up, so that they are known only to God who is
> named both charity and God. God is charity, and I have seen it
> written in holy scripture, and whoever lives in charity—Saint
> Paul tells us and I have read it—lives in God and God in him.
> (37–50) (my translation)

While this kind of commentary has the ring of a religious sermon, it is also a commentary on language, on names, and on how to read a text. In fact it is as much about the problem of meaning in language as it is about the virtues of Philip. Without breaking with the convention of the prologue, Chrétien has installed a lesson on reading. This gesture, combined with the wordplay on *conte* as story and *conte* as man, introduces two meanings into his prologue. He implies that he, Chrétien, the best of storytellers, is going to tell the best of stories for the best of patrons. From this premise it follows inevitably that the meaning of this tale must also be the best of meanings. What is more, with this strategy he has also prepared the ground for the great adventure of Perceval, the hero who is fated to search for not just the grail but the meaning of the grail. To complicate matters further, he also says that what his right hand writes must be hidden from the left. This would be a fair practice, for he tells us that hiding the good that you do is also a virtue. Concealing the truth must be inevitable, given the complex nature of God's meaning and human intentions, even more so when considering the ontology of language and its mysterious ways of signifying.

The nature of this challenge refers to the problem of re-reading and re-writing. What is at stake for Chrétien is nothing less that the interpretation of his own story. He as writer and Perceval as hero are both confronted with the problem of the meaning of the grail procession, and the story becomes a story about how to interpret signs. We have seen that heroes are heroes in part because of their ability to read signs. As gods or as semi-divine sons of gods they are empowered to know the hidden nature of the challenge put before them. This means they understand the nature of their destiny and accept it as part of their fate. CuChulainn is such a hero. He knows without question what to do, and as a result his human companions come to follow him. This is the surest sign of his divinity. However, we have seen that Peredur in the Welsh tale is not so clearly divine. He has a strong desire to become a knight, but he is clumsy at times and has to learn to achieve his destiny. This is clear at the point in which he cannot repair his broken sword; his full powers have not yet manifested themselves in his personality. Peredur has moved from the divine condition of CuChulainn, who suffers his "riastarthae" to empower him, to a more human condition in which he has to learn how to be a warrior. This shift from an automatic assumption of the heroic incarnation to one in which the hero grows into his heroic state is what is

found in *Li Contes del Graal*. Here the hero, although endowed with special capabilities, must proceed by trial and error. In fact the nature of his
errors will become the focus of the story. We find that he begins as a
clumsy boy and only gradually becomes competent as an ideal knight. It
is at this point that he confronts his greatest challenge, the problem of
reading the signs at the grail banquet. Here the narrator has his own
challenge. The hero, in order to follow the source and in order to be
confronted with a testing challenge, must err. This in turn will allow the
narrator to show him overcoming the error and achieving his full power.
This condition will enable the hero to return to the challenge and to
succeed.

That at least is one scenario. As a Romance it is the one we are led to
suspect. In Chrétien's case the heroic development of Cliges, Erec, and
Yvain all followed that pattern. Nevertheless, other narrative possibilities, ones not previously seen as part of Chrétien's repertoire, do exist.
Perceval could, for instance, fail to resolve the mystery of the grail. The
epithet "accursed" Peredur, found in the Welsh version suggests, such a
possibility. In that case the genre expectation of a positive resolution to
the problem would be modified. Celtic tales with tragic endings, such as
the story of Deirdre, formed part of the source material for Romance. In
the case of Peredur/Perceval there are other signs that such a possibility
is not ruled out. One of these signs is the fact that there is more than one
hero involved. The existence of the parallel Gawain story might imply
that one could fail and one could succeed. Modern editors take different
strategies when dealing with that problem. Some critics suggest that the
story of Gawain, which in the manuscripts is presented as part of the
total story, should be as a scribal arrangement imposed upon two separate stories that Chrétien had been working on at the time of his death.
We cannot be certain that he intended to conflate the two stories into a
single Grail configuration. The truth is that we can never know for certain what resolution he posited for this material.

We know for certain only that a story with two heroes is different from
a story with one hero. This change in narrative procedure would result
in a generic change from what Chrétien had earlier been doing. But as
Frappier has observed, there is no written law that such a change in
Chrétien's work could not occur. The problem reveals a fundamental
problem of genre itself. It must be seen that the problem has to do with
the question of *entrelacement*, the weaving of various narratives into a
larger *conjointure*, to use Chrétien's term. This practice was to be seen as

the fatal defect of Romance in the Renaissance battles concerning neo-Aristotelian aesthetics. One action or two meant the difference between epic and Romance. This distinction remained a crucial issue for Cervantes in the *Quixote*. He essayed one solution in part 1 and another in part 2. Nevertheless the possibility of a different narrative ordering is already inscribed in the grail text as it has come to us.

Three

Don Quixote: The Reluctant Romance

Hamlet: Then came each actor on his ass.
Polonius: The best actors in the world, either for tragedy,
comedy, history, pastoral, pastoral-comical, historical-pastoral,
tragical-historical, tragical-comical-historical-pastoral, scene
indivisible, or *poem unlimited.* (Emphasis added)

Hamlet

The Story of the Name and the Name of the
Story: Quijote/Quijada/Quesada/Quejana/Quijana/
Quijano, etc., or Paradigms of Referentiality

Much has been written about the hidalgo's *nom de guerre* and the prolonged confusion about his true *apellido*. Everyone knows him as Don Quixote, but the question of his original name is a notorious humanistic problem. Quijada, Quesada, Quejana are given as possible surnames in the opening paragraph of the work. The matter is introduced in this way: "They mean that he had the surname of Quijada or Quesada, for in this matter there is some difference among the authors that write about this *case*; although by verisimiliar conjectures it is

111

left understood that he was called Quejana" (emphasis added). One more variant form is inscribed in chapter five when a neighbor calls him Señor Quijana. All these names have in common a slightly ridiculous quality. The first signifies jaw or jawbone, while the second suggests a cheese tort. *Quesadilla, quixada,* and *quixotes* (sic) are all listed in Sebastián de Covarrubias's 1611 *Tesoro de la lengua,* so we know they enjoyed current usages and significations. While viable surnames, they lack, with the dubious exception of Quixote, heroic connotations. But what is even more significant is the fact that the as yet unnamed narrator comments that the precise form of the name is a matter of unimportant conjecture. The latter point has been generally overlooked, while the most authoritative modern critics have tended to see in the failure to give the protagonist's family name a fixed form a type of Ortegan *perspectivismo;* that is, the variant forms exist as linguistic indicators of a fragmentary perception of a referential reality These existential concerns are apparently buttressed by the fact that the phenomenon of shifting forms of names is not limited in Cervantes' writing to the *Quixote;* and, in effect, other examples of variant forms of names can be found in his other writings. Nevertheless, in no other work of Cervantes does this linguistic feature concern such a principal figure, nor are the other examples located in such a complex textual environment. The crucial difference in the *Quixote,* therefore, is this environment which is created by the narrator's commentary concerning the contradictory forms of the hidalgo's name found in the presumed source texts. These variants do not occur as possible errata or authorial lapses of memory. Rather, the narrator specifies from the first that different *autores* give different inscriptions of the name (Riquer, *Aproximación* 76).

The first consideration must be that the opening paragraph is a variant of the traditional Romance feature concerning the recovery of a story either lost in the past (the *Táin*) or imperfectly received from other languages (Geoffrey of Monmouth or Chrétien). In Cervantes' agenda the self-conscious narrator emerges as a Renaissance humanist trying to reform the language in the manner of Garci Rodríguez' *refundición* of the *Amadís.* This means that the first parodic gesture in the *Quixote* is referential to the story telling procedures of Romance and is not just a parody of the Romance hero. It is also a signal that the hero is a hero because he is a *product* of the way the story is told, and that the narrator is likewise part of the overall heroic *aventura* of the text's survival.

Thus, the result of all these inherited narrative gestures establishes the crucial existence of the "other texts" from which the editor claims to be working. One further procedure is that the work at hand brings into being a new linguistic artifact extrapolated from the *differences* found in other texts, which establishes a new language, not just a new story. Among these procedures is the narrator's assumption that the form of the name must be *Quejana*, a word not found in the source text. It is an invention grounded in two previous forms, *Quijada* and *Quesada*. This kind of arbitrary humanistic strategy, in effect, produces a new language fabricated out of unstable antecedents.

On another level the adjective *verosimiles* was a currently functioning critical term, particularly as it applied to theories of fiction. Thus, aesthetic questions, particularly ones that concern the truth of art, are also part of the narrator's story. What we have then is a parody of the editorial practices of the era, practices which included both problems of "correct" words as well as more refined words adjusted to a new Renaissance aesthetic. The immediate referential target of this commentary is the editorial statement with which Garci-Rodríguez de Montalvo prefaces the text of *Amadís de Gaula*:

> Aqui comienca el primero libro del esforcado y virtuoso cauallero Amadís, . . . el qual fue corregido y emendado por el honrrado y virtuoso cauallero Garci-Rodriguez de Montaluo, . . . y corregiole de los antiguos originales que *estauan corruptos* y mal compuestos en antiguo estilo, por falta de los *differentes y malos escriptores.* Quitando muchas palabras superfluas y poniendo *otras de mas polido y elegante estilo* tocantes a la caualleria y actos della. *(Amadís* 1, 243) (my emphasis)

> [Here begins the first book of the brave and virtuous caballero Amadís. . . . which was corrected and emended by the honorable and virtuous caballero Garci-Rodríguez of Montalban. . . . and he corrected it from the ancient originals which *were corrupted* and badly composed in the ancient style, though the fault of the *different and bad scriptors.* Taking out many superfluous words and putting in others of a *more polished and elegant style,* suitable to chivalry and the events that pertain to it.] (My translation)

This editorial attitude toward the faulty language of manuscripts becomes in the *Quixote* the referent for the initial parody. Most important of all, and in contrast to the editorial arrangement in the *Amadís,* this procedure incorporates the activity of the writing process into the story itself, with the consequence that both the editor/writer and the language itself are constituted as fiction. In this way the authority of the text and the authority of the language are self-authenticating gestures. The language of fiction turns out to be the fiction of language. This semantic liberation from exteriority, from anything beyond other language, creates a system of signification capable only of endless self-reflection and infinite regress. At the same time the story of the name, the narrator's self-indulgence in the onomastic formulations of Romance, is set up in such a way that *the life of the text* and *not the life of the protagonist* is the privileged subject of discourse. What follows is that both the story of the name and the story of the hidalgo emerge as prolonged, unending, and unendable, self-reflective meditations on the capabilities of language and on its power or failure to generate meaning.

At a narrative level this means that the narrator's editorial presence comes into being as the first parody, referential to Romance going back to both Chrétien and the *Táin,* while the subsequent parody of the chivalric hero forms the story of the hidalgo. Thus, the story of Don Quixote is entered into the text as a first interpolation, the first *entrelacement* gesture, while the narrator's story becomes the framing tale. With this device Cervantes has constituted the commentary of the narrator/editor as a parody, not of the hidalgo's story, but of the *rhetoric and language* of Romance. The result of this arrangement is the creation of a language of absence rather than a language of presence as the primary medium of narrativity.

In effect, the narrator seems to claim that all this worry about the name is not relevant to the meaning of his writing project, and he asserts that various forms of words exist but that he will proceed without bothering to verify which is the correct one. This is a subversive procedure with which to open a book since it challenges the idea of language as a system of signs representing an external reality. The impact of this arrangement is subsequently reinforced by the narrators of interpolated stories, in particular Pedro, the narrator of the tale of Grisostomo and Marcela (pt. 1, ch. 11), who also has trouble with the forms of words; by Sancho in his story of Lope Ruiz and Torralba (pt. 1, ch. 20); and, in an even more stylish way, by Dorotea with her feigned confusions about Don Quixote's name in her story of the princess Micomicona (pt. 1, ch. 30). In all these instances both names and nouns take on erratic forms, usually for comic purposes, but, like the unnamed narrator of the first paragraph, all three narrators claim that the verbal errancies are irrelevant to the meaning of their stories.

A significantly parallel manner of operation is found in the narrator's treatment of narrative sequences. In chapter two he problematizes the order in which certain episodes are to be inserted in the text. This question undermines even such key adventures as the windmill scene, since the narrator claims that his source texts disagree about where it comes in the story. He is uncertain therefore which comes first, the windmill adventure or the hero's encounter at Puerto Lápice. The latter name, of a still existent Manchegan village, has the meaning of the "pencil gate," which appropriately suggests both mark and beginning. But whatever significations can be teased out of these names, they remain grounded in the procedures of the linguistic and narrative strategies of Romance.

The important result of all this waffling establishes the ontology of the narrator's language as referential to other writing and, even more importantly, to his own writing agenda and to his own aesthetic concerns rather than to events in an external reality. He is saying in effect that he will name his characters and report their doings in the form and manner most suited to his storytelling procedures and, presumably, to his own search for meaning. This claim privileges the writing as product over what is being written about so that the language of narrativity emerges as an autonomous entity empowered to range freely without serious referential constraints.

This reflecting and self-reflecting condition of the language removes the problem of narrative sequencing from the matter of the flow of events in the hidalgo's life to the question of the narrator's methods of telling a story. The narrator in this way establishes the operations of language as the subject of the story. The partially hidden key to this arrangement can be found in his use of the word *caso* in the sentence already quoted in English: "alguna diferencia en los autores que deste *caso* escriben" [some difference in the authors that write of this case]. What he suggests with the multiple forms of the name is the idea of a case as a linguistic phenomenon. From this he also takes the matter of case inflection as a structuring device for his story. A second reference to the idea of case occurs in chapter two when the narrator, as noted, is discussing the narrative order in which the events should be sequenced: "Autores hay que dicen que la primera *aventura* que le avino fue la del Puerto Lápice: otros dicen que la de los molinos de viento; pero lo que yo he podido averiguar en este *caso,* y lo que he hallado escrito en los anales de la Mancha . . ." [There are authors that say that the first adventure that happened to him was the one of Puerto Lápice; others say that it was the one of the windmills; but what I have been able to find out in this case, and what I have found written in the annals of La Mancha . . .] (my translation). In both instances the word *caso* functions as the structuring principle the narrator invokes for his own writing agenda. Covarrubias's *Tesoro de la lengua* assigns three possible meanings to the word. First he lists it as a term for *fortuna,* as in *acaso;* second he indicates its legal usage as an event, "sucesso que aya acontecido" [an event that happened]; and last he points out its grammatical signification: "Casos, cerca de los gramáticos, son aquellos por los quales *se varia la terminación del nombre y el modo de sinificar"* [cases, according to the grammarians, are those (things) by which are *varied/changed the ending of the word and the mode of signifying*] (my translation, emphasis added). In the *Quixote* all these meanings to some extent come into play, but for the narrator, as he attempts to set parameters for the scope of his own problematic language and its possible inflectional manifestations, the idea of grammatical case does come to the fore. As noted, it is the differences in the forms of the name, and not the external referentiality concerning the hidalgo's possible existence, that is the focus of the narrator's discourse.

The problem of the form of the name installs a language in which the linguistic vector of referentiality is aimed at a *set* of names which constitute a grammatical *caso.* This phenomenon foregrounds the idea of language as language, and coming as it does as the first parodic gesture of the work, it conditions the ontology of the language in the text at hand. In this way the language used by the narrator presents itself as a linguistic system grounded in differences in other texts, and the *caso* of the hero's name posits a condition in which the form of the signifier is the result of differences of the form in the source texts and is therefore unstable. Thus, the meaning, the *querer decir* of the narrator's language, is conditioned by a set of variants, and the hidalgo's name is posited as having an inflectional paradigm of its own, one in which its variant endings or inner components shift about, but without, at this stage, the reader being able to interpret the significance of the changes. The tension in this condition is re-enforced by the everyday inflectional changes of the Spanish language in which changes in grammatical meaning are achieved by modifying the form of a word. Even though the five-case inflectional forms of its Latin origin have been lost, Spanish nouns retain masculine and feminine forms as well as terminal variations to distinguish singular and plural. Furthermore in the matter of verbs Spanish still operates with a wide variety of both stem and ending changes to identify tense and subject. The relevance of verbal inflections is important in this context because of the etymology of the word *caso*. Heidegger in his *Introduction to Metaphysics* devotes a chapter to the grammar and etymology of the Greek word for being (54ff.). There he points out that the original meaning of Greek *ptosis* (Latin *casus*) referred to both noun cases and verbal conjugations, and that the term itself comes from a root meaning "to incline" or "to fall away," hence the term *verbal declension*. Heidegger relates the term *ptosis»casus* to a concept of being as a coming-to-stand or a self-presentation. In this sense *caso* is linguistically appropriate in the context of the first paragraph, in that it defines language as a coming-to-stand within the parameters of a grammatical event. *Caso* functions as an attempt to set limits to the range of forms and meanings in language.

In precisely this way the idea of both verb conjugations and case inflections inhabits Cervantes' first paragraph, so that the variant forms of the name set up paradigmatic and syntagmatic axes of mutation in which meaning as well as form *might* be modified. The various forms of the name contain the possibility of changes in meanings such as singular/plural or masculine/feminine: quixotes/quixote and quejana/quejano. Later inscriptions of the name as well as later narratival developments (such as the niece's name in the last chapter of pt. 2) clearly confirm the existence of these lateral and vertical potentials already inscribed in the first paragraph. In fact the four inscriptions of the name already given suggest the fifth form found in the last chapter, which in effect completes the five-case paradigm:

Quijada/Quesada/Quejana/Quijana/Quijano.

We can observe, along with the multiple linguistic mutations of the protagonist's name, other kinds of inflectional possibilities in the operations of the narrative. We note first that two primary characters, the narrator and the hidalgo, engage the activity of the paragraph. What is most remarkable about them is the contrasting conditions of their identities. First there is what can be called the "generic status" of the hidalgo. The information that seeks to establish his identity is highly impersonal in that it tells us more about his social status as a typical "hidalgo aldeano" (village squire) than it does about him as an individual. The most specific information, moreover, is a curious recitation of his weekly eating and vestural habits, with particular emphasis on the differences between the days of "entresemana" (mid-week) and Fridays, Saturdays, and Sundays. This conjugation of his habitual behavior establishes the operation of time as a routine pattern of variation that confirms his belonging to a particular socioeconomic class. That is, the variations of the pattern mark the passage of time as a set of paradigm variants whose meaning resides not in the individual forms themselves (duelos y quebrantos los sábados) but in the fact that they operate as changing signifiers indicating a recognizable overall pattern. As with the variations of the name forms, it is the existence of the pattern of change as change that functions as signifier rather than the individual changes themselves. In this sense it is *the idea* of conjugation and declension in relation to the days of the week that sets time into motion. This factor coincides with the utilization of two verbal tense forms, the present and the imperfect, that report repeated, habitual action. Thus, what the reader learns about the hidalgo is that there are patterns of change both in the form of his name and in the modes of his behavior, but the signification of these changes remains on the level of a generic social identity rather than on an individualized level. We know about his potential for change before we learn about him as a person. This pre-figures his change into a madman, but it leaves his pre-change, pre-mad identity in a state of indeterminacy. Before we know him as a person we are aware of his curious potential for modification and change, and this characteristic is both a product and a condition of the language in which he is described. This arrangement, however, has consequences in that the volatility of the protagonist's personality begins to overshadow the ontology of the narrative language and to disguise the true power of the text.

In contrast to the generic description of the multi-named hidalgo's activities, the un-named narrator's business is quite individualized and even bizarrely specific. In addition to his linguistic funny business, it should be noted that of the eight sentences in the paragraph, the last two are devoted entirely to the problems of the narrator, and that both these sentences are divided by semicolons which effectively make them four sentences. Even more important, in these last sentences the ironic tone of the narrator effectively subverts the value of the rather precarious information already presented. That is, the seemingly unnecessary recital of the hidalgo's dietary and vesturaly habits is rendered even more problematic. We may know what the man usually ate and wore, but the value of that curiously detailed knowledge is called into question. This state of affairs privileges the activity of the narrator, since his quirky irony makes his behavior more individualizing than that of the hidalgo. The reader's curiosity is teased much more by the arbitrary and unpredictable procedures of the narrator's writing practices than by the routinized habits of the hidalgo.

There is one other crucial area in which the narrator's activities upstage his hero's. The second paragraph begins with the narrator recounting the reading habits of the hidalgo and his great affection for reading *libros de caballería*. It is in this context that the first preterit verb is used, one that begins the hidalgo's story (as opposed to the narrator's) and radically individualizes him: *olvidó*. Frye notes that some form of amnesia is characteristic of the change of consciousness in the hero (102). Thus the hidalgo forgets his own life and begins to buy all the books he can. In this way his madness sets the narrative parameters to the inflections and declensions of his *caso*, since the limits of the hidalgo's story are to be marked by the duration of this condition. A parallel is set up between the pattern of the *caso* and the patterns of mutation in the hero's life. As a narrative subject his vitality does not extend beyond these limits. So it is important to recognize that this is a madness originating in his interpretation of reading, in his various attempts to disentangle the meaning of texts. However, the problem of hermeneutics, of reading and interpretation of texts, has already been presented in the first paragraph, where it is designated as the primary domain of the narrator. Thus the text at hand is constituted as a product of reading, and the identifying activity of the narrator is that of a reader of texts. In this way, he and not the hidalgo is the first reader, and he asserts that the problematics of interpretation of language are his self-consciously assumed responsibility. So we see that hermenuetics is the challenge of both the narrator and the hidalgo, and the disposition of the story is to be a reading > interpretation > writing project on the part of the narrator as he reflects on the reading > interpretation > acting of the hidalgo. These two systems of reading constitute the critical problematics of the entire work.

We have seen that the narrator's project forms a constellation of questions and answers about writing that initiates the story of the narrator's progress. This procedure in turn distances the new text from the genres and the modes of writing that are being subsumed into his writing project, so that the emergent text is one born of the despoiling of other forms of writing, including *novelas*, ballads, tales, chronicles, songs, fragments of oral *formulae*, and other scraps of language. These corrosive actions not only establish the ontology of the text at hand but work to undermine the authority of the other literary forms, in particular their vulnerable concerns about the truth of history and the truth of fiction (see Williamson).

These contradicting aspirations about truth and fiction had long inhabited the Renaissance preoccupation with the function of both visual and linguistic art, and in part it was this type of anxiety that brought about the mannerist disruption of High Renaissance style. As an example of this disturbance, Cervantes in the opening paragraphs of the *Quixote* strategically positions his narrator as an examiner of an impressive arsenal of inherited rhetorical and narratival resources, and like his contemporaries in the visual arts El Greco, Tintoretto, and Parmigianino, he initiates a process of testing, discarding, and transforming the use of inherited aesthetic resources. (See Carilla; Hauser; Freedberg 52ff.). This procedure not only results in a severe disruption of the ontology of inherited literary language but establishes a new kind of language resilient enough for the conflictive tasks Cervantes' writing project required of it. Thus, in the first paragraphs of the *Quixote* Cervantes achieves a language that, as we have seen, not only undermines the external referentiality of language systems but, in addition, questions the rhetoricity of writing. With this arrangement, he creates a text in which the language is positioned to examine its own reflective possibilities. It is in this sense he moves toward a Mannerist fiction that not only tells the story of writing about writing but narratizes the problem of its own capacity to represent an external reality. In this way the writing comes to speculate on its own reflecting activity, and the narrator becomes the fabricator of a new language and a new agenda for narrative fiction, one that creates for the first time the possibility of a genre/non-genre we have, with understandable unease, come to call the novel/novela/roman/romanzo.

The etymons of these two terms set forth the ideas of "newness" and "language" and spell out the essential ingredient of the genre: *new language*. In this literary kind it is the ontology of the language and the operations of its self-reflective rhetoric rather than the formalist patterns of the narrative structure that inform the movement of the text. Recognition of this situation provides an answer to the hoary question of the definition of the novel as a genre. It is because of the condition of the language that no description of the formal components of the narrative is able to describe the novel. The matter of chapters, opening *formulae*, closure procedures, length, or even the condition of subject matter or treatment of subject matter as comedic or tragic, realistic, or fantastic cannot provide an adequate definition of the novel. Its procedures and contents are highly volatile, and no group of narrative or contentual features can define the essence of its operation. Rather, the initial factor of this new writing agenda, the one Cervantes sets forth here, is the matter of the rhetorical and referential procedures of its language.

As a genre, the novel subsists on the raw material of literary rhetoric and on its own concern with its own linguistic procedures. As a result the question of its vision of reality or illusion is undermined in the first paragraphs of the *Quixote*. This explains why the traditional thematic concerns of its contents, partially because of the nature of the *figura* of Don Quixote as a protagonist, have hidden the ontology of its language and distracted critical attention away from the more crucial problem of the self-reflective condition of a language that works to de-stabilize literature and rhetoric. In the *Quixote* this condition is achieved as the result of the invention of the narrator's story of the inflectional problematics of the hero's name. The fabrication of the *caso* as a narrative agenda renders the questions of content and narrative format obsolescent. Cervantes' fiction, like mannerist painting, holds up the mirror, not to nature, but to art and to the ability of art to reflect nature.

It is one of the great ironies of literary history that this miraculous invention of a "new language"/new genre was to be occulted by the figure of the new hero, Don Quixote, but it must be understood that this development was made possible by the fact that as a hero he incarnates the self-reflective condition of this same language. The invention of the story of his name allowed him to become the *figura* of the new hero, the new protagonist emerging from the disintegration of Medieval Romance. He is a recombinant figure made up, not only of the mysterious source texts cited in the first paragraph, but of the debris and detritus of a thousand literary ancestors. This achievement is explainable only by the ontology of the hero's text. It is the recombinant condition of the language, as we have seen in the fabrications of his name, that constitutes *Don Quixote* as a new *literary* myth, as opposed to a *folkloric* myth. The language of the text sets him up as a figure capable of escaping from that same text into the locus of modern imagination. The result, to a great extent, was that this same imagination became structured by the peculiar procedures of the new language of fiction, and this in turn explains why the resulting genre/non-genre became the paradigmatic instrument of post-Renaissance and in particular post-Romantic writing.

The process by which this is achieved begins in the very first words in the book. The text opens with what is certainly the most famous erasure in all literature, the suppression of the name of the hero's village, followed almost immediately by the repeated erasures of the hero's name. The first erasure (the name of the village) already establishes the existence of another text, one deliberately hidden by the narrator. In addition, since the language ("En un lugar de la Mancha" [In a place/village of La Mancha] is an inherited narrative gesture, the introduction of the place establishes the village as a rhetorical haunting, rather than as a specific geographic location. This feature has been studied extensively by various scholars (see Selig, "Cervantes" for discussion and bibliography). The "place" thus belongs to the horizon of the language of narrativity rather than to the horizon of la Mancha. And then the narrator confirms this ontology by utilizing a second traditional rhetorical phrase, "de cuyo nombre no quiero acordarme" [whose name I don't wish to recall]. This in turn establishes the existence of the narrator and at the same time the question of his volition in the storytelling procedures. By means of these inherited phrases the fabulist presents himself as an individual faced with certain ongoing choices in narrative strategies. In this way he leads into the all-important story of how he will tell the story and, at the same time, positions the initial vector of the language so that it is aimed at both "other" writing and self-consciously at its own writing project. Both of these strategies function as a means to introduce the activity of the hidalgo. This posits his ontology on the rhetoricity of the language at hand, establishing the problematics of his identity as a product of the activity of the writing rather than as the subject of the narration. The contrast to the opening of the *Amadís*, which merely states when and where the king lived, points up the radically distinct fictional situation fabricated by Cervantes. The matter is further complicated by the fact that the narrating "yo" (I) is introduced as part of this confabulating process. He operates, Druidlike, from a secret agenda, from a hidden store of privileged texts, which he will display to the reader in an order of his own willful choosing. In this way both the narrator and the hidalgo come into "being" as specific rhetorical operations of the story of the writing procedures, rather than as individuals situated in a mundane exteriority.

Unlike the more formally circumscribed Renaissance genres, most specifically the epic, the *caso* will be constituted not only by *what* the narrator deems to be relevant, but also by *how* he chooses to write about it. This factor effectively eradicates any exterior or pre-existent narrative format. What results instead is a casebook [caso/libro] into which the narrator, capriciously it would seem, may or may not inset/insert other material, including other stories, other heroes, other narrators, other kinds of writing, including critical commentary on his own writing. The complexity of this endeavor increases radically the complexity of the text, since each of these genre insertions also carries with it the linguistic possibilities of its own ontology. In the case of the *Quixote* this vast network of hauntings will come to include almost the entire repertoire of European narrative forms: pastoral, chivalric, epistolary, picaresque, Moorish, Byzantine, and "novella" fictions. Nor is this repertoire of generic horizons limited to narrative, since potentially anything could be incorporated: theater, poetry, song, ballads, *refranes*, *sententiae*, folktales, learned discourses like the *tratado*, but also commentary on dance, painting, drawing, as well as marginalia glosses, occult signs, and so forth. Not quite everything is, but the spectrum of rhetorical forms and *formulae* included in the work is functionally comprehensive. The work does come to incorporate, as the canon of Toledo is to comment in his dialogue with the priest and Don Quixote (pt. 1, ch. 47), everything the author *wishes*. This leaves the author free not only to include any rhetorical strategy or material he deems relevant to the *caso* but to indicate as well the existence of other material he has decided to exclude.

Nevertheless, the story of the protagonist's madness is still a very broad category. It could have included anything, given the nature of his infirmity, concerning the life of "nuestro hidalgo," but the narrator is going to take only a very selective advantage of this rubric. What it most certainly does not include is a full scale *vida* of the hidalgo, paralleling the structure of the *Amadís* or utilizing the *caso/vida* focus of the *Lazarillo*. These genres begin with the birth and ancestry of the protagonist and then proceed to relate the progress of his life. In contrast the focus here, as far as the life of the hidalgo is concerned, is the case/story of his madness. The narrative opens with the protagonist's decline into madness and closes with his recovery. There is no interest in the life of the person who becomes Don Quixote but only in the case of his madness and the telling of the tale of the case. The hero's death, which follows almost immediately upon his return to sanity, is relevant only because it functions to assist Cide Hamete's claim to conclude the story of the *caso* and its potential inflectional permutations. This feature becomes genre linked and serves to define the narrator's relation to his *materia*. Even so,

Cide Hamete's claim is precarious as well as erroneous, perhaps deliberately so, in the matter of the number of "salidas" (sallies) performed by the protagonist. Thus, there is no way that Cide Hamete can, so to speak, close the case of the hidalgo's madness; and this is to be an important genre-linked feature of the work, one that will function to enrich as well as complicate its hermeneutic horizons. This same condition will define the ontology of the protagonist. He too is an individual of vast and complicated horizons, and because of this condition he cannot close the hermeneutic circle that would complete his desired identity as a chivalric hero. He seeks to create and complete the story of a perfect knight by living a life marked by the prerequisite genre features of such a hero. But, unlike Amadís, his ontology is self-consciously based on a rhetorical case, which, given the infinite possibilities of inflectional and generic inclusions, cannot stylistically totalize, cannot possibly close its multiple hermeneutic circles (Dudley, "Ring" 2) In the same way Cide Hamete can only conclude his task with a warning to potential writers seeking to extend the adventures of the protagonist. Nevertheless, in spite of all Cide Hamete's protestations, the *caso* remains open, both on the contentual and stylistic levels, and this open-ended linguistic and generic agenda creates the ontology of both the hero and his story. This doubling of the status of the text and the identity of the protagonist can best be seen in Cide Hamete's concluding re-marks on the problem of the hidalgo's name.

The conclusion of the novel, the death of Don Quixote and the final commentary by Cide Hamete and the second narrator, have often been seen as insufficient in some sense. It has been suggested that Cervantes' became tired of his work and felt he needed to devote his remaining time and energy to conclude the *Persiles*. The truth of such a statement tells us more about the problem of reading *Don Quixote* than it does about Cervantes, even if we could confirm the biographical information. The ending of a work, as Kermode has observed, often has a hermeneutic function, telling us how to interpret what we have read. It is a type of metonymy, a miniature *reprise* of the work itself. Nowhere is this more relevant than in the *Quixote*, where the text reverts back to the opening agenda and its story of telling the story.

We have noted that there is an underlying competition between the role of the text and the role of the protagonist. In a radical sense the text itself seeks to be the hero of the work: it is the subject of the narrator's story. This situation becomes unbalanced as the story of the hidalgo begins to overshadow the story of writing, but the latter retains an autonomous and to some extent a directive role throughout the work as the narrator or second narrator comment from time to time on the problems of writing. What occurs in the concluding chapter must be seen as the inevitable engagement of both stories, the interlocking of the life of the hero and the life of the text. In a disturbing sense, the death of the writing has a fatal finality lacking in the death of the protagonist. The text does die but Don Quixote escapes such a fate. This arrangement has a sense of inevitability about it more powerful than any "fated" adventure of Don Quixote because to a great extent this encounter is already "written," already plotted in the functions of the grammatical *caso* that constitutes the hero's name. It plays out, so to speak, like a linguistic paradigm, and it reviews for us the inflections of the grammatical functions already explored. It does not, of course, exhaust the *caso*, since the possibility of other paradigms, still unsounded, haunt the landscape. For the narrator these hauntings assume the shape of possible continuations by other authors.

The hidden drama of this *mise en scène* can still be perceived through a re-reading of the problematics of the *caso* as they are narratized in the concluding pages. Here for the first time the two stories intertwine like the sudden meshing of two giant but unsuspected epicycloidal movements. One recalls the endlessly ingenious clocks of the era that synchronized calendric time with the astrological categories of planetary movements. Two disparate methods of counting/telling—"contar cuentos/contar números" [tell stories/tell numbers]—have abruptly coincided with an almost imperceptible shudder. The reader all at once becomes aware of unsuspected motion.

It is not until the hidalgo calls himself Alonso Quijano el Bueno on his deathbed and that this form of his name is verified by the Priest that the matter seems settled. But even this leaves us with question of what is the purpose of the apparently gratuitous contradictory evidence about his name. What is most remarkable of all is that this confusion occurs about the protagonist who became one of the most famous personages in all literature, but this only confirms the fact that the principal question to be asked should be: *Why* does this occur and what is the purpose of the persistent indeterminacy about the form of his name?

In the first instances in which the narrator refers to the problem of the hidalgo's name it is apparent, as noted, that he is parodying the humanistic affectations of Renaissance scholars. This confirms that Cervantes' writing is a stylistic gesture, a parodic strategy, a rhetorical joke. What is at stake is the condition of other kinds of language. He is writing with units of rhetoric, not with individual signs. The narrator is stating that his writing is a type of linguistic play, a game, and not an account of events that he claims have happened (Gadamer 91). The name of the hidalgo has become an instrument, a means toward creating a language of fiction not merely a matter of creating an identity for the hidalgo. We see that even though his family is known in the village, by his neighbors, by Sancho's wife, and so on, the narrator never, in all the thousand pages of text, specifies the exact form of the name. This is a deliberate omission, an erasure, as was that of the name of the village.

The existence of this non-information is further remarked by Cide Hamete at the conclusion of the work. There, even after the priest has specifically referred to the hidalgo as Alonso Quijano, Cide Hamete still refers to him as Don Quixote. In fact even the Priest's comments are noticeably evasive: "Acabose la confesión, y salio el cura, diciendo:—Verdaderamente se muere, y verdaderamente está cuerdo Alonso Quijano el Bueno . . ." [The confession (was) finished, and the priest came out, saying: Truly he is dying, and truly Alonso Quijano the Good is sane]. The statement has a sacramental ring to it. Alonso Quijano el Bueno is confirmed as his new name in his new condition of sanity and grace. There is no affirmation that Quijano was his name before the period of his insanity. He is reported to have acquired that name by virtue of his actions and it is confirmed as the form of his name by the priest now that Don Quixote is sane and in a renewed state of grace. The sacrament has erased past sins, past incarnations, past names. He is now born again as Alonso Quijano el Bueno. Both the name and the meaning of the name are new. But the possibility of this new form/new inflection already existed in the previous forms of his name. The work began with the narrator presenting the multiple forms of the hero's name, and it concludes with the priest sacramentally confirming not his name but the fact that there are endless forms of the name. The hero is an infinite paradigm, an infinite flux of form and meaning.

In the same way Cide Hamete is equally evasive in his editorial commentary. He states that—in reaction to the priest's words that Don Quixote is dying—Sancho, the housekeeper, and the niece begin to cry. Cide Hamete adds: "porque verdaderamente, *como alguna vez se ha dicho*, en tanto que Don Quijote fue Alonso Quijano el Bueno, a secas, y en tanto que fue don Quijote de la Mancha, fue siempre de apacible condición" [because truly, *as has been said at some time*, as long as he was simply Alonso Quijano the Good, and as long as he was Don Quixote de la

Mancha, he was always of a peaceful disposition/condition] (emphasis added). This unique reference by Cide Hamete to the surname of Quijano is stated in such a way that both names—Quijano/Quijote—remain inscribed and only in part equivalent to one another. It does not affirm that either is his "true" name, merely that they both are equally valid or equally non-valid, like a *nombre de guerra* and a *nombre de paz*, and both names were acquired by his deeds, and authorized by other people and by other texts ("como alguna vez se ha dicho") [as sometimes has been said], so that Cide Hamete does not claim to have originated this commentary either.

In this way the non-naming of the hidalgo by the narrator confirms the erasure of his proper name, and the question becomes one of examining the condition of writing itself and in particular the mysteries of naming. What this means is that both the text and the hero are inflectional linguistic units incapable of totalization. Don Quixote will live beyond the confines of the text, beyond Cide Hamete's attempts to achieve a "caso complido" as in Montalvo's *Amadís*. Don Quixote exists beyond that text because that was the way he was constituted. His fictional entity is one that comes into being as a *figura* that pre-existed in certain pre-texts, whose identity is as fictional as he is. Thus the hero's many texts can never be definitive nor complete. They truly constitute the generic possibility of Polonius's "poem unlimited." In this same way Don Quixote can never be complete. He is truly the Hero Unlimited. Cide Hamete is left fighting the fictions he has evoked. His battle is as hopeless and chimerical as any his protagonist undertook. The power of the chivalric challenge thus comes to rest on Cide Hamete, entrapped in his own engagement with the phantoms of the *libros de caballería*.

This fundamental condition of the text has inevitably been overlooked because the protagonist, by means of the operation of the language, acquires an unfinished ontology. It only appears that he is not born a hero when in fact he is endowed from the beginning with the ontology of a linguistic figure, an incomplete figure that can inhabit the empty spaces left in his text and the empty spaces in the text of the reader's imagination. His textual contemporaries Don Juan and Hamlet were born prior to the works of Shakespeare and Tirso (Feal). Their mythic condition was not conferred by the authors, who to some extent tried to fix or stabilize their heroes' identities by means of their own texts. The reverse is true of Don Quixote since the numinousness of his identity was the product of the inflectional potentials of the kind of textuality created by Cervantes.

Don Quixote is a linguistic *figura*, a configuration inhabiting the hidden capacities of language itself, and is therefore capable of endless incarnations, whether as an operation of a rhetorical trope or as the story of a narrative or even as a hermeneutic horizon attempting to read itself. In all these capacities he haunts modern fiction. Cide Hamete's uneasy claims about ownership are all in vain. He cannot even accurately claim his own writings, that is, his story of the telling of the name. However, whatever validity this part of the claim may have does not mean that Don Quixote will not escape from the tomb(s) and text(s) that Cide Hamete has created for him. Ironically, the tremendous signifying power of this genre based on an incomplete linguistic *caso* accounts for the fact that the fame of Cervantes' hero, the hieratic superscription of that text, has overshadowed that of Cervantes himself.

The power of the hero, hidden in the mutations of his *caso*, accounts for the curious critical failure to recognize Cervantes' impressive fabrication of a true fictional language. Instead attention has focused on the mythic dimensions of the protagonist. "Don Quixote lives!" has been the immortal graffito. "The novel lives!" has been the erasure.

The God of Thieves and Tricky Texts: The Inn of the Pig

> What caused the two pig-keepers to quarrel?
> It is soon told . . .
>
> The Táin

In the Welsh Medieval tale *Culhwch and Olwen*, the earliest Arthurian story, much of the action focuses on a prolonged hunt for a marvelous boar. This mythological hunt, undertaken by Arthur himself, rages through Ireland, Wales, Devon, and Cornwall, where at the end the indomitable creature vanishes into the sea. In this ur-romance, Arthur as a king is a great deal more active and competent than he appears to be in later literature, and he makes an astute comment about the nature of this extraordinary animal to the effect that prior to his porcine incarnation he had been a king, but because of his sins God had turned him into a boar. The comment about sin and God sounds like a Christian re-writing of a pagan shapeshifting, a phenomenon here related to a god/hero with an alternate porcine incarnation. The pig, along with the deer, was the pre-eminent Otherworld animal. Marija Gimbutas and others have shown that this attitude to be of very ancient origin.

The marvel-full condition of this pig is attested to by his extraordinary powers, which include his leading an army of piglets, one of whom can talk. Celticists point out also that the name *Culhwch* means "pig-run," a name given to the hero because as an infant he had been found next to a pig run by a swineherd. The episode suggests that his birth story is an onomastic tale, that is, an episode interpolated into the text by a later narrator in order to account for the hero's "funny" name. This kind of reading interprets the pig run as an episode that at one level of discourse *explains* the etymon of the hero's name but at another level *disguises* an earlier form of the story in which the hero is in fact sired by a swine god. This kind of explain/disguise episode can be found in a great many Romance texts where items have lost their originary meaning and need explaining. The explanations that the narrator gives of how Don Quixote and Rocinante get their names are a variant of this feature. As we have seen these explanatory gestures create other meanings of their own which add to the complexity of the text.

In Celtic mythology, however, the swine divinity, called Moch in Welsh, had great prestige and in fact was identified with Mercury by the Romans. In this Hermes/Mercury capacity we note a curious connection to the matter of interpretation, to a hidden hermeneutic capability associated with pigs. We see remnants of this attitude in the story of the three little pigs and the apple trees. Apples, as in the apples of Avalon and in the Bible, were also associated with wisdom, knowing, and hermeneutic capabilities. Other segments of the Culhwch tale also retain remnants of earlier versions of the story in which a variety of lost attitudes toward pigs still survive. How medieval Welsh readers were able to "read" such eroded mythological content is another question, but Arthur's comment indicates that he, as a special hero, appears to possess strange hermeneutic powers that give him access to the earlier condition of the text. This knowledge does not make him seem idiotic or funny at this stage in the development of Romance as a genre, but this capability does cause him to appear incompetent in later tales, as in the Lancelot and Guinevere story where he lets a strange challenger bargain away the possession of the queen. In that case, whether in Chrétien or Malory, Arthur appears inept, when at the level of myth his erratic behavior disguises a lost meaning in which the queen is possessed for part of the year by an alien deity or magician. Thus a modern psychological (mis-)reading of the king's mysterious epistemological powers imposes itself on much older narrative content.

Taking this process of gradual loss of meaning one stage further we have seen Chrétien's Perceval appear to be an idiot boy when he asks an ordinary knight if he is God. What has happened in both cases is that the hero is "reading" apparently "normal events" with their earlier mythological content still intact. To the modern reader of the tale the hero takes on an appearance of being insane in a "funny" way—in both senses of that term. This condition contains the possibility of the comico-realistic readings found in the *Quixote*. In his introductory commentary to the Culhwch tale the Celticist Patrick Ford traces the signification of the pig content back to earlier Irish myths in which heroes are often identified with horses, pigs, stags, or even fish, zoomorphic signs which indicate their divine ancestry (30, 119–21). The simultaneous birth of the hero and a colt as in the case of CuChulainn is a common feature which Don Quixote and Rocinante replicate in a realistic manner. This layering of different formulations of the narrative dating from successive time frames produces the double or triple or even multiple hermeneutic fixes on the text. At one stage an episode may have onomastic function that disguises earlier (suppressed) information, while at a later time the same episode seems to indicate a psychological quirk in the hero's temperament. Thus when various of these episodes are strung together by later storytellers the result leads to serious hermeneutic instability, since each episode contains material that half reveals, half disguises earlier versions. In this way the end product result becomes a "layered text" in which different horizons of meaning compete for interpretation.

In time the semi-decayed, semi-disguised mythic content itself becomes a type of literary intertextuality in which the partially forgotten meanings still operate within the text, and the shifting referential vectors provide the reader with a sense of vertigo. In fact this conflict of hermeneutic horizons creates the "unreadableness" that becomes a notable genre feature of Romance and contributes to the mixture of mystery and pleasure purveyed to the reader. It is just this kind of pleasure that Don Quixote invokes in his discussion with the canon of Toledo as the basis for his valorization of the *libros de caballería* (pt. 1, chs. 47ff.). The *libros* were a decayed form of Romance, and the authors knew nothing about the mythological and legendary sources of the genre, yet in their stylistic imitations of the archaic rhetoric something of this disguised potency to enchant the reader was still present. Cervantes himself would have absorbed, on an even more powerful level, this textual condition in his readings of ballad, chronicles, *Amadís*, and so forth, so that his own writings, in a new and self-conscious way, reproduced this same textuality.

Cide Hamete, that unreliable reader of Romance, consistently maintains that his hero confuses inns with castles. However, if a reader deprivileges Cide Hamete's assertion and instead "reads" Cide Hamete as lacking the capacity to definitively interpret the text, then his claim that the inns are merely inns loses authority. In fact, a genre reading based on extensive familiarity with chivalric Romances alerts readers to the possibility that narrators do not understand the stories they relate and that the hero's hostels can function as displaced mythological loci that do in fact have an Otherworld ontology. This in turn accounts for the claims by Don Quixote that Cide Hamete deliberately misreads the source texts in order to rob the hidalgo of heroic stature. In a similar way this kind of hermeneutic accounts for modern, if not postmodern, comments by such knowledgeable readers as Thomas Mann who see a basic contradiction between the narrator's insistent criticism of Romance and what is really happening in the story. Likewise, the comparison of journeys to inns or to the palace of the Sabia Felicia in the *Diana* and to the Emerald City in *The Wizard of Oz*, as noted by Avalle Arce (71), is a recognition of the operations of disguise and displacement of folk tales and medieval stories of wandering heroes arriving at a castle which does contain a world of marvels. This genre feature survives in modern fiction and films where the heroine or hero travels to a special place where strange things can happen: *The Fall of the House of Usher, Los Pazos de Ulloa, The Turn of the Screw, Los intereses creados* (where the scene is again an inn), *La casa de Bernada Alba, La casa de los suspiros*, and so forth. Popular "romances" found in drug stores endlessly repeat the paradigm of a lone woman going to a large house in the West country, the Outback, or another remote locale. It is certainly expected that readers of the *Quixote* in the seventeenth century would have been well aware of narrative patterns in which houses and castles took on various kinds of transformations and disguises, and that the inns, like the grail castle itself, could be locations existing under an enchanted disguise.

It is in this sense that Don Quixote's readings of what the inns signify do contain a validity, one that the narrator takes special pains to deny. What is radical about the *Quixote* in this respect is that the struggle between the hero's reading and the narrator's reading, not in itself new, becomes the founding fiction of the story. In point of fact, the diverse readings of the narrator and the hero constitute the plot itself. Such an arrangement places the reader inside the field of hermeneutic contention so that he or she is free to read/interpret/misinterpret the language and the episodes according to the multiple hermeneutic strategies offered. Such an arrangement deprivileges the narrator's authority and produces the possibility of interpretive indeterminacy.

The problem has been that these conflicting interpretive strategies have not been recognized as already existing features within the discourse of Romance. Therefore, in the *Quixote* these aporias have lead to endless scholarly and critical debates about meaning and interpretation which are in fact continuations of the interpretive operations of the plot line. By fictionalizing Cide Hamete, Cervantes has effectively incorporated both the reader and the reader's act of interpretation into the story line. In fact the act of genre interpretation *is* the story. In this way the reader is inscribed as a performer in the text and, to that extent, is also fictionalized. This constitutes the reader as a dramatic entity within the story, providing her or him with a spurious but seductive ontological identity. To some extent, as noted, this arrangement already existed in the earlier romances. The grail controversies in many ways continue debates already constituted within Chrétien's text and certainly within the texts of his successors who, like Wolfram von Eschenbach and others, believed that Chrétien didn't understand the "true" meaning of the grail episode. This happened, as we have seen, in part because later writers and certainly later critics and scholars have persisted in trying to read/interpret the grail episode as an allegory. The grail debate is thus the result of both a condition already present in the text and a subsequent radical shift in European hermeneutics, of readers searching for a different kind of meaning than what was found in the Celtic tales. In the *Quixote*, however, the hermeneutic conflict is self-consciously presented as a textual capacity, one that re-constitutes interpretation as part of the story. With this step Cervantes took a feature of Romance and made a new story out of it. That story is neither the story of the hidalgo nor the story of Cide Hamete. It is the story of how the text is told, and it is this that makes "the story of the story" a Romance *aventura*.

Included among the consequences of this arrangement is the fictionalization of the problem of genre. This topic, of intense interest in the Renaissance, moves the concept of genre away from the neo-Aristotelian (logocentric) agenda of the *preceptistas* toward an interpretative act originating in the reader's cultural conditioning. Such a formulation of genre becomes the underlying story of not only Don Quixote and Cide Hamete but of a panoply of characters that enter the hero's story in the fictional landscape of the interpolated tales. Starting with Cardenio, a succession of these figures create the fictional "action" of the Sierra Morena and the second inn. Within this arc of storytelling activity the conflicting generic articulations of what is happening become a series of genre wars in which the story concerns itself with "readings" of what is going on.

It is this phenomenon that gives the adventures of Dorotea their Romance flavor and make her in effect the heroine of part 1. She and not Dulcinea, who does not come into her own until part 2, creates the narrative thrust of Don Quixote's adventures. Her mercurial presence dramatizes the underlying thematic issue at risk in the text. At the same time this fictionalization of the genre problem de-constitutes the logocentric expectations of the prevailing neo-Aristotelian aesthetic, as well as those of the hermeneutic battles concerning the validity of the Bible. It is not surprising therefore that the same kind of hermeneutic conflict within the Quixote worked to create the novel as a new literary form of prodigious power.

The story of this text begins, as we have seen, in the very first sentence as Cide Hamete struggles to suppress the name of the village, and then the story of interpretation narratizes itself in the prolonged confusion about the protagonist's name. Likewise Don Quixote has his own language problems as he starts to write his own story by giving Romance names to himself and to his world. The story thus becomes a struggle over a process of creating language on the part of both the narrator and the protagonist.

What results is the drama of an opposition between two concepts of language. However, this difference of languages is in itself deceptive, since both the narrator and the hero are merely exploiting different aspects of the language of Romance. The differences between their readings erupt along an unstable border of genre signs and significations in which two signs have the same referent as in Quijada/Quijote, rocín/ Rocinante, venta/castillo, while at other times we find the opposite problem, in which one sign has two referents as in castellano meaning a man from Castile or alcalde de un castillo. The case in which the name of the fish at the inn has multiple forms (abadejo/bacallao/curadillo/truchuela) carries the situation one step further and seems to indicate confusion about the nature of the fish itself. Language thus suggests a problem concerning the ontology of an external reality.

In other instances the names often have onomastic functions that become stories in themselves, such as the naming of the hidalgo and his horse. These stories take on a life of their own, subject to various interpretations, just as the narrator invents the fiction of the source texts or the hidalgo gives the meaning/etymology of Rocinante's name. In these instances the reader is challenged to interpret the interpretation. This situation replicates the explanation that Arthur gives concerning the nature of the boar in the Culhwch tale. The beast is both a king/deity and a pig who ultimately escapes back into the sea, while the name Culhwch has its own onomastic function that explains the name and disguises the divine nature of the swineherd who found/sired him. Furthermore Arthur's explanation marks his own identity as problematic.

Applying the explain/disguise principle to the name *Rocinante* and to Don Quixote's explanation of the meaning of the name, the reader is invited to look for other meanings. While this may not discover that the name *Rocinante* is a disguise for a god, it is suggestive of the fact that horses were once read as having divine attributes. It also implies that the problem of the name does point to other "readings" about Rocinante's ontology. For one thing the horse is named first thus giving him certain privilege. The idea that the name contains a clue to the horse's former state is put forth by Don Quixote himself. Two critics, Rosenblatt and Riquer, have offered other interpretations of the form of the name and see the "ante" as being a gerund rather than signifying "before." The formulation *rocín andante* also comes to mind as a phonological echo of *caballero andante*. This kind of linguistic play does suggest, however, that there is more to the name because of what meets the ear, while the epigraphic dialogue between Babieca and Rocinante found at the opening of the *Quixote* suggests that Don Quixote and Sancho are themselves disguised *asnos* and *rocines*, thus extending the alternate equine ontologies to the heroes as well. This parallels the "external soul" condition of animals that accompany heroes as in the case of CuChulainn. Such pairings of men and animals have mythological roots that tell us something about the nature of the hero. Horse imagery is particularly powerful in Celtic myth, in which a major deity (a woman) was a horse. This background gave added magnetism to the idea of a horseman as a special kind of creature, raising his status above the level of mere mortals.

An important vestige of the special powers of horses does survive in the *libros de caballería* and in the *Quixote* as a genre-linked feature, and that is the practice of allowing the horse to chose the road to adventure.

Don Quixote comments on this more than once, and in fact Rocinante does lead him to Cardenio the wild man, another creature with zoomorphic characteristics. Historically also the endless pictures and statues of Don Quixote and Sancho usually depict them on their mounts, and this iconographic tradition has been reduced to its essentials in the famous Picasso profile drawing of them on their respective steeds. Not unexpectedly the horse and ass are prominent in the statuary grouping in the Plaza de España so that in many ways Rocinante is the most famous steed in literary history. All these conditions have multiple explanations, but it remains viable that Rocinante does function to both explain and disguise the nature of Don Quixote himself. This helps explain that the hidalgo and the horse have become mythic figures in the world's imagination, particularly when coupled with the windmill, an item which also has a mythic story of its own.

Thus the naming processes precede any encounter with the problem of the hero's adventures per se, but a fully operative Otherworld does not emerge until chapter two, when Don Quixote arrives at the inn for his first *aventura*. There, the hidalgo has his first meeting with pigs and with the language of the pig god that both explains and disguises the meaning of the episode. Effectively the pig images of the first inn adventure introduce the hero to the world of Romance, just as the herd of pigs running over him in chapter 68 of part 2 signals the approaching closure of his heroic incarnation. But among the denizens of the first inn are to be found not one but three porcine creatures.

The Hero's Arrival and Reception into the World of Romance

To a great extent the entire novel is situated between two incidents of reception and arrival: the hero's arrival at the inn in chapter two and the arrival back at his village in the concluding adventure leading to his death. Strung between these two arrivals is a prolonged search to come to terms with the hidden meanings of such moments. Don Quixote knows that these arrival scenes are a genre feature of Romance. To give but one example, they echo the arrival of the knight to a kingdom held under a malefic enchantment. Lancelot's arrival at the burning city in *The High History of the Holy Grail* is one example. The reception is, in fact, the recognition by the people of the *cité gasté* that this knight is the true hero,

the one foretold by ancient prophecies, who will break the spell. Some
scholars see behind the reception and recognition feature a narratized
version of the ritual arrival of the victim/hero whose sacrifice is required
by the gods. (Darrah 37–45). As such, the general rejoicing of the popu-
lace and the clamorous reception given the designated hero became in
Romance literature a sign this knight, as in the Lancelot ballad, is the
truest hero of all, even though the fateful meaning in its ritual source is
forgotten. For Don Quixote the search for such a reception becomes an
obsession never quite satisfied. Ironically, only in part 2, with his false
reception at the palace of the Duke and Duchess, does he finally confess
to Sancho that for the first time he then feels himself to be a true knight.
The search for this authentication by means of his identification with
Lancelot begins at the first inn and continues throughout the text.

Don Quixote's reception at the first inn is also strung between two
curious signs of disguised swine deities. These two figures, the swineherd and the swine castrator, appear fortuitously at the inn, marking his
arrival and the serving of his dinner. As Clemencín observed long ago:
"Un pito de capador solemnizó la comida de D. Quijote, como un cuerno
de porquero habia solemnizado su llegada al castillo" (Rodríguez Marín
87). [A gelder's whistle solemnized Don Quijote's dinner, just as a
swineherd's horn had solemnized his arrival to the castle.] (We note that
for Clemencín the inn has already become a castle.) The chance arrivals
of two swine figures equipped with musical instruments that mark certain moments in the hero's progress does not strain the appearance of
realism, but, nevertheless, the swineherd's horn that announces Don
Quixote's arrival into the world of the inn and the pig castrator's flute
that announces the arrival of his fish dinner are events open to many
readings. For one thing, in addition to the introduction of the pigs, the
castrador also brings to the scene the problematic of castration, an item
not easily introduced in a purely realistic depiction of an arrival to an
inn. Furthermore, Rodríguez Marín comments that the castrator's silbato
is "una zampoñilla de carrizos, como aquella con que pintan al dios Pan"
[a reed pipe like the one with which they depict Pan]. Thus echoes of a
zoomorphic deity are also heard. (The association of cañas with Pan is
also mentioned by Covarrubias in the Tesoro.) The presence of the swineherd and his pigs at the entrance to the inn foreshadows the chance
appearance of a hare pursued by dogs that greets Don Quixote on his
return to his village. These "coincidences" mark off the beginning and
the closing of the hidalgo's adventures with zoomorphic signs that both

disguise and explain not only the ontology of the hero but also the condition of the text itself.

A romance reading of the inn's ontology, however, is first provided by the narrator as he comments ironically about the manner of Don Quixote's approach: "[Don Quixote] vió, no lejos del camino por donde iba, una venta, que fue como si viera una estrella que, no a los portales, sino a los alcázares de su redención le encaminaba." [Don Quixote saw, not far from the road he was going, an inn, which was as though he saw a star that lead him, not to the gates, but to the palace of his redemption.] This commentary inscribes a double hermeneutic fix on the inn, establishing it as a locus capable of two readings. This interpretive doubling also replicates the problem with which the narrator introduces the entire episode when he comments that there is confusion in the source texts about whether the windmill scene or the inn scene is the first adventure. This confusion signifies an underlying accord between inns and mills and establishes them as the hero's interchangeable *loci*, where the hero most powerfully encounters his destiny. But the narrator decides that Don Quixote's first encounter with this Otherworld force is marked by the sound of the swineherd's horn, a porcine event that the knight reads as a sign of his arrival into the world of Romance.

The hero's passage into this world is further marked by other linguistic signs that evoke the role of chance or destiny in the sequence of events. The approach to the inn is carefully choreographed by the narrator. First, as noted, the hero suddenly sees the inn. It "appears" as he searches for a place to alleviate his hunger and fatigue, and the narrator specifically indicates that such a place would be either a group of shepherds or a castle, the two Romance lodgings for the knight. The abrupt appearance of the inn/castle replicates the similar scene of Perceval finding the castle of the Fisher King in Chrétien's tale. In both tales these apparitions signal the Otherworld ontology of adventurous loci in Celtic tales. Don Quixote's arrival at the inn at nightfall, which the narrator reports in two contradictory statements, marks the appearance of a "border" castle, his "castel de la marche" appearing at the day/night boundary. Then, in his first encounter with "human" figures, he sees the prostitutes at the gate of the inn. The ontology of the two is both undermined and co-opted, just as the ontology of the inn is, by the narrator's commentary.

Typically the narrator presents his own version of the event first: "Estaban acaso a la puerta dos mujers mozas, destas que llaman *del partido*, las cuales iban a Sevilla con unos *harrieros* que en la venta aquella

noche acertaron a hacer jornada" [There were at the door by chance two
young women, those that they call paid companions, who were going to
Sevilla with some mule drivers and who had made assignations with
them for that night]. The narrator's interpretation is then followed by the
narrator's putting down (in both senses) how the knight sees/reads the
scene, so that the narrator's interpretation is in the privileged primary
position: inn/castle, history/fiction. The Romance reading of the scene is
inscribed as a false interpretation of a deranged hero: "luego que [Don
Quixote] vió la venta se le representó que era un castillo con sus cuatro
torres y chapitels de luciente plata, sin faltarle su puente levadiza y honda
cava, con todos aquellos adherentes que semejantes castillos se pintan"
[as soon as he saw the inn it seemed to him that it was a castle with its
four towers and spires of shining silver, without missing its drawbridge
and deep moat, and with all those attendants with which similar castles
are described]. Thus the ontology of the building is entered into the
discourse in the deprivileged inn/castle position.

We note, however, the use of two adverbial forms *acaso* (by chance)
and *luego que* (as soon as), which are authorial commentary on the role
of chance in the event. Both adverbs bring to the fore the forces of time
and *fortuna*, two operations typical of a Romance narration, while *acaso*
evokes the *caso* with which the story began and relates it to its function
as a sign of fortune, thereby introducing a Romance feature of a "fortuitous event" into the narrator's "realistic" interpretation. In the descriptive language of how the inn appeared or "presented itself" to the hero,
we find also the apt usage of the Spanish reflexive for an event that
occurs without an agent. Like the ontology of the text itself, the inn
"comes to stand," "appears," or "presents itself" (se le presentó) as a
castle to the hero, just as it would in a Romance where the hero alone can
see the castle. The language thus appears to be playing the right tricks
on both the hero and the narrator.

In another attempt at undermining the hero's reading, the narrator
then presents the hero's image of what should happen next: a dwarf
should appear among the crenellations and sound a horn announcing his
arrival to the castle. This reading is then deflected by the narrator's own
version of what is happening. It is here that he relates the sudden appearance of a swineherd: "En esto sucedió *acaso* que un porquero que
andaba recogiendo de unos rastrojos una manada de puercos (que, sin
perdón así se llaman) tocó un cuerño, a cuya señal ellos se recogen" [At
this moment it happened *by chance* that a swineherd who was gathering

together the remnants of a herd of pigs (that begging your pardon are so named) blew a horn, at whose signal the pigs came together]. Thus we get both the swineherd and the swine appearing by chance (*acaso* for the second time in the same paragraph) at the crucial instant of the hero's arrival. The probability of the coincidence, this kind of event happening in real life is very low although not impossible, but the improbability factor is lost in the narrator's elaborate switches between his own version and the hero's version of what is happening. The result is that the reader's attention is misdirected to the comic effect of the improbability rather than to the improbability itself. In this way the narrator's ironic "realism" is privileged over the hero's more romantic interpretation, even though a genre reading of the features within the hero's hermeneutic has its own validity. It is just that the comic tone de-privileges the Romance content within a privileged "realistic" reading. This procedure is at least as old as Chrétien's formulations of the youthful hero's mistakes in *Perceval*, and to some extent can be found in both Welsh and Gaelic forerunners. The difference is that in Cervantes the narrator's authority is weaker because the story of the storytelling is itself part of the fiction. At the same time, moreover, the narrator's ironic reading of the hero is more critical, more undermining because the narrator presents the hidalgo openly as a fool and madman rather than as an innocent ingenue. The reader expectation in Chrétien is that the hero will grow up and triumph in some significant way, while in the *Quixote* the reader's expectations, carefully controlled by the narrator, shifts the attention to the ongoing drama of comic conflict between the madman and a deceptively articulated everyday reality. Remember that in Chrétien the story is placed in a misty past in which anything might happen. In Cervantes' text it is the transposition of the locus to the immediacy of contemporary Spain that, more than anything, undermines the authority of the hero's reading. The narrator in this way can appeal to the reader's shared familiarity with a topical reality in order to [enhances] the impression that the hero must be a madman.

Other factors of the language, however, do keep the Romance reading intact even though it is presented as only weakly subversive to the narrator's assumed hermeneutic privilege. In particular there is a curiously self-conscious concern on the part of the narrator with the problematics of naming associated with the ontology of pigs" "que sin perdón, así se llaman" [that without apology are so named]. The narrator's commentary in a deceptive way brings up the problematics of naming an item that exists outside the normal or acceptable range of discourse. Pigs, as "una cosa fea," are not to be directly named in proper language, but they can be so long as the speaker excuses his mis-speaking. The very fact that pigs are problematic has, of course its own story relevant to Spain's Semitic heritage. Nevertheless we note that within the chivalric tradition the loss of status of pigs reaches at least as far back as the Welsh tale of Culhwch, where already Arthur observes a lowered criminal condition for them. However, in another category of signification, boars as opposed to pigs did still appear in coats of arms, along with other chivalrically acceptable beasts like lions and stags. (The coat of arms of some branches of the Cervantes family utilized the etymon of their name by imaging a stag [ciervo-cum-cervantes]). Likewise the boar hunt remained a highly privileged aristocratic pursuit, as witness the boar hunting episode of the duke and duchess in part 2, where again the boar is associated with a trick. Thus the boar/pig image still retained a double hermeneutic fix, but the narrator elects the more comic pig formulation and then protects himself with a linguistic caveat, just as we might still say speak of the devil. At the level of popular discourse the inherent problem in naming any potency risked the hidden capability of calling forth the referent by the power of the sign. For Cervantes the doubled identity of pig/boar served perfectly for the doubled discourse of the narrator as he deals with the hidden romance energy of the inn.

Both the role of pigs and fortune are re-marked as Don Quixote attempts to eat while keeping his *contrahecha* helmet on his head. The fish banquet scene itself retains a grail energy as the two prostitutes assume roles of grail maidens bearing the food and drink. Although the maidens can feed him through the opening in the helmet, Don Quixote cannot drink until the inn keeper provides a hollowed-out *caña* (straw) through which he can draw the wine. The *caña* image then immediately reappears associated with a swine: "Estando en eso, llegó *acaso* a la venta un castrador de puercos, y así como llegó, sonó su *silbato de cañas* cuatro o cinco veces, con lo cual acabó de confirmar don Quijote que estaba en algún famoso castillo, y que le servían con música, y que el abadejo eran truchas, el pan candeal, y las rameras damas, y el ventero castellano del castillo" [And being so involved, a swine gelder *by chance* arrived at the inn and as soon as he arrived he sounded a reed flute four or five times, with which he confirmed to Don Quixote that he was at a famous castle, and that they served him with music, the codfish a trout, the bread a fresh white, and the prostitutes noble ladies, and the inn keeper the lord of the castle]. The narrator's list of linguistic oppositions that accompanies the pagan sound of the castrator's reed flute signals the existence of a hidden hermeneutic underlying the entire mis en-scène of the inn. At the same time the sound also evokes the problematics of reading/interpretation associated with pig signs. Sebastián de Covarrubias, like Rodríguez Marín, also associates the music of the *cañas* with pagan forces such as the mythological story of Pan's pursuit of the nymph Syringa. It is within this context of pigs and castration that the image of male sterility, a familiar grail sign, is inserted into the growing list of romance features: swine and swineherds, grail damsels who attend to feeding the hero, fortuitous coincidences that suggest Otherworld forces, curious fish plates, strange music, castration, and a disguised castle. But in the matter of the castration image it is the narrator who inserts the feature while the hero, like Perceval, is blinded to any meaning hidden in the image of castration by his immediate preoccupation with the problematics of the meal. In this sense Don Quixote fails to ask any question about the meal accompanied by this strange music. But it should be noted that key Romance features are introduced by the narrator's own discourse without reference to the imagination of the hero, thus undermining the Romance/ Realism dichotomy the narrator seeks to establish.

In the same way the narrator has repeatedly invoked the operation of fortune by the use of various verbal and adverbial terms. *Acaso* (by chance) is utilized three times: once for the *mujeres mozas* (young women), once for the *porquero* (swineherd), once for the *castrador* (gelder). In addition the fish dinner sequence is introduced with a double reference to the action of time: "*A dicha, acerto* a ser viernes aquel dia" [*By chance it happened* to be Friday that day]. Furthermore, Don Quixote's arrival at the inn on Friday echoes the curious list of eating habits attributed to him in the first paragraph. There it is clear that the hidalgo's week changes on Friday (the Moslem holy day) so that the day marks a time border for him. At the same time Don Quixote's Friday arrival at the inn recalls the Friday arrival of Perceval to the hermitage of the teaching hermit. In this episode, situated on Good Friday, Perceval learns crucial information concerning his redemption, a factor that parallels the hidalgo's apprehension that this inn is to be a place of redemption for him. No other of the hero's episodes occurs on a specific day of the week. Finally the role of time and fortune are also associated with the appearances and reappearances of the *ventero* (innkeeper) throughout this episode. By chance, he consistently appears at the crucial moment when his mediating

capacities are most needed, and his actions convert the inn into a teaching castle complete with a mercurial language and dubious hermeneutic
advice. In the same way the *ventero* is very adept at purloining the riches
of the road and hazarding dangerous crossings to his own advantage. In
all these capacities he evokes the imagery of Moch, Mercury, Hermes,
and thus emerges as the disguised master of thieves and tricky texts.

The Language of Chiasmus

The first appearance of the *ventero* occurs as an act of hermeneutic mediation, precisely at the moment in which the prostitutes cannot understand the language of Don Quixote. A conflict over laughter, appropriately
Don Quixote's first conflict, is about to lead to worse when the *ventero's*
appearance pre-vents further confusion. His arrival is specifically timed
by the narrator to emphasize his intermediary capabilities: "El lenguaje
[de Don Quijote], no entendido de las señoras, y el mal talle de nuestro
caballero acrecentaba en ellas la risa, y en el el enojo, pasará muy adelante
si a aquel punto no saliera el ventero que, por ser muy gordo, era muy
pacífico" (80, emphasis added) [Don Quixote's language, not understood
by the ladies, and the seedy appearance of our knight increased the
giggling of the girls and the anger of the knight. Things would have
turned out very badly *if at that point the innkeeper had not arrived*, who
being very fat was also very peaceful]. The interpretive skills of the *ventero*
facilitate (therefore) his first function and they foreshadow the hermeneutic
lessons he later gives to Don Quixote. Here the narrator remarks on his
being "muy gordo" and "muy pacífico." Under the entry for *gordo*
Covarrubias specifically mentions pigs, while under *pacífico* he comments:
"El que pone paz . . ." [He who imposes peace . . .] Thus both pig and
mediation are among the first associations with the image of the *ventero*,
but it is in the latter capacity that his linguistic powers are to emerge and,
with it, a special kind of language of which he is the titular master.

　　This language, the third discretely identifiable system of signification,
begins to establish its curious chiasmic capabilities in his first words to
Don Quixote. The illocutionary import of the words is that of a pacifying
gesture, to distract Don Quixote from his annoyance at the frivolity of
the prostitutes. The key to this new language is that its true "meaning"
is both deflective and deceptive. The import of the words themselves
reveals an oscillating referentiality as the result of a contradiction be-

tween their rhetorical import (ostensibly a welcoming gesture) and the obfuscation of a less positive attitude toward the new arrival: "Si vuestra merced, señor caballero, busca posada, amén del lecho (porque en esta venta no hay ninguno), todo lo demás se hallará en ella en mucha abundancia" (80) [If your grace, sir Knight, is looking for repose, let alone a bed (for in this inn there is neither), everything else may be found in it with great abundance]. (Commentators have had difficulty explaining the phrase "amén del lecho" since the usual meaning *además* (besides) seems here reversed to signify *menos* (less) [see Rodríguez Marín note 14, 80]. Covarrubias does not record this meaning, and Cejador confesses to finding no other instance of *amén* meaning *menos*. Whatever explanation for the linguistic inversion can be found, it is apparent that reversible signals are the identifying characteristic of the *ventero*'s language, a capacity he utilizes brilliantly in order to manipulate Don Quixote. To some extent his discourse seems a linguistic cross between the languages of the narrator and the hero. He combines the ironic subversive import of the narrator with the overblown rhetoric of the hero so that he seems to say the opposite of what the literal import of his words actually signify. All his verbal resources are mercurial and reversible so that he comes to stand as the chiasmic god of the crossroads and dangerous language. He is a herm figure marking the boundary between two generic discourses, the chivalric and the picaresque.

Most important of all, his language awakens in Don Quixote a subtle response to the meaning/non-meaning of his words and, in particular, to the problematic existence of the bed. The key words of the *ventero*'s speech, the ones that evoke Don Quixote's response, are *posada* (rest) and *lecho* (bed) buried within the rather lilting singsong of the *ventero*'s sentence. From this context Don Quixote responds with some well-known ballad lines of chivalric intent: "mis arreos son las armas, mi descanso el pelear" [my only adornments are my arms, fighting is my rest]. This in turn sets into motion an exchange of varying levels of intertextual discourse in which puns and verbal echoes, as well as the important reversals of meanings found in the language of *germanía* (criminal slang), come into play. The last in particular is a language of hidden meanings, such as the reference to *castellano* by Don Quixote which evokes various (mis)-readings: *castellano* (keeper of the castle) and *castellano* (person from Castile), and the *ventero*'s (mis)-interpretation, cited by the narrator, *sano de Castilla*, which signifies *ladrón disimulado* (disguised thief). The last reading evokes further comment by the narrator, who then identifies the *ventero* as a picaro from the coded region of "la playa de Sanlúcar," a notorious hangout for thieves and smugglers in Andalucia. This locale is also mentioned by the *ventero* himself in the next chapter when he recites a veritable "mapa picaresca" of Spain. Rodríguez Marín comments here (94) that since the *ventero* was born in the playa de Sanlúcar that he belongs to "aquella gente picaril, medio terrestre, medio marítima" [those thieving people, half terrestrial, half maritime]. The reference is of course to the criminal smuggling by both land and sea, but the double citation to the *playa* (beach), itself a border marker, also identifies the *ventero* with maritime or water activities. His land/water ontology further connects him with the pig in Culhwch and with the imagery surrounding the Fisher King himself, who is first seen on water and whose grail contains all the jewels of the sea. Likewise in Loomis's story of the Irish folktale concerning the problem of asking the right question, the disguised king is again of maritime origin (*Arthurian* 382). There the castle/island is visible only to select heroes once every seven years. All these sea references suggest Celtic Otherworld powers which appear as realistic items in Cervantes' text: *cañas*, the multi-named fish dinner, the beach of Sanlucar, the fish market of Malaga, and so forth, as well as Don Quixote's arrival at the inn on Friday—the day of the sea born goddess of love. All this occurs within a context of sea/land reversals common to both Celtic tales. The same matter survives in the figure of Amadís of Gaul, "el doncel del mar" [the boy/page of the sea], a hero born along a river and cast out to sea in a floating ark. In a parodic reversal, Lazarillo de Tormes replicates the river imagery, and it should be remembered that in one of the many sequels to *Lazarillo*, Lazarillo himself turns into a fish. While each of these items in itself suggests very little, the gradual accumulation of references does gain a recognizable profile. What is at issue is the chiasmic reversals in both the linguistic signs and the contentual items of the unstable ontological environment in which the hero operates. This kind of fluctuation is found in Romances as a recognizable genre feature: lovers turn into swans, knights suddenly come upon ruined cities or waste lands that at the reverberation of a hidden signal reverse themselves into thriving kingdoms, just as the Celtic tales tell of waves and fishes turning into meadows and sheep. Shapeshifting is thus one of the most powerful Celtic forces, and it underlies both the condition of language and the ontology of events. In this context the piglike figure of the *ventero* is a perfect disguise for the shapeshifting ontology of the inn itself, which in many ways is the Inn of the Pig.

Nowhere is the linguistic capacity of the innkeeper better displayed than in his use of a remarkable language of reversal. By means of carefully orchestrated rhetorical rhythms and phrasings he manages to converse with Don Quixote, who remains deaf to the referential import of what is said. This factor is particularly in evidence in the *ventero*'s long autobiographical account of his youth spent in criminal adventure. His picaresque reversal of the language of chivalry is a tour de force performance. The litany of criminal hangouts, which he makes sound like a list of chivalric courts, accords perfectly with Don Quixote's highly charged view of the condition of the inn and its keeper. At the same time the *ventero* does not lie; rather, his guest cannot read what is being said so long as the rhetorical tone of chivalric adventure is maintained. It is a triumph of rhetoric over referentiality in which two systems of signification cancel each other out. In effect the *ventero* explains perfectly well his long criminal past if one reads the conversations from the viewpoint of the language of *germanía*, and yet it exhibits the same ridiculous rhetoricity of Don Quixote's chivalric language. In fact its overblown rhetoric critiques the lack of precise referentiality that deprived the *libros de caballería* of any serious validity. In this sense he makes fun of the Don Quixote's language while at the same time appropriating it for his own intents.

It is within this environment of hermeneutic and referential volatility that Don Quixote provides a remarkable intertextual reading for his own name, one that will underlie its possible meaning throughout the remainder of the text. With the mention of *posada* (inn) and *lecho* (bed) the *ventero* has already called into being some lines taken from an old ballad about the condition of knights. Specifically the lines refer to the lack of sleep or rest enjoyed by fighting men. We have also been told by the narrator that the hidalgo himself slept little. This habit of little sleep, of course, means little access to the dream world in which gods have traditionally communicated with their favorites. Thus the warrior often relies on visual signs such as the passage of birds. At the same time, when he does sleep he is likely to have a significant dream, as Don Quixote does in the second inn or in the cave of Montesinos. Thus the first ballad lines concern sleep with or without dreams, and this topic is a significant one for the hero who is later to have his most meaningful dream in an inn, a dream which provides the resolution to Dorotea's dilemma.

Don Quixote's second citation of ballad lines follows almost immediately, as the hero weaves an invisible text of chivalric identity about himself. The second set of lines describe the scene of arrival of Lancelot to a welcoming castle. The parallel of inn/castle is the immediate meta-phorical trigger, but the lines are significant in multiple ways. As the attendant *putas/doncellas* (prostitutes/maidens), in the best chivalric manner, help the hero disarm, Don Quixote suddenly adapts an ancient *romance* (ballad) about Lanzarote to the immediate situation. His adaption in this case contains an important modification of the original text in which he inserts his own name into the metrical pattern for the name of Lanzarote. This substitution and repression provides a magical pun on Lanzarote/Don Quixote and, by so doing, sets into motion a mercurial chain of cross-references between the poor hidalgo and the supreme knight and lover of the entire meta-text of Arthurian Romance:

> Nunca fuera caballero
> De damas tan bien servido
> Como fuera don Quijote/[Lanzarote]
> Cuando de su aldea/[Bretaña] vino:
> Doncellas curaban del;
> Princesas, del su rocino. (pt. 1, ch. 2)

> [Never was a knight
> so well served by ladies
> as was Don Quixote (Lanzarote)
> when from his village (Britain) he came:
> Damsels looked after him;
> (while) princesses served his steed.]

These ballad lines with their name substitution are to echo throughout the entire text, both on the level of the interchangeable names and on the level of the protagonist's preoccupation with a chivalric reception that will verify his identity. The choice of Lancelot rather than any other chivalric hero has itself become a chiasmic problem. Some critics have suggested that the name Don Quixote is the result of its metrical fit into the Lanzarote slot of the ballad line (Riquer), while others suggest that Lancelot was chosen because of its fit with Don Quixote (Rodríguez Marín). But in either case the pun inscribes Lanzarote as the mimetic source/echo of Don Quixote, so that we read two names for one and associate the hidalgo with the Arthurian panoply of euhemerized heroes: Arthur, Tristan, Merlin, Perceval, Lancelot, and so on. The choice of Lancelot may indeed be "fortuitous" because of the sound pattern, but it also serves important purposes within the text. For one thing it is re-enforced by the hero's subsequent references to the love scene between Lancelot and Guinevere in which they are guarded by the dueña Quintañona. The latter is a purely Spanish fabrication, but her role is adapted from Celtic patterns of the fatal libation server. Don Quixote himself refers to her as "la mejor salxador de vino del mundo" [the best server of wine in the world]. In this capacity of wine server she serves the warrior a special brew that authenticates him as the hero chosen for a specific destiny. Thus the Lancelot ballad underwrites a grail identity for Don Quixote.

Echoes of these scenes of reception and love occur in several crucial instances throughout the book. Don Quixote himself cites from the ballad or provides echo of the lines in his dialogue with Vivaldo about love and chivalry (pt. 1, ch. 13), in his love scene with Maritornes in the second inn (pt. 1, ch. 16), in his debate with the canon of Toledo (pt. 1, ch. 48), in his fabrication of the tale of the Caballero de lago (pt. 1, ch. 1), and in his Bodas de Camacho adventure (pt. 2, ch. 19). At the same time, he experiences similar receptions in key episodes such as the cave of Montesinos (pt. 2, ch. 23), his arrival at the palace of the Duke and Duchess (pt. 2, ch. 31), during his meeting with Merlin at the time of the boar hunt scene (pt. 2, ch. 35), and finally when he arrives back at his village just before his death (pt. 2, ch. 71). Thus the ballad provides a subtle pathway of words and images through the myriad adventures and continually evoke verbal and thematic echoes of half-forgotten Arthurian meanings.

It should be remembered that Lancelot is a failed grail knight, failed because of his adulterous love for Guinevere, love that is a betrayal of his allegiance to his king. So the loves of Lancelot and Guinevere are a curious model for the hidalgo. Yet this image is a primary pattern for Don Quixote's articulation of his own love for Dulcinea. Curiously or not, Don Quixote himself never makes the connection between the betrayal of Arthur and the fatal love between Lancelot and the queen. Various interpretations come to mind in this matter. For one thing Don Quixote sees his love for Dulcinea as platonically pure and, therefore, not an adulterous betrayal. But also it must be kept in mind that Lancelot as an euhemerized god was not originally part of the Arthurian cycle of tales. He was a proto-Arthur himself and so his contention over Guinevere did not appear until the conflation of the stories occurred, probably fairly late in the evolution of the Arthurian cycle. Nevertheless the fact that

Don Quixote sees Lancelot as the perfect lover leaves open interpretative
questions of love, failure, and identity concerning his own role.

This kind of contradiction also replicates the shifting identities of other
mythic and legendary heroes who appear one way in certain ballads or
stories and then another way in other sources. The Cid, for instance, has
a double identity seen in the differences between his portrayal in his epic
incarnation as opposed to his youthful (*mocedades*) image in the ballads.
In the *Quixote* the problem of the shapeshifting ontology of heroes is
narratized during Don Quixote's dream in the cave of Montesinos and
during his explication of the dream to Sancho and the humanist. Thus
traditional stories, like heroes, have more than one profile and are rarely
self-identical even within one redaction.

The *ventero*'s knighting of Don Quixote, a crucial event for the entire
career of the hero, fittingly takes place amidst this environment of volatile referentiality and fluctuating hermeneutic horizons. Again the hero
stands on the edge of various levels of discourse which provide glimpses
of not only the chivalric world but that of its generic opposite, the world
of the picaresque. At the same time the *ventero* himself assumes new and
powerful roles that relate him to Perceval's tutors and to his even more
remote ancestor, Hermes, the god of thieves and texts. This aspect is
particularly apparent during the lessons in hermeneutics that he gives
the hero concerning the problem of how to read the *libros de caballería*:

> Preguntole si traía dineros; respondiole don Quijote que no traía
> blanca, porque el nunca había leido en las historias de los cabal-
> leros andantes que ninguno los hubiese traido. A esto dijo el
> ventero que se engañaba: que, puesto caso que en las historias no
> se escribía, por haberles parecido *a los autores dellas* que no era
> menester escrebir una cosa tan clara y tan necesesaria de traerse
> como eran dinero y camisas limpias. (97, emphasis added)

> [Then he asked if he had any money with him, to which Don
> Quixote replied that he had not a cent, as in the histories of
> knight-errant he had never *read* of any of them carrying any. On
> this point the landlord told him he was mistaken, for, though not
> recorded in the histories, because in the *author's opinion* there
> was no need to mention anything so obvious and necessary as
> money and clean shirts.]

This lesson brings into focus the problematics of the layered texts of Romance and of the multiple hermeneutic fixes of successive audiences. Here the idea of lost meanings and of faded readings giving way to new (mis-)readings is fully narratized. In this way the *ventero's* lesson replicates the condition of the text we are reading and in a haunted manner the statement questions the lost identity of the speaker, a god of a lost language. Don Quixote is going to be suitably knighted by his true tutelary deity.

The ceremony begins with the hero's vigil over his arms, a necessary prelude to the knighting ceremony. The mis en scène for this endeavor includes again a series of items that are recognizable from the landscape of Romance. The site where the hero places his arms is a well, a traditional challenge locus in Romance and a passageway to the Celtic Otherworld. Traditionally damsels inhabit such wells before the kingdoms fall under a malefic spell. These damsels bring food and other sustenance to knights, but they are absent in the belated, postlapsarian times in which Don Quixote sees himself struggling. Other Romance items here are Don Quixote's posture of leaning on his lance, the appearance of the moon, the interruption of the mule driver, and the invocation to Dulcinea.

The moon has numerous meaningful associations with Don Quixote, such as the connections of the moon with madness and with the etymology of *lunático*. Astrologically the moon is the sign for late July, the time of his birth as a hero and madman (see Covarrubias), when the overly powerful influence of the unconscious is associated with the moon in Cancer. Also involved in the episode is the choleric and violent anger of the warrior which echoes the image of the warriors' moon or halo (cited above; this signified the descent of the hero's "riastarthae" in the story of CuChulainn). There the hero's capabilities as a supernatural warrior descended upon him like an empowering fit of madness that made him invincible. This type of martial enabling is most suitable for Don Quixote, since his *padrón* does not provided him with lessons in bearing arms, such as occurred with Chrétien's Perceval. Instead, Don Quixote, more like the earlier Celtic heroes, receives his warrior status as a fit of madness directly descending from the heavens.

In contrast to Perceval's tutor, Gornemont the innkeeper gives only social lessons to the aspiring knight. It should be remembered that in Gornemont's lessons was the warning against speaking too much, the very warning that lead to Perceval's disastrous failure to ask the spellbreaking question at the grail castle. Thus the kind of lessons voiced by the tutor can have profound and fatal effects on the knight himself, much as the powers of enchantment that befall a hero because of a "geiss" or malediction. Culhwch's love for Olwen is evoked in this manner and leads to all the adventures found in the tale. In other cases the pronouncements spoken at birth foretell the fate of the hero or heroine, as in the story of Deirdre of the Sorrows. Her fatal beauty leads to not only her own demise but to the destruction of her lover as well. In the case of Don Quixote, the presence of the moon not only suggests madness and fits of warlike anger, such as his attack on the *harrieros*, but also has a more general connotation of foreshadowing fateful energies that result from the words of the *ventero*. Among the most prominent of these is the advent of Sancho, who is ultimately to deceive Don Quixote in regard to Dulcinea's enchantment and disenchantment. Just as Perceval fails to disenchant to the grail castle because of Gornemont's interdiction, so Don Quixote follows a trajectory that is to be thwarted because of his entrapment in the hoax of Dulcinea's enchantment. In both stories the hero's major challenge is complicated because of the tutor's advice.

The situation of Don Quixote's posture of leaning on his lance as he performs his vigil replicates a number of very early Irish tales of the hero or heroine being enchanted by sight of an image of drops of blood in the snow or the appearance of a black bird pecking at the spots. Such moments are indicative of the protagonist (sometimes a woman) thinking of his or her beloved. The blood and color are missing for the moment in the initial stance of Don Quixote: "otras [veces], arrimado a su lanza, ponia los ojos en las armas sin quitarlos por un buen espacio dellas" (pt. 1, ch. 3) In this case the hero is transported by the sight of his arms but Dulcinea's image is only briefly delayed. The situation in general, however, recalls the situation of a similar episode in Chrétien's *Perceval*, one that occurs just before Perceval's entrance into the court of Arthur. Perceval, leaning on his lance and staring at the drops of blood in the snow, is transported with the thoughts of his lady. The intensity of his preoccupation is such that Arthur's knights have difficulty intruding on his thoughts without arousing his battle fury. Kay, always rude and ill-willed in Chrétien, abruptly addresses him. Perceval is seized by his battle fury and breaks Kay's collarbone and arm with the blow from his lance. After this failure, Gawain, the paragon of courtesy, manages to cajole Perceval out of his trance and introduce him into Arthur's presence without bloodshed. Here we see two fallen deities, Cei and Gwalchmai (Kay and Gawain), interact with a special hero of whom it was foretold that he would break Kay's shoulder. One is rude the other courtly. In the *Quixote* these roles are taken by the *harriero* and the *ventero*, with exactly the same results. Dulcinea also appears in the Quixote sequence when Don Quixote invokes her aid (for the first time) after the *harriero* has moved his arms from the well. Then Don Quixote in a rage hits the *harriero* and his companion on the head with his lance and is pulled out of his fit only by the mollifying words of the *ventero*. In the same way the Perceval episode occurs just before the hero is incorporated into Arthur's court. Both the *ventero* and Gawain replicate the role of the uncle in the CuChulainn episode in that each functions to incorporate the new hero into the warrior group. Thus Don Quixote enters the world of chivalry accompanied by much the same kind of misadventures that mark the comparable transitions of Celtic and Medieval warriors.

The relationship of the *ventero* to his mercurial ancestry has been apparent in more than one instance in this adventure, but the appearance and role of the *harrieros* also contains a story. Their function in the *Quixote* is to serve as a foil to Don Quixote, and he fights with them in both inns. Specifically they represent the non-chivalric condition of everyday life on the roads of Spain. They are not evil but they are an obstacle to the chivalric vision of the hero. In the same way the role of Kay in Chrétien (but not in earlier Welsh tales) often contrasts to the courtly and generous ideals of Gawain and Perceval as embodiments of all chivalric virtues. In *Culhwch and Olwen*, however, we see clearly the supernatural ancestry of Cei/Kay, who in that tale still retains traces of a deity and performs marvelous deeds of various kinds. In one he is closely associated with an all-wise salmon who assists him in his adventures. This suggests a water ontology for him and access to hidden supernatural knowledge. Chrétien, however, generally depicts him as ill spoken, ill willed, and jealous of more perfect knights like Gawain and Perceval. His beating at the hands of Perceval has been foretold by the court fool, so he is destined to clash with a chosen hero.

The *harrieros* have the same lack of courtesy and impatience with Don Quixote that Kay displays toward Perceval. Furthermore, in one episode in the *Quixote* one *harriero* does reveal something of a connection with the Otherworld. This occurs in the second inn at the outset of the love scene between Don Quixote and Maritornes. This episode has clear antecedents in various Irish tales and medieval Romances, including *Li Contes del Graal*, which will be discussed later. The *harriero* misadventure is relevant to both inn scenes. In the *Quixote* love scene, the second narrator comments that Maritornes' would-be lover, the rich *harriero* from Arevalo, is said to be a relative of Cide Hamete himself. Now this bit of information seems irrelevant and inconsequential to the matters at hand. In Romance texts, unmotivated and unconnected events of this sort often indicate the presence a fragment left over from an earlier redaction of the same story, and whatever meaning that fragment had is now eroded. In the *Quixote* the information is inserted as an editorial intrusion and suggests that the main narrator, Cide Hamete, a Moslem, is not entirely friendly toward Don Quixote. This situation contains some of the ambiguity that Fergus has in narrating the *Táin*. Now Cide Hamete's role is also that of a hermeneut and he does claim the same occult powers as the *sabios* who narrate the stories in the *libros de caballería*. That means that Cide Hamete is empowered with supernatural capabilities associated with enchanters and with Moslem necromancers (Stagg "el sabio..."). The family relationship of Cide Hamete with the mule driver is typical of the Morisco ancestry of most *harrieros*, particularly those from the region of Valencia or Arevalo, the *patria chica* of this particular *harriero*. The inclusion of these apparently trivial details concerning a minor character does not effect the action at hand, but it does suggest that Otherworld factors are guiding the events in the inn. The intrusive information about Cide Hamete's family seems like the onomastic episodes found in Romances that attempt to explain inexplicable items but, in effect, often work to disguise an unacceptable pagan meaning or event. This kind of reading also accords with Don Quixote's hermeneutics when he comments that the inn seems to be inhabited by an enemy Moorish enchanter who seeks to possess the beauty of Maritornes.

Such a reading, beautifully comic, nevertheless does contain a more complex validity. The protagonist seems to possess powers of interpretation that are the mark of a divine hero, powers that make him seem ridiculous but at the same time exceptional. This meaning is achieved because Cervantes has replicated in a more realistic manner the layered intertextuality of the medieval Romances. Again the Romance textuality is created by the narrative strategies of Cide Hamete and not by the knight's imagination.

In summary, we find that the text, by means of an impressive list of chiasmic signs, produces a Romance reading of the events at the first inn. In each of these items we find first a privileged realistic topic which suggests a de-privileged Romance equivalent: pig, piggish/Hermes; Quixote/Lanzarote; inn/castle; prostitutes/damsels; fish/grail, advice/riddle; picaresque/chivalric; *ventero/aventurero;* well/Otherworld entrance; mule driver/Kay; lunacy/"riastrarthae"; moon/warrior's halo; idiocy/special knowledge.

By means of this linguistic indeterminacy the misadventures of the aging hidalgo assume the pattern of an *enfances* narrative of a semi-divine hero. The story has assumed the condition of what Northrop Frye calls a realistic displacement of a Romance, a development he considers closely related to parody (36–37). However, even in the matter of parody there are clear antecedents in Celtic tales (Rees and Rees 211). The result, in Don Quixote's case, confers a hidden validity onto the hidalgo's "funny" interpretation of what is happening to him. His reading is based on the fact that the pattern of events at the inn fulfills a recognizable Celtic and Romance generic horizon, one found in the childhood stories of CuChulainn, Peredur, and Perceval.

In this way the Romance configuration finds in locus, not in the hero's imagination, but in the narrator's agenda. At the same time Don Quixote possesses curious interpretive powers that, like Perceval's, empower him to see things denied to mere mortals. In other words his epistemological capabilities make him appear "funny," that is, both mad and comic. This in turn marks him as a grail hero and creates an anticipation of his success in his special quest. This arrangement awakens the reader's sympathy for the knight and likewise undermines the narrator's authority.

The precarious condition of the narrator's privilege further contributes to the Romance horizon of expectations. While in the opening scene of writing the narrator sets himself up as the adjudicator of the hero's story, his version of events has limited authority and accounts for the later shift of reader response to the viewpoint of the hidalgo. This parody of the storytelling methods is an inherited feature of Romance which stacks the cards against the narrator's view of what is happening. He is no more than a bungler, as Eschenbach said of Chrétien, while Don Quixote moves into Perceval's role as the innocent ingenue who is pure of heart.

It is therefore the narrator's mis-reading and mis-handling of the story that is at issue. While earlier Romance narrators in general had trouble understand their own stories and were in this sense incompetent story-tellers, they nevertheless were sympathetic to the hero's trials. Initially at least, this sympathy is missing in Cide Hamete, who enjoys too much the

nasty tricks that other characters play on the hidalgo. In several instance
the beatings and bruises received by the knight are genuinely brutal and
not funny. In contrast, in *Li Contes del Graal* Perceval's humiliations are
limited in their painful effects both because of the narrator's attitude and
the hero's youth. Neither of these attitudes is found in the tone of the
Quixote. The result is that Cide Hamete becomes, as Kermode says of
Mark in his Gospel, the first person to misunderstand the import of the
hero's story.

The Hidden Story of a Hero

> The knight Don Quijote who greets the sunrise over the fields of La
> Mancha is as much a descendent of the gods of solar mythology as the
> paragons of chivalry he emulates
>
> Luis Murillo

Enough of the disguised Romance text is now in place for a subversive
counter-reading to emerge. Most important of all, this hidden story exists
entirely within the narrator's discourse and is not the product of Don
Quixote's "romantic" interpretation of the events. Rather a recognizable
set of signs comes into being that is clearly referential to other texts and,
ironically, to the kind of text the narrator claims to oppose. Furthermore,
because of the chiasmic power of the language, the hero is depicted as
living on the edge of an Otherworld where events follow a Romance pattern
of the kind found in the very texts the narrator appears to be attacking. At
the linguistic level there is a language of chiasmus in which a new narrative is made up of "realistic" substitutions or distortions of Romance features. Thus the flow of events, while presented as taking place within a
realistic environment of random occurrences, is in fact a recognizable
Romance configuration. In the opening section of the *Quixote* the partially
obscured outline of a Romance can be read in the following story:

> A male protagonist lives in a remote and isolated environment.
> As in *Perceval* he inhabits a household of women who are op-
> posed to the male world of heroic chivalry. The only sign of his
> future destiny is his dedication to the hunt. In spite of his soli-
> tariness a type of "geiss" or word spell in the form of the books

of chivalry takes possession of his mind and will power. This causes him to become a member of a warrior class. The hero's "change of consciousness," as in Frye's analysis, marks the beginning of a Romance adventure. The radical alteration in his personality, however, makes him appear crazy and out of contact with the world around him. Even though he has no first hand knowledge of war or battles, he determines to leave his home and go in search of this ideal warrior brotherhood. Like Perceval he assembles a ridiculous collection of arms and armor and, mounted on an unsuitable horse, sets out for the court of a ruler who can initiate him into the world of the warrior caste. At the same time he is also possessed by the image of a woman he has never seen. As in the story of Culhwch his madness is motivated by desire for this woman who exists only as a "word spell" which takes the form of her name. He then embarks on a long series of unrelated adventures loosely strung together in a quest for this woman no one has ever heard of.

This sequence of events, give or take an item or two, clearly signals the opening of a well-known story. The combination of genre features constitutes a tale of adventure found in stories of heroes like CuChulainn, Finn, Oengus, Culhwch, Peredur, and Chrétien's Perceval. Here, within Cide Hamete's tale, a Romance narrative configuration has come to stand.

Gradually the hidden Romance story begins to take over the formulation of events in the life of the "crazy" hero. At the entrance to a *Chastel de la Marche*, the hero is greeted by the significant figures of a pig herder and two degraded women. The phenomenon of women transformed into lower life forms is an echo of women like Pryderi's mother who was originally a horse goddess but appears in the story as woman servant condemned to carry visitors on her back. This condition is then "explained" by the fact that she is being punished for the supposed killing of her son, Pryderi. Her "condition" is, of course, cured by the subsequent revelation of Pryderi's true identity. In the *Quixote* this story pattern is repeated at a realistic/ironic level when the hidalgo, once knighted, bestows titles on the two prostitutes. Another degraded figure, the innkeeper, who is fat and piglike, speaks a strange language which is (mis-)understood by the hero.

By means of these disguises and contradictions the validity of the hidalgo's "reading" of the inn as a castle begins to undermine the narrator's authority. In its essence this problem becomes one of the reader's approach to genre: if the episode is read as a Romance, the protagonist does in fact recognize the disguised ontology of the hostel as a teaching castle like the Gornemant's episode in *Perceval*; contrariwise, if the passage is read as a realistic novel, the hero's interpretation of events indicates he is out of his mind. While this double reading problem could be true of many realistic novels, in the *Quixote* the hermeneutic conflict is deceptively narratized as a struggle between the narrator and the hero, a conflict that at first seems to favor the narrator's assertion that the inn is in fact only an inn. At the same time, the strange language of the innkeeper performs the function of another Romance feature. The innkeeper's double talk is chiasmic and riddlelike. The true meaning of this kind of language can be understood only by the special hero.

In the Romance reading of the situation we recognize that the innkeeper is a retired adventurer who can instruct the hero about many things heroes need to know. This in turn picks up the teaching function of the uncles or other relatives (as in the cases of CuChulainn, Culhwch, Perceval) that the hero meets. At an earlier stage of this kind of narrative these figures can also appear as tricksters or gamesters whose advice contains hidden messages. In the CuChulainn episode just cited, the gamester problematic is encoded in the game of fidchell the uncle is playing with the narrator. The game board and the game of fidchell perform the same function as a special goblet served to the hero in the story of Oengus. Both the game board and the goblet have something to do with verifying the heroic destiny of the protagonist. He who drinks of this cup is the truest hero. Likewise, in a much later tale, *The Dream of Maxen*, the hero sees an ancient figure carving fidchell figures out of gold, which signals that the adventure about to take place has a predestined function. In the *Quixote* the figure of the innkeeper is also associated with the world of gambling, a motif that re-appears much later in the cave of Montesinos. As we have seen, the innkeeper belongs to a border world of criminality (such as law courts) and sea smuggling (such as the playa de Sanlúcar). As a component of the linguistic ambiguity of the inn keeper the protagonist begins to speak in verse forms as he adapts two old ballads, both of which evoke the discourse of a lost world of chivalry. Likewise in the oldest prose tales of the Celts we find inserted verse passages used as dialogue. These poetic inserts are often verse remnants of earlier forms of the story. Thus, in the *Quixote*, the ballad lines bring to life an alternate version of the story we are reading, one that encodes a lost hermeneutic having to do with the loves of Lancelot. This intertextual reference seems to suggest an alternate incarnation of the hero we are reading about, just as Culhwch was originally a swine god or Yvain was a lion deity. In the same way the pun Lanzarote/Don Quixote contains a hidden "message" concerning the ontology of the protagonist who, in a lost or suppressed version of the story, was a warrior of divine dimensions before he assumed his present "degraded" ontology.

In both the Celtic tales and in French Romances the heroes or heroines assume animal or other "dumb" forms except when spoken to by the enchanter. This condition is particularly common in love stories, as in Renaut de Beaujeu's *Le Bel Inconnu*. An alternative strategy is found in a tale like *Yvain*, where the hero is accompanied by an animal companion. This creature is in fact an avatar of the hero carried over from an earlier mythological formulation of the tale. In the inn episode the apparently random appearances of the swineherd and the swine castrator, with their pagan pipes and flutes, also suggest an earlier form of a story in which a swine deity is active in this locale. The castration image, a grail item unnoticed by Don Quixote, introduces the fertility problem of a figure like the Fisher King. This condition encodes a challenge that can be remedied only by a virgin knight.

The knighting of the hero and the conferring of his arms often takes place in a significant locale associated with water. In the medieval ritual of knighting the warrior was actually bathed, a sign that, like Lancelot, he and his sword had a water origin. In the CuChulainn stories he visits loch nEchtrae, the lake of adventure, a site frequented by new warriors. In *Culhwch and Olwen* the heroine has her hair washed in a special bowl, as a replacement for a bath in a lake. In other versions we may find a special well or fountain. In the *Quixote* the locus is suitably the patio of the inn which contains a well. The water also relates to the water-pig ontology of the boar who returns to the sea in the Culhwch tale and with the innkeeper who comes from the Playa de Sanlúcar in the *Quixote*. In Celtic tales a well or a lake usually signals the Otherworld origin of the hero's arms. Both Lanzarote del lago and Arthur obtain their armor from water fays, while medieval illustrations often show women presenting a sword to the knight. At the inn Don Quixote appropriately places his arms on the *pila* of the well which suggests an appropriate water source for his arms.

Then, leaning on his lance as Perceval does outside the tent of Arthur, the hero falls into a love trance from which he is rudely "awakened" by

an uncouth Otherworld figure (Kay/the *harriero*) who opposes the evolution of the strange youth into the perfect warrior. A fight ensues in
which the knight uses his lance to clobber his opponent, breaking his
bones or otherwise wounding him gravely. This situation is remedied by
the arrival of a mediating figure (Gawain/the innkeeper) who succeeds
by means of a special language in peacefully introducing the hero into
the world of the warriors. The teaching figure (Gornemant/innkeeper)
then instructs the hero about the social ways of the warriors and gives
him advice that, in an unforeseen way, mis-leads the hero into a profound error concerning the grail question. In the *Quixote*, the innkeeper
tells the hero to get a squire to carry his magic balsam, money, and clean
shirts. The subsequent introduction of Sancho as squire is presented as
the result of this advice, and in fact it is Sancho who deceives Don Quixote
about his most important adventure, the enchantment and the disenchantment of Dulcinea, so that the hero never does succeed in finding
her. Likewise, the magic balsam leads to other misadventures. Both items
work to prevent Don Quixote from breaking the spell which would presumably reveal the true ontologies of the inn, the heroine, and the hero.
Like his model Lancelot, a thwarted grail knight, Don Quixote will fail
to disenchant the castle or achieve his rightful ontology. It must also be
remembered that the Lancelot image which Don Quixote takes as his
referential identity is a highly arbitrary choice, and this choice inscribes
a condition that cannot be definitively "read." This is one of the most
characteristic features of Celtic art, which presents indeterminate forms
whose meaning is left to the mood of the viewer (Kruta 94).

In the *Quixote* one of the degraded women, a daughter of a miller,
usually considered a thief, and called by the equally degrading name of
La Molinera, presents the hero with his sword. This bit of onomastic
wordplay also indicates a water source for his armament. Other associations with mills and millers are found in the early tales, as in the Miller
of Hell episode in the *Voyage of Maelduin*. In that tale, to be examined
further in connection with Don Quixote's windmill adventure, the mill
seems to connect things of this world with things of the Otherworld. In
this same connection we can also note the link between the *molino de
batanes* episode, where the adventure does concern a water mill and water
sounds, and where the hero finds the magic helmet of Mambrino (pt. 1,
chaps. 20–21). There, Don Quixote refuses to take refuge from a very
arbitrary rainfall by going into the mill and instead goes out on the road,
where he immediately sights the barber's basin being worn as a hat. This

links his most essential piece of armament with a most unlikely water source, since it never again rains in the entire course of the story. Back at the first inn the figure of La Molinera also foreshadows the hero's fight with the *molinos de viento*. In various ways we will find that the inn and the mill episodes are sometimes placed in an either/or situation where one can be substituted for another, indicating that they both deal with Otherworld challenges.

Among all these genre items, one in particular marks the hidalgo as a Romance hero. This is the factor of his change of consciousness, articulated as his "madness." In a Romance tale this mental derangement can take many forms. It may appear as a dream or psychic possession which carries the hero off to a fairyland where he must confront the powers of the Otherworld. In other cases some odd behavior, such as Arthur falling asleep or gambling away the possession of Guinevere, signals the collapse of the normal sequence of cause and effect and the onset of a new order of strange and threatening challenges. Today the best-known modern articulation of this feature is the cataclysm of the tornado in *The Wizard of Oz* when the heroine is hit on the head and carried off from her home in Kansas.

In a more disguised realistic formulation we can recognize instances in which the hero or heroine suddenly takes it into mind to find a new job or get married or go on a trip. These features are easily introduced into a larger "realistic" fabric, where they nevertheless work their powerful magic. In *Fortunata y Jacinta*, the most complex of all Galdós's texts, we find that the madness of Maximiliano or the derangements of Mauricia la Dura all shift the direction of Fortunata's life. In the same way, in Dickens's novels numerous behavioral quirks mark the roles of many secondary characters, the so-called English eccentrics of Victorian London. But even main characters suffer some loss of identity at the outset of their adventures. Oliver Twist, with a patronymic suggestive of his condition, cannot find out who he really is until the string of "adventures" finally leads him back home. In the most famous Spanish picaresque novels the protagonists, Lazarillo and Pablos, are examples of the displaced Romance hero who goes in search of a new identity. In more modern versions of the story the hero may be looking for this hidden identity in a subjective or psychological way, such as we find in the novels of Baroja or Hemingway. These masked forms of strangeness or eccentricity are stock features of realism, but they signal the operation of Romance energies operating within the flow of "ordinary" events.

In the history of the realistic novel the hidalgo is the first and foremost of these disguised protagonists, a man whose *caso de locura* is targeted as the narrator's topic of investigation, a problem subjected to "reasoned" analysis. The "reasoned" motivation, of course, is a camouflaged formulation for the narrator's sense of *aventura*, a factor made clear only at the conclusion of the novel. The nature of Don Quixote's madness has received a curious mix of critical analysis. Sometimes his condition has been more talked about than studied. Often it has been taken as a given in the story, and critical discourse has quickly moved on to other matters. At other times it has been seen merely as a device, as a gimmick that allows the story to go on. In part 2 this attitude is itself both narratized and thematized within the operations of the plot line as the hero discusses his "improving" mental condition. Other analyses have approached this feature as a study in the psychology of madness, subjecting it to a Freudian analytic, while still others have addressed it as part of a new Erasmian attitude toward folly. In most of these approaches, however, the case of madness becomes the focus of the specific analytics of a reasoned modern scientific discipline. The madness is thus "read" according to the highly organized hermeneutics of one or another human science.

Such readings are valuable in themselves and highly persuasive, since we want to rationally understand the mysteries happening within the story. Nevertheless, there is in such approaches an inevitable focus on conflicts that are continuations of the narrator's agenda. They are in this sense wonderful elaborations of forces already at work within Cide Hamete's text. This does not deprive them of heuristic value, but, at the same time, they cannot achieve the force of closure that they aspire to since they are part of the fictions of the text and not, as they claim, genuine examples of external commentary. In this way the critics are like the continuators of the grail romance who set for themselves the goal of re-explaining the story in their own terms.

In effect their weakness is the assumption of the limitless authority of reason. Art by its nature, and paradigmatically the art of Romance, cannot be contained or explained away by the workings of reason. Romance is not a reasoned discourse, and this feature has been and continues to be seen as the prime defect of its discourse. This attitude emerged as soon as Chrétien began adapting the wild, weird, unreasoned Celtic stories for his Flemish audience. The conflict is already articulated within Chrétien's prologues and tales, and it becomes spuriously "externalized" as soon as other writers, including the author of the *Chanson des Saisnes*, categorized the "matière de Bretagne" as vain and foolish. The critical offensive against the disturbing Otherworld authority of Romance achieved a compelling intensity in the neo-Aristotelian aesthetics of the Renaissance, even though most readers persisted in their addictive reading of the romances of chivalry.

In the *Quixote* the crux of this critical contention finds its source in the puzzling ontology of the hero's madness and in *how* this dysfunction comes to signify within the narrative placements and dis-placements of the narrative. By remembering that what we read, presented to us as the *caso* of the hidalgo, is itself an interpretation of Romance signals, we can see that our own reading task has the challenges of addressing two questions: (1) How does such madness present itself in the discourse of Romance? and (2) how does the *Quixote* text alter the formulation? In other words, What does the story do with the problem? In this way the madness must be viewed not as the *cause* of the story but as the *product* of the story. The madness of the hero is an inscribed feature of Romance. The story dictates a change of consciousness, itself a disguise for the Otherworld happenings of a Celtic hero. Such an arrangement relocates the question of his madness within the problematics of how meaning is achieved, rather than within the problematics of psychology. The answer to this kind of question is best found by examining the narratival and textual formulations of the Romance hero's story.

The earliest Celtic tales we possess reveal the textual history of their own transmission. Today we are probably better at reading this transmission history than we are at reading the stories themselves. This means that we can recognize that the hero is presented as a euhemerized being still showing signs of an earlier formulation of the story in which the protagonist was still an Otherworld being. This kind of figure possessed divine attributes, and this accounts for his extraordinary powers usually having to do with love, war, and the ability to read mysterious signs. Such heroes are bound to overcome their adversaries in battle, and in later versions this power takes the form of supreme bravery and self-confidence in situations which would dismay a mere human. But among these capabilities there is also an access to knowledge, including a self-knowledge, which allows them to read the situation in a way not accessible to ordinary humans. Nevertheless poor Peredur/Perceval thinks that deer without horns are goats and that a knight in shining armor is God. But it is his bifurcated epistemological capability that marks him as a Romance hero, and he is fated to triumph in impossible situations.

In the history of Romance this situation is complicated because in the stories of Chrétien and his followers there is already an earlier meaning partially re-written for a new audience. From an anthropological viewpoint we find that the function of the tale is in a state of transformation from a religious telling which in some way reveals the "true" nature of things, to a kind of telling which is closer to the idea of entertainment. This re-categorization as entertainment is a way of de-privileging a kind of knowledge that is not in accord with the dominant beliefs of the society. In the case of Romance the tale is suffering the same fate as its hero: it is falling from a divine state to a more human one. Its "truth" must assume a disguise, so that its pagan ontology (and pagan meaning) doesn't offend a powerful new Christian hermeneutic.

The Song of the Singer and His Song

In the earliest form of the CuChulainn narrative that we possess, the hero's disguised status already makes him exceptional on one level but distinctly odd on another. He is not like the other youthful warriors, and this "condition" is to have a long literary history. The episode from the Childhood Deeds of CuChulainn already cited relates the boy's attempted passage into the band of boy warriors. The boys referred to here are the groups of fifty youths being trained for war. The narrator is an older warrior, now an enemy of the Ulaid clan whose champion CuChulainn is: "When he reached Emuin, he went to the boys without first securing their protection—at that time, no one went to the playing field without a guarantee that the boys would protect him. *CúChulaind was unaware* of this" (Ganz, *Early Irish Myths* 136, emphasis added).

This lack of knowledge is curious for a god. As the son of Lug he is the heir to the categories of knowledge that that deity, a Mercury figure, represented. Of course there is the delimiting of this knowledge represented by his double paternity, since his mother also had a human husband and in one version she is twice impregnated, and in all likelihood there is an incest subtext to boot. Thus Sétentae (his original name meaning "knower of roads") has a more restricted access to the categories of knowledge than those exemplified by his divine father who was master of all skills. In this episode he therefore lacks an awareness of the human rules by which the game of war is played, and his mis-adventures illustrate the spectacular descent of his divine war power (his "riastarthae") and his initiation into human society. Both of these components must be brought into focus before he can begin his adventures. It is in these youthful blunders that the comic element, perhaps a form of primitive unease when dealing with the divine, first appears. The formulation signals a specific story which reads in this way: the boy is an unlikely hero because he is odd and often foolish, but in time his real powers will become evident. As we have seen, the opening adventures of Don Quixote fit comfortably into this narrative pattern. What is significantly different is the age of the hero, which makes him even more comic, and the fact that the early deeds, his *mocedades*, are going to be much prolonged. In fact this narrative phase is never entirely transcended in the *Quixote*. Such distortions of genre features are commonplace in the transformations they suffer, as Alastair Fowler has shown. For instance, the traditional descent into hell of the epic hero, originally just one episode in the *Aeneid* becomes in the *Divina Commedia* the entire *Inferno*. (172).

The CuChulainn's initiation process will have two stages: first he will conflict with the other boy warriors, and then a teaching uncle will take over his education and provide him with the necessary social competence to assume his rightful place as a leader in a purely human clan or warrior caste. This scenario is the model for countless later stories of a youthful hero coming from a world of women and, after initial difficulties, establishing himself as the most glorious hero of his time. The situation has endless variations, but Perceval's entry into the court of Arthur is perhaps the most famous example. However, similar situations appear in modified ways in almost all the heroes' tales: Finn, Culhwch, Yvain, Erec, Peredur, and so on.

It is this sequence of events that programs the story of Don Quixote's visit to the first inn. What is consistent in all the articulations is that the protagonist instinctively knows he is a special hero, but he lacks what we would call the "necessary social competence" to function effectively in the society in which he lives. He is in fact a throwback, a survival from an earlier mythological version of the same story. He knows many things but not the social codes of the belated world in which he is trying to operate. A clear separation of his powers of knowing and not knowing is not possible because he can shift his frequencies with mercurial facility, so to speak, and at unexpected times speak with impressive eloquence. At these moments he, like the solar knight, is invincible while at other moments this power dissipates and he merely seems disoriented.

In the *Quixote* this everyday social incompetence is the ever available source of comic effect, but all this is the result of a powerful personal hermeneutic which he can call into action. In this sense the capabilities of his fractured epistemology provide the necessary foreknowledge that shapes his hermeneutics. Like all great teachers, like Buddha or Christ, Don Quixote astounds with his disturbing way of looking at everyday reality. This kind of hermeneutic event makes us see the world anew, the certain sign of a radical teacher with a subversive agenda.

The refractive angle of his insights, twisted away from the trivia of a quotidian reality, reveals the hidden contents that inform his vision. Like the genre, whose icon he becomes, Don Quixote's archive includes a broad spectrum of texts that include both Romance and non-Romance stories he has read with his own hermeneutic. As with the structure of Romance itself, these stories interlock; that is, they fit one into the other to form an overarching metastory, and they are understandable only in that narrative context. A reader has to know something of the stories of Arthurian and other Romance figures before being able to "read" the nature of Don Quixote's madness. This body of other stories is not sharply defined or delimited, and the hero will refer to some of them, but Druidlike, he picks and chooses from this hidden repertoire of texts in mysterious ways. As both Cide Hamete and other characters in the work comment, Don Quixote has surprising capabilities that allow him to set forth his ideas in highly articulate ways. The famous sermons on love (pt. 1, chap. 11) or arms and letters (pt. 1, chap. 32) are the most impressive of these discourses. When he so speaks, he is enjoying moments of high inspiration in which he ranges broadly over the multiple horizons of knowledge. At these times he expresses a type of truth informed by access to a more abstract Truth that seems to lie behind the nature of his vision.

Myles Dillon discusses the ordering power of a transcendent Truth that informs both Celtic and Vedic texts (74ff.) The basic factor of this belief is that the Truth is the basic ordering and sustaining force in the universe, and it endows the language of the storyteller with divine presence. This explains the ultimate logocentric power to which the language of Romance aspires. This special language is the language of the gods, to which the poet or storyteller has access through the strange capabilities of genius. This arrangement accounts for the Celtic belief in the immeasurable power of storytelling. Rhetorically, remnants of this belief still survive in the formulaic phrases used by Irish storytellers, reminding their listeners that divine or magic benefits could be derived from listening to the tale (Dillon 75; Rees and Rees 17). This tag is the key back to the ancient belief in a Truth that was the ordering power of the universe. This attitude became demonized during the Middle Ages, which accounts for the multiple attacks on the "vanity" of the Matter of Britain. In the *Quixote* just such a belief in the demonic power of language is what underlies the housekeeper's and the priest's fear of the books of chivalry that "cause" the hidalgo's madness. The difficulty today in reading the "meaning" of this madness is due to our diminished capability to recognize the narrative function of madness in Romance.

Within the structure of primitive Celtic society only kings, heroes, and Druids had access to the ordering energy of this sustaining Truth, and in moments of fateful decisions the Druid was needed to advise the king. This arrangement can still be read in the role of Merlin in the Arthurian fictions, and it is the survival of this situation that allows for the effectiveness of the Merlin tricks in part 2 of the *Quixote*. In the same way Don Quixote's imaginative archive of Truth is a potent mix of a special language and a secret knowledge that in the earlier tales would be clearly divine or sacred. The fall in the prestige of that kind of knowledge within the relentless rise of neo-Aristotelian rationalism in the twelfth century and of the new science in the seventeenth century accounts for Don Quixote being considered a crazy fool. But at the same time the suppression of the old magic by the new scientific dispensations created a sudden need for another kind of expression of the old repressed modes of knowing. *Don Quixote* as a work of art provided a new habitation for that kind of release. Cervantes' achievement was a re-articulation of Romance for the modern rationalized world of the seventeenth century. In this sense Don Quixote's madness provided the vehicle for an expression of the struggle between the "wild" Truth of the old Celts within the rigid world of Bacon's *Novum Organum*. In the *Quixote* Cervantes produced a new kind of story and a new kind of hermeneutics with which to read the history of this radical change in the human condition. His seventeenth-century readers found their own epistemological situation narratized for them in the endless encounters of Don Quixote with the quotidian reality of the new dispensation of truth. Like a new Perceval he was the hero of the epistemological border crossings of the modern world, and the innkeeper's chiasmic language provides access to both the world of reason and the world of unreason.

The way this story is told is defined by the unstable ontology of the narrator. The question is what he knows and *how* does he know it. Like the hero he too exists with fractured epistemological resources; he too lives on the edge of kinds of knowing. Like Chrétien's narrator he is positioned so that he is knowledgeable about the society in which he lives and the rules by which it operates, and while his ways of knowing are much more socially acceptable than those of the hero, he too has a secret archive. Ostensibly the story is told with a certain amount of patronizing humor directed at the hero. He sets up a conspiracy of knowledge between himself and his audience as they both laugh at the socially foolish mistakes of the hero. It is this conspiracy that makes the hero seems like a middle-aged idiot, as opposed to the idiot child formulation found in the cases of CuChulainn and Perceval.

At the same time there are serious lacunae in the narrator's epistemological resources. He really does not know about the divine energies which are the source of the hero's power. Thus a crucial element of the novel is the narrator's failure to understand the meaning of his own tale. His blindness means that he lacks the proper hermeneutics with which to decode the narrative, and this factor is also an inherited genre feature. For this reason the narrator's conspiracy with the audience is vulnerable, and it slowly collapses as the audience gradually shifts its allegiance to the hero. Since the story depicts a hero with curious epistemological resources that gives him access to an important but overlooked truth, the hidalgo ultimately proves to be more right than wrong. By definition, a true hero is the person who best reads the situation, so that in time the audience for his story will come to partake of his "strange" hermeneutic. In that way the listener of the tale is improved and endowed with some of the power the tale ultimately encodes. For ordinary people the access to this Truth and its dynamic and controlling power provided the basis for the fear that the story seemed to have the power to enchant.

In primitive Celtic societies it was the general acceptance of this belief that accounts for the immense prestige of the storytellers, but this prestige declined as the old magic became demonized. The special class of trained narrators vanished as the Druids were replaced by the Christian priesthood. Thus, the stories we have are the productions of later less powerful storytellers, but nevertheless something of their original more powerful ontology still clings to them. The important but more modest position of court entertainers in the Welsh Middle Ages represents a serious loss of authority and prestige, and this social adjustment in effect epitomizes the collapse of the old order of things. It is from these Welsh storytellers that *The Mabinogion* tales receive their final redaction. In this

formulation the narrator is already alienated from the original understanding of the story, and a new articulation of the story is developed for
a new audience.

In the case of Chrétien this condition is even more true, since his
prefatory statements about simple *contes d'aventure* indicate that he believed they lacked what he considered sense or coherent meaning *(sen)*.
As a result he sought to impose an entirely foreign meaning on the
stories which expressed a new beliefs in reason and *courtoisie*. In his
successors this new *sen* moved increasingly toward a Christian
allegorization of the story in which the meaning of the mysterious grail
seemed to tell a story of spiritual redemption. The prevalence of an allegorical hermeneutic in the Middle Ages made these kinds of stories the
favored readings of cultivated audiences throughout Europe. Nevertheless the original ontology of the barbaric tales remained sufficiently intact beneath the veneer of an allegorizing hermeneutic to account for
their curious and disturbing appeal. Somehow the hidden image of a
primitive grail platter containing a severed head floating in blood seemed
to remain visible behind the representation of a chalice containing a mass
wafer. Even the idea that the grail contained such a wafer, it must be
remembered, was not present in the grail scene itself. Perceval did not
see a wafer. This interpretation is only an assertion of the hermit Perceval
meets much later in the story, a hermit who attempts to explain to Perceval
what has happened to him. Likewise the external reader of the tale never
directly perceives the wafer in the grail. No doubt the fact that the Christian wafer is itself a substitution for a blood sacrifice contributed to the
strength of this ghost reading of the scene. At the same time a sense of
unease surrounds the appearance of the hermit in the tale, and it is at
this juncture that violent anti-Semitism finds its expression. This would
indicate that the Jews have become the substitute for the ritual victim
role originally belonging to the knight himself. What is most important
to remember, therefore, is that the wafer interpretation exists in the text
as only one of various explanations presented to Perceval to explain his
failure.

In this way the half-survival of a more primitive version of the story
endowed Romance with the feeling of enchantment that so disturbed the
warriors and churchmen who ruled the new society. Within this historical development the stories achieved an unprecedented popularity, but
at the same time they remained—and still remain—outside the approved
canon of a literature that celebrates the power of reason, of cause and

effect, and of a male commonsense reality in which the lurking energy of the old magic is kept out of sight. It was perhaps only the total dis-empowerment of women in medieval society that allowed for the survival of the Matter of Britain. Since women legally did not exist in the new order, what they read was not so rigidly controlled. Thus we see that even today the literature of and by women has still not emerged into the canon of approved texts.

This story of the unresolved tensions within the ontology of Romance received its ultimate re-formulation in the *Quixote*. There the conflict between the threatening energy of Romance and what is deemed acceptable or normal by an increasingly "rational-ized" culture is what creates the extraordinary power of Cervantes' text. To a great extent it is the drama of the survival of Romance as a genre that is at risk in the *Quixote*. Nevertheless the articulation of this epistemological dichotomy within the story line is not a simplistic struggle between the narrator and the hero. In fact they are both enmeshed in the same struggle, a struggle of the narrator's agenda against a suppressed countertext found within the story. The authority in the narrator's interpretation is already a Romance item and therefore cannot contain the appeal of the knight's adventures. The narrator tells the tale but never recognizes that he himself is the propagator of this Romance. He cannot see that he is in fact telling the story of an ancient hero returned to the modern world in the disguise of a foolish hidalgo. Because of these buried contra-dictions, Cide Hamete's discourse creates the diverse readings it has received.

Cide Hamete never does have his supper at Emmaus in which he suddenly is able to recognize the deity disguised within the appearance of a common traveler. Perhaps it is not coincidence that Cervantes' younger contemporaries, Caravaggio and Rembrandt, created the two most powerful images of that fateful supper. The scene must be read as a dramatization of a profound hermeneutic break, a re-imaging of what was happening in seventeenth century science. Not only does Cervantes' narrator remain blind to the ontology of his hero—at the end of his story Cide Hamete is left fighting the shades of Romance that he himself has unleashed. The scene of writing with which the story ends is thus the narratization of the danger inherent in certain kinds of art. The question of nobility of Don Quixote could achieve institutionalized status only with the coming of the Romantics, and this reveals their enthusiasm for the transcendent meaning hidden in the story of a crazed hidalgo.

Nevertheless, for the postmodern world Don Quixote as a hero can be seen as inhabiting the dangerous borderland between divinity and a dyslexic dementia. Though admired and beloved he is still often not taken "seriously" because the raucous humor of his story is not recognized as the sign of the divinity hidden in his tale. For this reason the work is still generally ranked below that of "serious" works like *Oedipus*, the *Divina Commedia*, *Hamlet*, and *Faust*. In this context it is significant for instance to realize that Erich Auerbach's curious chapter "The Enchanted Dulcinea" in his masterwork *Mimesis* was not originally part of that book. It was added for purposes of the completeness of his dominant thematic "The Representation of Reality in the Western World." Yet it doesn't "fit" within that rubric. Whatever the validity of Auerbach's reading, both the essay and its topic remain precisely on the edge of the dominant hegemony of Western culture that he attempts to define. Rather, as a narrative work the *Quixote* still belongs to a pre-Western articulation of the "reality" that civilization has tried to suppress. In this sense the *Quixote* is the most non-Western of the Western masterworks because it radically subverts the modes of knowing and being created by that civilization. In spite of the brilliance of its best readers from Dostoyevsky to Borges, the text of the fallen Druid Cide Hamete and his un-named editor still awaits its most radical reading.

The accumulation of "unreadable" Romance signs within the text is impressive, but whatever sum that list achieves, one of the most basic indications of its Romance ontology is the limited understanding of the self-presented narrators and editors found in the text. The story as an entity is always beyond the totality of their contradictory presentations and readings, a factor that signals the existence of a source of long forgotten and all powerful knowledge within the text. This kind of knowledge does not present itself as a seamless totality. At its source in Celtic culture such Truth exists only in the multi-categoried crafts of the gods like the Dagda or Lug, and in the lesser craftiness of their illegitimate warrior offspring. These creatures are fated to pass through the world as wanderers, half-admired and half-scorned. They are at one moment cherished as the redeeming hero and at other times the butt of jokes and, like Lancelot, pelted with dung and killed off as sacrifices. Don Quixote is the most comic of these heroes but that very fact further enhances his hold on his audiences, who both love him and laugh at him, even as they weep at the curious scene of his death. Cide Hamete evokes no such adulation; he is forgotten as a disposable item. That is his punishment for not understanding the story.

Cervantes is also sometimes forgotten. At least his fame is much less than that of his hero. Many people know of the crazy knight who tilts at windmills who have never heard the name of Cervantes. The account of that particular *aventura* constitutes the single most famous scene in all of secular literature. The question of how such an achievement came about is perhaps unanswerable, but the story of how the knight's attack on a windmill came to signify is not.

The Windmill of Hell

> The wall of Paradise is built of contraries, nor is there any way to enter but for one who has overcome the highest spirit of reason who guards the gate.
>
> Nicolas of Cusa

For some as yet unexplained reason the entire world knows about the lunatic knight who attacked the windmill. Hundreds of thousands, perhaps millions of drawings, paintings, statues, and other representations of it have circulated the globe like a coinage of uncertain value. In the same way, linguistic echoes of it are found embedded in most European languages. In English the phrase "tilting at windmills" is proverbial, and it can be used without any overt reference to Don Quixote. The exact reasons for the worldwide fame of this episode are not at first sight easy to comprehend. In fact the meaning of the scene as Cervantes presents it is not at all clear in the sense that a reader reading it for the first time today would necessarily come to any single pre-determined interpretation. Nearly five centuries of reading have endowed it with a sense of struggle between the nobility of courage and failure, but it has never received an institutional reading, and perhaps because of that condition, it has remained open to gradual shifts of meaning. As a result this indeterminacy has endowed it with the power to engage the human imagination. Like the grail, it has escaped the prison house of an exact signification and remains a floating signifier. But at the same time we can only surmise that buried somewhere in its articulation there lies an occult power, a numinous appeal, which speaks softly of eroded meanings and forgotten messages. Nothing else could account for the enduring attraction of Don Quixote and Sancho's first *aventura*.

What this tells us is that what we read is "the half-said thing" and that outside the story there exists another story, different from the one we have before us. This story seems to exist in that secret archive from which the Cide Hamete works, like some latter-day Druid who has half forgotten his own wisdom. It is that other text, that other wisdom that propels the story, urges it forward, and ignites Don Quixote's, and the reader's, imaginative powers. The operation of this other text, not visible to the eye of reason, seduces the reader into wishing Don Quixote well, into joining him in his passionate search for adventure and in his desire to find a meaning hidden in the banal commonplaces of the quotidian reality that oppresses him. In that enterprise the reader finds the secret appeal of a personal freedom and the forbidden fulfilment of an existence reserved only for gods and sons of gods. But the exact nature of that appeal remains amorphous and unarticulated. The flow of meaning for the reader lies concealed somewhere in the text, but we are not certain whether its source is buried in the past, disguised in its present state, or still to be discovered in a future revelation.

The humor itself verifies that there has to be another meaning of the event in order for the event to appear comically inappropriate. No event can be funny without some other text, some other reading, some other wisdom. It is that aspect of all humor that inscribes the existence of another interpretation. The windmill scene is funny in the comic sense but "funny" also carries the implication of uncanny.

It is well known that a certain kind of obscurity is the hallmark of Celtic art. This characteristic is found in both their linguistic and visual artifacts, in the swirling decorative patterns of their metallic work and in the elliptical rhetoric of the their poetry. In his discussion of Irish and Welsh poetry the French Celticist J. Vendryes states: "It is obscure because by tradition the poets wished to keep it so. It conceals as much as it suggests, perhaps more so." Myles Dillon has identified a similar quality in Sanskrit poetry, where we have more evidence to work on. The quality of the obscurantism there has been given a name by Hindi theorists. "It is known as dhvani, that which is not expressed in words." An early treatise on poetics (ca. A.D. 850) states: "a good poem must have two things, that which is said in words and fittingly adorned in diction, and that which is unsaid and must be imagined by the hearer. This that is unsaid is the true soul of poetry" (Dillon 67–68). Anyone familiar with contemporary reader response criticism will recognize in this concept an anticipation of current hermeneutic concerns. For the critic of

Romance, however, such a condition is a familiar enough feature of the text, since each reader may dredge up from unknown sources unique meanings and interpretations. The grail banquet in Chrétien and the hero's attack on the windmill in Cervantes are the two most famous instances of this kind of writing in Western literature. Their success is due to what is unsaid, to what exists outside the language in which they are articulated. The question then becomes how this is effected in the *Quixote*.

The narrator, we remember, questioned whether the adventure of the inn, Puerto Lapice, or the windmill came first in the narrative sequence of the hero's actions. This gesture in one sense equates the three episodes, at least in the mysterious source texts from which the narrator claims to be working. The equivalence of temporal precedence suggests also an equivalence of function for the three encounters, and we have already seen that the ontology of the inn is not as clear cut as the narrator would like us to believe. While it remains an inn or hostel, it seems inhabited by persons and forces that are suggestive of other states of being, states of being (familiar to readers of Romance) in which Otherworld forces can be activated. The misadventures of the hero in this environment put him in contact with a strange language, a challenge well, the power of the moon, degraded women, special armaments, and curious pig identities not often found in real-life inns. While the surface realism is never strained, or is barely strained, the actions remain consistent with Romance patterns suggestive of the adventures of Lancelot and Perceval, two heroes who seek the grail. Thus in all these situations we find the ontology of the inn to be haunted by the same kind of Otherworld forces that operate in the various castles visited by Romance heroes. It follows that the next edifice the protagonist encounters may also be invested with an ontological presence other than the one insisted upon by the narrator. The windmill, like the inn, has a secret story of its own.

Explorations of this story can take two directions: (1) the extra-textual associations with mills and (2) the other mill adventures within the *Quixote* itself. Starting with the second point we find that a significant capacity that all the mill scenes have in common is their effect on Don Quixote: they all represent for him a hostile force that challenges or tests his chivalric identity. Such a capacity within a Romance articulation would of course represent an Otherworld threat that the hero is called upon to overcome. Furthermore, the recognition of this challenge is part of the singular hermeneutic capacity of the hero, one that defines his heroic identity. In all three mill episodes, and more so than in any other adventure he encounters, Don Quixote recognizes the mills as a personal summons to a meeting with his destiny. The three encounters or *echtrai* are the attack on the windmill (pt. 1, ch. 8), the night adventure with the *molino de batanes* (pt. 1, ch. 20) in which Sancho is physically endangered, and the escapade with the *barco encantado* (pt. 2, ch. 29) in which both Don Quixote and Sancho are genuinely at risk. In all three episodes Don Quixote is defeated and has to fall back on ingenious explanations for his failure.

However, another kind of significance seems to be attached to these adventures and to the role they play in the knight's story: all three encounters are followed by a fundamental change in narrative procedures. The first one is followed by the Puerto Lapice encounter with the Vizcaino which introduces the name of Cide Hamete and the entrance of a second editor into the narrative strategy. The second mill adventure is immediately followed by his finding of the helmet of *Mambrino* which introduces an elaborate narrative *entrelacement* referential to Ariosto's *Orlando furioso.* In part 2 the third mill episode immediately precedes Don Quixote's meeting with the duchess, a development which provides the central narrative focus of this part. Thus the three adventures are significant not only for the hero's identity but for the way in which the story is to be told. They seem to stand out from the landscape like three signposts, three herms that mark fundamental border crossings for both the hero and his story. In this way the mill episodes achieve a special hermeneutic power because they stand for the self-referential agenda of the text itself.

At the same time all three adventures threaten to undo the chivalric incarnation because, as hero, he should be able to recognize his fateful *aventura.* Yet he appears to err in his "reading" of the nature of the mill's challenge. For this reason he is particularly at risk when he ignominiously fails, even though his interpretation had been rhetorically seductive in its own right. In the windmill episode he names for the first time the actions of an enemy enchanter; in the *molino de batanes* he produces his most poetic and evocative exposition of the nature of the challenge awaiting the true hero; while in the *barco encantado* failure he insists that the river mill holds important personages imprisoned by an Otherworld force that only he, the grail knight, can overcome.

The last encounter replicates the Modena Architrave adventure in which Guinevere, held captive by an Otherworld lord, is rescued by Arthur and Gawain. This challenge has a strong hold on Don Quixote's imagination as we have seen in both the cave of Montesinos episode and during the puppet show staged at an inn. The third mill adventure prefigures the central importance of this motif for part 2 since it immediately precedes Don Quixote's meeting with the duchess. The importance of this chance meeting becomes clear at the house of the duke and duchess when they create the subterfuge of the knight's climactic meeting with Merlin. It is there that he learns how to disenchant Dulcinea, a trick that provides the narrative vehicle for the remainder of part 2. Thus all three mill adventures signal fundamental changes in Don Quixote's story. The first mill immediately precedes a radical alteration in the way the story is told. The second mill foreshadows the shift to an elaborate *entrelacement* configuration of interpolated stories which dominates part 1. The third mill dramatizes the force of a rescue challenge that provides the narrative core of part 2, the enchantment of Dulcinea by Merlin.

The Danger at the Mill

Before examining the three mill encounters, we must review the traditional views associated with mills, both in Romance texts and in popular beliefs about mills in Hispanic and in foreign cultures. In the latter category it is probable that associations similar to the one prevalent in Spain enjoyed a wide acceptance because of the scene's immediate success all over Europe. For one thing, mills of various kinds were a very ancient technology so that long familiarity with them had allowed for a considerable folklore to develop and spread. This phenomenon has been extensively studied by Giorgio de Santillana and Hertha von Dechend in *Hamlet's Mill*, where the worldwide knowledge of the Hamlet tale is examined. Their analysis reveals the mill's universal association with the idea of fate.

These beliefs in fact found expression within the very oldest Celtic texts. An episode concerning the Miller of Hell is found in the Irish tale of the *Voyage of Maelduin*. This tale belongs to the Celtic genre of the *immrama*, a tale of sea wandering best known today in the Christianized Voyage of St. Brendan. In the Maelduin story the hero travels by boat from island to island seeking a way in which to avenge his father's murder. Each island locale has its special enchantment and danger with which the hero and his companions must contend. Rees and Rees have suggested that what we have is an eroded version of a Celtic Book of the Dead in which a hero voyages to a series of Otherworld locales, each of which represents the state of the soul as it journeys to its final resting place (325). Readers of Cervantes will recognize this narrative pattern in the first two books of his *Persiles* where the hero and his troop have a succession of mysterious adventures as they sail through the same northern seas found in the Maelduin story.

In the Miller of Hell episode the hero's ship comes to an island in which there is a mill whose function is to grind up all the unwanted things of this world and ship them off "to the west," a metaphor for the Celtic Otherworld. The story reminds us how very ancient the technology of mills is and that even at such an early time associations with the Otherworld were already part of its image. On the island Maildun asks the miller the meaning of all they have seen. The miller, a "huge-bodied, strong, burly man," replies:

> This mill is called the Mill of Inver-tre-Kenand, and I am the miller of hell. All corn and all riches of the world that men are dissatisfied with, or which they complain of in any way, are sent here to be ground; and also every precious article, and every kind of wealth, which men try to conceal from God. All these I grind in the Mill . . . and send them afterwards away to the west. He spoke no more, but turned round and busied himself again with his mill. And the voyagers, with much wonder and awe in their hearts, went to their curragh and sailed away. (Joyce 96)

This story, which is preserved in the oldest manuscript of Gaelic tales, provides us with a base line, so to speak, of beliefs associated with mills. The terms *hell* and *God* undoubtedly represent Christianized versions of pagan concepts, but the tone of revealing an ancient belief still survives. The mill clearly functions as an access point to the Otherworld, generally believed by the early Irish to be located in islands to the west. Such islands, like O'Brasil, were often times visible only once every seven years and then only to special heroes. As in the nineteenth-century tale of the drunken Watty O'Neil cited by Loomis, these locales were associated with a treasure held under enchantment. In the Loomis tale, as in the case of the grail castle, the enchantment could be broken by the formulation of a question. But the mode of disenchantment was variable. In the instance of the island of O'Brasil the hero had to ignite fire on it in order to keep in from disappearing beneath the waves. This story has been associated with the Portuguese naming of Brasil (Sharrer). Thus these kinds of locales contained a hidden ontology which could possibly be revealed by ritual performances. However, even if they were not associated with enchantment, the hero, as in the case of Maelduin, is privileged and in some sense enriched by merely seeing such places. In the final episode of the *Voyage of Maelduin* the hero is relieved of the burden of avenging the murder of his father. Thus the accumulated adventures lead him to a resolution of a problem and to a new appreciation of his home. While specific meanings are difficult to identify in this tale, the feeling of wonderment as the hero and his friends wander from island to island, all of which contain enigmatic content, creates the pattern of prolonged episodic encounters leading back to a home from which the hero is in someway estranged. This format is endlessly repeated in Romance literature where the heroes and heroine are involved in a sequence of strange encounters. *Alice in Wonderland* and *The Wizard of Oz* utilize both the narrative arrangement and the thematic content of this kind of tale.

The lack of a finite closure typical of these tales is the same factor that Don Quixote himself recognizes as a genre feature of the endless books of chivalry, and it must be remembered that the task of finishing such a story was the first challenge faced by the hidalgo. The pattern is universal in world folklore but the particular articulation of it for the *Quixote* is the one found in the Celtic tales and their Romance progeny. For this reason it is likely that Don Quixote's mill adventures contain an Otherworld challenge in which he must discover a truth hidden in the mill. This pattern is also encoded in the image of the "rich Fisher King" whose wealth, sexual and otherwise, is constrained by his wound. The feature of the hero's spell-breaking question is repeatedly assayed in the Cervantes' text by Don Quixote habit of interrogating the people he meets. Sometimes, as with Cardenio, Don Quixote's questions do begin a process of "disenchantment"; in that case the process eventually leads to Cardenio's transformation from his wild state to his status as a true Christian and gentleman (Dudley and Novak 115–39). In other cases, Don Quixote fails to achieve a disenchantment. Ginés de Pasamonte (pt. 1, ch. 22), for instance, cannot be redeemed by Don Quixote's questions, nor do we ever read his unfinished picaresque tale. That genre remains unredeemed by Cervantes novelistic powers, since it contains entrenched devilish forces beyond the reach of the hero's capability. But in all the interpolated tales told by afflicted heroes and heroines to Don Quixote we sense something of the power of a verbal disenchantment, of a breaking of a wordspell or geiss such as those found in the primitive Celtic tales. In this sense the *Quixote* presents the story of a question-asking hero who seeks to disenchant the protagonists of the interpolated tales in part 1.

At first glance it would seem that such primitive beliefs would have been forgotten by Cervantes' time, but the association of mills with forces beyond human control has persisted into our own time. Even today this sense of a hidden danger has not fully disappeared. One thinks, for instance, of Hitchcock's successful evocation of evil in the film *Foreign Correspondent,* where a peace seeking diplomat is kidnaped in Holland and held prisoner in a windmill. The camera's careful exploration of the internal mechanical movements of the mill add to the eerie and fateful atmosphere of the locale. Ingmar Bergman explores this same sense of evil in *Virgin Spring.* Likewise, in fiction, Le Carré is not above utilizing a similar ambience in *Smiley's People,* also for a kidnap episode, while the title of a popular bestseller like *Windmill of the Gods* still evokes a vague idea of fate associated with the image of the wheel of fortune.

In Spanish this survival is linguistically recorded in popular sayings comparing the *rueda* (wheel) of the mill stone with the *rueda de fortuna,* an image cited in the *Quixote* text itself: "Que la rueda de la fortuna anda mas lista que una rueda de molino" (see Fernández Gómez 916 for this and other citations in Cervantes) [For the wheel of fortune turns more rapidly than the wheel of a mill]. This traditional metaphor evokes a deep seated association of mills with the workings of fortune. The literal image of the turning of the millstone is also specifically pictured by Sancho as he tries to explain the function of the mill to Don Quixote. Thus something infernal lingers around the curious mechanics of mills and the popular idea of getting something for nothing, an achievement traditionally associated with danger. Both Correas and Horozco record similar sayings in their collections of *refranes* (popular sayings) under the topic of the mill. According to Professor Barbara Heinemann, the association of the mill with demonic forces is also found in Germany, where mills are popularly referred to as "the devil's house." This popular sense of the sinister is utilized by George Elliot in *Silas Marner,* where the outcast takes refuge in a remote mill symbolizing the outer limits of the society and where more than one chance event changes the protagonist's life. The same referential force may lie at the source of Blake's celebrated phrase "dark satanic mills" where "satanic" expresses the idea of an infernal force.

Other Hispanic instances which associate mills and millers to the matter of tricks, deceptions, and petty criminality are fairly common. Lazarillo de Tormes' father is obviously part of this tradition, although we sense there is also the echo of Amadís de Gaula having been born along a river. Likewise, the river house to which his Amadis' mother repairs in order to secretly give birth to the hero, although ostensibly a type of hermitage, is also a place of deception. Later in Spanish culture we have also the tricks performed in Alarcón's *Sombrero de tres picos* as well as in Manuel de Falla's ballet of the same title. Falla's original title, *El corregidor y la molinera,* gives even more prominence to the miller/trick motif. This same association is also recorded in a sixteenth-century linguistic item cited in Peter Boyd Bowman's *Lexico Hispanoamericano del siglo XVI.* He records the following reference to tricks associated with mills from a letter written in Mexico City by an ordinary citizen: "me allano por el suelo y pecho por tierra pido perdón de lo que los *he molido con embustes* de que me pesa en el corazón" (597, emphasis added). Another Hispanist, Professor Juan Fernández, tells me that in his native Navarra a belief that a mill is a place of trickery and deception is still extant.

A crucial association with mills is inscribed in the *Quixote* text itself with Sancho's famous reference to madness and windmills: "que no eran sino molinos de viento, y no lo podía ignorar sino quien llevase *otras tales en la cabeza*" (pt. 1, ch. 8, emphasis added) [for they were nothing but wind mills, and no one could ignore that who didn't have similar ones in his head]. Similar association are found in proverbs listed by Horozco relating wind to instability, love, madness, fortune, and even deceiving words. In all these citations mills, windmills and millstones suggest meanings associated with Otherworld forces, and the consistent response of Don Quixote to mills that confirms this meaning. His reaction consistently takes the form that the mill represents a call from destiny, a call that locates threatening forces of madness, the Otherworld, and deception in the figure of a mill. One must suppose that some or all of these associations strengthened the universal appeal of the scene of a mad knight and a windmill, two icons representing an ideal form of human identity pitted against a powerful infernal force.

Evidence that something of this meaning still clings to the image of windmills and is found in the work of the Chilean poet Vicente Huidobro. In *Altazor,* his long poetic meditation on the role of language and creative genius in the modern world, he makes repeated references to *molinos* which play with the multiple significations still associated with the image. His litany of *molino* rhymes—*molino de viento, molino de aliento, molino de cuento,* and so forth—express a remarkable list of associations that echo those found in the *Voyage of Maelduin,* where the mill grinds up the multiplicity of earthly things for transit to another level of existence. Mireya Camurati finds Huidobro's mill images often associated with the idea of time (126 ff.) The final two stanzas of his celebrated *molino* poem evoke the haunting feeling of irreparable loss of being to the workings of time:

> He aquí el verdadero molino
> No olvidéis jamás su canción
> El hace llover y hace el buen tiempo
> El hace las cuatro estaciones
> Molino de la muerte Molino de la vida
> Muele los instantes como un reloj
> Estos también son granos Molino de la melancolía
> Harina del tiempo que pondrá
> a nuestros cabellos blancos

> [Here is the true mill
> Don't ever forget its song
> It makes the rain and the good weather
> It makes the four seasons
> Mill of Death Mill of Life
> It grinds up the moments like a clock
> These too are the kernels
> Mill of Melancholy
> The flour that turns our hair white]

No post-Cervantine text in Spanish can be certified free of Quixotesque intertextuality, but at the same time Huidobro's wordplay also invokes associations that recall Maelduin's infernal mill as well.

This overview of the referentiality of mills provides a useful threshold from which to approach again the most celebrated adventure of the aging knight.

The Story of the Three Mills as the Story of the Text

The story of the three mill episodes provides us with a reading lesson of unquantifiable dimensions—unquantifiable in that three is a mystic number whose value is not limited to its *ratio* value. Numerology, the belief that certain numbers possess a value not based on their numerical count, is perhaps as old as the science of numbers itself. Alwyn Rees and Brinley Rees devoted an entire chapter to the numerology of the ancient Irish in their *Celtic Heritage*. It would seem that most numbers had some "other" meaning, three being particularly prominent. The sign 666 as a mark for the anti-Christ is a universal symbol, one we can also read as meaning an anti-logos or for anti-meaning in the sense of loss of meaning or, more radically, for the loss of the possibility of meaning. The relationship of this kind of reading to the system of numbers signifying six hundred and sixty six units is not at all clear.

In the same way we recognize that three, as half of six, is a mystic number, both for Christians and for Celts, and that in Ireland the two traditions easily conflated. Trinity College, Dublin, can be read as a sign of devotion to the Christian belief in a triune Godhead, but we also note that the pagan Celts carved three-faced gods and worshiped a configuration of three goddesses. Triplication seems to have enhanced the power of almost any item, horses, women, kings (Green 214) In Wales there is a legend of three Guineveres indicating her divinity and mercurial presence. The pious legend of St. Patrick utilizing the shamrock to preach the truth of the Christian Trinity combines the two traditions without totalizing the dominance of the Christian signification. So it happened that in its historical development the new Irish church proceeded to refurbish the old symbols without suppressing much of the earlier content. Druids were replaced by priests, but the people's attitudes toward the Christian clergy retained the attitudes always assigned to the earlier caste. In this sense both sign and meaning often survived with a modicum of disruption.

Even in the revival of Irish literature associated with Yeats and Joyce we can still read another mode of meaning surviving within their use of modern English. Joyce spoke of re-creating the Celtic consciousness in his writing and proceeded to distort the forms and meanings of English words. In another way Yeats's reversion to emblematic imagery as opposed to "natural" metaphors, a process traced by Paul de Man, has the same arrangement of two meanings inscribed in each metaphor (145–238).

In one crucial category of thought, however, a rupture of meaning did occur. The role of the poets and their stories did suffer a radical (at the root) change. Liberated from their earlier sacramental or ritual status, the stories told by the poets took off on a new road toward a separate kind of meaning. The storytellers still retained much of the status of divine *vates*, but they also became free to develop stories whose value remains today curiously uncertain. Since these stories no longer enjoyed an institutional meaning their purpose became uprooted, and we have noted that even the storytellers themselves became unsure of their original intent. No doubt the process was gradual, but in time the purpose of storytelling took on a different dimension. The idea of entertainment in the sense of a celebration of a suppressed truth comes to mind, the purveying a de-valued truth suitable for members of de-valued castes, such as women. Thus the idea of *entertain* in its root sense of engaging the motion of the imagination, an imagination whose power often challenges and overshadows that of reason, came to indicate the role of the old stories in new societies.

Medieval Welsh and Irish cultures, however, never fully succumbed to the spell of the rational that has dominated European civilization since the re-introduction of Aristotle in the twelfth century. This old but new rationalism was to be the organizing principle of a kind of thought that ultimately created Thomistic theology. With this development European thought became fascinated with the idea that God is rational. This agenda installed and privileged a new critical attitude toward the workings of nature. There was to be nothing irrational in the new Christian universe. The eruptions of theological violence that accompanied this transformation can be traced in the early opposition of the churchmen to Aristotelian thought. Nevertheless, in little more than a century Aristotelianism went from being an alien Moslem strain of thought to a position of overwhelming dominance in the Roman Church.

Remnants of this conflict are inscribed within the narrative strategies of medieval Romance and survive still in the storytelling rhetoric of the *Quixote*. We read them in the first paragraphs of the work when the rationalistic narrator comments that the poor hidalgo went crazy trying to understand the language of the books of chivalry when even Aristotle himself could not have deciphered them if he had been resuscitated for that sole purpose. The narrator's comment is a way of asserting that the language of the texts in question had no meaning. The narrator is trying to claim that no one could find meaning in the language of Romance. Yet we have the story, a very long story, of a man who against the prevailing winds of rationalism did just that. If the hidalgo had found no meaning in the texts we would *ipso facto* have had no story at all. The narrator's book would have had no point of departure. The story however did come to be since the hidalgo found a world of meaning in those texts, those collections of officially "unreadable" signs. The difference is that he did not use the hermeneutics of reason to read them. He read them as another kind of sign, one not used to add up, to totalize or reach an end sum. He read them as numerology reads numbers. They are signs that contain another system of signification. This is why the narrator insists that the hidalgo *perdió su juicio*. He lost his judgment because he had refused a rational hermeneutic. Instead he affirmed another kind of reading, one based on a powerful use of the irrational, precisely the human capacity that had been under fire since the twelfth century. What better texts could he find for this enterprise than the texts of Romance, the kind of story that does not depend on the use of reason for its meaning.

Instead these stories encoded a more ancient wisdom that placed events in a contiguous position or sequence for reasons unknown to reason. Addition and totalization have nothing to do with the value of these stories, nor does cause and effect. In fact the value of the words is not easily contained. They signify in various ways because of an inherited tradition of irrational forces. The difference between words and numbers (in their ratio code) is best seen in contrasting arithmetic with etymologies. The former adds up and is rationally explained; the latter does not totalize and is irrational in its methodology. The hidalgo opts for etymologies, not mathematics.

In the *Quixote* the parameters of this opposition is beautifully explicated in the debate between Lotario and Anselmo over the value of Camila. In that dialogue, the issue of meaning is debated in the best Renaissance manner, specifically in the genre of the Neoplatonic dialogue. This genre came into fashion with the rise of humanism, partially in reaction to the reasoned discourse of Aristotelian syllogisms, the favored methodology of the scholastics. The dialogue forms gained new favor with the revival of Platonism as articulated by Ficino, Pico, Leone Hebreo. Hence the Renaissance nurtured a great tradition of literary and philosophical dialogues, among which Cervantes favored Leone Hebreo's *Dialoghi d'amore,* which he claimed to have read in the Tuscan language.

The debate between Lotario and Anselmo clearly sets out two different systems of signification by which men can supposedly read women. Both interlocutors wax eloquent. Lotario appeals to the power of the humanists, who place their faith in a core of beliefs based on texts from the Bible and pagan antiquity; but his methodology eventually loses out to Anselmo, who argues, as Lotario notes "like the Mohammedans" who insist that one plus one equals two.

> "Pareceme, oh Anselmo!, que tienes tú ahora el ingenio como el que siempre tienen los moros, a los cuales no se les puede dar a entender el error de su secta con las acotaciones de la Santa Escritura, ni con razones que consistan en especulación del entendimiento, ni que vayan fundadas en artículos de fe, sino que les han de traer ejemplos palpables, faciles, inteligibles, demostrativos, indubitables, con *demostraciones matemátics* que no se pueden negar, como cuando dicen: 'Si de dos partes iguales quitamos partes iguales, las que quedan también son iguales;' y cuando esto no entiendan de palabra, como en efecto, no lo entienden, haseles de mostrar con las manos, y ponérselo delante de los ojos." (pt. 1, ch. 33, emphasis added)

> "It seems to me, Anselmo," Lotario went on, "that your present state of mind is like that of the Moors, who can never be brought to see the error of their creed by quotations from the Holy Scriptures or by reasons based upon speculation or founded upon the articles of faith. They must have examples that are palpable, easy, intelligible, capable of proof, not admitting of doubt, with *mathematical demonstrations* that cannot be denied, like, 'If equals are subtracted from equals, the remainders are equal.' *If they do not understand this in words*, as indeed they do not, it has to be shown them with the hands, and put before their eyes, and even with all this, no one succeeds in convincing them of the truth of my holy religion."

Taken out of its context the debate has a surprisingly postmodern ring to it concerning the failure of logocentric language. Placed back into the narrative context, the debate becomes an argument about two systems of deception utilized by two men who want to sleep with the same woman. Camila as an individual has little to do with their debate. She exists there only as a philosophical proposition, when in fact another kind of proposition is at risk. Ultimately both men are destroyed because they cannot or will not read their own languages. As we will see this crisis concerning the ability of language to signify came to dominate both religion and science in the seventeenth-century debate about Galileo.

So in Cervantes' story, Camila, the free woman, is also destroyed because she reads herself entirely within the terms of a male language system and thus comes ultimately to signify nothing. The triumph of the anti-logos is complete. However, Camila's story is placed between the equally compelling stories of the wily Dorotea and the willful Zoraida. Dorotea, in contrast to Camila, begins her story as already signifying nothing. In contrast to Camila, however, she tells her own story and eventually comes to know how to read her own language. In a very literal sense she "finds" herself as she creates the story and the language of Princess Micomicona. This enables her to return to Fernando as more than his equal. By re-acquiring the language of Romance, Dorotea triumphs. "Venciste, Dorotea, venciste: porque no es posible tener ánimo para negar tantas verdades juntas" [You triumph, Dorotea, you triumph: because it is not humanly possible to deny so many truths]. Thus Fernando surrenders as he abandons the privilege of his male language. Her triumph is with a language in which she has discovered a "truth" but not a logos.

Camila, by contrast, is vanquished. "Rindiose, Camila; Camila se rindió" [Camila surrendered herself: Camila surrendered] the ironic narrator tells us. She is vanquished by a male system of meaning because she had accepted the men's words of love in the first place. In a reverse way, Zoraida imposes her will on a group of men, including both her father and her knight, by remaining true to the language of her female Christian slave who provided her with a new discourse in which the soul, not the body, is the ultimate unit of value. Zoraida can not be "had." She cannot be raped either by her father or her would-be lover nor even by French pirates. She has achieved her own language, which for her is a language of transcendence. It is significant that of all the pairs of lovers in part 1, she and the captive cannot speak to one another in human languages. Her Arabic and his Castilian are not viable means of communication. Yet they alone achieve a love match. Like the alchemical royal couple their oneness has no basis in reasoned systems of discourse. In all these stories Cervantes addresses the failure of logocentric language. This issue is already inscribed in the first paragraphs of the *Quixote*. There the hidalgo emerges as a reader of an unreadable language and ultimately he becomes himself a new kind of language.

Mills, Herms, Marks, Borders

In much the same way the story of the three mills can be read like the intertextual stories of the three women, Dorotea, Camila, Zoraida. They can be read backward or forward or from the center to either extremity. Together, however, they provide an accumulation that never quite sums up. This kind of reading takes its unquiet meaning from the language of *fábula* and Romance, not from the language of *historia* or verisimilitude. Here the hermeneutics of Romance overwrites the hermeneutics of reason, just as the hermeneutics of belief informs the Bible with a meaning that overwrites the hermeneutics of history. In each instance there are two readings, neither of which can vanquish the other, since each hermeneutic contains within it the meaning of the other. In the same way the Christianity of the Irish contains the paganism of the Celts within its own meaning. The Church in Ireland became a unique incorporation of the past and the present.

The intertextuality of the sequence of the three mills reads in the same way that each of the interpolated tales re-reads the other tales. The fact that Cervantes himself seems to have experienced uncertainty in the ordering of the interpolated tales displays the arbitrariness of in their present order (Stagg "Revision..."). To a great extent this problem of sequencing episodes is one that functions to distance the novel from Romance. So within the *Quixote* the tension between Romance and the novel, between an emblematic sequence of *aventuras* and a rational sequence that can be numerically numbered to illustrate the idea of cause and effect, generates both the story of the story and the story of the hidalgo. In this way the problematic of meaning in language becomes a genre-linked feature of the novel. The history of this conflict goes all the way back to the Celtic tales themselves. What, for instance, is the meaning of the sequence of island adventures in the *Voyage of Maelduin*? We have no definitive text of the story since the earliest manuscripts of the work both show symptoms of lacunae as well as an instability of the order of the encounters. Do they build in some way, or are they sequenced according to a system we can no longer read, or does the sequence itself not "mean" anything? The entire history of the evolution of the tales from the Celts to Chrétien is a struggle between newer concepts of cause and effect and older "irrational" modes of sequencing. (Owen, *Evolution* 102–29). If, in effect, the repeated encounters of knights at wells, castles, fords, trees, islands are no more than narratized equivalents of ritual actions, then the order in which they are related may have everything to do with lost rituals and nothing to do with our idea of a reasonable story.

The same tension seems to be contained in the repeated love adventures of Romance heroes. Each episode seems to be presented as complete in itself, yet ultimately the hero must chose between his Isoldas, his Blanchefleurs, his Dulcineas. The conflict is clearly seen in such Romances as Beaujeu's *Le Bel Inconnu* and where the choice between La Blonde Esmeree and La Pucelle de les manes blanche has no satisfactory resolution from the point of view of either Christianity or courtly love. This problem even appears in the *Quixote* and comes to the fore in Don Quixote's dilemma when offered the hand of Princess Micomicona. In that episode even Don Quixote seems to waffle as he triumphantly tells Sancho that he has a queen to wed. His loyalty to Dulcinea ultimately prevails but the conflict was written into the story long before when he had told Sancho that the chivalric hero would gain the love and the kingdom of a princess or queen and thus be in a position to bestow an island on his squire. When just this option suddenly appears in the ingenious story of Princess Micomicona, Don Quixote is forced to reject the princess and remain loyal to Dulcinea. Sancho rightly feels that he has been betrayed.

This struggle to maintain the privilege of one story line over another in a Romance text woven out of endless *entrelacement* gestures stems precisely from the editorial practices of early bards. "The Wooing of Etain," in which a woman is constantly being transformed from one being into another as she is wafted from one husband to another, is perhaps the most sophisticated Celtic articulation of this dilemma, and in its present form it suggests the possibility of another kind of meaning. Nevertheless, the story remains unsatisfactory from a the view of a Christian European hermeneutic because it utilizes an idea of reincarnation rejected by the institutional Church. The story thus becomes just a "fairy tale," a designation intended to deprive it of meaning. Yet viewed from a hermeneutic of belief in reincarnation the story creates various alternate meanings. With the realization of the story's relationship to Hindu or Vedic beliefs the tale seems significant in a new way. However the designation of the story as a fairy tale allows the story to survive because the hermeneutic has been adjusted to disguise its pre-Christian origin.

The story of the three mills exists in the same way, a sequence of three *aventuras* placed at some distance from one another but nevertheless constituting what can be read either as three versions of the same story or as a metastory containing intertextually significant repetitions. Their similitude therefore exists according to different ideas of sameness and repetition. They differ and signify by changes of formulation, but they also achieve meaning or special meaning as they become parts of a system rather than as discrete units of self-contained *aventuras*. Both these signifying systems functioned in early Romance tales, as we can see in the story of Culhwch and Olwen. There, perhaps for the first time, a series of discrete adventures whose interrelationship is now unknowable, were strung together under the rubric of an Arthurian quest. This allowed for a prolonged narrative in which many heroes—Culhwch, Cei, Arthur, Gwalchmei, and even the marvelous boar Twrch Trwyth—could each operate their special magic within the context of an overarching challenge. The rest is literary history. But the fact remains that this "history" can be read within the organizing fiction of the tale itself. The quest pattern adds another horizon of meaning to the multi-layered text.

In the metastory of the three mills the precedence of the windmill encounter over the adventures of the *molino de batanes* (fulling mill) and the *barco encantado* (enchanted bark) must be acknowledged as only an arbitrary precedent, a fact of narrative order. In many ways the other two mill episodes contain much more readable material. We can use that material for our own purposes, but it must be recognized that it is the unreadable or less readable windmill episode that captured the imagination of seventeenth-century Europe and has since retained this eminence. No doubt the relative brevity and simplicity of the first encounter with a mill is in part the cause. In the 147-word segment of text that begins with the description of the windmills and concludes as Don Quixote and Sancho move on to the next adventure, we find portrayed a powerful encounter between two emblematic icons, the knight and the mill. Each of these images brings a distinct system of meaning to the encounter. We recognize that the knight is the most evocative and most prestigious representation of the ideal male in Western culture, while the mill, one of the most ancient human machines, contains an equally primitive organization of meaning. The conflict between these two systems contains the story of an unresolvable struggle between two hierarchies of meaning and wisdom. We cannot perhaps reduce the struggle to merely two cultural patterns but amid this plenitude of meaning we can discern two differing but still similar modes of knowing.

In part they overlap, like non-concentric hermeneutic circles. In this way the relationships between them seem endlessly fascinating, like the workings of an elaborate mechanical system of interlocking wheels that make up the varied motions of a windmill itself. Our emphasis must remain on the interlocking mechanisms themselves, the idea of which provided mankind with a convenient conceptualization of the movements of the stars. R. S. Loomis examines the Celtic articulation of this problem in the Irish tale *Bricriu's Feast*. There CuChulainn sits on the roof of a revolving fortress in which the movement of the structure replicates the circling course of the stars around the sky (*Arthurian Tradition* 444). Rotating fortresses in other Celtic tales make this same comparison between the movement of a millstone and the revolving of the stars in the heavens (Rees and Rees 138). The same movement is later found in the instability of Gawain's bed in the Castle of the Women, an episode that underwrites the fragile condition of Don Quixote's bed during his love scene with Maritornes. An even closer connection is found in the windmill scene with its double wheel of both the mill stone and the rotating vanes. The same connection of the wheel of the millstone with the wheel of fortune underwrites the power of the knight's attack on the windmill. Don Quixote is not wrong in seeing the operations of *fortuna* in this adventure.

Historically differing systems of readings overlaid the successive human projections of order upon stellar movements. The problem of these contrasting readings reached a crisis in Cervantes' own time and rendered obsolete the hermeneutics of astrology, one of mankind's oldest and most cherished systems of interpretation. As we will note this crisis further enflamed the primary interpretive crisis of the time concerning Galileo and the problem of reading the Bible. All these tensions came into an abrupt comic focus as Don Quixote proclaimed the validity of his own reading of the windmills moving arms and then set off into a "divinely" inspired chivalric charge. It is in the conflation of these disparate yet related interpretations that the power of the scene finds its source. Love, madness, reason, lunacy, common sense, and the collapse of a powerful epistemology all inspire the ridiculous yet appealing gallop of Rocinante, the failing steed of the old equine order of things, as he attacks a new hermeneutics of suspicion incarnated in the windmill. In that charge he carried the confusing burden of human epistemological aspirations into battle with the unknowable. The result underwrites the emblematic fame of the knight's attack.

Disguise and Explain but Take No Prisoners

The best sign of this struggle is encoded in Don Quixote's "disguised" explanation of what he is doing. As with the ancient Celtic tales, the meaning of the explanation is to be found not in the mundane referential value of his language but rather in a more deeply coded valorization of the signs involved. His explanatory passage reads: " 'Bien parece' respondió don Quijote 'que no estás *cursado* en esto de las aventuras' " (pt. 1, ch. 8) ["It clearly seems," responded Don Quixote, "that you are not *versed* in this matter of adventures"]. The entire discourse of the book is found in this sentence. From the etymological root of *cursado* (English "versed") we get an impressive panoply of significations in Covarrubias's *Tesoro: ocurrir* (meaning something that places itself before us); *incurrir* (incurs); *curso* (an academic course) and ultimately *discurso* (discourse), a reasoned ordering of expression. Thus Cervantes' utilization of the past participle of *cursar*, which also refers to the passage of time and the act of running, tells us that a crisis in modes of knowing is at hand. Sancho is not *cursado*, that is, instructed, learned, or versed in the matter of adventure, nor does he have the special modes of knowing of a hero. Here Don Quixote opposes his secret knowledge of the ontology of the mill to the claims of reason and to the kind of knowledge that is based on sense perception. This is emphasized by the narrator's commentary: "Pero él [Don Quixote] iba tan puesto en que eran gigantes, que ni *oía* las voces de Sancho, ni echaba de *ver*, aunque estaba bien cerca, lo que *eran*" [But he (Don Quixote) was so convinced that they were giants that he neither heard the words of Sancho, nor was able to see, although they were very near, what they were]. Don Quixote cannot see nor hear what they are because he is *versed* in the modes of knowing of a Romance hero. This special epistemological ability allows him to *know* that the demonic forces resident in the satanic mills constitute a challenge to his ontology as a hero. In this way the mills constitute an *echtra*, a fateful call from the Otherworld. He is not just reading his life as a book of chivalry; he is also reading the mundane reality of the windmills according to a venerable system of knowing encoded in traditional stories that reach back to the earliest recorded Celtic tales. It is out of these stories that chivalry was fabricated, and therefore an old man on an old horse, guided by the wisdom of the ages, opposes himself to the forces of the Otherworld.

Don Quixote's coded text reveals other wisdoms than those of either Sancho, who appears here very much as a man of the seventeenth century in touch with the workings of everyday technologies, or to the validity of a science based on *ratio*, on counting and adding up. The scene narratizes the conflict between traditional narrative arrangements and a new story based on observation and numerical measurements. The windmill as a demonic force is no longer "readable" according to the new hermeneutic of science, just as astrology, alchemy, and other organizations of knowing were to lose their hermeneutic validity. Traditional tales were being reinterpreted as stories of the occult and their meaning was to be invalidated by the new scientific hermeneutic.

In this double reading the scene of the knight and the windmill appears before us like a palimpsest manuscript in which the shadow of the old text still presents itself behind the bold markings of the new script. In this way the history of the story we read has a different intent than the literal reading of the scene. Yet both "meanings" remain in effect just as the old magic of the shamrock underwrites the new Christian Trinity. The double hermeneutic fix is installed in full force, just as the knight begins his adventures; and his subsequent encounters all partake of this textual condition, yet endlessly varying the shifting content for ever new and surprising configurations. The validity of this arrangement has proved to be one of the most enduring systems of narratival meaning in all literature, and the workings of that system can be found in the repetition of the mill episode in the adventures of the fulling hammer and the enchanted bark. In these instances we have conceptually richer if poetically less powerful reprises of the basic profile of the struggle between the knight and the mill.

The contradiction between knowledge based on reasonable sense perception and a more intuitive mode of knowing remains consistent in the three episodes, even though the manner in which the hero encounters the mill varies. In the case of the windmill, Don Quixote clearly sees the mills but rejects that information for his learned (*cursado*) knowledge of Romance. It is a clear opposition between the sequence of reason and the sequence of storied fiction, between new cause and effect stories and traditional narratives, between a system of logic and an emblematic hermeneutic. In the case of the second mill episode, the *molino de batanes* adventure of chapter 20, Don Quixote and Sancho cannot see the mill in the darkness and are forced to rely on other means of perception. Nevertheless Don Quixote's reaction remains consistent as he "recognizes" the sound of the mill as a call to glory. In fact, here more than in any other episode, he fully explicates his sense of his own ontology as a hero destined to accomplish feats for the benefit of all mankind. Almost nowhere else in the book is his language more genuinely poetic. The seduction of his chivalric rhetoric transcends but does not fully erase an ironic counter reading. In fact the irony works to lighten the traditional and tired heroic diction and lifts it to a new level of expression, one in which the reader both feels the appeal of a lost tradition of rhetoric while still sensing the futility of its ancient import.

In the third episode Don Quixote neither sees nor hears the mill but rather responds to the sight of a small boat beached at the side of a river. He "recognizes" the boat as enchanted and as an invitation to a fated adventure. In this arrangement the boat will carry him to a perilous encounter. With this reading he is more right than wrong since the boat inevitably does carry him downstream and into a dangerous mill race from which he is rescued at the last moment by a group of white-faced millers. Thus each version of the episode is read from a different perceptual perspective, and in each system it achieves meaning in a different manner. At the same time the two interpretations operate as variants of the other. Each version comments on the other, while in itself signifying both an affirmation and a subversion of the protagonist's identity.

In essence even though each of the three mill encounters narratizes a different problematic of perception, the nature of the protagonist's response is always a sense of challenge. In each encounter he reads the mill as a threatening call from the Otherworld which must in some mysterious way be overcome.

There is, however, another feature that all three episodes have in common, one that reveals the nature of the text itself. In this reading the mills come to stand as the hermeneutic sign not only of the condition of the hero but of the ontology of his story. They are the sign of the text's encounter with its own challenge, with the problem of how to tell the story. This function is recognizable when read as relevant to the workings of the story. They need to be recognized as a sign concerning the changing nature of the hero's story. In this sense they stand as three herms, as border signs marking the entrance of the hero into a new phase of the world of Romance. After each mill adventure the story changes so that the three episodes indicate a turn not only in the nature of the hero's adventures but in the rhetorical composition of the text itself. The profile of the mills rises up along the fault lines of the Romance text, which, we have seen, play a hidden role in the operation of the discourse. In this arrangement the problematics of the text become the real hero of the story of the story and challenge the primacy of Don Quixote himself.

This phenomenon is written into the text from the first paragraph, where the challenge of writing such a strange story is introduced before we come to the story of the hero's name. It emerges even more dramatically in the conclusion of the text when both Cide Hamete and the second narrator move themselves to center stage after the death of the hidalgo. There Cide Hamete, having related the "cure" of the hidalgo's reading madness, himself succumbs to the power of reading Romance and proclaims himself the hero of his own story. His fated adventure of writing the story is also a call from the Otherworld, every bit as powerful as what Don Quixote had had in the mill episode. In his own change of consciousness, Cide Hamete at last recognizes the Otherworld dimension of the task of writing the story. The ancient debate of arms and letters resurfaces at the end as the narrator claims the palm, as in Palm Sunday, of the true hero. In this manner Cide Hamete ironically achieves the Romance incarnation that always eluded the hidalgo.

The mill adventures in this reading emerge as moments of conflation when the story of the hidalgo becomes, at the same time, the story of the text. The two hidden wheels of fortune, the one marking the movement of the hero and the other marking the movement of the text, mesh into a powerful synchronicity. Just as the movements of the millstone call out to the hero, sounding the fatal signal of his destiny, so they also inform the imagination of the storyteller as he contends with the Otherworld forces of fiction. In this way the narrative energy of the mill episodes asserts its pre-destined role. They become moments when the poet's confrontation with his muse comes-to-stand with the hero's confrontation with his most enigmatic challenge. As when the horse chooses the road and confirms the direction of both the story and the hero, so the mill episodes mark a similar crossroads for both the storyteller and the story.

Such moments are not rare in the history of the novel as a genre but they are usually either more disguised or seen as awkward narrative gestures. In the latter case they may be read as defects in the art of telling, while in the former case they are not "read" at all since they become invisible within the prevailing hermeneutic the work has demanded. It is only within the hermeneutics of Romance that such fault lines allow themselves to be read as part of the repertoire of viable features. In Romance, for reasons not entirely readable, the genre presents its narrative agenda both as the subject of its own discourse and as numinously important for the workings of the hero's fate.

The Romance of Hermeneutics

If poets' verses be but stories,
So be food and raiment stories;
So is all the world a story;
So is man of dust a story.

Betha Colaim Chille

One of the great scholarly Romances of modern Hispanism has been the
long history of conjectures concerning the composition of *Don Quixote*.
There, if one is patient and persevering, one can read the story of how
the work has been read by generations of scholars who have sought to
write the "true history" of how Cervantes wrote the work. Since we have
neither manuscript nor valid external documentation, this story has been
fabricated—often with great wit and insight—from the text itself. Few
works of literature have enjoyed this kind of critical attention, particularly in the absence of external data concerning the daily life of the author. In fact Cervantes himself has more than once been the subject of
Romance-like conjectures about the chronology of his life, his family, his
ancestry, his marriage, his sex life, the sex life of his sisters, his religious
beliefs or dis-beliefs. The temptation to read his personality along the
lines of the personality of his most famous creation, the figure of Don
Quixote, is particularly strong. That effort is no doubt due to the seductive power of the hidalgo's personality.

Mixed in with this conflation of author and hero, there is also the
inevitable fascination of how the author, always *andante* himself, man-
aged to write such an immense work under such difficult circumstances.
This history has become part of the critical fame of the author, because
the inevitable contradictions and apparent lapses of memory within the
text itself have challenged critics to interpret and/or justify the more
blatant confusions. The appearing and disappearing condition of Sancho's
donkey in chapter 21 of part 1 is the most famous of these contradictions.
In the opening of part 2 Cide Hamete himself comments on this problem
but without offering a satisfactory explanation. The acknowledgment of
this "error" however not only is an autocritical gesture but must be seen
as a continuation of the narrator's story of his own writing project. In
this way the "errors" are re-created as an essential feature of the fictional
ontology of Romance as a genre.

Another aspect of the problem of internal contradictions is addressed by Luis Murillo in *The Golden Dial*, where he traces the marvellous history of the temporal sequences in the work. Questions of how many days, weeks, or months the hero and his squire spend on the road have teased readers since the eighteenth century, when an inspired military officer attempted to establish the first calendar-based account of how much fictional time elapses from the moment Don Quixote starts on his adventures until his death. Murillo also shows how this preoccupation itself is the result of eighteenth-century preoccupation with the measurement of time that formed part of the cultural, scientific, and philosophic concerns of the Enlightenment. Likewise Murillo traces the history of this concern through the nineteenth century and into modern times. His study reveals that each age has sought to read the question according to the lights of its own scientific and cultural hermeneutics. Thus, as Murillo observes, the readings tell us more about the era in which they were made than they do about the text itself.

Murillo's study also reviews the history of the compositional theories critics and scholars have put forward about specific parts of the novel, particularly speculations about when the various interpolated tales may have been written and whether or not they formed part of the author's original conception of the work. This concern, as we shall examine further, is essential to the problem of Romance as a genre.

Since the time of Murillo's study we have also had Robert Flores' ingenious analyses concerning the history of the printing of the first editions of the novel, an approach which in fact does yield verifiable compositional data. In this endeavor the problem of Sancho's disappearing donkey is again addressed with great vigor and conviction. Other evidence found in Cervantes' works also has provoked speculations about his methods of composition, in particular his prologue to the *Persiles*. There Cervantes specifically refers to his failing health and his intense concern for the fate of his last fiction. The date of the prologue, just four days before Cervantes' death, increases the sense of ending that haunts the final words of a great fabulist. All these critical commentaries have further enhanced the sense of human drama that surrounds the creation of works of art. In this way the problem becomes the topic of both careful critical studies and imaginative leaps of great insight.

This kind of commentary is of course not limited to Cervantes' works but can be found circling around many great figures from Homer to James Joyce. What is curious about this kind of questioning is the fact that it occurs both when we know nothing about the writer (Homer) and when we know a great deal (James Joyce). In fact, knowing more seems to generate even more problematic questions than knowing little. In his study *Novels in the Making*, William E. Buckler presents data on a series of novelists from Defoe to Elizabeth Bowen. What is noteworthy is that the mystery of composition remains mysterious no matter how much we know. We discover, for instance, that even such a stylistically self-conscious writer as Conrad found himself confronted with unresolvable problems about the final form of his novels. In *Nostromo*, his prolonged poetic evocation of nineteenth-century South America, the final form of the published version was achieved on the basis of editorial decisions made by the publisher. Certain segments of considerable length, exquisitely written, were omitted in the published work and remain today external to the text of which they were once integral. In this arrangement, what was said becomes the Vedic "unsaid." It comes to exist on the periphery of what we read, an unknowable narrative just beyond the horizon of our cognizance.

In the case of modern novels we do know that other kinds of problems have intruded themselves in the editorial decisions concerning their published format. F. Scott Fitzgerald, for instance, could never decide on a "correct" narrative sequence for *Tender is the Night*. Thus the first published version which begins *in medias res* has become an alternate to another version published much later in which the action begins at the beginning of the protagonist's life and continues to his death. Such arbitrary decisions are known to have affected many novels about which we have a great deal of compositional information. No doubt the history of the writing and publishing of *Don Quixote* would be as varied and curious as any of the actions recounted in the work itself.

However, the question of the compositional history of the text of the *Quixote* has other sources than those found in the intriguing mysteries of the author's life. As we have seen, another compositional story is written within the text itself and is there constituted as a fiction. The story of the name is merely the first adventure in this *historia* which surfaces from time to time to remind us that another action is taking place. The story of the story underwrites all Don Quixote's adventures like the invisible attraction of a rarely seen planet.

This is related to Romance as a genre which contains within its form a paradigmatic feature that has critically overshadowed all others and cannot passed unnoticed even for the most casual reader. That problem

is the question of *entrelacement*, of the interweaving of diverse and separate stories into a metastory which provides an overarching schematic
for the whole. It was the debate concerning this feature that exercised
Renaissance *preceptistas* and drew the battle line between the partisans of
Ariosto and Tasso (Forcione 27–42). It came to be seen as an unstable
border land, a *marche* dividing the world of medieval Romance from the
new ideal of the "unified" Renaissance epic. In this way the interlacing
of various story strands came to define Romance as a genre and to further isolate it from the acceptable canon. Whatever the validity of this
criterion, however, we have noted that *entrelacement* can be found in the
earliest Irish tales, such as *The Voyage of Maelduin* and the Welsh ur-
Romance *Culhwch and Olwen*. In these narratives we know almost nothing about how the writer or perhaps writer-editor deploys the various
inner narrative sequences and creates the configuration of the text as we
have it. The same is true of the *Li Contes del Graal* manuscripts, where the
first continuator tells us of Chrétien's death.

Textual situations of this kind create at one level of reading the
hermeneutics of Romance but at another horizon of reading they produce a Romance of hermeneutics in which the reader is challenged to
look for meanings that are referential to the text itself. In the *Quixote* this
aspect of the text presents itself as the privileged subject of its own discourse, as a framing tale, while the story of Don Quixote becomes the
first interpolation.

This challenge feature of Romance is inherited from the earliest Celtic
texts as we have seen in the "How the *Táin Bo Cuailgne* Was Found
Again" fragment. There the story of the story is clearly an Otherworld
adventure and the narrator is the first "reader." In one way or another
this feature survives through the many transformations of storytelling
from the tales of CuChulainn to Culhwch to Perceval to Amadis and Don
Quixote. The ultimate Romance in this series of shapeshifting narratives
is the challenge to the reader to find the answer or perhaps the question
that will reveal the meaning of the tale. The difference is that not until
the *Quixote* does this storytelling process fully surface as part of a self-
conscious narrative agenda. What had been a quaint but conventional
genre feature emerges as the story of the hero's name, that is, the story
of how language comes to signify and how meaning comes to mean.

In this matter of the *entrelacement* of different stories or episodes, the
meaning of each episode we read will be conditioned by *when* we read
it. Each episode or tale both reads and counter-reads what precedes it

and at the same time anticipates what is to follow. Thus the introduction of the windmill scene in chapter 8 of *Don Quixote* shapes our response to all that follows. To a great extent it creates the dominant hermeneutic for the entire work and, because of this, has come to stand for the book as a whole. Much of its fame is due to its success in narratizing the problem of hermeneutics. It stands as the archetypal adventure that causes all readers to question how anyone should read anything. As such, it functions as an organizing myth that sets forth the limits of the human capacity to read and interpret. In this sense it is the ultimate icon of the human condition, and this has insured its universal appeal.

The fact that it occurs as the first adventure in which both Don Quixote and Sancho participate likewise accounts for the sustained potency of its influence over the remainder of the text. Not only does the windmill challenge assume precedence over all that follows but the same energy that informs its articulation also underwrites the other mill adventures of the hero. This is why the repetitions of this problem in the *molino de batanes* and *barco encantado* episodes tell us that all three encounters stand at crucial turning points in the course of the action and in the discourse of the text's composition. Thus the mills come to function as signs or herms in the text pointing the way toward a change in the environment of the hero's adventures and a change in the manner in which the story is told and a change in the way the story can be read. They mark crucial moments in the composition of the text, moments signaling a type of fault line as the story begins to unfold in a new way. It is in this sense that they form part of a Romance of hermeneutics, of the story of how to read the text. The hermeneutic challenge to the reader has become part of the fiction.

This arrangement means that we must examine not only how we are reading the story of the hidalgo but also how we read the story of the narrator and the story of the editor as simultaneous gestures. Thus, the first windmill adventure marks the reconstituting of the text after the failure of the first sally and introduces a new narrative phase in which Sancho and Don Quixote function as hermeneutic antagonists, a change so fundamental that it is impossible to imagine the work without it.

At the same time the windmill scene presages the introduction of the next challenge, the adventure at Puerto Lápice, where the hero's battle is interrupted as an unsuspected second narrational voice emerges from the storytelling project. This surprising development in effect creates another level of discourse which can query the procedures of the first narrator so that the overall narrative arrangement incorporating two narrators replicates the dialectic of the Sancho and Don Quixote. The two protagonists argue about the truth of their adventures while the two narrators argue about the validity of what is written. In this way the text becomes fully autocritical and the adventure of storytelling becomes the counterplot of the novel.

Thus the windmill marks the advent of the struggle of how to tell the story. In the same way the *molino de batanes* appears just before the finding of the helmet of Mambrino from Ariosto's *Orlando Furioso*, an adventure that moves the story toward a sequence of Ariosto-like interpolated stories, a development that puts the paradigmatic narrational procedure of Romance to the test. The completion of interpolative structure disappears with the end of part 1, while part 2 begins with a rejection of interpolation and the introduction of a new narrative stratagem. This reformed narrative program, however, does not find its self-marking herm until Don Quixote sees the "enchanted " bark on the shores of the Ebro. There, in a final assertion that he has found a new adventure, the last echo of his entrelacement incarnation, he enters the boat and is carried down the river to the water mill. The mill run destroys the bark and Don Quixote and Sancho are saved just before they would face their deaths. This salvation leaves them free for the immediate appearance of the deceptive duchess. Her role, like that of Dorotea (whom she resembles both with her green dress and her imaginative leaps) will be to structure part 2. Her country estate will form the locus of the Don Quixote's adventures while her invention of Merlin's recipe for disenchanting Dulcinea will provide a quest structure for the narrative configuration of part 2. It is this development which imposes a new kind of unity for part 2, but it should be noted that the quest is another Romance structure. In the subsequent history of the modern novel it is the quest structure that comes to dominate the narrative format, although from time to time interpolated stories still appear.

From this perspective we can see that each of the mill episodes functions as a herm that signals a fundamental turn in the shape of the story. They appear in effect as signs that new hermeneutic and narratival developments will disrupt the narrative agenda. In this sense the mill profiles come to stand along radical fault lines that mark the textuality of Cervantes' novel. They tell us, however subliminally, that the hero is crossing a frontier into a world of different kinds of challenge. This feature repeats the moments in earlier Romances during which the hero chooses a road that presents a challenge fated for him alone, as when Lancelot crosses the sword bridge to enter the kingdom where Guinevere is held by an infernal power. It is this act that makes him worthy to achieve her freedom and, at the same time, to possess her sexually. The function of this moment of choice replicates the metastory of the compositional challenges faced by the narrator. As with all Romance fault lines, such junctures bring to the reader's attention that a story is being told and that at this textual shift a new hermeneutic challenge is being posed.

These compositional clues become readable when the mill episodes are deciphered within the sequential arrangement of the episode situated before and after their appearance. The genre of Romance, partially because of its weaving of unrelated episodes into the tapestry of its textuality, was always ready for the procedure that we find in *Don Quixote*. There the story and the metastory become readable by means of a strategy that turned the storytelling problem into the meta-Romance challenge faced by the narrator. This challenge was called forth by Chrétien, who set out the difficulty of his project in the prologue: to tell the best of stories to the best of audiences. He failed, perhaps because of death, and became the first named martyr in the struggle to find the holy grail of meaning. But the challenge had always lurked in the earlier tales. It remained for later tellers, like Wolfram von Eschenbach, to boast of having found the "true" meaning. But not until Cervantes was the problem of the writer's *maniera* sufficiently self-conscious for a story to be written that encoded both the hero's and the narrator's *aventuras* within the same agenda. The *Quixote* itself stands like a herm, like a windmill, marking its own enterprise as a grail-like encounter with the threatening gods of narrativity.

Hermeneutics as Eros

To think that *Don Quixote* is not an erotic work is an easy error. The so-called comic story of the aging would-be knight, would-be lover disguises a deeper intentional thrust in the fiction. Nor is it the overt eroticism of the many interpolated love stories that generates the text's eroticism. The feeling is already there in the Celtic tales, where images of eroticism and meaning are intertwined like serpents ascending the tree of temptation. In the *Quixote* there is a more complex interweaving of two stories, two narrators, two protagonists restlessly circulating around a case of hermeneutic instability.

To mean, to wish to mean *(querer decir)*, to achieve meaning are all erotic acts, a form of action that in order to be complete must reach another being. In Genesis, Adam names the animals, an act that writes his power over them. Giving men the right to name is tantamount to giving them sexual and social dominance, empowering them to confer being through language, as a substitute for women's power to give birth. All this is deeply enmeshed in the patriarchal lore of the Jewish Bible that re-wrote an earlier version of the story. In this way the story we have, as in the Celtic tales, is a disguise for an unacceptable meaning which one suspects is not patriarchal. This story has already been told in various ways by numerous feminists: Marija Gimbutas, Merlin Stone, and others. Adrienne Munich has related Genesis to the story of Grisostomo and Marcela, where the two versions of their story, the man's and the woman's, compete for the status of truth. Not surprisingly the story of Grisostomo and Marcela is a re-written version of a story told in the *Galatea*. In the original version the woman seems more to blame for the tragedy, while in the *Quixote* it is the man who fabricates his own destruction.

Eros and meaning, sex and power, love and language, nescience and knowledge are stories that are endlessly re-told. So Don Quixote sees himself as the erotic surrogate of Lancelot, the hero who achieved his fulfillment in the bedchamber of Guinevere. Lancelot is a troubled image. We read beneath the text of Chrétien's *The Knight of the Cart* a disturbing story of deception, incest, patricide; and by means of later fabulists like Malory, we find also the cause of the destruction of Camelot. The whole panoply of these adventures read much like a more pagan version of the destruction of the house of Atreus, the tragedy of Oedipus, the fall of Adam, the betrayal of Joseph, and so on. As a Romance, the grail story is forever incomplete.

The story of Etain best exemplifies a tradition of male renewal found in the wasteland imagery of old king/captive goddess/young warrior triad. Such stories survived only in the discourse of Romance with its tales of Lancelot, Guinevere, and the enigmatic regenerating grail. Even these stories, with their suggestion of forbidden desires, were harshly derided by the dialectic of reason and fell from favor. It is in this sense that *Don Quixote* is a Romance about a hero who seeks the grail of renewal in a mythic realm of madness, death, and a rebirth into a state of youth and eternal sexuality. It all depends on his finding the right language, not a language that does not reflect reality but rather one that calls into being the desired state. It is in this sense that *Don Quixote* as a text is an examination of eros as meaning and meaning as eros.

The Inn of the Two Genres

"[Cervantes'] respect for the creature of his own comic invention grows during the narrative. This process is perhaps the most fascinating thing in the whole novel; *it is a novel in itself . . ."*

Thomas Mann

The hermeneutic signals inhabiting the episodes of the three mills, each signifying a change in the nature of the hero's story, constitutes a pattern replicated elsewhere in the unfolding of the novel. Their closest parallel can be found in the three inn episodes that structure part 1. This is to be expected, since the narrator has already indicated that in the source material the windmill adventure was interchangeable with the adventure of the first inn. The inn, however, is the first *aventura,* and appropriately, as we have seen, it marks the entrance of Don Quixote into the world of his Romance identity. There he learns to read his own destiny in the disguised forms of his everyday reality: the swineherd is a pagan god of signs, the inn is a castle, the innkeeper teaches the new knight how to read, the fish meal has an unstable ontology, the prostitutes are grail maidens bearing him food and drink and arms, and so on. The inn adventure, like the mill episode, reproduces itself in two subsequent visits to the second inn. The first of these visits to the second inn provides Don Quixote with his Lancelot/Gawain adventure of the perilous bed, in which he suffers his first amorous test, while the second visit occurs when he returns with Dorotea as Princess Micomicona. In this adventure he overcomes the second challenge of his loyalty to Dulcinea and then enjoys a climactic dream in which he, like Lancelot, beheads the giant of lust.

While the repetition of similar challenges is a Romance feature, the mills and the inns in the *Quixote,* however, function in diverse ways in relation to the hero. The mills are always challenges to his power of "arms"; they are external threats from the Otherworld that lead to battle. In contrast, the inns constitute more intimate adventures with "letters," which present challenges of both love and reading. For Don Quixote these adventures climax in his second visit to the inn of Juan Palomeque el Zurdo where he triumphs in his championing of Micomicona and where the reading of "El curioso impertinente" and the telling of the captive's tale provide negative and positive readings of the problem of love and arms. Thus the inn sequence traces an *entrelacement* pattern of amorous adventures that weaves in and out of both the hidalgo's story and the narrator's adventure of the story of the story. The latter is auto-referential to the act of writing, repeatedly reflecting the scene of writing and the search for meaning in the author's writing project. Thus the mills and inns remain in the mind of the reader with particular force, not only because they are vividly portrayed but because they form segments of a signifying system.

At the level of novelistic discourse the inn/mill episodes recreate in realistic terms the repeated visits of the grail hero to special castles where he finds adventures ultimately marking out his destiny. In Romance these encounters are never chance events but are, rather, orchestrated occurrences of challenge sites that lead the hero step by step to his predestined fate. Often the sudden appearance of the castles before him clearly marks them as Otherworld sites, a factor re-invented by Cervantes in his description of the first inn. The second inn also "appears" fortuitously just after Don Quixote's beating by the Yanguenses. This indicates its double function as a locus for his healing as well as for his first amorous adventure, an encounter that continues the motif of misadventure in love already suffered by Grisostomo and Rocinante. In the case of Rocinante's amorous misadventures we recall that the hero's animal companion functions as an alternate incarnation of the hero himself, an arrangement already inscribed in Cervantes' text with the epigraphic verses. It may be that Cervantes moved the Grisostomo story to this position in order to re-focus the direction of the novel at the thematic level with a new emphasis on love.

Since the castles in Romance function as slightly altered versions of one another, each exploring differing aspects of the hero's destiny, Cervantes achieves the same effect with his realistic "distortions" of the imagery. Fundamentally the interpolated tales function as expansions and explorations of the hero's ontological needs. In the *Quixote* this situation has moved the crucial step toward the realistic novel in that the inns function both as "real constructs"—that is, external entities—and as locales for the hero's interior development. The inns are thus both internal and external to the hero, and their existence functions to expand the scope of the hero's challenge.

A number of other factors corroborate that the second inn is also an Otherworld castle for the hero. He alone recognizes its true character and successfully translates its contents into Romance formulae that constitute a testing site. The innkeeper, Juan Palomeque el Zurdo, signifies a hidden negative force in that he is left-handed (and therefore sinister). At the same time, his unusual patronymic suggests a disguise, for the dovecote of the goddess as an Otherworld ontology, this being consonant with the nature of the hero's adventure while lodged in the hostel. His wife, as is often the case, is a positive and helpful creature, while his daughter and her maid come to play romantic roles that challenge the hero's loyalty to his lady. The official of the Santa Hermandad with his Hermes rod and lantern takes the role of a storm god lodged in the site, while the other lodgers are impish pranksters with carnivalesque energy, as Sancho is to discover. The Gawain-like adventure of the perilous bed indicates that an enchantment of some sort affects the castle and strengthens Don Quixote's interpretation that the locale is enchanted by an enemy force. This observation distinguishes the negative character of the second inn as a test for the hero in contrast to the positive force of the first inn which functioned primarily as a teaching site. More than anything else, it is the appearance of Maritornes that denotes the Otherworld condition of the place. To a reader of Romance she is clearly a form of the loathly damsel figure who announces the nature of the challenge facing the knight. Her prominent role in both visits to the inn reveal the character of the forces inhabiting the inn.

In addressing the question of the loathly damsel it is necessary to look back not only to Chrétien's version of her role but also to the Celtic presentations of such creatures. The most important aspects of these figures is their unstable appearance and their uncanny ability to define the fortune of the hero. Partially fateful, partially helpful, they function to set forth the nature of the challenge. In this capacity they are sometimes ugly and dwarfish like the loathly damsel in Chrétien and sometimes beautiful like the maidens of the cart in *Perlesvaus*. In the *Quixote* Maritornes incorporates many of these qualities. The first description of her is a stroke of comic exaggeration which produces a rupture in the realistic tone with which the inn is otherwise depicted:

> Servía en la venta, asimesmo, una moza asturiana, ancha de cara, llana de cogote, de nariz roma, del un ojo tuerta y de otrono muy sana. Verdad es que la gallardía del cuerpo suplía las demás

faltas: no tenía siete palmos de los pies a la cabeza, y las espaldas,
que algún tanto le cargaban, la hacían mirar al suelo mas de lo
que ella quisiera. Esta gentil moza. . . . (pt. 1, ch. 16)

[There was also a servant in the inn, an Asturian lass with a
broad face, flat head, and snub nose, blind in one eye and not
very sound in the other. The elegance of her shape, to be sure,
made up for all her defects. She measured no more than five feet
from head to foot, and her shoulders, which weighed her down
somewhat, made her contemplate the ground more than she
would have liked. This graceful lass . . .]

To begin with it is her physical appearance that in itself calls attention to
her presence as an Otherworld creature within the conventional setting
of the inn. Not only is Maritornes the only figure described physically
(always a sign that the personage will play a significant role), but the
details of her misshapen appearance give her an emblematic profile among
the mundane personages inhabiting the inn. We recall that in Chrétien it
is the dwarf at Arthur's court that first recognizes the heroic identity of
Perceval. Thus it is Maritornes who asks the crucial question concerning
Don Quixote's name and then interrogates Sancho about his profession
as "caballero aventurero." With these actions she sets about establishing
her role as a troublesome intermediary, sometimes helping, sometimes
obstructing the knight's progress. It is also Maritornes who at the end
ties Don Quixote's wrist to the post in the hayloft and leaves him hanging "enchanted" from the window.

A look back at Chrétien's description of the loathly damsel indicates
specific features that anticipate Maritornes, in particular, the disfigurment
of her eyes, nose, and back:

> Her eyes were tiny holes; those eyes
> Were small as any rat's in size.
> Cat-like or ape-like was her nose (*Perceval* 4621–24)

or again:

> With hunchbacked spine,
> the maiden's haunches seemed to be
> like twisted wands of a willow tree (4634–36)

In *Peredur*, the Welsh version of the tale, the ugly maiden possesses even closer similarities to Maritornes:

> her face and hands were blacker than pitch, and yet it was her shape rather than her colour that was ugliest—high cheeks and a sagging face, a snub, wide-nostrilled nose, one eye speckled grey and protruding, the other jet black and sunken . . . Her backbone was shaped like a crutch; her hips were wide in the bone, but her legs were narrow, except for knobby knees and feet. (Gantz, *Early Irish Myths* 248)

Here the narrator not only differentiates her eyes from one another (a common device in Celtic tales) but also compares one part of her physiognomy with another—two descriptive devices utilized by Cervantes.

In both the *Peredur* and the *Perlesvaus* this maiden is also a variant form of the grail maiden herself, a feature read into the *Quixote* by critics who see her as the anti-Dulcinea. While this physical change is never displayed by poor Maritornes, a similar characteristic is retained in Cervantes' articulation of her persona. For one thing we are told that in her own eyes at least she does have another form of existence than the one presented to the world. Cide Hamete tells that she has given her word to the *harriero* to come lie with him that night and to satisfy his every pleasure. Overt sexuality is a common Otherworld characteristic, and likewise Maritornes herself conceptualizes her actions in a significant way:

> Y cuéntese desta buena moza que jamás dio semejantes palabras que no las cumpliese, aunque las diese en un monte y sin testigo alguno, porque presumía muy de hidalga, y no tenía por afrenta estar en aquel ejercicio de servir en la venta, porque decía ella que desgracias y malos sucesos la habían traído a aquel estado. (pt. 1, ch. 16)

> [And it is said of this good lass that she never made promises of this kind without fulfilling them, even though she made them in the woods and without any witness present. For she prided herself greatly on being a lady and felt it no disgrace to be employed as a servant in an inn, because, she said, misfortunes and bad luck had brought her to that position.]

Thus she herself sets up another "estado" for her being and in this anticipates Don Quixote's perception of her as a princess when she inadvertently stumbles into his clutches in the famous bedroom scene. Here Don Quixote, like all good heroes, perceives the "true" status of a heroine mis-perceived by everyone else. What Cervantes has done is re-formulate the Romance situation in realistic terms acceptable to his audience. In Maritornes he accomplishes one of his most successful novelesque transformations of Romance features into the rhetoric of realism. But it must be noted that Cervantes does not negate the Romance reading. Rather, he retains the advantages of both modes of fiction by satisfying both Romance and realistic horizons of expectations. This function is further enhanced by balancing Maritornes against Dulcinea as binary opposites. In this sense Maritornes as the anti-Dulcinea vitalizes the reality of her binary opposite, the beauteous grail maiden.

The Maritornes/loathly damsel formulation is only the first of several basic rhetorical features that signal the double genre readings of events at the inn. Other signs, as we have seen, are found in the left-handed innkeeper, who proves hostile to Don Quixote and Sancho. Like the giant Isbaddaden in *Culhwch and Olwen*, he represents a force opposing the hero's quest; in this case he typifies the world of money and commerce resistant to the ideals of chivalry espoused by the hero and is finally "neutralized" by Fernando's wealth. Likewise the rich *harriero* from Arevalo opposes Don Quixote's *colloquio de amor* with Maritornes. His relationship to Cide Hamete, commented upon by the second narrator, likewise brings into the scene the problematics of blood relationships within the grail castle. The commentary also precipitates Cide Hamete himself into the flow of action, so that he becomes an actor in the hero's story. This indicates that it is the narrator's bloodline and not Don Quixote's that is at risk and in this way introduces the subversive question of who is the protagonist of the story.

In another category of opposition, the official of the Santa Hermandad represents the forces of law and order at the level of realistic discourse, but in the world of Romance he acts out the role of the storm god who strikes the hero with a lightening bolt as he reclines in the perilous bed. At the same time the healing balsam, first brewed in the inn, brings into the story the important magic cup that can be served only to the true hero. We also have noted that the mischievous guests, who otherwise have had no existence in the inn, suddenly appear at the moment of departure and toss Sancho in the carnivalesque blanket scene. The latter event seems to paralyze or enchant Don Quixote, foreshadowing his later enchantment at the same inn, while for Sancho this indignity remains in his memory as the severest of his many misfortunes, presumably because it seems somehow to undermine his identity.

At the center of all these components is the famous love scene of Don Quixote and Maritornes, a scene that re-constitutes the adventure of the perilous bed for the grail hero. From this matrix all the other Romance components found at the inn take their meaning and force, and it is this adventure that convinces Don Quixote that the inn is an enchanted castle. As in the case of the grail castle, a spell hangs over the inn that is the very essence of the challenge confronting the hero. His mission in one sense is to break the spell and restore Maritornes to her beautiful and noble ontology. However the problem is not quite so simple for Don Quixote. So as we see at the end, after all the happy resolutions of the stories of the four sets of lovers (Cardenio/Luscinda, Dorotea/Fernando, the Captive/Zoraida, Don Luis/Dona Clara) have been achieved, it is Don Quixote who becomes enchanted while the inn presumably resumes its quotidian existence. In order to re-read this conundrum we will have to look closely at the perilous bed adventure and then at the dream adventure that focuses Don Quixote's second visit to the inn.

The paradigmatic articulations of the adventure of the perilous bed are to be found in the Gawain segment of *Le Conte du Graal* although many components of this test can be found scattered through various Celtic ur-romances. It is a fairly common feature in Celtic source material. Loomis cites the adventure of CuChulainn in *Bricriu's Feast* as one source. There, as in all the subsequent formulations, the episode contains a test which the hero must undergo in order to prove his primacy over other warriors. The siege perilous of the Round Table has the same purpose. Whoever enters the bed or sits in the chair will suffer destruction unless he is the hero destined to overcome the challenge in question, whether it is a matter of finding the grail or, as in Gawain's case, disenchanting the castle of the ladies.

In Loomis's analysis of the parallels between the various French articulations of this scene in Chrétien and in other writers, he finds at least fifteen features which parallel Celtic episodes of similar formulations (Loomis, *Arthurian Tradition* 207–8, 443–44). In the *Quixote* twelve of these items appear in inn scenes of chapters 16 and 17, while three crucial items, the connection with the shameful cart, the inn as a land of women or castle of ladies, and the beheading test appear during his second visit to the inn. Furthermore, these three components are anticipated by events in the first adventure of the perilous bed.

Taking these features in their order of appearance in the *Quixote* they are:

1. The host, although initially present to greet the hero, is absent during the test but reappears in a hostile form after the conflict

2. The hostess initially provides for the hero's needs

3. The daughter or maid (sometimes the wife) comes to the hero's bed and sexually tempts him

4. There are three beds in the room

5. The bed or chair is on the roof of the hostel and the stars are visible

6. The bed is on wheels or is otherwise unstable

7. The test occurs during the night

8. The hero has some foreknowledge of what is to come

9. The lights around the bed go off and on

10. The hero is alone on the bed

11. He is attacked by a giant or churl

12. He is struck by a flaming lance or some other fire bolt

A final item is the fact that as a result of the test the hero should be proclaimed the special hero for whom the adventure was created. This is reversed in the *Quixote* when the knight himself announces that the treasure of the castle is reserved not for him but for an enemy Moor.

Likewise the matter of the chessboard imagery in the Gawain castle comes from earlier narrative formulations such as the Welsh tale "The Dream of Macsen" and ultimately from "The Boyhood Deeds of CuChulainn" [Owen, *Evolution* 36; Chrétien, *Perceval* 204] Gaming imagery in the *Quixote* tends to rely on both card games and chess. Card imagery appears both in Don Quixote's Princess Miulina story and again in the cave of Montesinos dream. In the same way the first innkeeper makes reference to card sharking, so that the inn episodes all have some sense of trickery associated with games even though the chessboard itself is absent. At the same time the perilous bed adventure itself evokes other formulations of this kind of encounter, just as Don Quixote himself embarks on the scene with his own internal literary agenda. In all the Romances, the images of beds and game boards are found to harbor the forces of chance and fate that pursue the hero.

In Chrétien's version of the scene, Gawain loses sight of the evil maiden just before he comes upon the Castle of the ladies which contains the wondrous bed. Her abrupt disappearance signals the end of one configuration of his challenge and the re-formulation of its forces into a new adventure. He also has trouble with his horse just before coming to the castle, and this is suggestive of the misadventure of Rocinante just before Don Quixote comes to the second inn. Troublesome horses are also signs of change in the nature of the hero's journey. At the castle Gawain finds a great queen (needless to say one of his relatives) and a huge band of maidens and youths. The castle exists under some sort of supernatural restraint that holds the women prisoner and attempts to incapacitate the hero as well. At the source of this situation is a Celtic story of the hero in an Otherworld "land of women," an adventure that fictionalizes an underlying pre-Aryan matriarchy that survived to a very late period in Ireland. The feminist focus of this kind of adventure survives also in the opening episode of the *Táin Bo Cuailnge* where the "pillow talk" reflects the underlying matriarchy/patriarchy conflict between Queen Maeve and Conchubur (Kinsella xii). Gawain's challenge is to overcome the enchantment of the women without becoming imprisoned himself, a factor that anticipates Don Quixote's problems on his return visit to the second inn. As we will see below when we examine that component of the *Quixote*, it too contains echoes of the Celtic hero's visit to the land of women, just as it narratizes a feminist challenge to the dominance of the warrior's discourse.

The key components of the perilous bed adventure come during the night when a beautiful but forbidden woman visits the hero's bed. Taking her into his arms precipitates various pyrotechnical effects even as the hero is set upon by a charging demon, fiend, giant, or animal. According to Celticists this adventure is a re-articulation of warrior's visits to the castle of the storm god where the hero challenges the god's possession of the woman. *Sir Gawain and the Green Knight* contains another version of the testing of the knight's integrity by the wife of his host. Whatever the version, in the Maritornes episode Don Quixote's

intertextual memory clearly evokes this kind of story when he tells Sancho
after his beating by the *harriero* that the beauty of Maritornes is reserved
not for him but for a Moor who holds the castle under enchantment.

This bit of hermeneutic insight has a curious twist to it in that his
opponent is the Moorish *harriero* who is the relative of Cide Hamete. The
second narrator observes that Cide Hamete, as a Moor, is jealous of Don
Quixote's fame as a Christian hero and that this factor causes him to omit
or mis-relate his adventures. But in this episode Cide Hamete's prejudice
takes on the form of an enemy force operating within the inn and within
the story. Don Quixote's two fights with *harrieros* occur at inns and at
crucial moments in his ascent to chivalric incarnation: the first during his
arming vigil at the well in the first inn and second during his first love
adventure at the second inn. Thus the knight's interpretation of the condition of the inn is perfectly consistent with his view of his life as a
Romance, but at the same time we also note that Cide Hamete himself
is part of that Romance story and not an outside interpreter as he pre-
tends to be. He is a player in the Romance of Don Quixote, not a critic
of it. Therefore his opposition to the hero is internal to the story not
external as he claims. In this way the Romance formulation is part of
both the story of the hero and the story of the narrator's story. It is this
double articulation of the Romance energies at both narrative levels that
undermines Cide Hamete's claim that Don Quixote is not a hero. Cide
Hamete's interpretation of the story is always already compromised by
his own participation in the events, and this condition is highlighted by
the commentary of the second narrator, who here presents Cide Hamete
as compromised by his Moslem loyalties. The second narrator's commentary as a narrative device also compromises the precarious borders
that should mark off the inside and outside of the textual identity of the
story. To some extent the second narrator himself is also both inside and
outside the story, just as he is both a reader and editor of the tale.

From this vantage point the content of the Maritornes love scene reveals another story. Don Quixote as hero is challenged to disenchant the
inn and thus free the women held prisoner there. This group includes all
the later "heroines" who come to lodge at the inn: Dorotea, Luscinda,
Zoraida, and Doña Clara. This challenge in effect is the narrative focus
of part 1 and anticipates another articulation of the same challenge in the
problem of Dulcinea's enchantment in part 2. In this sense both parts of
the *Quixote* re-invent the basic feminist energies of the Land of Women
Romance as a genre, and the hero's conflicts are a carry over of the

original formulations of the Irish and Welsh tales. In a way not entirely traceable this conflict is carried forward by the genre of Romance into the Renaissance. Cervantes' writing both in the *Quixote* and in other texts always engages this problem, whether in overt assaults on gender definition or more generally in his resistance to the formulation of reason as the dominant conceptualization of Western culture. In the case of Don Quixote's adventures at the second inn, the recognition of them as a representation of the "land of women" *echtrae* provides a new reading of its content.

The fact that the adventure of the perilous bed takes place within the castle of the ladies suggests not only the same formulation in the Gawain story but also serves to re-enforce the rescue of the maidens from enchantment as the focus of the hero's quest. Among the specific items of the Don Quixote/Maritornes scene we find an impressive list of features found in both Chrétien and the Celtic sources. For example, the fact that the bed is unstable and capable of movement suggests the wheels found on either the castle itself or on the bed. The meaning of this detail seems related to the solar condition of the knight and of the castle which rotates "like a mill stone" during the course of the night, just as the panoply of the stars revolve in the heavens. In *Bricriu's Feast* CuRoi's castle rotates and CuChulainn spends the night on the roof awaiting the challenge of the giant. If he survives he will be proclaimed the greatest hero in Ireland. We note also that Don Quixote's bed is in the loft of the inn and that the stars are visible through the numerous gaps in the roof. The three beds are arranged for Don Quixote, Sancho, and the *harriero*. In the *Quixote* the arrival of the maiden temptress is foreseen by the hero because he recognizes the nature of the test before it begins, just as CuChulainn awaits the arrival of the giant. In a similar away Gawain is forewarned of dire consequences if he sleeps in the bed. Part of the comic power of Cervantes' scene is of course due to the fact that the scene develops against an intertextual awareness of the general outline of the Romance archetype in question. That the first attack will come from the *harriero*, who takes the role of the churl, is also anticipated by the reader but not by the hero, thus heightening the comic suspense. The Romance hero is always vulnerable to comic embarrassment as he enacts a ritualized testing program, a feature found in the adventures of CuChulainn, Perceval, and Lancelot.

What Cervantes has achieved is a reversal of the hero/fool into a fool/ hero format while at the same time retaining the haunting ambience of a Romance enactment. The *harriero*, as noted, is the Moorish enemy and, like his more famous relative Cide Hamete, misunderstands the intent of Don Quixote's actions. This motivates the first attack on the hero, who, like Gawain, is injured but not killed. Like his prototypes he will subsequently be "healed" by a magic ointment. The collapse of the bed, the arrival of the host, the melee, and the loss of light all reproduce the storm features of the ritual test. The subsequent intervention of the officer of the Santa Hermandad introduces the arrival of Otherworld powers symbolized by his lantern, a miniaturized version of the storm god's flaming lance or thunderbolt. This aspect is more specifically represented when the officer returns with his oil lantern and then strikes Don Quixote on the head with this "lightening bolt" (Loomis, *Arthurian Tradition* 442). With these types of realistic substitutions, the comedic grace of the entire sequence still contains the elements necessary to a Romance adventure. Even the parody, as we have seen, is part of that heritage.

In fact the source of the humor of Don Quixote's reading of the events is due to the precise concordance between the pattern of a Romance testing of the hero and a comedy of errors. This humor is not at all "realistic" but rather contains the frantic energy of early Greek comedy that cuts close to its sacred sources. Cervantes here has created a supremely comedic episode re-enforced with just enough of the necessary Romance features to keep his hero a hero. The result is close to a romantic comedy found in the theater of Lope and Calderon in that it generates a dominant feeling of romance, yet it does not resemble a denigrating parody that seeks to destroy the validity of its hero. The crucial element of Romantic verve is partially infused with the compromising link between Cide Hamete's narrative agenda and the actions of his surrogate *harriero*. The result makes fun not only of Don Quixote's Romance but also of the narrator's intentions, and it thereby undermines Cide Hamete's subversive attack on the authenticity of the hidalgo's heroic virtues.

Ginés versus Cardenio

> No one ever wrote the novel they started out to write.
>
> Robert Penn Warren

The critical concern with the re-ordering of the chapters beginning with Don Quixote and Sancho's entry into the Sierra Morena may itself have been "in error," in the sense that it ignored deeper issues in Cervantes' text. To some extent the obvious "error" concerning the theft and reappearance of the donkey disguises a more important contradiction in the sequence of events. The nature of the tension in the text has to do with the arrival of Ginés and the challenge that the picaresque as a genre presents to the Romance agenda we have been documenting. If the reader recalls the series of adventures Don Quixote encounters after leaving the inn of Juan Palomeque (ch. 17–21), it is obvious that they accumulate as repeated assaults on the interpretation of events, each providing some affirmation of the hero's reading. The adventures of the flocks of sheep, the cart of death, the finding of the helmet of Mambrino all assert the validity of the hero's hermeneutic fix. In each he proclaims that this adventure is an affirmation of his identity. On the other hand, Chapter 20, the *molino de batanes,* is the most problematic of his adventures since it introduces the narrator's challenge to the interpretive powers of both Don Quixote and Sancho. However, immediately after this, Don Quixote finds his long-sought helmet of Mambrino, which constitutes his paradigmatic piece of armament, in that his power resides in his head and not his arm.

Such a development also signals a turn in the direction of Ariosto's *Orlando* and the narrative pattern of entrelacement. In effect the helmet marks the beginning of the long and complex sequence of interpolated stories, beginning with Cardenio and ending when the "truth" about its identity is established in chapter 45. Only between these two markers does the *entrelacement* dominate the narrative sequence (Dudley "Don Quixote as Magus"). Before and after the helmet question the story proceeds on a day-by-day schedule that follows the unfolding of the protagonist's life. Thus, only in the helmet section is the discourse about his life, so to speak, removed as the controlling code in the story line. This fundamental change in the way the story is told is what is at risk as Don Quixote moves into the Sierra Morena. The disappearance and reappearance of the donkey is the result of a conflict between two narrative modes (Flores). Significantly, Ginés also stole Don Quixote's sword, another event missing from the text and about which we learn only later when Don Quixote can't find his arms. The "meaning" of these two lacunae has to do with the story of the story and not with the story of the hidalgo. In this sense they belong to the repertoire of Romance features that give us the history of its transmission. However, from the point of view of sixteenth-century aesthetics and its condemnation of *entrelacement*, the introduction of a set of interpolated tales also indicates a turn toward Romance as a genre. Critically Cervantes was to pay a high price for this "error".

Given this configuration of an initial sequence of *aventuras* followed by the insertion of an interpolative structure, we can read chapter 23 as a profound genre conflict in which features of both Romance and the picaresque novel appear. From this overview, what suddenly becomes intrusive is the appearance of Ginés with his picaresque novel. In a larger sense we can also read that Cervantes himself was never comfortable with the picaresque as a genre. His picaresque *novelas ejemplares*, like *Rinconete y Cortadillo*, all lack basic features of the genre, in particular the thematic insistence upon the picaro's failure to escape his destiny, his inability to not be a picaro. For whatever reason this attitude toward life is not at home in Cervantes' fiction. Likewise we discover that in the general review of fictional forms of the sixteenth century inserted into part 1 only the picaresque is omitted. We have the description of the picaresque genre by Ginés, but his novel is not included among the interpolations in the text we read. This is a curious gap from one point of view but quite consistent with other concerns of the *Quixote*. The question then emerges as to why we have Ginés at all. Why didn't Cervantes remove chapter 22 if he became dissatisfied with the overall direction of his episodic structure? The question lacks force since Ginés performs other functions for the hero, but both thematically and narratively the removal of the Ginés episode does make sense.

This may account for the fact that we have an unusually self-conscious insistence in the first paragraph of chapter 22 that links Ginés solidly with chapter 21:

> Cuenta Cide Hamete Benengeli, autor arábigo y manchego, en esta gravísima, altisonante, mínima, dulce e imaginada historia, que despúes que entre el famoso don Quijote de la Mancha y Sancho Panza, su escudero, pasaron aquellas razones que en el fin del capítulo veinte y uno quedan referidas, que don Quijote alzó los ojos y vio que por el camino que llevaba venían hasta doce hombres a pie, ensartados como cuentas en una gran cadena de hierro por los cuellos. (pt. 1, ch. 22)

> [Cide Hamete Benengeli, the Arab and Manchegan author, relates in this most grave, high sounding, minute, delightful, and

original history that after the discussion between the famous Don Quixote de la Mancha and his squire Sancho Panza which is set down at the end of chapter 21, Don Quixote raised his eyes and saw coming along the road he was following some dozen men on foot strung together by the neck, like beads, on a great iron chain.]

This kind of opening, while not unique, is not the most common transition formula for chapter change in the *Quixote*. As well as being unusually number specific in its reference to chapter 21, it also belongs more to the style of those transitions that signal a break in the continuity of events. The naming of Cide Hamete occurs, for instance, each time Cervantes inserts a section division of the four "parts" of part 1 (ch. 9, 15, and 28). In other cases the chapter divisions are not consistently remarked upon by the text, nor is Cide Hamete invoked. Thus this opening signals a change in the shape of the upcoming adventures. It anticipates the introduction of a new and disruptive force (Ginés and the picaresque) which brings into question the type of episodic structure the text has been utilizing, to wit, the sequential narrating of events that seeks to replicate realistically the ordinary flow of time in the protagonist's life.

This narrative procedure is identical to that of the *Lazarillo* and is often employed in later realistic novels as well. It also has the advantage of obeying the regulations of the neo-Aristotelian *preceptistas* who praised Virgil while criticizing Ariosto's use of medieval *entrelacement*. We know from many studies—Forcione's *Cervantes, Aristotle, and the "Persiles"* gives us a full discussion of the question—that Cervantes was aware of this problem and in fact introduces it as part of the debate about the success of part 1 reported by Sanson Carrasco at the opening of part 2. The fact also remains that in spite of this interdiction Cervantes embarked on a highly sophisticated use of *entrelacement* beginning with the story of Cardenio. So again the question arises, Why Ginés?

The answer is already at hand. At the level of thematic focus the problematics of destiny and free will found in the picaresque are relevant to Cervantes' agenda. It is merely that the picaresque resolution of this conflict is not to be part of Cervantes text. However, by introducing Ginés at this point, he clearly defines the issue between picaresque and Romance at both the structural and thematic levels. Only after Ginés does the narrative pattern shift to a complex *entrelacement* configuration of stories which addresses the conundrum of free will. Romance as a genre provides the possibility of never ending challenges to the hero and usually, but not always, leaves open the opportunity for a happy resolution of the problem at hand. In contrast, the picaresque consistently closes off the chance for a happy ending. Thus thematically the two genres are opposed. At the same time they also conflict at the stratum of narrative structure, since the picaresque moves ineluctably from the birth of the hero to the moment of writing, while the Romance interrupts the flow of time by means of its intricate interplay of various stories. The youthful Cervantes had essayed this interpolative structure in his first long fiction, the *Galatea*, and, starting in chapter 23 of part 1 he returns to the same narrative technique. In fact the limitation of fiction attempting to follow closely the minute-by-minute sequence of events is already narratized in Sancho's tale of the goats in chapter 20, where the problem of the reader's attention to the details of the story line becomes an issue. Likewise Cardenio, with a reverse intent, also makes the denial of interruption a feature of his story. This tells us that Cardenio is originally as resistant to Romance as Ginés is; only after his meeting with Dorotea does he become open to a fundamental change in the way he looks at life.

A comparison of the language of Ginés and Cardenio will bring into focus the nature of the generic conflict at issue. These two languages can be identified by the condition of the protagonists: for Ginés it is the language of *germania*, that is, a language of criminality, while for Cardenio it is the language of the wild man. The question then becomes, What constitutes the difference between these two modes of signification? In the case of Ginés his argot is merely a matter of substitution or metaphoric replacement so that the linguistic change occurs only at the level of the lexicon. Ginés himself sees the function of his language, in spite of its deceptive intent, as clearly logocentric in that its signifying power is "present" prior to the moment of expression. In the same vein, he also sees language as an expression of an already existent meaning. His "story" is fully present in his thought before he begins to narrate, and the language is merely a means of re-presenting an already formulated series of events. With Cardenio the problems are not so simple. He too has his story ready in his mind and insists that he be allowed to tell it without interruption. The fact that this is not what happens when he actually begins to narrate is what his story is really about. In fact his insistence that he not be interrupted indicates that he recognizes that he has trouble with language. Like the traditional wild man that he has become, he either cannot speak or, if he does, it is in a language no one can understand. Hayden White has discussed the importance of language or lack of language in the figure of the wild man. Thus while Ginés is certain that he can relate his *verdades* (truths), Cardenio is hesitant to speak at all, and when he does he tries to build protective walls around his discourse so that it won't get out of control. In this aspect Cardenio already displays a healthy respect for language, an important factor in his redemption.

The difference between the two can be designated by the literary topoi they represent. Ginés is the urban con man who seeks to deceive the world, while Cardenio represents the autistic recluse who has withdrawn into the wilderness in order to escape verbal discourse. Thus Ginés cannot be redeemed, Cardenio can. The titles of their two stories indicate their genre orientation. Ginés's *Vida de Ginés de Pasamonte* and Cardenio's *librillo de memoría* (little book of memory) mark out specific narrative formats in the terrain of sixteenth-century fictions. While the first is clearly picaresque and logocentric, the second finds its roots within the tradition of neo-Platonic tales of unhappy lovers. Nevertheless both are in the category of autobiography, a genre strongly represented in Renaissance Spain with travel accounts and religious confessions. Thus the oppositional dichotomy of Ginés/Cardenio also contains the story of two kinds of narrational languages. These two stories of language come to be told during the course of their conversations with Don Quixote.

The Stolen Language of the Picaresque versus the Forgotten Language of Women

From a very basic point of view Cardenio and Ginés are reverse articulations of the same thematic concerns. Their stories take their form in opposition to one another. They also set forth the underlying contradictions of Cervantes' text which here becomes a story of the struggle between two kinds of language, one which leads to freedom and the other to entrapment. The differing articulations of the two stories become meaningful within this thematic opposition. Without the power of a preordained destiny there can be no free will; without free will predestination lacks meaning. This binary struggle is not only the history of the Reformation and the Counter Reformation, it is also the story of the decline of the Romance and the rise of the modern novel. *Don Quixote* comes-to-be along the fault line between these literary kinds. As is often the case in Romance, the people the hero meets represent further explorations of the conflicts within his own identity. In Don Quixote's case Cardenio is the dominant factor, representing a commitment to the thematics of love, while Ginés articulates the forces that overwhelm the hero, who exists on the criminal margins of society without the possibility of love.

At the same time their intimate similarity can be found in a list of parallel functions they perform. They both tell the stories of their lives, physically attack Don Quixote, see themselves as victims of fate, seek to justify the course of actions which have led them to their life situations, address the problems of how they learned what they know, resent external comments on their condition, and assert the validity of how their language relates to an external reality. Since we never read Ginés' story we cannot judge its effectiveness, but because his situation parallels Cardenio's in fundamental ways, we can put forward the possibility that his story, like Cardenio's, undermines its own agenda. What is more certain is the fact that Cardenio produces a discourse that—like his efforts to win Luscinda—is deeply self-defeating. At the same time, however, it is Cardenio's story that crowds out Ginés's and sets forth a powerful new agenda concerning love. It is this thematic that will dominate the spectrum of tales centered on Don Quixote's third visit to an inn.

The problem of the definition of the picaresque as a genre has been studied by Claudio Guillén in *Literature as System*. He finds that the essential features of the picaresque are identified by the dialog between the knight and the picaro in chapter 22. More recently this study has been critiqued by Alastair Fowler in *Kinds of Literature* (56ff.). The outline of Fowler's genre re-definition is as follows: Guillén identifies eight universal features in the early picaresque novels. Fowler fully accepts this analysis but finds the synchronic approach utilized by Guillén as limiting, since it can't trace the "life and death of literary forms" motif of his own study. He rejects the restriction of identifying features to universal ones, since many other features appear in some picaresque novels but not in others. Fowler posits a broad spectrum of possible features for a given literary kind, but he stresses that not all such features can be found in any single exemplar of the genre. While Fowler still holds to logocentric views of language, the flexibility of his schema allows for viewing a genre as a system of communication rather than as a closed form.

Returning to Ginés's self-portrayal in his *Vida* we find the crucial features of autobiography: the author's attempt to escape from his family's social history, self-centered and self-justifying prejudices, and a tendency to generalize from a very specific personal experience. These are all features that create an ideologically closed view of life. These same three features are found in Cardenio's narrative: he seeks to justify his actions; in a symbolic way he is alienated from his father; and he generalizes dogmatically about love and women, basing his opinion on his own limited experience. In this way his story also struggles to remain ideologically closed. Nevertheless the two autobiographies are based on radically distinct concepts of language, and it is these differing linguistic ontologies that place the two stories on differing roads of development.

The fact that Cardenio "steals" the main story line away from the thief Ginés determines the shape and function of the remaining fifty chapters of part 1. In this way Cardenio's story re-defines the formulation of language used by the text. At the same time the identity of his language is created by its binary opposition to the language of Ginés's picaresque novel. The importance of the latter is that it constitutes a radical challenge to the validity of the Don Quixote text. It is this function that justifies the inclusion of the picaresque within the plethora of genres represented in *entrelacement* configuration. The fact that Ginés re-appears in part 2 indicates that Cervantes had not finished with him at the time that he, along with Don Quixote's sword, vanishes from the story of part 1.

The challenge the Ginés factor presents to the fabric of the text is precisely spelled out in his dialogue with Don Quixote as he describes his methods of composition. The first segment of his book—the part left in pawn back at the prison—narrates his life from the time of his birth until his first period of confinement in the galleys. For Ginés, writing and incarceration are dual forms of enclosure. He boasts that the part already written deals with "truths": "trata verdades, y que son verdades tan lindas y tan donosas, que no pueden haber mentiras que se le igualen" (pt. 1, ch. 22) [it deals with truth, and they are truths so beautiful and so gracefully entertaining that no lies could be their equal]. Thus he asserts that his language is clearly referential to external reality and it likewise represents that "reality" perfectly. He suffers no doubts about the adequacy of his language and asserts that this "truth" is superior to any fiction. In practice, however, his claim to an unproblematic language is undercut by the referential substitutions of the criminal language of *germanía* that he utilizes: *cantar* for *confesar*, sing for confess, and so forth). He has ignored the fact that this language exists as already referential to a prior language and is thus at least one remove from any possible exterior reality. In fact the most urgent force of this language is the ironic impact of the substitution. The use of *esposas* (wives) for restraining hand irons, for instance, can achieve meaning only in relation to a complex set of attitudes about women and marriage. In this instance one must share the specific feelings about women that range beyond their dictionary definitions in order to understand the language of *germania*.

No such language is free from references to the complexities of other systems of signification. It can function only within a spectrum of signifying possibilities so that Ginés's "truths" are referential to the compromised condition of all language rather than to an unmediated exteriority. In fact this referential dependency on other language is perhaps one of the most paradigmatic features of the picaresque as a literary form since its agenda seeks to explode unexamined beliefs about the language by which society functions; that is, hidalgos, beggars, priests, and so on are not like the dictionary definitions of the terms, nor do they fulfill the accepted ideas of their roles in society. Rather, their social reality is different from lexical terms which attribute specific characteristics to them. The picaresque as a genre, in spite of the assertions of the narrators, is a deconstruction of the possibilities of meanings in certain kinds of language. The relevance of this project to the linguistic condition of the *Quixote* text is obvious, in that the picaresque seeks to undo the social respectability of a certain kind of lexicon just as Cide Hamete aims to undermine the validity of the language of Romance. In this sense both the picaresque and the *Quixote* are concerned with the problematics of language, and this general accord validates the importance of the Ginés episode within Cervantes' text.

The contradictions within Ginés's assertions about his language are increased as he continues to describe his writing project. The next section of his book, he asserts, will easily be finished during his new period of confinement: "y no me pesa mucho de ir a ellas [las galeras], porque allí tendré lugar de acabar mi libro, que me quedan muchas cosas que decir" (pt. 1, ch. 2) [and it doesn't bother me much to go in the galleys again because there I will have time to finish my book, since not too much remains to be said]. This confirms his view that *what* he will write already exists in a pre-text and that his written "language" is perfectly transparent and fully adequate to the task. Even without going into problems of a fully deconstructed language we are presented with an already existent text that only needs to be transcribed from the marks in his head to the marks on the page. By means of these claims he tries to forestall a further "deconstruction" of his "truth." He insists that the language will say what he wills it to say—nothing more nor less. However, his *verdades* about the human condition are already fully compromised by his own status as a liar and by his failure to recognize his own linguistic inadequacy.

Perhaps the reason Cervantes did not include the text of Ginés's *Vida de Ginés de Pasamonte* is already evident. Given the problems of language already narratized in the story we realize that no such language as the one Ginés claims to possess exists. Such a language, as Don Quixote has pointed out in his first sermon (pt. 1, ch. 11), has already been lost in the fall from the Golden Age. In this way Ginés's *verdades* are already inhabited by *mentiras*, (lies), as can be seen in the text of the *Lazarillo* invoked by Ginés as his model. The language of the picaresque novel is fully compromised in spite of Ginés' arrogant claims to full logocentric presence.

In contrast to the assertion of full linguistic presence in Ginés, the language of Cardenio is fully compromised by a sense of absence, even before he speaks. His sudden appearance as a naked wild man, emerging like a chthonic force from the bowels of the Sierra Morena, already signals a problem with language. As Hayden White has discovered, the typology of the wild man marks him as a figure that has trouble with language (White 18–20). Either he has no language or speaks in terms that cannot be understood. In the *Quixote* this condition is further weighted by the broken condition of Cardenio's voice. Like his persona, his language has already been emptied of meaning.

This is the dilemma that confronts Don Quixote in his efforts to repair the collapsed state of Cardenio's identity. Within the possible horizons of a Celtic story, Cardenio has suffered a transformation from a handsome young man into a zoomorphic creature, a subhuman form indicated by his nakedness and animal movements. The change is clearly remarked by the shepherd's statement that Cardenio, after a few months in the Sierra, became unrecognizable. In the same vein it is Don Quixote's special epistemological gifts that allow him to see Cardenio's true state hidden within his present appearance:

> Y si es que mi buen intento merece ser agradecido con algún género de *cortesía*, yo os suplico, señor, por la *mucha* que *veo que en vos se encierra*, y juntamente os conjuro por la cosa que en esta vida más habéis amado o amáis, que me digáis quien sois y la causa que os ha traido a vivir y a morir entre estas soledades como *bruto animal*, pues *moráis entre ellos tan ajeno de vos mismo*

cual lo muestra vuestro traje y persona. (pt. 1, ch. 24, emphasis added)

[If, then, my good intentions deserve any reciprocal courtesy, I entreat you, senor, by the courtesy you clearly possess in such a high degree, and by whatever love or have loved best in your life, to tell me who you are and the cause that has brought you to live or die in these solitudes like a *brute beast, where you dwell in a manner so unsuited to your station [since you dwell among them so alienated from your true self]*, as is shown by your dress and appearance.]

We observe here the phenomenon of Celtic shapeshifting translated from a primitive idiom to the terms of a modern psychological novel. In this way the story of Don Quixote's confrontation with the paradox of language and identity of the characters in the interpolated stories will constitute his central challenge in part 1. Since language in the *Quixote* lacks transcendence, all identity is compromised, but this predicament does not become fully narratized until he meets Cardenio.

Nevertheless, while Cardenio is less confident about the efficacy of his language than is Ginés, he still retains strong logocentric yearnings. Cardenio, like Rousseau after him, admits to being unable to fully present himself in spoken language and as a result privileges writing over speaking. He comments about this problem when discussing the fact that Luscinda's father had forbidden him access to her.

. . . aunque pusieron silencio a las lenguas, no le pudieron poner a las plumas, las cuales, con más libertad que las lenguas, suelen *dar a entender* a quien quieren *lo que en el alma está encerrado*; que muchas veces la presencia de la cosa amada turba y enmudece la intención más determinada y la lengua más atrevida. ¡Ay cielos, y cuántos billetes le escrbí! . . . donde *el alma declaraba y trasladaba sus sentimientos*, pintaba sus encendidos deseos, entretenía sus memorias y *recreaba su voluntad*! (pt. 1, ch. 24, emphasis added)

[. . . for though they forced silence on our tongues they could not impose it on our pens, which *can reveal the heart's secrets to a loved one more freely then speech*. Often the presence of the beloved disturbs the firmest will and strikes dumb the boldest tongue. Heavens, how many letters did I write her, and how many dainty modest replies did I receive! How many songs and love poems did I compose in which *my heart declared and made known its feeling*, described its ardent longings, reveled in its recollections, and *dallied with its desires!*]

In contrast to Ginés's fully formed pre-text, Cardenio addresses language as a translating function that re-creates in new terms a non-verbal phenomenon. In this sense he recognizes that the process is not without problems even though he feels a certain sense of adequacy in relation to his letters. It is this feature that identifies his story as an epistolary novel (Dudley in *Wildman* 115–37).

The fact that Cardenio conceives his love story as an epistolary adventure has important consequences for both himself and Don Quixote. On a narrative level Don Quixote, who had already mentioned the intent to send a letter to Dulcinea, is further stimulated by Cardenio's example to undertake his letter to Dulcinea. This in turn results in poor Sancho attempting to carry the letter to her and subsequently having to invent an entire encounter with Dulcinea that never takes place. This lie subsequently forces Sancho to invent the enchantment of Dulcinea in part 2. To this extent the letter to Dulcinea provides the narrative vehicle of the sequel. It is therefore precisely at the juncture of Don Quixote meeting Cardenio that parts 1 and 2 are linked, further establishing the Cardenio episode as a crucial turning point in the story of the story.

On a more immediate level, the introduction of the epistolary novel provides a voice for the woman and deprives the male of his unchallenged linguistic advantage. This generic possibility is first suggested when Don Quixote and Sancho find Cardenio's farewell letter to Luscinda in his *librillo de memoria*. The incompleteness of this memoir is symptomatic of the condition of Cardenio and his story, while the title "little book of memory" is referential to the importance of memory in the Renaissance theory of love. From this precarious and incomplete foundation of language and memory, Cardenio struggled to bring forth his story of love. Renaissance Neoplatonism had assigned a privileged position to the function of memory within the epistemology of love. Since whatever is known must be recalled from the soul's previous life, love takes its birth from the soul's memory of its pre-earthly existence. The function of memory is to recognize the original soul mate in his or her mortal form. The Spanish phrase "la mitad de mi alma" (half of my soul) still survives in the language from the amatory lexicon of the sixteenth century. Without the memory of its Otherworld engendering, love could not come into being in its earthly form.

This memory of Platonic forms constituted love as a transcendent force within the literary production of the era. Mystical poetry, pastoral novel, Moorish novel, epistolary novel all took their force from this belief. In his search for meaning Cardenio is imprisoned within the restricted categories of this epistemological arrangement. When he speaks of love his language is referential to the endless archival accumulation of love songs, letters, laments, and so forth, rather than to his unmediated experience with Luscinda. Therein lies his downfall, since he ignores her language and unwittingly casts her into the literary role of the unfaithful female. The practical message of her letters is very different from the one he reads in them. Like men in general he is programmed to not "hear" what women say. Until he liberates himself from this misconception he is trapped in the web of his own misunderstanding.

Cardenio's linguistic situation is one of yearning for male logocentrism as he comes into conflict with the language of love and more specifically with the unreadable (to him) language of women. But for Cardenio, as for the Celtic hero, the miracle of transformation can occur because he does discover the forgotten language of love, a language of women that generates its meaning out of its own complex operations.

This means that Cardenio's re-formulation can occur only in the subsequent *entrelacement* of his own story with that of Dorotea. Her intervention is effective because it adds another stratum of language, one invented by Dorotea herself. This in effect places woman's language in the highest level amid the hierarchy of discourses that constitute the text.

In retrospect the stories of Ginés and Cardenio differentiate between an ideal of logocentric language and an exploration of a post-logocentric discourse. Within this linguistic agenda Cardenio's story narratizes the failure of Neoplatonic rhetoric to come to terms with the amatory confusion he has experienced. His story demonstrates the inadequacy of Neoplatonic terminology to tell the kind of story he needs to tell. In this sense his defective language is a primary contributor to his schizophrenic break. From a Neoplatonic enthusiast he degenerates into a wild man without a language. At the next stage Dorotea takes this linguistic order of business one step further by attempting a formulation of a language that opens the possibility of dialogue between the sexes. She achieves this goal in her generic passage from one discourse to another: as farmer's daughter, shepherdess, Byzantine princess, and finally as a "new" Dorotea confronting the enigma of Fernando.

It is this flight from the limitations of linguistic formulations that makes the Romance feature of *entrelacement* a necessity. Cervantes' achievement of genre mix marks part 1 of *Quixote* as a post-Renaissance and post-modern Romance, and at the same time Cervantes creates Dorotea as the first heroine of the modern novel. In the process of storytelling Dorotea is forced to create a new female identity, a *figura* very different from the image of woman that is written into the rhetoric of male storytellers.

The Revenge of Romance

Es todo milagro y misterio el discurso de mi vida
[everything is miracle and mystery [in] the discourse of my life]

Dorotea, chapter 30

As for *Don Quixote* . . . I cannot but shake my head over the single tales scattered through it, so extravagantly sentimental they are, so precisely in the style and taste of the very productions that the poet had set himself to mock.

Thomas Mann

In many ways the introduction of Dorotea announces the eruption of the forces of disjunction and dispersement into the text. Her resonance goes far beyond the edges of her stories. As an emblem of *entrelacement* her numinous and contradictory appeal suffuses the entire span of Cervantes' writing schemata from the *Galatea* to the *Persiles*. Her role in the *Quixote* narratizes the contentious forces of self and other within a thematic of onto-hermeneutic operations. Like Etain she assumes multiple shapes and creates a confusion about which epiphany represents the "real" woman. Even her name, "gift of God," implies a divine source for her ontology, and like many feminine names in pastoral romances, hers can be read forward or backward (e.g., Teodora/Dorotea, Belisa/Isabel, etc.), suggesting a shifting chiasmic persona.

She herself formulates this disturbing agenda in each of the stories she relates. As "herself" she describes the volatile nature of her being to the enigmatic Fernando in a language as reversible as her name:

"Si como estoy, señor, en tus brazos, estuviera entre los de un
leon fiero, y el librarme dellos se me asegurara con que hiciera,
o dijera, cosa que fuera en perjuicio de mi honestidad, así fuera
posible hacella o decilla como es posible dejar de haber sido lo
que fue." (pt. 1, ch. 28)

["If as I am, sir, in your arms, I were in the grasp of a wild lion,
and liberating myself from him could be achieved by doing or
saying anything in prejudice of my chastity, it would be as possible to do it or say it as it would be to undo the past."] (my
translation)

Considering her heavy reliance upon subjunctive and conditional clauses,
it is not surprising that this chiasmic statement comes just moments before
she accedes to Fernando's sexual demands.

Later, as Princess Micomicona, she even recognizes something of her
linguistic errancies when she affirms: "así, es todo milagro y misterio el
discurso de mi vida, como lo habreis notado" (ch. 30) ["thus everything is
miracle and mystery [in] the *discourse of my life,* as you will have noticed"]. *Discurso* here puns on its two meanings: the verbal *story* of my
life as well as the *passage* of my life. The gaps between narrating a life
and living a life are the essence of her being. Like Don Quixote himself
she sees herself living a novel, although in her case she lives a congeries
of novels. She doesn't find a definitive genre/gender fit.

Within the parameter of these two statements she brings into being an
impressive compilation of narrative and thematic problematics: fiction and
"truth," self and other, closure and indeterminacy, continuity and disjunction, fate and free will. This is achieved by creating a miraculous discourse
woven out of narrative disguises and subterfuges that tell not just the story
of her life but the story of her story's coming to be.

It is not by chance that the presenter of this discourse is a woman who
speaks first disguised as a boy and then later as a princess. The former
is a genre feature of the pastoral novel while the latter belongs to the
Byzantine novel. Her linguistic masks indicate her attempts at genre
identifications for herself and her stories. Reading her stories with the
advantage of this backward and forward motion we come to realize that
Dorotea/Teodora is the master/mistress of all her discourses.

It is only by this kind of reading that we also come to recognize *why*
the introduction of Dorotea marks the fourth and final of the original

"parts" into which Cervantes' divided part 1. Since the fourth "part" begins at chapter 28 out of a total of the fifty-two chapters of part 1, the imbalance has aroused some critical concern.

It is Flores who connects this phenomenon with the "disappearance" of Cide Hamete during the last sections of part 1. Flores sees this as part of the problem of the stolen ass and the relocation of the Grisostomo/Marcela story. I concur, if we add the condition that this shift in narrative arrangement results also from the text's fundamental engagement with its own programmatics. To put this into other critical terms, the narrator's commentary at the opening of chapter 28 concerning the entry of Dorotea constitutes a moment of deconstructive disguise and revelation. Like the onomastic tales in the Celtic ur-Romances that disguise and reveal the intentions of the original narrative, the Dorotea commentary allows the reader to glimpse briefly the generative engines at work behind the production of the text. Reading backward from the conclusion of part 1, we can recognize that this commentary provides an important clue in the unmasking of the text's economy:

> Felicísimos y venturosos fueron los tiempos donde se echó al mundo el audacísimo caballero don Quijote de la Mancha, pues por haber tenido tan honrosa determinación como fue el querer resucitar y volver al mundo la ya perdida y casi muerta orden de la andante caballería, gozamos ahora, en esta nuestra edad, necesitada de alegres entretenimientos, no sólo de la dulzura de su verdadera historia, sino de los cuentos y episodios della, que, en parte, no son menos agradables y artificiosos y verdaderos que la misma historia. La cual, prosiguiendo su rastrillado, torcido y aspado hilo, cuenta que, así como el cura comenzó a prevenirse para consolar a Cardenio, lo impidió ua voz que llegó a sus oidos, que, con triste acentos, decía desta manera. (pt. 1, ch. 28)

> [Happy and fortunate were the times when that most daring knight Don Quixote of La Mancha sallied forth into the world. Because of his so noble resolve to seek to revive and restore to the world the long-lost and almost defunct order of knight-errantry, we now enjoy in this age of ours, so poor in merry entertainment, not only the charm of his true history, but also of the tales and episodes contained in it. These, in their way, are no less pleasing, ingenous, and truthful than the history itself which,

resuming its thread, carded, spun and wound, relates that just as
the priest was about to console Cardenio, he was interrupted by
a voice he heard speaking in a plaintive tone.]

The multiple narrative concerns encased here point first to the differences between the story of the story and the story of the hidalgo, an
opposition that begins in the first paragraph of the book. We return to
the problem of the case of the hidalgo and to the question of the language of fiction. The story of the hero, who doesn't know who he is, is
to be told in the text that cannot define itself.

We also find that at the beginning of each of the four sections the
narrator uses this kind of self-conscious commentary: The opening paragraph, as we have seen, sets up the scene of the narrative voice working
its way through conflictive source documents. The second part, beginning with chapter 9, reveals a rupture of the original narrator's story line
and introduces a second narrative voice over. The third part, chapter 15,
comes just at the conclusion of the first interpolated story and specifically refers backwards to Grisostomo and Marcela. (This backward glance
may or may not confirm the theory that the Grisostomo story was moved
there in a later editorial adjustment.) In either case the comment of Cide
Hamete posits the existence of the interpolation and links it thematically
to Don Quixote's next adventure, the frustrated love story of Rocinante
and the Gallegan mares. As noted this zoomorphic insertion forms a link
between the erotic frustrations of Grisostomo and those of Don Quixote
with Maritornes. The next and final division, for whatever reason, is
postponed until chapter 28 and includes the commentary just quoted
about the function of the interpolated stories. Thus all four division commentaries have to do with changes in narrative procedures and bring to
the foreground the question of multiple stories and multiple narrators.

Ten years later, in chapter 3 of part 2, the critical question of interpolation is again discussed, this time from the viewpoints of the characters
within the novel. There Sanson Carrasco tells Don Quixote that the interpolated stories were perceived by some readers as an unjustified intrusion of material not relevant to the history of Don Quixote. Even though
this commentary is not made by the narrator, it does point up the fact
that part 2 does not make significant use of interpolations. This is all the
more noteworthy when we observe that of all Cervantes' longer fictions,
only part 2 of the *Quixote* does not utilize an interpolative structure. It
stands as a unique narrative configuration in that the focus is entirely

fixated on the two main characters. It is within this context that we can read the singular importance of the narrator's commentary in chapter 28, since the question of interpolation/no interpolation is relevant to the entire spectrum of the author's fictions.

From this vantage point we also see that the *Persiles* and not the *Quixote* represents the mainstream of his work and should not be viewed as an aberration or a decline into senility. Since it was written more or less throughout the period in which he composed part 2 of *Don Quixote* it is a product of his maturity not his decline. Thus the overall trajectory of Cervantes' work indicates a persistent commitment to interpolative structure and to Romance. In this way it is part 2 that emerges as an aberration, however welcome some readers have found it. Even part 2, however, can be seen as utilizing the quest structure so that in this manner it too carries forward a Romance agenda.

This overview of narrative procedures sets into relief the importance that the entrance of Dorotea serves as a vehicle for unpacking the narrative and thematic anxieties of fiction as a kind of writing. In one sense, however, the fourth division heading seems to come a bit late in the procedure. As a justification for the use of interpolation it belongs at least as early as chapter 23, the take off point for the *entrelacement*. In point of fact, however, Dorotea's story interrupts Cardenio's adventures and not Don Quixote's. This feature is a paradigmatic Romance strategy of holding various earlier stories in abeyance, while an apparently new character emerges into the story line. The real importance of Dorotea is that she weaves the entire interpolative structure back into Don Quixote's *historia*, and it is in this sense that the editorial commentary does pertain to both her dispersive and integrative functions within the overall narrative strategy.

It must be observed, in addition, that the ironic tone of the editor's self-reflection on the storytelling methods contributes still another layer of signification to the story itself. Since editorial intrusions in themselves were not new to the books of chivalry nor to the genre of Romance as a whole, the ironic tone is a specific Cervantine addition. At the same time, the narrator's commentary reveals a sense of apprehension about warding off critical attacks on the wandering story line, attacks that in effect do come to pass.

The reader is also struck at the complexity of the grammatical structure of the first sentence. Not only is very long but its intricacies wind back upon themselves, in the manner of *entrelacement* itself. The sentence seems to perform its own stylistic anxieties. What also bears notice is the ironic repetition of the term *verdadero*/(truthful). The narrator puts in question, as he has before, the veracity of the Don Quixote story and then asserts that the inserted *cuentos* are just as "true," that is, they too are fictions. In this way the unasked question of what is relevant or irrelevant in fiction hovers behind the commentary.

Two other attributes of fiction are also at issue. First the narrator refers to the "dulzura" (sweetness) of Don Quixote's true history and then asserts that the interpolated stories are as "agradables y artificiosos y verdaderos" (agreeable and artificial and true) as the history itself. The "dulzura" and "agradables" compliment one another, but "artificioso" enters a new factor into the equation. Self-conscious artifice was one of the primary virtues of sixteenth-century mannerism, as is easily seen in the work of El Greco. But this kind of artifice was to lose status within the aggressive neo-realism of the seventeenth century. S. J. Freedberg's detailed description of the abrupt transition from mannerism to a new realism is particularly relevant to the this topic (52–79). Velázquez's youthful *Water Vendor* (1619) appears only four year's later than part 2 of *Don Quixote*. Given this development the pleasant artificiality of the pastoral novels like the *Diana* and the *Galatea* was already at risk in 1605. Thus the term *artificioso* is problematic here, as is born out in the question of *artificio*/ *engaño* (artifice/deception) in both the priest's *artificio* of taking Don Quixote home and in the less benevolent deceptions of Lotario, Anselmo, and Camila in the *Curioso* story. Nevertheless within the context of Dorotea's stories, where lying and artistic intentionality have overlapping roles, the term *artificioso* still finds a positive connotation. Its relevance to her manipulations of Don Quixote in fact is very much at issue. Dorotea as a person is a product of *artificio* and this feature accounts for the contradictory nature of her behavior. She is, more than any of the other heroines, the most "guilty" of evasions and role playing. In this characteristic Dorotea is the mannerist re-interpretation of the Celtic banshee or fairy woman of the Otherworld *sides*, and this accounts for the contradictory readings of her personality. But whether she is morally "good" or "evil" is not the relevant question. She is rather the paradigmatic Romance gesture of the text, and, like the text itself, she is not only reliable/unreliable—she is at times "unreadable" in the terms of realistic fiction.

The artifice of her entrance into the text is an inherited strategy of the sixteenth-century pastoral novel, one that Cervantes had repeatedly used in his *Galatea*. In this sense she emerges as an abstracted interruption, perceived only by her voice, which splices into the Cardenio situation. She is still disembodied, and her Otherworld condition is emphasized by the thematic import of her opening statement. "¡Ay Dios! Si será posible que he ya hallado *lugar*...." ["Oh God! If it were possible that I have now found a *place*...."]. The absence of a place/*lugar* for her is repeated a few lines later: "estos riscos y malezas ... me darán *lugar*..." (Selig "En un lugar de ...) [these peaks and thickets ... will give me a *place*..."]. Not only does this echo the opening rhetorical gesture of "un lugar de la Mancha" [a place in La Mancha] but the thematic situation emphasizes that she is a person (not yet a woman) without *lugar*/place in the world of men. To use the current lexicon, she is a non-person in the society of her time, but in the language of Romance she is also the Otherworld woman of the Celtic *sides* and the enchantress of passing warriors. In fact the folklore of the time already points to her as a wild woman, that is, as a creature not belonging to the social world of man.

This thematic is further developed in this same sentence: "para que con quejas comunique mi desgracia al cielo, que no la [compañía] de *ningún hombre humano*, pues no hay ninguno en la tierra de quien se puede esperar consejo en las dudas, alivio en las quejas, ni remedio in los males!" ["so that with complaints I may communicate my disgrace to heaven, and not to the companionship of *any human man*, since there is not one on earth in whom one can expect counsel in doubt, relief in complaints, nor help in suffering!"]. At one level, she has lost faith in men is as the result of her experiences, sexual and otherwise, and at another level, she is anticipating the interventions of the priest and Don Quixote, neither of whom is your everyday male on the make. But in another, more remote sense she is also anticipating Fernando, whom she will convert by means of her storytelling powers into a suitable Otherworld figure for her own ontology. She is already a lorelei, a water fay, a "belle dame sans merci" found in a stream or pool who has the power to enchant her listeners. Fernando merely proves to be the most resistant of these listeners, but he too will reluctantly succumb to her words.

Entrelacement versus Logocentrism

The question of Dorotea engages the larger issues of part 1 of the *Quixote* text as they weave through the ever more intricate interpolative maneuvers of her stories. These theoretical questions are most approachable within the debate of interpolation versus no interpolation, or medieval Romance versus neo-classic epic. Echoes of this debate inform Don Quixote's dialogue with the canon of Toledo (pt. 1, chs. 47–48), as well in the change of narrative structure between parts 1 and 2. In his study of Sannazaro, William J. Kennedy points out that the vogue of *entrelacement* was wedded to the early Renaissance delight in adjusting to the changing horizons of expectations such works required of the readers, while later readers with new ideals of "unity" became impatient with such tasks [104]. This joy in the deferment of an ever receding closure point is one of the characteristics of the Romances of Chivalry commented on by both Don Quixote and Cide Hamete. The critical commentary concerning the function of the *Curioso impertinente* at the opening of part 2 marks the end of that manner of reading within the *Quixote*.

To some extent this shift in reading habits marks the end of the Renaissance and the rise of the commitment to causality in science, and to realism in literature and the arts. El Greco gives way to Velázquez; the pastoral to the picaresque; the Romance to the epic; *Quixote*, part 1, to *Quixote*, part 2. Other considerations distinguish this change, but reader impatience with *entrelacement* established itself in the 17th century and dominated narrative discourse until the rise of the moderns and postmoderns starting with Joyce's *Ulysses* and *Finnegan's Wake*. In this sense *Quixote*, part 1 is already postmodern just as *Quixote*, part 2, prefigures the realistic novel of the eighteenth and nineteenth centuries.

This preoccupation with logocentric consciousness obviously favors a fiction that replicates the illusion of its own condition. Hence the rise of narratives that begin with the beginning and proceed forward in an orderly progression of time's unfolding. The intellectual commitment to a sequential cause-and-effect universe that took place in seventeenth-century science favored the expectation for this kind of narratives. In contrast, the continual shifting between narrative time sequences in Romance was viewed as a disturbance and quickly fell from favor. This neo-realism in painting and literature is, however, compromised by a forgotten awareness of its mannerist ancestors. Thus in a master strategist like Velázquez his achievement in his *Las Meninas* is precisely the disguising of a disjunctive universe within the effects of its illusionism. The painting appears realistic but contains disguised mannerist references to its awareness of its own subterfuges. In that achievement it is anticipated by Cervantes' similar maneuvers in *Quixote*, part 2, where the reader is reminded by means of the Avellaneda references that fiction fictionalizes itself. In fact a similar gesture initiates the entire narrative program in the first paragraph of *Quixote,* part 1, where the fictional narrator fictionalizes his mysterious sources. Thus Cervantine "realism" in part 2 is thoroughly compromised from the start.

The difference between this compromised realism of *Quixote,* part 2, and the extravagant sentimentalism that Thomas Mann finds in *Quixote,* part 1, is nowhere more in evidence than in the story of Dorotea and Fernando. In this instance both the manner of telling and the evolution of the narrative content call for careful critical attention. Yet the problem of why the Dorotea situation forms part of the text has remained invisible in broad daylight, and instead critical attention has focused on humanistic concerns about Cervantes' methods of composition (i.e., he might have written the stories earlier and then "inserted" them here) or on questions of how the stories "fit into" the thematic schemata. All this has focused attention on what Dorotea's stories may "mean" in relation to the "totality" of the book. Whatever validity these questions have ignore the more fundamental operations of a text that in this instance circles back on its own genesis. The need for disguising the text's concern with its own hidden movements alerts us to the importance of the question. With Dorotea, rather than with Cardenio in chapter 23, the *entrelacement* energy has found its moment of self-authentication. If we can trace how Dorotea performs her role as the *figura* of *entrelacement*, we will reveal how Romance inhabits the ontology of the novel. At the same time, given the historical relevance of the *Quixote* as a literary document, we have moved very close to discovering the emergence of a new literary kind, not only for Cervantes but for early modern Europe. We are witnessing what in the history of the natural sciences would be called a "shift of paradigms" (Kuhn 43ff.). Here, the future of narrative strategies hangs precariously over an epistemological abyss.

The deceptive energy of the Dorotea/Micomicona sequence as it unfolds is due to its complicity with the power of Romance. Ostensibly the target of an organized attack and supposedly undercut by the force of parody, Romance here makes its most effective effort to usurp control of the text's schemata. The success or failure of the attempt is less important than what it reveals about the constitution of the *Quixote* and the nature of the Romance dynamism it displays. The paramount attribute of this development is the voice of Dorotea herself, the woman hidden in the story as Cardenio has already (mis-)presented it. The historic importance of the voice of the Romance heroine cannot be underestimated. The intervention of the woman's voice has already been accomplished for the *Quixote* with the discourse of Marcela, her famous "I was born free" speech, but the nature of that instance has limited its immediate impact because Marcela as a heroine opts out of the sexual economy of the text. She rejects not only Grisostomo but love itself, and thus she herself has no viable future within the story line. If she were to reappear she would do so as already a victim of love, just as her prototype the cruel Gelasia did in the *Galatea*. But this convention is not actuated by Cervantes in the *Quixote*. Instead he introduces the mercurial Dorotea, who, unlike her predecessor, becomes the heroine of this or any other story that she come in contact with.

It is a commonplace of courtly love that the voice of love is that of the man. In this tradition the lady had little to say other than no. However, Chrétien's Romances, under the influence of Celtic source tales, refocused the erotic landscape so that the women played a more aggressive role. Guinevere openly celebrated her control of Lancelot, but this "aggressiveness" contributed to the lowered social valorization of Arthurian Romance within the hierarchy of genres. In the Renaissance the pastoral tradition, at least after Montemayor's *Diana*, provided an even more overt role for the language of women who emerge as the dominant storytellers of the pastoral novel. The popularity span of the pastoral novel coincided with Cervantes' youth, and he himself entered the arena with his never-to-be finished *Galatea*. Nevertheless his effort to create a fictional language for women finds its most forceful expression in the figure of Dorotea. She thus constitutes the disguised presence of Romance within the text. She is hidden in plain sight because she is both astonishingly visible and at the same time "under erasure." Like her Celtic ancestry she is both there and not there, appearing and vanishing as she assumes different epiphanies in the workings of the text. Next to Don Quixote himself, she is the most vigorously articulated protagonist of *Quixote*, part 1, while in *Quixote*, part 2, her spirit seems to inhabit the stylish *bizarría* of the duchess. In this sense it is meaningful to refer to the Dorotea factor rather than just the figure of the new heroine. Her function becomes nothing less than the operation of Romance as it manipulates the multiple fictional horizons of the story.

Romance in this sense incorporates all the subversive textual forces operating below the surface not only of Don Quixote's adventures but of the Cide Hamete narrative. This energy includes the resistance to logocentrism found in her feminist language. The moment of deconstructive revelation presents itself very innocently at the side of the stream in the Sierra Morena as the essential Romance heroine takes hold of the rhetoric of interpolation and turns the story back upon itself.

The Language of Dorotea and the Discourse of Disjunction

Unlike Cardenio's narrative rhetoric, Dorotea's language does not aspire to logocentric presence. Instead, the linguistic environment in which she comes-to-be deprives her multiple personae of a clear referential basis. Much like her Celtic shapeshifting predecessors, Dorotea seems to have no privileged form in which to express her mercurial personalities: daughter, runaway, shepherd, peasant, wild woman, enchantress, woman, wife, mistress, majordomo, princess, and storyteller supreme.

In the last capacity she is like the Welsh bards, the entertainers who weave old stories into new fabulations without concern for their original meaning or purpose. Her goal, like that of the orator, is to convince her audience, and in this she belongs to the Renaissance tradition of privileging rhetoric over philosophy. As a result, the reader can never be certain when her mercurial language liberates itself from mundane referentiality. There is an exuberance to her various linguistic strata, and her fictions partake of truth, just as her truth partakes of fiction. Whether the "Dorotea" version of what happened with Fernando is more true than her princess Micomicona version is doubtful, and neither version in itself presents the whole story. Never in the *Quixote* is meaning so evanescent or so opaque. Never is the language so luminous or so shadowed. Her sign is Gemini and she shares a linguistic cusp with Don Quixote's Cancer.

Her first narrative traces her trajectory from the privileged but enclosed habitat of the *hija mimada* (sheltered and spoiled daughter) to the unenclosed world of the wild woman. Reading beyond the letter of her story (she invites this practice) one finds the source of her problem is not merely the question of her relationship to Fernando, but rather her transgression beyond the boundaries of a male language utilized to inscribe and prescribe her status as a woman. In the terms of the rhetorical limits with which she is described and circumscribed she remains "unreadable." Like her lover Fernando she also ruptures the linguistic categories of the various languages in which she has to operate. All the possibilities

of meaning are exhausted without containing her shifting modes of being. As in the Vedic description of poetry, what is unsaid about her is
more powerful than what is said.

Among the many levels of discourse that attempt to contain the identity of Dorotea, three stand out: the Petrarchan lexicon of love, the rhetoric of the Spanish *novela pastoril* (e.g., the *Diana*), and the narrativity of
the Byzantine Romance of Heliodorus. Fragments of other special languages, most notably legal argumentation and epistolary interchanges,
are woven into the narratives that bring forth Dorotea. The first signs of
the hidden/apparent condition of her linguistic ontology can be discovered by the interweaving of Petrarchan commonplaces used by the narrator to describe her beauty as she washes her feet in the mountain
stream. The abrupt appearance of these well-worn poetic tropes clashes
with the unadorned language of the description of what, at first glance,
appears to be a rustic shepherd boy with dirty feet. In this context four
commonplace Petrarchan metaphors for feminine beauty introduce
Dorotea:

> los pies. . . . no parecían sino dos pedazos de blanco cristal
> [the feet . . . seemed like nothing more than two piece of white
> crystal]
>
> la pierna, que sin duda alguna, de blanco alabastro parecía
> [the leg, which without doubt appeared to be of white alabaster]
>
> los cabellos, que pudieran los del sol tenerles envidia
> [the hair, which could have caused the envy of the sun's rays]
>
> las manos semejaban en los cabellos pedazos de apretada nieve
> [the hands in (her) hair seemed like pieces of crushed snow]

The familiar lapidary imagery applied to the beloved female is doubly
displaced here. It belongs within a poetic lament spoken by a lover, not
embedded in a realistic description of a shepherd's body. These are
metaphors to be used in the song of a lover and not in the prose of a
narrator. Scattered along the developing story line this imagery evokes
not just the person described but rather the emotional environment from
which its rhetoric has been lifted. Thus Dorotea first appears partially
wrapped in a language little suited to her immediate situation. It does

evoke, however, both her beauty and her amatory past. As the woman abandoned to the forces of the wilderness, she still trails clouds of poetic immortality. In this way, what was hidden by her shepherd's disguise emerges from the rustic setting so that she is born amid lexical contradictions indicative of both her past and her present conditions. In fact there is an ironic cruelty in applying the language of the love complaint to an abandoned woman. It is a discourse which still wears the rhetorical shreds of a language used to deceive her.

In this sense the appropriate/inappropriate rhetoric announces its own inadequacy in its attempt to describe the "reality" of the woman and her social situation. In fact she is located beyond the language of men and their erotic expectations. She is, in effect, a creature for which there is no name, except that of a wild woman, a being belonging to no known language. This, then, is the dilemma she faces in attempting to tell her story within the rhetoric of human society. No matter what she says, it will be in part a lie. In the lexicon of current critical usage she is doomed to "misspeak." The truthful/lying Dorotea enigma is in place. She becomes unreadable because at its deepest level her story is untellable in the language of men.

Communicative Incompetence

The pastoral tradition, both in its poetic and novelesque formats, provides other resources and other problems for the expression of the Dorotea situation. Perhaps because the condition of lying obtains within the decorum of the pastoral roman à cléf, its expressive possibilities are richer and more complex than in other rhetorical environments. Fifty years before the *Quixote* Montemayor had effected a renovation of a narrative language which privileged the voice of the woman, and Dorotea is heir to that change. Among the important expressive features at her disposal were a self-conscious theatricality that was part of the mannerist movement and a type of autobiography encapsulated in the pastoral masquerade. The underlying playfulness of this arrangement is to be a significant aspect of her storytelling performances. The question is not whether she plays certain pre-scribed literary roles (shepherdess, princess, etc.) but *how* she utilizes the resources of these various languages. Her "performances" must also be measured against the similar role-playing by Cardenio and Camila, the interpolative hero and heroine most closely related to her. This panoply, of course, also plays off of Don Quixote's role-playing as the *caballero andante*, a baseline that informs all the interpolated stories from Marcela to Leandra and from Grisostomo to Vicente de la Roca. Against this spectrum Dorotea is the most prominent actor/actress. She differs from the others only in degree and complexity.

Nevertheless the pastoral tradition cannot contain Dorotea's many forms. Her being and expressiveness extend beyond the reach of the narrative possibilities of the genre. In this sense the pastoral components of her storytelling repertoire function as do the onomastic tales in the Celtic tradition: they explain and disguise a hidden formulation of her personality. While in the Celtic situation that device had to do with the suppressed pagan content of the tales, in the case of Dorotea the reader is induced or seduced to imagine a "real" Dorotea existing behind the masks she puts on. It is this condition that leads to the impression of a deceptive, manipulating Dorotea who utilizes a false self-presentation as an innocent village girl abused by an exploitative nobleman. To a great extent this "interpretation" is "true" at one hermeneutic stratum. She is a skillful storyteller, but her success is undermined by an overtly self-serving design. As she herself states:

> Esta, pues, era la vida que yo tenía en casa de mis padres, la cual, si tan particularmente he contado, no ha sido por ostentación ni por dar a entender que soy rica, sino porque se advierta cuan sin culpa me ha venido de aquel buen estado que he dicho al infelice en que ahora me hallo. (pt. 1, ch. 28)

> [Such was the life I led in my parents' house, and if I have depicted it thus minutely, it is not out of ostentation, or to let you know that I am rich, but that you see how, without any fault of mine, I have fallen from the happy condition I have described to the misery I am in at present.]

As is characteristic of Dorotea's rhetoric it is impossible to separate the elements of truth and fiction. She is both saying and unsaying at the same time. Like Cardenio she does intend, at one level, to excuse/justify her actions; but at the same time her story also tells us how self-conscious she is both as a narrator and as a heroine of her own tale. The touch of theatrical excess to the "particulares" of her lifestyle undermines the impression of her as an innocent victim of circumstances beyond her control.

An example of this duplicity is her account of how Fernando's letters found their way into her hands. Although she doesn't admit it at this point, her personal maidservant is obviously the carrier of the letters regardless of Dorotea's protestations of ignorance: "Los billetes, sin saber como, a mis manos venían" [The letters, without my knowing how, came into my hands]. The linguistic slights of hand of this phrase speak volumes. She seems to say that the letters on their own power "arrive" into her hands. The grammatical structure omits the all important agent or even the need for an agent. What she hasn't said, of course, is that the maid's [correct?] decision to pass the letters on to her is the result of the maid's "reading" of Dorotea's desires. As in the case of the "Curioso impertinente," the maid functions as an agent of Camila's unconscious wishes. This social arrangement provides another insight into the maid's crucial function in introducing Fernando himself, and not just his letters, into Dorotea's bedroom. The letters also perform functions similar to the ones found in the Cardenio epistolary novel. The pen and letter are the signs of very obvious male sexual intentions. The letter seduces the reader, by Dorotea's own admission; and the pen foreshadows the penis. Her personal maid, trapped by her precarious social situation under a willful mistress, took the risk of introducing Fernando into her bedroom because she read/misread the real nature of Dorotea's intentions.

If Fernando had immediately lived up to his many oaths concerning a marriage to Dorotea, the maid would have reaped the benefits accrued to her mistress. Fernando's backsliding doomed the hapless maid, who is subsequently punished by Dorotea. Again like Cardenio, Dorotea is unable to accept responsibility for her own actions and refuses to admit her complicity in originally accepting the letters at all. The maid's tragedy, also unacknowledged by Dorotea, was that she was caught in the web of Dorotea's conflicting desires to have her cake and eat it too. At the same time Dorotea herself is caught between the conflicting claims of honor and desire.

Another reading of her story can be found if we re-situate the story into a Celtic context. There the conflict goes back to the patriarchal/matriarchal wars that are the source of *The Táin*, where Queen Maeve states her sexual situation openly: "If I married a jealous man that would be wrong, too: I never had one man without another waiting in the shadows. So I got the kind of man I wanted" (Kinsella 53). While Dorotea may not aspire to such sexual freedom she nevertheless has to balance the demands of her public situation with her private desires. She is trapped not just by the inadequacy of the societal arrangements in which she finds herself but by the inadequacy of the male language at her disposal. Like her maid, Dorotea must choose between two unacceptable choices: remain the village maiden or sexually engage herself with Fernando. The suitability of Fernando as a partner for her, the "kind of man" she wants, is the other story that remains unexpressed in Dorotea's account of her misadventures. We only note that, like other meanings of her narrative gestures, her recognition of Fernando's sexual appeal is both denied and celebrated.

It is in this way that the mannerist pastoral agenda becomes the underlying message of Dorotea's tale. As with the *Quixote* text, the telling of the story becomes, in a mannerist illusionistic slight of hand, the subject of the story. Dorotea incarnates herself as the ultimate mannerist shepherdess, the woman who seeks to achieve the triumphs of both language and love. But, like her language, she must resort to illusionistic devices and hence earn the reputation of being deceptive and manipulative. She lives up to the priest's and Cardenio's expectations: "Todo esto dijo sin parar la que tan hermosa mujer parecía, con *tan suelta lengua*, con voz tan suave, que no menos les admiró su discreción que su hermosura" (pt. 1, ch. 28) [She who appeared (to be) a most beautiful woman said all this without stopping, with such a quick tongue, with such a soft voice, that they admired her discretion as much as her beauty]. Again the language in which she is portrayed raises suspicions about her state of being. She is linguistically seductive, and the erotic pun on *lengua* may indicate something of her sexual appeal to Fernando.

The extravagance of her person and language may in effect work to frighten Fernando away after his first two sexual encounters with her. He, above all, wants to feel in control of women, and his instincts tell him that he is not adequate to the challenge Dorotea presents. It is here that we see a parallel with the limitless sexuality of Otherworld women like Queen Maeve. The hero who involves himself with the women of the fairy *sides* will not be able to go home again; and Fernando, once he encounters Dorotea, is no longer the happy seducer of village girls he once was. At the same time he has reached the point in his sexual maturation that allows him to be captivated by a powerful equal. His immature self then re-asserts itself as he tries to recoup his emotional freedom and its adolescent sexuality. This explains the nature of the challenge he presents to her. One of the few good things that can be said about him is that for once he has become vulnerable to a woman he has seduced.

The difficulty for Dorotea is that the resources of her pastoral rhetoric do not provide the means to resolve the impasse. The bankruptcy of the inherited linguistic resources finds its true expression in the contradictions of the rhetorical set phrases that she employs. She develops her story out of the punning possibilities of two terms, *cuento* (story) and *doncella* (maiden). The first of these also exists as its doublet *cuenta*/account, an economic subtext of the possibilities of counting/telling, when she recounts her experience keeping the "accounts" of her father's farm. Dorotea presents herself as a very competent "counter/teller" with suggestions that she is also a very good re-counter or teller of a tale. This device is further extended with the use of a pun phrase current in the narrative strategies of the time: "Mas por acabar presto con el cuento (que no le tiene) de mis desdichas . . ." [But in order to end quickly the story/account of my endless misfortunes . . .]. The phrase also contains a second pun with "des-dicha" (un-said), which couples the concept of fortune and misfortune with what has been said and unsaid. (Covarrubias makes this same pun in his *Tesoro* entry for *desdicha*.) This type of language that is self-referential to its own referential possibilities fits comfortably within the *artifcio* of mannerist wordplay in the sixteenth-century pastoral. At the same time it is consistent with the Celtic use of puns to indicate a dangerous border land, a place where Otherworld forces could intervene (Rees and Rees 265–66).

The second instance of this kind of punning occurs, tellingly, at the moment of her seduction by Fernando. Here again she passes quickly over what in many ways is the climactic event of her story with the use of a well-worn pun. After Fernando has promised to be her husband and sworn oaths before the image of the Virgin and the witness of the problematic maid, Dorotea recounts: "Y con esto, y con volverse a salir del aposento mi doncella, yo dejé de serlo" [And with this, and with the exit of the maid from the bedroom, I stopped being one (a maiden)]. What is left unsaid here speaks the true story. As a result while Dorotea remains open to further erotic development with Fernando, he quickly removes himself from the scene, and abruptly seeks to marry Luscinda, a traditional girl he believes will not challenge him. The latter development seems motivated by hidden reasons, since he has no need of a wife except to protect himself from Dorotea. Thus, whatever story can be extrapolated from her account, it is apparent that Dorotea has moved beyond the signifying possibilities of the restrictive categories of polite rhetoric.

The relevance of this linguistic dilemma to her social situation is found in the contradictions of another pastoral trope with which she opened her discourse. The reader will recognize that the conventionality of this expression was also apparent in Cardenio's story. Dorotea's formulation comes in response to the priest's equally conventional offer of help or consolation: "temo que la relación que os hiciere de mis desdichas os ha de causar, al par de la compasión, la pesadumbre, porque no habéis de hallar remedio para remediarlas ni consuelo para entretenerlas" [I fear that whatever relation I may make of my misfortunes will cause you, along with the response of compassion, grief, because you will not find the remedy to relieve them nor consolation to allay them]. The repeated punning of this kind of highly manneristic language ultimately undermines its own validity. For instance, she states near the conclusion of her story that she was relieved to find that the marriage of Fernando and Luscinda had been aborted by the suicide attempt of the bride: "Esto que supe, puso en bando mis esperanzas, y tuve por mejor no haber hallado a don Fernando, que no hallarle casado, pareciéndome que aun no estaba del todo cerrada la puerta a mi remedio" [As soon as I found this out it gave renewed strength to my hopes since it seemed to me that finding Fernando not married left open (not closed) the door for my recovery]. This commentary provides the unsaying of the formulaic pun about *lugar* (statement) with which she opened her story. It is like the contradictions between the *sen* and the *aventure* found in Chrétien's stories. It is a kind of hindrance to meaning found in Romances which attempt to retell a traditional story and add a new meaning on to its decayed rhetoric.

These examples indicate the linguistic problems Dorotea encounters in telling her misadventure. She has bankrupted the linguistic devices of her genre and now has to find a new rhetoric in order to communicate her emotional and social situation. Unexpectedly her involvement with the priest, Cardenio, and Don Quixote provide her with new expedients and artifices.

Otherworld Languages

Given the volatility of Dorotea's linguistic situation it is to be expected that the events of the story are but narratized exempla of the mercurial messages encoded in all discourse. This story unfolds in descending stages of communicative incompetence. At the simplest level it begins with

Fernando's misreading of Dorotea as a naive country girl. This in turn creates an uncontrollable sequence of consequences for the people who deal with him. The problem of untangling Fernando's intentions is experienced by everyone: Dorotea, the servants, her parents, Cardenio, Luscinda, the priest, and so forth. In her seduction scene Dorotea mounts a rearguard action to this challenge by attempting to bind Fernando with performative statements that would constitute the nature of their relationship as a secret marriage. In this effort we find the performance of a ceremony complete with oaths, icons, and witnesses. Since she realizes that language is not logocentric, Dorotea seeks to bolster its efficacy by embedding it in a ritual situation. This device is not foolproof, and it indicates more about her intentions than it does about his. At its core the problem has become centered on the ontology of Fernando's language. As with the riddle in a mythic tale, only Dorotea as heroine will be able to "read" its message. Her challenge has become a search for a Romance hermeneutic that will make Fernando readable.

This scenario brings to light crucial glimpses of material left out of Cardenio's story. The reasons for these omissions, relevant to Dorotea's relationship with Fernando, reveal what has been hidden in the discourse of the metastory of the four lovers. One is that Cardenio, who suffers from another version of adolescent male sexuality, also can't accept the responsibilities of marriage and therefore attempts to forget the binding conditions of his promises to Luscinda. Those promises too have performed a secret marriage along the lines of the one Dorotea describes. Thus Cardenio, contrary to what he said, had been sleeping with Luscinda prior to the time in which her father forbade him access to the house. This information comes to the surface only in Luscinda's final letter found at the time of her fainting during the aborted wedding ceremony with Fernando. This information, omitted by Cardenio, is only implicit at the time of Dorotea's story, but a quick-minded girl like Dorotea would have easily read the message in Luscinda's actions. In this way the two narrative events (Cardenio's and Dorotea's discourses) interweave their implied meanings, each providing material missing from the gaps in the other's story.

A particularly secret omission is that Cardenio not only wants to suppress the nature of his sexual relationship with Luscinda but also secretly wants Fernando to marry Luscinda, an arrangement that will enable him to play the Lotario in their marriage. This stratagem would allow the substitution of the husband's prohibition for the father's in the paradigm of his sexuality, since by his own admission neither his father nor her father has forbidden the marriage. He therefore half seeks to arrange the marriage which will allow him to continue the adolescent enjoyment of a forbidden delight. This reading is one of the subliminal messages suggested to Dorotea by the story of Lotario and Anselmo and Camila. Since both she and Cardenio listen to the priest's reading of the *Curioso* story, the interpretation of that story becomes part of their own stories since it suggests subversive counter readings of their own narratives. If Cardenio and Dorotea learn anything from the *Curioso* story it would have to do with the disruptive possibilities of unfaithful marriages, disruptions that come about because of the suppressed sexual fantasies of adolescent males. Within this perspective, Cardenio's story can be read as an account of his persistent efforts to place a barrier between himself and Luscinda. Since by his own admission there is no real obstacle to their marriage, which was the expected goal of both sets of parents, his "story" has to do with the invention of obstacles, impediments he needs in order to operate sexually. In this way Dorotea's story provides the necessary supplements, sexual and signifying, to Cardenio's attempt to create "events." In this sense both Dorotea's story and the *Curioso* subversively supplement his discourse, while in a larger view, all three stories form a metastory in which the erotic subtleties of forbidden sex are exposed.

The importance of this phenomenon is that it provides a clue to a crucial aspect of Fernando's role within the *entrelacement* of the three tales. The curious thing about this clue is that it is almost invisible in the operations of Cardenio and Dorotea's stories. Of the four "enamorados andantes" only Fernando has no unmediated presence. We see him only through the highly biased eyes of Dorotea and Cardenio until the moment he appears, behind a mask, at the inn of Juan Palomeque. His arrival scene anticipates the similar first entrance of Don Juan in Tirso de Molina's *Burlador de Sevilla* or the initial entrance of the duke in Lope's *Castigo sin venganza*. All three of the moments seem to say that Don Juan has to hide his real identity from the world (Feal); the person that he is cannot operate within society. Of all three writers only Cervantes tries to portray the redemption of Don Juan. Many modern critics have likewise found this portrayal of Fernando's transformation unconvincing, and we are left with the impression that his belated marriage to Dorotea is a patched up affair, sexually and emotionally unsatisfying for both of them.

Yet the most interesting aspect about him is precisely what Dorotea tries to suppress in her account of her seduction. Not surprisingly, this trick comes immediately after her punning on *cuento* and *desdichas* and reveals her attempt to omit the most interesting part of her story: "Mas por acabar presto con el cuento (que no le tiene) de mis desdichas, *quiero pasar en silencio* las diligencias que don Fernando hizo *para declararme su voluntad*" (pt. 1, ch. 28). [But in order to end quickly the count (which it doesn't have) of my misfortunes, *I want to pass in silence* over the efforts that Don Fernando made *in order to declare his will to me*]. In other words, she seeks to hide his powers of communication, precisely the component we need to know in order to understand her story, since this would inevitably reveal her own motives. It is the latter topic that she needs to conceal if she is to proceed with her insistence about her own lack of culpability, but in this attempt she is only partly successful. The focus of the problem is simply the power of Fernando's language.

In order to evaluate the importance of Fernando's language we have to step back and take a view of his position within the multiple interpretations in which he is presented. He is the first person identified in the unfolding of the tales, since Cardenio names him during one of his seizures of madness and before he begins telling his story to Don Quixote: "¡Ah, fementido Fernando! Aquí, me pagaráis la sinrazón que me hiciste!" [Ah treacherous Fernando! Now you will pay back the injustice you did me!]. This language refers back to Don Quixote's ravings in his library, where he imagines he is beset by giants and enemy enchanters, and thus links Cardenio's paranoic madness to Don Quixote's world of Romance. The term *fementido* is also used by Dorotea in reference to Fernando, to which she adds the name of Galalon, the betrayer of Roland at Roncesvalles. The latter figure is also invoked by Don Quixote as a paragon of treachery in his inventory of enemies in chapter 1. Thus Fernando is "set up" by both Cardenio and Dorotea as a Romance *figura* who embodies the idea of treachery.

Cardenio, while never examining his own motives, further expostulates in a sonnet on the mystery of Fernando's reasons for betraying him. This sonnet opens his second narrative attempt to complete the story of his misfortunes, and it places the problem of Fernando at the center of the negative forces Cardenio creates to impede his marriage to Luscinda. In a similar way Fernando's betrayal also appears to be the focus of Dorotea's dilemma. At least that is the story each tries to tell, but, as we have seen, the real story is not just about Fernando but about the roles that Dorotea and Cardenio cast him in.

In many ways he is their victim rather than the other way around. He just happens along as Dorotea and Cardenio are groping about for a way out of their respective situations, and they both seize upon him as a vehicle for escape. For Dorotea he is a way out of the prison of her boring village life and an entry into the world of Romance. For Cardenio, Fernando constitutes the perfect obstacle to impending responsibilities of marriage and, in addition, the necessary erotic stimulant for a life of great adulterous sex with Luscinda. The latter is almost achieved in that the wedding of Luscinda and Fernando is completed, at least to the stage of her equivocal si/si (yes/if). Here again a pun is necessary for the ultimate outcome of the story line, and, as in the case of Dorotea's word-play, the pun allows for a polysemous resolution. Nevertheless Dorotea's need for Fernando has a more complex linguistic challenge. The nature of that challenge could not find a more satisfactory resource than the Byzantine novel, a genre she utilizes in her Micomicona story.

Sailing to Byzantium

The generic inter-relationships of the two tales Dorotea tells constitute in themselves a story of polysemous intricacy worthy of the contemporary postmodern novel. In fact the sequence of tales from the printing errors of chapter 23 until Don Quixote leaves the inn in chapter 45 forms a generic *entrelacement* unexcelled in complexity. The adventures at the second inn provide a re-ordering of all the generic languages utilized. The recurrence of the metaphor of tapestry throughout these episodes provides a self-awareness of what the text is about. Cardenio himself is the icon of this process, as his epithet *El Roto* (broken thread) indicates the rupture in his personality.

The task of analyzing these linguistic interactions must be attempted if we are to achieve an understanding of what is at issue in the stories. From a linguistic viewpoint the text seems intent on foregrounding the communicative power of certain genre-specific messages. This means that to "read" the signifiers the reader needs to be aware of the genre systems at work. If we consider that each genre installs specific meanings to key words and phrases, we can recognize the multiple possibilities of signi-fication in this interchange of genres.

In this sense the interpolative phase of the novel converts the resources of *entrelacement* into the subject of its own storytelling procedures. We find not only miniaturized formulations of longer forms, such as the Byzantine, pastoral and chivalric Romances, but also briefer coding systems which also come into play. Throughout these chapters there is a mercurial referential volatility to the language that produces a mannerist tour de force. In fact the contradictory force of Dorotea's personality obtains its energy from this linguistic situation. Her "story" creates a polygeneric system of signification, an *entrelacement* configuration with fluctuating horizons of referentiality. Her personality becomes unreadable because her words simultaneously exploit meanings that ordinarily occur only in separate genres.

Cervantes has in this way replicated the condition of multiple meanings or systems of meanings found in Romance, where the confusion is due to a layering of changing hermeneutic systems. In this way he has established a triumphant new mannerist Romance self-referential to the problematics of meaning in all art.

At the same time he has also produced a language that presents the multiple generic strata as referential to the psychological dilemmas of the four lovers. The Dorotea story, for instance, presents one of the most telling examples of the problems of lying and honesty that exist in autobiography as a genre. This means that at every instance her language is so constituted that she cannot contain the referential possibilities of her story. When she says *cuento* she unleashes unnumbered referential possibilities of counting and saying. In the case of her Micomicona story these numbers are further complicated by the fact that her Byzantine story retells her pastoral story, which is already a partial retelling of Cardenio's story. At the same time her story also echoes the situations of the previous stories of Grisostomo and Lope Ruiz and anticipates the story of Anselmo and Lotario and Camila. At the same time, all this generic linking and overlapping plays off Don Quixote's generic madness. The result is that part 1 of *Don Quixote*, part 1 becomes a mannerist Romance of unparalleled expressiveness, and the language of entrelacement is able to deal with the polymorphic ontologies of Dorotea, Cardenio, and Fernando.

The Micomicona Artifice

Mannerism marked a revolution in the history of art and created entirely new stylistic standards; and the revolution lay in the fact that for the first time art *deliberately* diverged from nature. (emphasis added)

Arnold Hauser

Artificio is a dangerous word in the *Quixote*. Mannerist fascination with the self-referential possibilities of art became both an ethical and aesthetic vice in the judgment of later eras. To some extent this shift in attitude toward *artificio* is inscribed in the interpolated tales, where it sometimes appears as a virtue and sometimes as a vice. The clearest instance of this vacillation can be found in the contrast between its use in the priest's invention of the artifice of Dorotea's role as Princess Micomicona and the sinister invention of Anselmo's test of Camila's virtue in the "Curioso impertinente." The latter invention leads to Camila's ingenious reversal of the artifice to disguise her sexual relationship with Lotario. In the first instance the intention of the artifice is to help Don Quixote by rescuing him from his penance in the Sierra Morena, while the second is a purely selfish device needed to increase Anselmo's—or later Camila's—sexual pleasure.

This arrangement places the good or evil of artifice entirely in the hands of the user. Like language itself, artifice has endless possibilities for truth and lying that make it a dangerous supplement to the already deceptive resources of art. It was the general unease with the "lying" potential of art that made mannerist artifice a convenient whipping post for later critical pieties. It survived into both the baroque and rococo periods, first becoming an illusionist device in the visual arts for Bernini and Velázquez, and then becoming a decorative Trompe l'oiel in the eighteenth century, a development that deprived artifice of its seriousness. In the *Quixote*, however, Dorotea's triumph of *artificio* lies about midway in this progression and helps explain the shifting positive and negative responses she generates. In order to understand this development her device must be seen against the pattern of other considerations which make artifice in Cervantes' text a self-conscious resource of Romance.

The cultural devaluing of *artificio* coincides inevitably with the rise of scientific analytics and the concomitant *privileging* of realism as the dominant aesthetic mode. The obverse of this process places *artificio* as a favorite resource in both the pastoral and the chivalric Romance of the sixteenth century. For this reason the linguistic mannerist excesses of Feliciano de Silva are among the first targets of parody in the *Quixote*. Likewise Don Quixote himself produces a mannerist tour de force to mark his own passage into the world of Romance in chapter 2. His self-referential description of his own sunrise exit from the corral onto the plain of Montiel is an instance of *artificio* in which the metaphorical resources of writing block out the referential value of the language. The reader's attention is focused on the manner *(maniera)* of writing rather than on what is being said. Don Quixote's representation of the style establishes the crucial features of the language of Renaissance Romance and at the same time incorporates the exact amount of exaggeration to create a balance between mannerism and the necessary parody of mannerism. In some sense this passage deflects the Romance parody of the hero himself and initiates a parody of the language excesses of the books of chivalry. This arrangement, however, serves to disguise the "serious" comicity of the Romance hero's condition, a feature that goes back to the semi-divine Celtic heroes like CuChulainn and survives intact in Chrétien's *Perceval*. But in the first paragraph of the *Quixote* the comic focus has lost its force as a sign of a hero. This development, this shift in generic signals, becomes the basis for the comic/romantic debate of Cervantine scholarly criticism, particularly in British and French contexts. Cervantes has added a twist to the comic feature of Romance by exploiting an ancient component of the Celtic ur-romances in a new manner *(maniera)*.

The effectiveness of this re-arrangement of the feature takes new strength from the mannerist tendencies in the sixteenth-century books of chivalry. Sentences very like the parody of de Silva can be found throughout the literature of the sixteenth century, whether in Spain, France, or England. This common denominator guaranteed the easy success of the *Quixote* in English and French. The excesses of euphemism in England and *preciosité* in France were ready made for the comic effects of the Oudin and Shelton translations. Seventeenth-century readers, already committed to a new aesthetic, found robust enjoyment in laughing at the outmoded language of the previous century. What is forgotten is that mannerism was a serious attempt to explore the boundaries between modes of representation and the possibilities of meaning. Cervantes in his equally serious use of comic exaggeration was uniquely able to exploit both the comic and serious significance of this language. In so doing he inscribed into his own language an erratic vitality which empowered him to express the contradictory, polymorphic personas of Cardenio, Dorotea, and Fernando.

To speak of the genre of Dorotea's Micomicona story is already a contradiction. Instead it should be seen that she thrives on generic indeterminacies. The logocentric question about who she is founders on its own inadequacies. As we have noted, she is in turn a sheltered daughter, a peasant boy, a shepherd/ess, a water nymph, a wild woman, a virgin, a fallen woman, an enchantress, a farmer's daughter, a princess, a damsel in distress, an actress, and above all the ultimate storyteller. This panoply of *personae* in which her "being " finds expression indicates at least three genre formulations—Byzantine, chivalric, and commedia del'arte—coupled with numerous folkloric, social, and biblical archetypes.

The contradictory condition resulting from her multiple signifying powers is that she is both seductive and seduced, both enchanting and enchanted, both a teller of truth and a liar. She produces a chiasmic language that is almost always reversible. When she first appears at the side of the stream she is capable of enchanting the priest, the barber, and Cardenio; but at the same time she herself is enchanted in that she cannot escape from the stream. She thus becomes a *silvestre* water nymph imprisoned in her no-man's-land. She can't find a way out of her stream ontology until the priest provides her with the role of damsel in distress in Don Quixote's chivalric Romance.

At the same time this "escape" is programmed through not only the linguistic resources of the *libro de caballería* but also those of the Byzantine novel and the commedia del'arte. In the last instance she is the actress performing under the direction of the priest/prompter who invents the role and provides direction but leaves the dialogue to the improvising capabilities of the actress. This triple generic incarnation creates an exciting range of rhetorical possibilities that she successfully utilizes to "enchant" Don Quixote and lead him back to the inn. In this sense her role is pivotal for the narrative vehicle of part 1, just as Cardenio's epistolary novel leads Don Quixote to write his letter to Dulcinea, an event that leads to the quest structure of part 2. All these developments reveal the directional function of the interpolated tales within the spectrum of Don Quixote's adventures. The turn away from Ginés to Cardenio in chapter 23 marks the emergence of the shaping force of a Romance, as opposed to realism, in the subsequent agenda of the novel.

Generic indeterminacy is not the only situation to produce unreadable items in Dorotea's storytelling performances. The shifting ontologies she displays for her male audiences run the gamut of the unreliable woman images found in male fictions. It is the expediency with which she achieves these successive incarnations that brings forth the impression of manipulative female that undermines her reputation among modern readers. Questions as to her sincerity proliferate. Is she reliable? Does she really love Fernando? Is she merely trading up in her rise from village maiden to daughter-in-law of a ducal grandee? All these doubts undermine her every statement.

A male graduate student once observed in class that if Dorotea's luck holds out Fernando's older brother will die and she will become duchess, while a female student once insisted that Dorotea was lying from the first word of her story. Both these insights deserve serious consideration and both have an element of truth in them, but at the same time we must question the validity of either comment. The presuppositions of their formulations are to be found in the categories of male discourse and its imposition of logocentric anxieties in Western metaphysics. Here the cultural de-privileging of Romance fictions works against Dorotea's ability to explain herself in terms other than those allowed in the linguistic and literary resources at her disposal. If she "lies" with the first word of her story, the fault can be found in the unsound ontology of the word she is forced to use. She is constrained by her language and by the situation, moral and physical, and by her male audience that has asked for her story. As a beautiful wild woman found in the deserted fastness of the Sierra Morena she has no social place (lugar) of her own with which to authorize her language. She herself sets forth this difficulty in her first expostulation:

> ¡Ay Dios! Si será posible que he ya hallado *lugar* que pueda servir de escondida sepultura a la carga pesada deste cuerpo, que tan contra mi voluntad sostengo! Si será, si la soldad que prometen estas sierras no me miente. ¡Ay, *desdichada,* y caún más agradable compañía hara estos riscos y malezas a mi intención, pues me darán *lugar* para que con quejas cominique mi desgracia al cielo, que no la de *ningún hombre humano,* pues no hay *ninguno en la tierra* de quien se pueda esperar consejo en las dudas, alivio en las quejas, ni remedio en los males! (pt.1, ch. 28, emphasis added)

> [O God! . . . could this place perchance serve as a secret grave for the weary load of this body I bear so unwillingly? It could indeed, unless the solitude these mountains promise deceives me. *Woe is me*! What company can be so pleasing to my mind as these rocks and thickets that permit me to complain to Heaven of my misfortune, rather the *human* (male) *companionship,* since there is no one (man) on earth from whom I might seek counsel in doubt, comfort in sorrow, or relief in distress!]

Like all of Dorotea's language this lament, formulated in the traditional lexicon of a love complaint (*queja*) is both a call for an Otherworld language in which to express herself and an Otherworld man to listen to her. This invocation in effect inspires Cardenio's perspicacious perception of her beauty: "Esta, ya que no es Luscinda, *no es persona humana, sino divina*" [This person, since it is not Luscinda, *is not a human but a divine being*]. In the same way the explicative "Ay, Dios!" with which she initiates her complaint is referential to her own Otherworld condition as well as to her awareness of the inadequacy of human discourse. The mention of *lugar* (place) is referential to Don Quixote's unnamed *lugar* in the opening line of the novel and to the same term in Sancho's and the captive's tales. In all these instances the term also signifies a social locus for a human language which can exist only as a product of a human community. Since she is at this point effectively "wild" and not part of any such community, she can only hope than heaven will understand her lament, a condition she shares with Marcela. For this reason she begins her "story" where Marcela's left off: A woman can hope to communicate with heaven but not with men.

Marcela vanished into the forest pursued by Don Quixote so that Dorotea's predicament is precisely what is needed for the knight, as an Otherworld being, to fulfill his mission and confirm his incarnation. Like a Celtic fairy queen this is a role Dorotea will perform. In all these capacities she is entering into the gaps of a text marked by its arbitrary sequential progressions and lack of closure. As a type of Otherworld enchantress she will re-weave the unraveled threads into a meta-text that hovers over the multiple story lines. With her Micomicona web she will provide Don Quixote with his paradigmatic *aventura* of part 1 and at the same time release Cardenio from his unrealistic and untrue conception of Luscinda. Likewise she will greet Zoraida with courtly gestures of welcome to a strange land and provide Doña Clara with a supportive female audience for her tale of adolescent love. Finally it is her reduction of Fernando to a normal size that allows for the resolution of her own dilemma.

The most curious thing about Dorotea is that she has never been critically recognized as the female protagonist of part 1. She is the only one who is equal to the many tasks of interlinking the multi-storied ontology of the text and providing a sufficiently mercurial persona to confront the unraveled psychic needs of Don Quixote, Cardenio, and Fernando. The fact the she has never received this recognition in the untold number of critical studies of the novel is probably a tribute to her Celtic Otherworld ontology. Like Etain she has many epiphanies that allow her to relate to men in the multiple forms required by the story. Her ontological shifts are not signs of moral instability but expressions of her resilience and resourcefulness. Unlike Cardenio, who has a fragile male rigidity, she has a flexible but powerful drive to survive which enables her to meet the challenges placed before her. Only from the pre-suppositions of a logocentric viewpoint does she appear inconsistent or unreliable.

The questions cited above concerning her motivations are not relevant within the horizon of expectations of a Celtic tale. Rather, she incorporates the operations of the text's entrelacement into the orderings of her personality and her language. Her "lies" are referential to the borderland nature of her ontology. She exists as an elfin creature who vanishes and re-appears, just as the story of an Otherworld heroine requires. In this she provides a necessary competing story line for the adventures of the hidalgo, an alternate focal source that appears to draw energy away from Don Quixote's story but in reality functions to complement his incomplete ontology. Together the Dorotea and Don Quixote agendas program the Romance schemata of part 1.

In part 2 the interpolative structure is repressed and the Romance energies are re-programmed along different lines which allow Dulcinea to take a primary role in the trajectory of Don Quixote's quest *aventura*. Seen from this perspective, Dorotea's stories must be read as expressions of what the Romance text is doing. She becomes the mysterious queen of the borderland, of the Marche, who regulates the *aventuras* of a lost hero. Like Lancelot's water fay who provides him with skill and arms, like Urganda la desconocida for Amadis, she is a shaping Otherworld force. At the same time her primal feminine energy performs the role of a euhemerized goddess who falls in love with Fernando, a problematic hero in his own right. In this way she and Fernando both exist with double ontologies as fays and as humans. The price they pay is that the are both perceived as unreliable because they express important human needs that our logocentric decorum condemns. At the same time they share with Don Quixote the fate of existing as emblems representing the functions of language itself. They are super-scriptural forces incarnated into figures that exist beyond the limits of human society and human discourse. As such they appeal to some people but are seen as deceptive by others. Like the revenants of a supposedly dead religion, they hover over the operations of the language of the *Quixote*.

The lack of *lugar*, the absence of grounding for Dorotea's language, is replicated in the peripatetic condition of Byzantine stories. The profile of this genre, inherited from the Alexandrine Greeks, reached new heights within the humanistic horizons of the sixteenth century. Its appearance in the *Quixote* provides useful insights into Cervantes' fascination with Heliodorus's *Aethiopian Romance*. There are sound reasons for this interest. At the most personal level Cervantes' own life had prominent Byzantine features. His own *peripecia* from Spain to Italy, to Africa, and maybe to Flanders or even England; his wanderings as tax gatherer in Andalucia; his desire to emigrate to the New World suggest a life lived as a Byzantine Romance. Even more markedly Byzantine were his naval encounters at Lepanto and his subsequent capture at sea by pirates resulting in a prolonged imprisonment in Algiers. No doubt a literary genre that allowed for all these improbabilities would seem "real" to a society committed to a world empire in the sixteenth century. The added cachet that Erasmus himself privileged Heliodorus over all other fiction writers guaranteed the high position of this genre in the hierarchy of literary forms. It is not surprising that with Cervantes we have a writer who committed his final energies to an elaborate re-working of the generic possibilities of Byzantine fiction. Within this overview the Micomicona story provides a miniaturized formulation of a major literary phenomenon of the time.

How the tale is situated within the text is even more complex. The priest offers Dorotea the role of the damsel in distress, a standard feature of the *libro de caballerías*. It is then that Dorotea boasts that she can easily perform the task, because she has read many such books and knows the style very well. This confession, of course, was omitted in her discussion of her reading habits in the story of her life she fabricated for the priest. Obviously the devotional books, which she does include on her reading list, would give her more credibility than the defamed Romances of chivalry. It is this opportunistic selection of evidence that contributes to undermining her honor from the point of view of the society from which she has fled. The situation is now reversed because it is precisely her familiarity with Romance that provides access to Don Quixote's madness and serves a practical purpose in the priest's stratagem. The *libros de cabllería* as a genre shared many features with the Byzantine novel, and in Spain as early as *El caballero Zifar* the genre had shown Byzantine influences. While this general condition facilitated the intrusion of a Byzantine tale into Don Quixote's story, there were more specific reasons for the genre of Dorotea's story.

In his *Secular Scripture* Northrop Frye observes that the protagonist of a Byzantine novel, as in the case of Heliodorus, is often a woman. This coincided perfectly with the damsel-in-distress tales found in the *libros de caballería* since their roles called for an account of their wanderings and misfortunes. By combining these two features Cervantes was able to find the appropriate rhetoric for a heroine who tells a tale of shipwreck and pursuit by a giant. Moreover, the shipwreck feature itself provides the story with its necessary escape from closure since such occurrences function to hold one story line in abeyance and introduce a whole new sequence of adventures. This linking device can be seen operating in the carefully orchestrated opening sequence of the *Persiles* as well as in the captive's tale. Dorotea, as a self-conscious narrator, appends a shipwreck to the end of her story. Significantly the shipwreck serves as the necessary link between her story and Don Quixote's, and anticipates the ambience of the captive's tale.

Another characteristic of the Byzantine novel in Dorotea's Micomicona story is the question of geographical indeterminacy, a feature that operates effectively both for Dorotea's Byzantine *persona* and for the status of her language. Specifically this feature also functions to underwrite the significance of Dorotea's fictional name and title: Princess Micomicona of Guinea. What is even more significant perhaps, the contradictory signals in the name find their source in the condition of geographical knowledge of the era. This aspect is important because we find the same "error" and indeterminacy in Covarrubias's *Tesoro de la lengua*. The contradiction appears first when the priest introduces Dorotea, now disguised as a princess in a green dress, to Sancho as Princess Micomicona of *Guinea*. In his entry for Guinea, Covarrubias reveals the nature of the confusion:

> GUINEA. La tierra de los negros o *etíopes*, en África, ado contratan los portugueses. Orosio la llama Gangines, y Abraham Ortelio dize ser ésta la que oy llamamos *Guinea*. (emphasis added)

> [GUINEA. The land of the Negroes or *Ethiopians*, in Africa, where the Portuguese (slave traders) do their business. Orosio calls it Gangines, and Abraham Ortelio says this (land) is what we today call Guinea.] (my translation)

According to my colleague Henry Richards, this confusion between east coast Ethiopia and west coast Guinea may originate with the earlier use of *Ethiopian* as a term applicable to all blacks. The fact that the Portuguese slave trade to which Covarrubias alludes was historically situated in West

Africa, here designated as Guinea, has not yet been clearly differentiated by Covarrubias from the east African location of Ethiopia.

In the *Quixote* the problem is further complicated by the popularity of Heliodorus's *Aetheopian Romance*, a literary reference that emerges by stages in the words of both the priest and Sancho. The priest's introduction of her as a blonde princess from an exotic non-European kingdom is a clear echo of a literary convention found in both Heliodorus and Ariosto.

> "Esta hermosa señora" respondió el cura, "Sancho hermano, es, como quien no dice nada, es la heredera por línea recta de varón del gran reino de Micomicón, la cual viene en busca de vuestro amo a pedirle un don, el cual es que que le desfaga un tuerto o agravio que un mal gigante le tiene fecho; y a la fama que de buen caballero vuestro amo tiene por todo lo descubierto, de Guinea ha venido a buscarle esta princesa." (pt. 1, ch. 29)

> [This fair lady, Brother Sancho," responded the priest, "is no less a personage that the heiress in the direct male line of the great kingdom of Micomicona. She has come to beg a boon of your master, for she would have him redress a wrong or injury that a wicked giant has done her. Because of the fame your master has acquired far and wide as a good knight, this princess has come from Guinea to seek him.]

Sancho in turn further elaborates on this information when he subsequently urges Don Quixote to undertake her rescue:

> "Bien puede vuestra merced, señor, concederle el don que pide, que no es cosa de nada: sólo es matar a un gigantazo, y esta que lo pide es la alta princesa Micomicona, reina del gran reino de Micomicón de Etiopía." (pt. 1, ch. 29)

> [Your worship may very safely grant the boon she asks," he said, "it's nothing at all: only to kill a big giant. And she who asks it is the exalted Princess Micomicona, queen of the great kingdom of Micomicon of Ethiopia.]

Sancho's addition of the phrase "de Etiopía," whatever its geographical referentiality, reinforces the literary link to Heliodorus and endows

Dorotea/Micomicona with the aura of a Byzantine heroine. At the same time it introduces geographic indeterminacy as a genre-linked feature that Dorotea seems to stumble over in the discourse of her feigned story. What is unreadable in both the priest's and Dorotea's use of the feature is whether they genuinely make errors in geographic nomenclature or whether they do it as a deliberate parody of the genre. As in the case of Dorotea's "forgetting" Don Quixote's or her own names, it becomes an "unreadable" feature. Does she really forget what the priest has told her, or is she pretending to be a confused damsel in distress? Is her humor directed at the genre, or is she not as smart as she thinks she is?

Errancy as Artifice

The fact that the first errancies in the Micomicona story are introduced by the priest indicates an unstable literary ontology for both the story and the heroine. Like Don Quixote Princess Micomicona is the product of an unreliable narrator, and both her name and homeland have a shifting referential value. Editors have disagreed on the possible meaning of Micomicona. Rosenblatt (170) and others have asserted that it is a play on *mico* and comes from her status as a woman deceived by a man. Rodríguez Marín's footnote indicates that this is a risky assertion but recognizes that the term has even less chaste connotations. Casalduero emphasizes the erotic association of the term *mico* with a deceived woman. (148) However there is a general agreement on a strong sexual implication in her name.

The priest further confounds the geographic location of her kingdom when he makes reference to their impending voyage to confront the giant:

> "y si hay viento próspero, mar tranquilo y sin borrasca en poco menos de nueve años se podrá estar a vista de la gran laguna Meona, digo, Meotides, que está poco más de cien jornadas más acá del reino de vuestra grandeza."

> [if the wind is fair and the sea smooth and tranquil, in somewhat less than nine years you may come in sight of the great lake Meona, I mean Meotides, which is little more than a hundred days' journey this side of your highness's kingdom.] (pt. 1, ch. 29)

This geographic muddle places her kingdom in the Black Sea area, possibly a reference to the Asiatic home of the faithless Angelica la bella of Ariosto's *Orlando furioso*. This would undermine Dorotea's sexual reliablility and at the same time highlight the eroticism of her long blonde tresses and peripatetic condition.

Dorotea's challenge to the priest's estimate of nine years for the journey is the first instance of her resistance to his direction. She insists that it has not taken two years to arrive in Spain. In doing so she also "corrects" his assertion of good weather, since the absence of smooth sailing is an important part of the genre's repertoire of features. In effect Dorotea's re-reading of the genre begins to assert itself, a factor that helps empower her re-reading of her own life as a Romance.

This self-reading is a fundamental characteristic she shares with Don Quixote and further reinforces her role as the female protagonist of *Quixote*. But at the same time she radically differentiates herself from the male "heroes" and offers a viable feminist re-interpretation of fashionable literary genres. Her difference from Don Quixote is that she makes Romance work for her in a way that escapes his powers. The key to her triumph is to be found in a powerful feminist hermeneutic which allows her to move beyond the male view of genre configurations. For Dorotea Romance is her true country, her absent *lugar*, and her habitation there allows her to break loose from male dominated categories of truth, being, and language.

Rescued by Romance: A Feminist Hermeneutic

> Thus we return again to the fact that the excluded, the wild, the dead, the young, the female, the Other World have their place in the total scheme of things.
>
> Alwyn Rees and Brinley Rees

The history of women's discourse is a difficult topic to extract from the formulations of male rhetoric and literary genres. Mostly women's language has been created by men and put in the mouth of heroines of the sort Dorotea is about to play. Cervantes seems to have made use of the work of Santa Teresa, the one significant woman writer of his era, when he created the "discurso de Marcela." There he achieved a workable variant of the traditional phrase "nací libre" in order to express the validity of Marcela's rejection of love. The phrase was traditionally used to express the status of the soul before succumbing to the irresistible power of love. Juan Rodríguez had played with this usage in the first of the Spanish erotic romances by having the narrator sing the song "nací libre" as he recalls his happy state before he fell in love. In fact the title "Siervo libre de amor" further puns on this phrase. Marcela, however, creates a more radical reading of the term by proclaiming that she will not fall in love but will reserve her soul for God. She is effectively able to make her argument on the basis of this and other conventions of the love lyric. She is a re-reading of the cruel beauty archetype that Cervantes had used in a more traditional way in the *Galatea* with the figure of Gelasia. The similarities between that story and the Grisostomo and Marcela situation are obvious, but the crux of the change is found in the differences that separate the two heroines. Each belongs to the stereotyped image of the woman (or man) who refuses love only later to fall victim to its greatest excesses. In the case of Marcela this consequence is aborted by her spiritual commitments and by her vanishing into the woods. However, at least for Cervantes' readers, the literary expectation of her return as the victim of love is left hanging. She remains merely a variant of the disdaining beauty and has in this sense not entirely escaped the landscape of literary conventions of the era. In another sense, however, she has radically validated her case by the use of reason, an acceptable male resource. Thus her argument is airtight, and no reproach can be made against her.

Nevertheless, while she sounds a clear cool note of feminine freedom, she is at the same time a prisoner of her own formulations. In the terminology of Karen Horney's study *Neurosis and Human Growth,* she is seduced by "the appeal of freedom." She has achieved her liberation at a price acceptable to her, since as an orphan raised by a priest she is presented as incapable of human love. As such she is not a viable model for Dorotea, who seeks involvement and has been trapped by her risk-taking proclivities. Her betrayal by Fernando has led to her social and spiritual isolation in the Sierra Morena. Contrary to the vestal-like Marcela, who chooses to live at the margins of society, Dorotea has been forcibly excluded from human discourse. Hence her lament about her lack of access to a viable language with which to re-insert herself into the society of her time.

In the same way, Dorotea is inevitably caught within the male horizon of expectations: She will either die or be reconciled to Fernando. Within the discourse of the abandoned woman either resolution is possible, but it is difficult to imagine Fernando undergoing the fundamental character change necessary for a convincing reconciliation. In fact most modern criticism has failed to produce a believable reading of his repentence. From the viewpoint of a modern psychological reading, his acceptance of Dorotea at the inn seems contrived or at best temporary. It is just a matter of time until he will again be back to his old tricks. The practicing Don Juan makes a poor risk as a husband. In this light Dorotea will have to make do with him because she has no other social choice. For this reason the story proves to be an unsatisfying example of compromised expectations.

An intellectually more acceptable hermeneutic is provided by Joaquin Casalduero's venerable but durable *Sentido y forma en el "Quijote."* There he successfully argues that Fernando is presented as the ideal Baroque hero, the man who rationally overcomes his passions for the sake of a Christian ideal of marriage. This reading is in its own way "correct" but nevertheless emotionally unsatisfying for the modern reader who does not accept the hierarchy of values of the Counter Reformation. This is probably accurate in itself: this reading consigns the story to the literary trash bin of history. Even if Cervantes did conceive the reconciliation of Dorotea and Fernando as a satisfying exemplum of Counter Reformation sophistry, later readers are under no obligation to buy into an archaic value system. From this point of view the episode needs a new validity.

At the same time the alternative reading of the conventional happy ending for a Romance is not any more satisfactory. Even the powerful analysis of Northrop Frye succumbs in this instance to the modern belief that Romance leads to positive resolutions. At its sources however the Celtic ur-Romances obey no such imperative. The classic example of Deirdre, whose name means "sorrow," suffices to make this expectation unreliable. While Romance sometimes does, as say in *La Traviata* or *Madama Butterfly*, offer an emotionally satisfying unhappy ending, that also is a nineteenth-century convention alien to the mythmaking power of Celtic narrative. So too we find in Chrétien an ambivalence about the emotional expectation of human happiness. Even though *Li Contes del Graal* remains unfinished, it is difficult to program a Romance ending in which Perceval walks off into the sunset hand in hand with Blancheflor. As later sequels added layer upon layer of interpretation to the enigma of the grail procession, nothing of that sort was envisioned. While it is always acceptable for a later age to re-interpret a story, it is often not always possible to entirely undo earlier meanings. At first sight this impasse seems to remain as an enigma at the heart of the story of Dorotea and Fernando. However, once Fernando's repentence is recognized as logocentrically "unreadable," the reader is alerted to the existence of other unreadable items in the story and a different hermeneutic begins to emerge.

Among the unreadable items we have elaborated, a Romance landscape for Dorotea is already in place. From a woman without a place or name, she moves into a Romance geography of indeterminant specificity. From Guinea, Ethiopia, the Black Sea, she moves into a garbled Spanish scenario where she presents Osuna as a seaport and has to be rescued by the priest's stratagem as re-presenting Osuna as the place where she first heard Don Quixote's name. The priest's hermeneutic cover-up has been noted as an item suggesting that the model for Dorotea is to be found in an historically recorded instance of a girl who was seduced by the scion of the house of Osuna (Márquez Villanueva). The evidence for this missing patronymic is inscribed in the opening line of Dorotea's story to the priest where she is careful not to reveal her full name and in fact situates her lack of name as part of her lack of place. The missing place name of Osuna hangs in the air as she begins: "En Andalucía hay un lugar de quien toma título un duque." "In Andaluccia there is a place from which a duke has taken his title." (pt. 1, ch. 28). As already noted, the missing name of Don Quixote's *lugar* provides a link to the main narrative vehicle along with Sancho's "un lugar de Estremadura" and the captive's "un lugar de León" to form part of a larger intertextual fabric (Selig, "un lugar de…"). This web of missing place names forms the linguistic landscape of Dorotea's search for a viable language community.

Given this context of circumscribed rhetorical and narrative tropes, Dorotea's situation does not seem promising. The role of the damsel-in-distress is the most limited and conventional of heroine paradigms for a woman to assume. In this situation all the woman has to do is provide the hero with a challenge situation. Once this is defined, she has no active role in her own redemption. Her narrative function is complete, and emotionally she vanishes from the narrative horizon. In spite of these severe prescriptions Dorotea overturns the convention by creating a radically subversive feminist re-constitution of the language of chivalric

Romance. To do this she utilizes, as already noted, the feminist resources of both the pastoral and Byzantine novels as well as the unpredictable improvisations of the commedia dell'arte theatrical tradition. The result is inevitably theatrical and manneristic but unexpectedly serious and powerful. To achieve this she also taps into the earlier suppressed matriarchal energies of chivalric Romance itself. She sets up camp in the heart of the enemy enclosure and proceeds to destroy Fernando's destructive advantage. In this endeavor she is dead serious, despite what surface gestures indicate to the contrary.

We have observed that one of the causes of the historical rise of Romance in Western culture was the suppression of the originary matriarchal situation of Celtic women. Both in the traditional tales as they come down to us from the monastic scribes and as further re-worked in twelfth-century France the role of women is inscribed as excluded from political and intellectual discourse but at the same time curiously powerful in the domain of emotions. Since men were proscribed from expressing their emotions, they were left particularly vulnerable to the powers of "unscrupulous" (i.e., persons not committed to the establishment) enchantresses. This situation produced an endless succession of *belles dames sans merci* who took the forms of archetypal "evil women": Morgan le Fay, Eve, Isolde, Lorelei, and so forth. Even Guinevere's capricious sexual adventures with Lancelot result finally in the destruction of Camelot. The blame is entirely hers however and not Lancelot's or Arthur's. This interpretation of the love triangle is the result of intricate attitudinal forces constructed to circumscribe women outside the centers of societal power. At the same time, the setting aside of the matter of Britain as a literature dedicated to women readers provided a marginal space for feminist concerns. After all men were not supposed to read this "vain" literature. The fact that they did shows the power inscribed in its articulation.

In the *Quixote* this male fascination with Dorotea is undoubtedly erotic at its source but is nevertheless intensified by men's limited access to their own repressed emotions. This phenomenon may be as old as civilization itself and works its spell on all of Dorotea's male listeners: Cardenio, the priest, the barber, Sancho, Don Quixote. Only Fernando seems resistant, and that is because as a Don Juan his male erotic responses are conditioned by his greater fear of women. At the same time Don Juan is a known male type that threatens society's concern with safeguarding its property and genetic arrangements. Thus, like Dorotea, Fernando also has a "wild" status. Their incorporation into the prevailing societal structure is problematic but achievable within the rhetoric of Romance norms. No other literary mode of the time would comfortably accommodate them, and Cervantes attempted this same goal in both his "romance" novelas and in the *Persiles*. Therefore, the Dorotea/Micomicona configuration is central to the total agenda of Cervantes' art, and it is his best example of a subversive story decked out in conventional trappings. That it is neither conventional nor acceptable to the social conventions of his era provides the underlying cause of its unreadable features. As is always the case when the Romance story seems to provide a "pointless" episode, it is in fact engaged in serious underground activity. The result is that what is really going on is kept out of sight and the episode may seem out of place. The very fact that it appears awkward within the apparent agenda of the work is the sign of its real power.

Fortunately, Romance narratives accommodate this type of action while it fits poorly into the decorum of realism. This situation is what obtains in the Dorotea/Fernando story. What is happening is not acceptable to either the fictional norms or the referential social reality in question. Hence both the numinous appeal of its self-conscious theatricality. These features, instead of trivializing its discourse, are the signs of its unacceptable seriousness. Most readers, then and now, are not ready for what it reveals about the human condition. This in part accounts for the critical neglect the episode has suffered and the unwillingness to accept the Dorotea factor as central to the textual discourse of the *Quixote*. Instead she has been treated as an embarrassing failure of the master and relegated to the external interpolative rhetoric of the text rather than seen as the central climax of part 1. What I am positing is that this narrative component is part of the radical if disconcerting energies of the work as a whole. Our embarrassment with it and our need to "explain" Dorotea alerts us to the importance of our discomfort. Instead of being trivial, the Romance unreadablility indicates our unwillingness to know what is going on. In fact the stress on the comic importance of the *Quixote* helps accommodate our unease. This may indicate that it is the reader and not Dorotea who needs to be rescued by Romance.

The Importance of Losing Your Head

Within the *Quixote* these anxieties are orchestrated in the male narratives of the text, that is to say, both the structure of the Cide Hamete/second

narrator complex and the Cardenio, priest, and barber configuration reveal their masculine anticipation of seduction. At risk is their personal
fear of falling out of the prescribed decorum limiting them to being "serious" men involved with important male business. For this reason the
narrator begins the chapter in which Dorotea is introduced with an apo-
logia for Romance *entrelacement*. At the same time, the "odd" male triad
of wild man/priest/barber displays an unusual sense of pleasurable
anticipation of the storytelling performance of "la muchacha de la suelta
lengua" (pt. 1, ch. 30) [the quick-tongued peasant girl], as Princess
Micomicona. There, the male listeners reveal their expectation of erotic
seduction and release from conventional male constraints. The fascination with this kind of female performance is comparable to the eternal
appeal of all female enchantresses from Delilah to Dietrich. No doubt
Klimpt's spectacular depictions of beheading females, like Judith and
Salome, performed a similar aesthetic function in the early stages of
modernism. In the same way, Dorotea's story of Micomicona and
Pandafilando must be read as another "serious" story of a beheading
female. As such it is not an entirely pleasant experience for men, even
though it is ultimately a liberating one.

The range of problems addressed in the four-part configuration of
Quixote, part 1, are difficult to circumscribe. Obviously the challenge of
part 4 proved fatal for the original concept of the novel, since the sec-
tional divisions are abandoned after the fictional "resolution" of the
Dorotea and Fernando segment. It may be that the inclusion of the Zoraida
and the captive material proved unmanageable for the sense of section
divisions of the earlier episodes. Or it may also be that in a serious way
the text moves on to address the complexities of Don Quixote himself as
he moves toward the situation in *Quixote*, part 2. In any case the early
division into four parts collapses at this point for various reasons, some
of which can be read in the Dorotea situation. Though her role persists
until Don Quixote leaves the inn, her most dynamic functions decline
after her confrontation with Fernando; this indicates that the Dorotea
performance is winding down even before the entrance of the captive
and Zoraida in chapter 37. Their arrival, in turn, designates a new agenda
within the *entrelacement* structure, one more directly engaged with problems of Cervantine autobiography.

The "Romance climax" of Don Quixote's story therefore belongs to the
Micomicona space of the novel and, not uncharacteristically for Romance,
comes in the center not at the end of the larger fictional structure. This

is the arrangement in the *Diana* and perhaps also in *Li Contes del Graal*. The location of a climax or denouement may be of more concern to a logocentric decorum rather than to a Romance organization of narrative. Thus its position in *Don Quixote*, part 1, is another bit of unreadable rhetoric for the realistic horizons of expectations.

Why, after all, cannot the reader expect to enjoy the fruits of the denouement rather than have the whole fabric swept away the moment the story reaches some sort of resolution? Such questions belong to the history of taste. Nevertheless a recognition that in some sense Don Quixote as a knight has his ultimate challenge in his confrontation with the giant Pandafilando de la Fosca Vista is not a surprising arrangement in Romance, however disconcerting it may be within the history of the realistic novel. The fact that this climax coincides with a major feminist challenge to the conventional order of language and eroticism is appropriate for the rhetoric of Romance as a genre.

In addition to the accumulating Romance features of rhetorical and geographic indeterminism, we have to consider the crossover of gender roles in Dorotea. This aspect must be coupled with the sexual reversal proposed by the priest, who, interesting enough, originally had programmed himself for the role of the damsel in distress. This arrangement was quickly aborted by the arrival of Dorotea, who resolves clerical unease about the appropriateness of a priest playing the part of a woman. We recall that it was the Church in Spain that promulgated the ban on men playing women's roles in the theater, so we know it was a sensitive issue at the time. The double reversal—Dorotea as shepherd boy, priest as *doncella menesterosa*, with which the Dorotea episode begins—is parallel to the opening of the *Persiles*, where Periandro is disguised as a girl and Auristella is disguised as a boy. While this "scene" is never presented in the *Quixote*, the arrangement potentially exists at the opening of chapter 28. This partially suppressed schema again indicates the "seriousness" of the issues at risk, and foreshadows the hidden challenges Dorotea presents to the situation. Her "male" drives are consciously pushed to the background as she herself admits at the opening of her confession to the priest:

"Los ratos que del día me quedaban , despúes de haber dado lo que convenía a los mayorales, a capataces y a otros jornaleros, los entretenía en *ejercicios que son a las doncellas tan lícitos como necesarios*, como son los que ofrece la aguja y la almohadilla, y la rueca muchas veces" (pt. 1, ch. 28)

["As for the leisure hours left me after I had given the needed orders to the head shepherds, overseers, and other laborers, I spent in those *occupations that are not only allowable but necessary for young girls*, such as the needle, embroidery cushion, and spindle.]

Not by coincidence alone are the tasks she cites the paradigmatic symbols of male and female occupations in the organization of culture. In particular her managerial capacities in directing men workers are obvious echoes of the matriarchal role of Queen Maeve and an anticipation of the Doña Perfecta/Doña Barbara syndrome of later Hispanic literature. The manner in which she introduces her "female" occupations indicates an awareness of her basic unease with her conflicting roles. As for her awareness of her sexual situation she is again overly explicit in her narrative:

"Es, pues, el *caso* que, pasando mi vida en tantas ocupaciones y en un *encerramiento tal, que al de un monesterio pudiera compararse, sin ser vista*, a mi parecer, de otra persona alguna que de los criados de casa, porque los días que iba a misa era tan de mañana,y tan acompanada de mi madre y de otras criadas, y yo tan cubierta y recatada, que apenas vian mis ojos mas tierra de aquella donde ponía los pies, y, con todo esto, los de amor, o los de la ociosidad, por mejor decir, a quien los de lince no pueden igualarse, me vieron, puestos en la solicitud de don Fernando, que este es el nombre del hijo menor del duque que os he contado."

[The truth is that I led this busy life in a retirement that might have seemed monastic, and unseen, as I thought, by any except the servants of the house. When I went to mass it was so early in the morning, and I was so closely attended by my mother and the women of the household, and so thickly veiled and so shy, that my eyes scarcely saw more than the ground I trod on. Despite all this the eyes of love, or idleness, more properly speaking, that not even the lynx's can rival, discovered me, with the persistence of Don Fernando. For that is the name of the younger son of the duke I told you of.]

The intertextual referentiality of this language brings to the fore the problem of her already precarious relation to the *place* with which she opened her initial lament, and at the same time her situation anticipates that of Zoraida who likewise lived a life of "encerramiento" except for the eyes of the servants and slaves, among whom was counted the captive himself. This arrangement suggests also that Fernando, like the captive, will end up as the woman's *siervo/criado,* (slave/servant), in accordance with the dictates of Courtly love.

The question of Dorotea's veracity also hovers over this account of her lifestyle. Two different hermeneutic possibilities are offered. The most obvious is that she is lying—or at least indulging in major exaggeration about the enclosure of her life. If this were literally true Fernando would never have seen her at all, nor would she have seen him on those early trips to mass. Mass, of course, served for centuries as the most convenient place for young males to look over the village virgins. However since Fernando (like the hidalgo) was a hunter and by definition "un gran madrugador" (an early riser), he could have easily observed the family procession on its jaunt to early mass. She leaves this possibility open by her later commentary on his hunting habits. This information leaves open another hermeneutic arrangement: Fernando in fact never did see Dorotea's beauty; he only saw the procession of her monastic seclusion. Ortega suggests that Don Juan is most attracted to women who are inaccessible and hence his fix on doña Inés as a nun. This would mean that Fernando was at first attracted to her status as a highly protected daughter rather to her beauty. It may be that both literally and figuratively he doesn't really see her beauty until the unmasking scene at the inn. Only after gaining access to her in the bedroom, where he still did not see her beauty, did he become aware of her strength and resourcefulness—and this is what frightened him off. His subsequent attempt to marry Luscinda was likewise motivated not by Luscinda's beauty but by the protection of being married. This alone would shield him from the power of Dorotea.

Fernando may not be too perceptive about women but even an insecure male instinctively knows when he is out-manned. The reverse of this weakness is also relevant in that he fears adult male responsibility and is therefore attracted to a resourceful female. Hence he is both attracted to and frightened by Dorotea's personality. Whether she is fully aware of these problems is another unreadable item, but his weaknesses nevertheless provide viable psychological motivation for his behavior. The fact that this emotional sequence exists connects it with a hidden Celtic story pattern and suggests a Romance reading. But whatever the reading, we are left with Fernando's unstable ontology that functions as a challenge for Dorotea's hidden feminist agenda. As a Romance heroine she knows that this *aventura* is reserved for her alone.

The convergence of multiple Romance strategies must be seen as the necessary landscape for the showdown between Dorotea and Fernando that takes place in the linguistically charged ambience of Juan Palomeque's inn. Dorotea must accomplish a basic Romance reading if she is to escape the desperation of her moral and social isolation. Her invocation of the Otherworld god in her lament indicates that she has no role in the world of everyday men. Without the intervention of strange men like the priest and Don Quixote she is at a dead end. Only the resources of situating her life as a Romance will suffice to "save" her. Fortunately she herself possesses the capabilities for this hermeneutic challenge. She will be saved by means of this maneuver, and in the process she will also carry along with her the priest, Cardenio, and Don Quixote to *un buen puerto*. Like the Sabia Felicia she will untangle the snarled threads of all their stories. In this capacity she becomes the female enchantress at the center of a web of deceptions that holds every one under enchantment. She is the female Percival who can ask the spell-breaking question that will release the entire kingdom. She must become the heroine of a new language and a new narrative.

While many Romance circuits are operative in the locus of the inn, it is not at all certain whether the resolution will be happy or sad; and in fact something of each does come to pass. Dorotea and Fernando will be married, but the outcome of that arrangement will remain unwritten. Equally ambiguous is the fact that Don Quixote will be returned to his village where he will die. Both these "conclusions" fit within the spectrum of Romance fiction, but the text astutely does not seek logocentric closure. Perhaps Cervantes reserved that resolution for the *Persiles,* where its effectiveness, although questionable, may have in fact fulfilled the author's desires. Whether it achieved the satisfaction of his readers is another matter. Nevertheless these considerations indicate the importance the feminist/ logocentric opposition plays within the trajectory of his fictions.

In the *Quixote* the Romantic key to the secret code, the one the heroine must find, lies in the dual figure of Fernando/Pandafilando. The first figure, the handsome young man, has been presented to her by fate, and the second, the giant, is her own reading of his condition. In effect she now has to supply the solution, but first she must to have the perspicacity to recognize her own power of observation. Like all the heroes and heroines of Romance she has the power to win but she has to articulate this fact at the conscious level. The mystery lies in how that power is hidden from her view and what she can do to reveal its true condition. Perceval has the question at the tip of his tongue but fails to ask it. After that failure, is it possible to regain the lost advantage? That is the question Chrétien never answered. Cervantes re-positioned a similar fictional situation for Dorotea. In the process of this endeavor the *Quixote* as a fiction created the possibilities of both the modern and postmodern novel. This reading of the Dorotea dilemma within the context of Romance provides a schemata for a history of the hermeneutics in the seventeenth century.

Spelling and Un-Spelling Languages

The double ontology of Fernando/Pandafilando establishes his presence as an Otherworld force within Dorotea's Romance discourse. Nevertheless Dorotea has remained blind to the truth of this situation because she is still "reading" Fernando within the rhetoric of her original formulation of his *persona* that she created in the tale she told to the priest. This blindness is an essential factor in both Romance and folklore where the protagonist can't see the truth when it is first presented to him/her. Thus Percival misreads his role at the grail banquet and fails to ask the un-spelling question. In same same way, Dorotea remains a captive of her original view of herself as a farmer's daughter taken advantage of by the Duke's evil son. This failure persists even though there are in her Romance descriptions of Fernando clues as to his redemption. For instance her insistence, like that of Cardenio, that he is a traitor of the dimension of Vellido or Galalon, fails to see that these terms give him a mythic dimension reserved for an enchanted villain who abuses his wife. The rhetoric of her tale raises the dimensions of his actions to the level of a Romance ogre.

It is typical of her blindness about herself that she can't or won't read her own contradictions, but at the same time if she truly is a Romance heroine her insights are in fact revelations of a secret ontology hidden within everyday appearances. Just as Don Quixote's misreadings contain revelations about the nature of mills, so Dorotea's language contains clues to another kind of truth about Fernando. In this case her insight is buttressed by Cardenio's reference to the same archetypal villains as comparable to Fernando. At the very least she has targeted Fernando as a traitor of legendary dimensions. The result is that either she is a histrionic liar or a prescient reader of realities hidden from mere mortals.

Another symptom of Fernando's Otherworld powers, at least from her point of view, is his ability to appear and disappear at crucial moments. His sudden entrance into her bedroom, even though it is later explained by her maid's betrayal, has the appearance of a realistic re-writing of a Romance situation in which an Otherworld lover suddenly presents himself in the maiden's chamber. The legendary vision of such a lover survives in fact in the Christianized tradition of the feast of St. Agnes, according to which the maiden will in a dream see the face of her future husband. Dorotea's first story—to the priest—is again a realistic re-presentation of a mythic story. The fact that Dorotea sleeps with Fernando is a recovery of a less-inhibited version of the same story. Keats recovered the same event in a more poetic arrangement in his "Eve of St. Agnes." In either case the story has the same essential features: the lover, called forth by a forbidden ritual, mysteriously appears and sleeps with her in spite of her enclosure within barriers set up by her family. In the Dorotea articulation reading, we note also the inclusion of overt Christianizing features in the shape of religious invocations to the Virgin and saints, adeptly utilized to authorize the lover's language. In most cases these references are clearly accretions added to make the story acceptable to a Christian hermeneutic. In Dorotea's story we recall the Casalduero reading which formalizes this arrangement even though to a modern reader it all seems added on to a simpler story of a villain seducing the village beauty. Any way these "Christian" oaths are read, they seem a transparent cover-up for what was going to happen in any case. Whatever he said she was not obliged to believe him, and in fact her behavior does not clearly indicate that she did. Her subsequent shame and her refusal to see her parents reveal a deeper layer of mistrust, not of him, but of herself.

The Performative Power of Language: The Celtic Geiss and Other Traumaturgical Acts

The oaths themselves are only part of the general view of the power of language and more specifically the power of Fernando's language. It is here that he outmaneuvers her, and her subsequent wonder at her foolishness may be sincere. She takes considerable pains to attribute her seduction to his power of language which sets out the conflict between them as a struggle between two kinds of language. This in turn is necessary if she is to triumph during the final showdown at the Inn of Juan Palomeque where she must establish the performative truth of her language over his. The scenario for this linguistic duel is carefully inscribed in her own account of her seduction.

The nature of this problem is not confined, of course, to the story of Dorotea and Fernando. It is first introduced by Don Quixote himself in his sermon on the Golden Age. There he states directly: "Entonces se decoraban los conceptos amorosos del alma simple y sencillamente del mesmo modo y manera que ella los concebía, sin buscar artificioso rodeo de palabras para encarecerlos" (pt. 1, ch. 11) [Then the love-thoughts of the heart clothed themselves simply and naturally as the heart conceived them, without endeavoring to commend themselves by force and rambling verbiage]. Such a language is a self-contradiction in which the thought *(concepto)* exists as self-constituting in the soul and seems to need no self-presentation. This transcendental language is now lost, and the love stories preceding Dorotea's each show the failure of the lovers to communicate effectively. Grisostomo and Marcela, the two most literate combatants, each has his/her own fully developed rhetoric of love. His "Canción desesperada" clearly delineates the consistent failure of language to express his own despair. His suicide in this context is a final desperate attempt to communicate with her. This sets up suicide as part of a system of communication in which the lover endeavors to express the impossible. Luscinda, at her wedding with Fernando, attempts suicide because she feels Cardenio did not believe she loved him. Camila, in a false suicide, communicates the lie that she is faithful to her husband. Likewise Marcela explicates a perfect Platonic love that exists without need of carnal expression. This duel between two languages of love reoccurs in each of the successive love situations: Rocinante and the *yeguas galicianas,* Don Quixote and Maritornes, Miulina and Alifanfaron, Torralba and Lope Ruiz, Cardenio and Luscinda. The latter story stands as the fundamental example of two lovers that have known one another all their lives but fail to communicate either in letters or in bed. The chance intervention of Don Quixote followed by the priest and Dorotea is their only salvation.

In this story sequence the climactic position of the Dorotea narratives is obvious. If she is to successfully communicate with Fernando she will have to resolve the enigma of the language of love.

Dorotea's positioning of Fernando's language as the operation of an Otherworld force governs the entire seduction confrontation in her bedroom. This scene is the most fully explicated event in her story and presents more than one viable reading. However, given the linguistic context in which she speaks, she cannot tell an honest story. As the famous dictum of Mary McCarthy says of Lillian Hellman, Dorotea lies when she says "of" and "the." But the important consideration is that her problem is due to the inadequacy of language and not the result of her own motives. As the disinherited offspring of a matriarchal tradition of language she cannot make the patriarchal discourse of society tell her tale. This situation constitutes, in effect, what she is talking about. She is telling the story of language and not just an account of what happened in her bed. To a great extent the "events" of her story are the attempt to tell the inevitable consequences of certain speech acts. She, like the other heroines of part 1, is the victim of the fallen state of language spelled out by Don Quixote in his first sermon.

The communicative challenge dominates the discourse of her narrative in a series of comments she makes about Fernando's powers of deceptions. This linguistic power is necessary both for her seduction and for her salvation. Whether his deceptions constitute lies in the ordinary sense is another problem but they do in effect reveal some inner truth about Fernando that can be read at the level of a psychological hermeneutic. This means that perhaps his declarations of love are true even though he himself does not recognize their validity. That is another story, one inscribed in a logocentric humanism but inadequate for present purposes. Instead the question is not one of personalist motives, for speech acts, but one concerning the nature of language itself. Here again it is the operation of a Romance meaning that is at stake. This is what is involved in the sense of an Otherworld language whose vector of referentiality is directed at the nature of the hero/ine's *aventura*. In this sense the question of lying loses its humanist significance and becomes instead an emblematic sign.

This problem in turn leads us back to the questions of the ontology of language and to an exploration of the limits of knowing. We are looking at questions of philosophic and scientific fallibility. In this context Descartes's formulation "cogito ergo sum" is a last stand to shore up meaning within some workable humanistic operation. Instead Cervantes has positioned the text as a story, like a Celtic tale, which does not reveal an intelligible universe but rather is itself a metaphor for a barely contained chaos. In this effort he positions the *Quixote* with the postmodern, poststructuralist universe. The text has moved beyond humanism and beyond knowing, and reading this story is not always a comfortable experience since the threat posed by the underlying chaos makes itself felt. As a result Romance and not realism becomes the more viable narrative vehicle, the "truer" presentation of a precarious condition in which human consciousness is at risk. In this context a radical Mannerism achieves its ultimate extension, a moment in which its self-conscious uncertainties reach their greatest expression.

The first sign of Fernando's special language comes appropriately in an observation that Dorotea makes about his letters. Here she assigns to them a curious communicative power of writing: "Los billetes que, sin saber como, a mis manos venían, eran *infinitos, llenos de enamoradas razones* y ofrecimientos, *con menos letras que promesas* y juramentos" (pt. 1, ch. 18) [The love letters which, without my knowing how, came into my hands were *infinite, full of enamored sentences* and offerings, *with fewer letters [of the alphabet] than promises* and oaths] (my translation).

The playful exaggeration of her rhetoric is self-referential but at the same time is a serious engagement with the question of signs and numbers. As we have noted she is lying about her ignorance of how the letters arrived, or perhaps the problem of not knowing is misplaced in her syntax, since what is unknowable is what the *letras* communicate. She obviously thinks that she is aware that he is lying by the numerical excess of his promises. What is at risk however is that in his skilled utilization of the strategies of seduction, he himself doesn't recognize that he has in fact fallen in love. The situation is comparable to that of Luis's letters in *Pepita Jiménez;* everyone but Luis knows he is in love. Fernando's later behavior might indicate just that. After all Dorotea is no legal threat to him, and as for his father, it cannot be the first time he has overstepped his aristocratic privilege. Rather he is afraid to be in love.

The possibility of this reading is re-enforced by the story of Camila and Lotario, where the procedure of Lotario's courting of a beautiful woman brings about the downfall of not only the woman but of the man as well. An intelligent woman might very well feel that she understands her lover's intentions better than he does. The same kind of ambiguity is found in the recent film *Dangerous Liaisons* where the unreliable but skilled Valmont falls victim to his own endeavors to seduce the chaste Madame de Tourval. Unfortunately for him he fails to recognize what his own feelings are until it is too late. The more perspicacious Mme de

Merteuil, however, immediately see what is going on. The question is that if Fernando did not love Dorotea, in what way was he vulnerable to her after the seduction? He merely had to move on to the next conquest. Instead, his unrealistic pursuit of Luscinda is more motivated by the protection from Dorotea she would provide him than a genuine attraction to her passive beauty.

Dorotea's next textual commentary presents the contradictory power of Fernando's language of seduction in a manner that sets the stage for what is to follow. She is speaking of Fernando's promises: "Todo lo cual no sólo no me ablandaba, pero me endurecía de manera como si fuera mi mortal enemigo, y que todas las obras que para reducirme a su voluntad hacia, las *hiciera para el efecto contrario*" (pt. 1, ch. 28) [All of which not only didn't soften my resolution but hardened my feelings as if he were my mortal enemy, and that all the efforts that he made to *overcome my will worked in the opposite manner*] (my translation).

There are two crucial insights here that reveal what is at stake in her story. The reversal of meaning, the *efecto contrario*, is a commonplace of the love narrative, which nevertheless underscores the chiasmic reversals that language can produce. What she observes about language is that it can reverse its stated intent due to the reader reading not the words but a hidden motive in their articulation. The language by its excess brings out a hermeneutic focused on the originary energy of the statement and not its lexical import.

Her other critical insight, which anticipates this reading, is her assertion "como si fuera mi mortal enemigo" [as if he were my mortal enemy]. The use of the subjunctive marks a recognition, presumably, that Fernando is not her mortal enemy. Instead that condition is only the appearance of hostility, not a genuine threat. In the long run this awareness of the contradiction between his surface appearance and behavior on the one hand and his possible motives on the other will have to be factored into a suitable response on her part. At this stage she seems not aware of what she has intuited in the situation. This reading provides a psychological interpretation of a common story pattern in both Celtic tales and medieval Romance. This kind of narrative constitutes a testing function for the protagonist which makes use of the shapeshifting capacity of Otherworld creatures. In this instance Dorotea has set out, in a disguised formulation, the first clues that Fernando functions like the testing ogres of Celtic Romance. Beauty and the beast, the princess and the frog are fairy tale formulations of this same situation. What you see is not what you get if you are true and brave. The beheading challenge in *Sir Gawain and the Green Knight* is a masculine version of the same test. Dorotea has entered the world of Romance, a place where the everyday orders of reality are suspended. In the famous movie metaphor, Dorothy is not just in Kansas anymore.

The next step in this drama is already prepared. Her responses to him have the same contrary effect on his intentions. Because of the compromised status of the language, she further arouses his lust rather than restrains it: "jamas quise responder a don Fernando palabra que le pudiese mostrar, aunque de muy lejos, esperanza de alcanzar su deseo" (pt. 1, ch. 28) [I never intended to respond to Don Fernando any word that might indicate to him, even faintly, any hope of fulfilling his desire] (my translation).

In this environment of unstable meanings her own reactions inevitably come into question. As to be expected, her awareness of the unreliability of his language does not prevent her from falling victim or at least from trying to present herself as falling victim. In effect she has created a linguistic habitat in which it is impossible to tell what is appearance and what is the emotional reality of her own actions and responses. The reader cannot know what is the external referentiality of her words because she has established the intrinsic inadequacy of her language. Is this a story of sexual or linguistic seduction? The two questions can no longer be separated. When we read her account we are forced to consider the possibility that her inevitable seduction is as much an expression of the genre of her story as it is a revelation of her personality. In either case we are carried along by the charm of her performance:

> Y así, no fui poderosa de dar voces, ni aun él creo que me las dejara dar, porque luego se llegó a mí, y tomándome entre sus brazos (porque yo, como digo, no tuve fuerzas para defenderme, según estaba turbada), comenzó a *decirme tales razones, que no sé como es posible que tenga tanta habilidad la mentira, que las sepa componer de modo que parezcan tan verdaderas.* . . . Yo, pobreceilla, sola entre los míos, mal ejercitada en casos semejantes, comencé, no sé en qué modo, a tener por verdaderas tantas falsedades. (pt. 1, ch. 28)

> [And in this way I was not able to call out for help, nor do I believe that he would have let me do so, because then he came up to me, and taking me in his arms (because I, as I said, didn't

have the strength to defend myself, since I was so disturbed), *he begin to say to me such phrases, that I don't know how it is possible that deception had so much power, that it knows how to invent such a way that the lies appeared so true*]. (my translation)

By moving the focus of the drama away from the trite story of seduction to the question of Fernando's unreliable language, she has infused the situation with a powerful dimension of Romance. Is she the victim of her own desire or of language? Can anyone know the multiple conditions of the polyvalent power of words, sentences, metaphors, and so forth? What is the nature of the story she is telling? Does it belong to the genre of a sordid village seduction or to the genre of a testing Romance? There can be no certain answers. We can only follow her fascinating storytelling procedures, which have begun to overshadow the story itself. This places the reader, along with Cardenio, the barber, and the priest, in the position of waiting to see how she will pull off her story to Don Quixote. This arrangement re-constitutes her language in a radical new way that further removes the import of its external referentiality. In effect the Micomicona story places all its emphasis on achieving a result and on performing a spell that conveniently removes any constraints about its referential truth. It is the language of sortilege and Dorotea is the performative enchantress.

Within this linguistic context and with Dorotea's knowledge of the *mentirosa/verdadera* word, she insists on Fernando performing a speech act as an authorizing device. This speech act, of course, is Fernando's oath, his assertion of marriage. However, given the progressive de-authorization of language as a referential sign there is no possibility that Fernando's words have any validity in relation to his intentions. In the same way, Dorotea is fully apprised of this situation, as she herself admits. Yet whether in desperation or with intent to outmaneuver him, she insists that he enunciate the promise and that he constitute it as a social and religious act. He invokes the matriarchal image of the Virgin that she has at her bedside, and she makes him repeat it in the presence of her maid. The failure of this oath is the basis of the moral and linguistic isolation in which the priest finds her in the Sierra Morena. There, given her experience, she can no longer accept male language as a viable element in her life. Thus she invokes the deity ("¡Ay Dios!") in her hopes of finding a viable means of communication with Otherworldly powers. By a different route she has come to the same emotional and philosophical situation that characterized Marcela: a woman can find no truth in the words of men. The consequence of this situation makes her truly "wild." Unfit for traffic in men's society, she no longer exists as a legally consti-tuted being within the parameters of human discourse. This realization is her most authentic act in the story. It is at the same time a small apocalypse. There comes with it not only the end of meaning but the end of the possibility of meaning in human terms.

Her salvation, as she herself has stated, cannot come from human men. Within the religious terms of the time this would leave open the possibility of a priest, a man who is about to enter her domain. However, within the context of the *Quixote*, the entry of Don Quixote also brings something of an Otherworld man into her situation. Both of these exempla do, in effect, assist in her recovery of social status. She will move from the condition of a non-being to a member of the ducal house of Osuna. Yet neither the priest nor Don Quixote provides the kind of man she seeks. Only in the strata of Romance can the Otherworld man she seeks exist. The question of whether Fernando is this *kind* of man has not at this point entered her consciousness, even though in her story she en-dowed him with certain characteristics that are recognizable Romance features. He appears and vanishes as though at the beckoning of her secret desires, he uses an Otherworld language in which falsehood and truth have no clear distinction. The traditional binary opposition of truth/falsehood does not signify in his language, a poststructuralist condition that confounds Dorotea's view of discourse. Her desire for a valid oath is the last gesture of her logocentrism. From that point forward she exists beyond the possibility of men's language, and beyond the possibility of meaning, in postapocalyptic void.

The role of the priest in the *Quixote* is another of the many unreadable items. He claims to help Don Quixote, yet we find that the success of returning the hero to the village brings about his death. At one level he operates as helpful and motivated by generous intentions, yet at other levels he is deceptive and self-serving. He is the one that invents the lie about Micomicona, an *artificio* that performs both helpful and destructive acts. One can only attempt to re-read him in Romance terms, akin to Merlin as a Druid or enchanter who helps Uther Pendragon seduce Igraine by means of shape shifting. Here the man's shapeshifting disguise occurs within Dorotea's story in a reverse way, while the priest works to re-invent Dorotea as a princess.

In this situation she moves beyond failure into a perilous new region of untraveled roads and threatening ogres. As the most important feature of this role she begins to recognize that she is armed with a powerful weapon she did not realize she possessed: an ability to read Romance. It is the excitement of this possibility that energizes her performance and captivates her male audience. In a profound way the story of Dorotea not only provides the main action of part 1 of *Quixote* but also brings into play the fundamental problematics of language that were established in the first paragraphs of the novel.

The Riddle of the Name

The eye of the other calls out the proper names, spells them out, and removes the prohibition that covered them.

Jacques Derrida

Far from the heated debates of the Holy Office, the problem of the relationship between name and substance presents a similar enigma for Dorotea. From the very beginning of their stories both Dorotea and Cardenio had failed to find an adequate language in which to name Fernando. They both had recourse to evoking the names of two archtraitors of legend and Romance: Galalon, the betrayer of Roland at Roncesvalles, and Vellido Dolfo, the assassin of Sancho II. Epithets like *fementido* and *traidor* were also used by both narrators. Cardenio's description of Fernando is, if anything, more contradictory than Dorotea's. He initially depicts him as "mozo gallardo, gentil hombre, liberal y enamorado" [a handsome youth, a gentleman, generous and much in love], only later to sputter into incoherence and fall into an epileptic fit at the mention of his name. In both stories, Fernando appears in his dual incarnations as ideal young man and unspeakable traitor, and both narrators fail to find adequate terminology for him.

For Dorotea, however, once presented with the paradigm of a Byzantine Romance, she easily accommodates him as the arch-ogre Pandafilando de la Fosca Vista. The name is her own invention, and it suggests in its etymon the activities of *hilando* (weaving), thus picking up again the thread of narrative entrelacement. The giant's epithet "de la Fosca Vista" refers to his deliberate crossing of his eyes as a means of frightening his enemies. Within the text, the condition of his eyes relates him to both the trickster Ginés de Pasamonte and to the loathly damsel Maritornes. However, within the larger world of Romance, there continues the tradi-

tion of the Celtic heroes and monsters who possess deformed eyes, sometimes a single eye that possess multiple pupils, or, as we have seen, the
phenomenon of CuChulainn's battle frenzy in which specific distortions
of the eyes occur as he goes into combat. Willy-nilly Dorotea has picked
up in her Romance readings something of this tradition. In endowing her
enemy with this capacity she is suggesting that his eyes have certain
powers with which he protects himself and confounds his enemies:
"porque es cosa averiguada que, aunque tiene los ojos en su lugar y
derechos, simepre mira al revés, como si fuese bisco, y esto lo hace él de
maligno y por poner miedo y espanto a los que mira (pt. 1, ch. 30) [for
its a verified fact that, although his eyes are set in their proper place, he
looks the reverse, as though he were cross-eyed, and he does this out of
spite and in order to frighten those he looks at] (my translation). At the
same time she ignores another meaning buried in the image, one that
refers to the warrior's special visual powers that allow him to better
interpret his adversary. In either case, however, her language attempts to
single out negative features that characterize a sense of evil and forebod-
ing in the giant.

In this context it should be observed that there is within the narratives
of Dorotea and Cardenio an untold story. The reader never directly enters into Fernando's perceptions of what is occurring. Motives are attributed to him by others, but at no time are we told how he interpreted
Cardenio's or Dorotea's actions. His story remains hidden within their
view of events. This narrative arrangement, however, is also a Romance
storytelling pattern. Only at the end does the ogre sometimes say a few
words about his own situation as is the case of the Chief Giant in the ur-
Romance of *Culhwch and Olwen* or of the giant in *Carl of Carlisle*. Thus,
within the *Quixote*, among the four lovers it is Fernando who remains the
enigma. As a feature of Romance he is the challenge faced by the heroine.

It should be noticed that within the *Quixote*, part 1, there are only
two female narrators, of whom Dorotea is both the first and most significant. Pedro, the shepherd boy, tells the story of Marcela; Sancho tells
the story of Torralba; Cardenio tells the story of Luscinda. The male
portrayal/betrayal of women is unmasked in Pedro's misreading of
Marcela as "la endiablada Marcela" when Marcela speaks for herself. In
the same way Cardenio paints Luscinda as immature and changeable
when, as later developments show, she is steadfastly loyal to him even
when he is immature and unreliable. These stories reveal the problems
of men trying to read women. In contrast, the Dorotea/Micomicona

stories depict, as in the pastoral Romances, a woman trying to read
men—and, at the same time, the inadequacy of narrative language for
such a task. This underscores the problematics of rhetoric in the two
versions of his persona as a handsome young man and an ogre. And it
is here that Dorotea will triumph. The recognition "victory" is pronounced by Fernando himself when he finally accepts her as his wife.
"Venciste, hermoso Dorotea, venciste," he intones as he raises her from
her kneeling position.

The difficulty of this scene has always been related to the image of
Dorotea prostrating herself before him and imploring him to accept her,
if even as a slave. Such a scene, from a modern point of view, rankles
because it seems that, having no other choice, she is reduced to accepting
him at any cost. At the same time his acceptance of her is so delayed and
begrudging that his "repentence" seems equally forced and contrived.
The Romance factor in this arrangement seems only a conventional happy
ending tacked onto a fatally compromised situation. She cannot really
love him because of his betrayal and he cannot love her because she is
a manipulative female. The only reading seems to be that, while they
may deserve one another, that they do not deserve the reader's belief in
the validity of their love.

There is, however, another Romance narrative pattern that provides a
more relevant reading of the situation in which Dorotea finds herself. As
a skilled reader of Romance Dorotea applies this hermeneutic to the
riddle of Fernando. In this context, Fernando's eloquent and contrived
pronouncement "Venciste" [you have conquered] can be read as his tribute to her remarkable reading of the motives behind his behavior. Since
the language of the story by this time is both theatrical and mannered,
his rather formal pronouncement of her victory serves to mark the moment as the end of her test. This places her actions into the context of a
Romance challenge and reveals that the events at the hostel of Juan
Palomeque belong to a perilous castle pattern where the hero must face
a validating adventure. This reading is consistent with the condition of
the two earlier inn sequences (ch. 3 and 16), where we found that
Otherworld testing forces were also at work. Within this hermeneutic we
can see the scenario that Dorotea plays out belongs to a recognizable
paradigm found in the fictions of Irish myth and medieval Romance.
*Bricriu's Feast, Li Contes del Graal, Perlesvaus, Sir Gawain and the Green
Knight,* and *Carl of Carlisle,* among many others, all make use of similar
testing procedures. In this schema the hero finally finds out who he is,

and in fact the sole purpose of the story pattern is the revelation of the hero's "true" identity. The difference in the *Quixote* is that the hero becomes a heroine and it is Dorotea, not Fernando, who overcomes the challenge.

In addition the triumph of the protagonist will also release the castle from its enchanted state and allow for the rescue of all its inhabitants, in which case everyone, including the giant, is saved. In the *Quixote* this feature applies suitably to Cardenio and Luscinda, who will be free to marry since Cardenio will finally be released from his crippling vision of himself. Likewise the artifice of the Micomicona fiction will allow Don Quixote to complete his mission of rescuing the princess. The simultaneous resolution of these story lines is what provides a "romantic" impulse to the events at the inn. Similar scenes are found in the popular *comedias* of the epoch in which the various couples are marched off to the altar in the final scene. The ritual of multiple weddings, whether here or in Lope, marks the return of the protagonists to the immediacy of everyday life after their sojourn in the land of Romance.

In the *Quixote* this spirit of Romance informs the happy resolutions of their problems for the four couples at the inn: Dorotea and Fernando, Cardenio and Luscinda, the captive and Zoraida, and Doña Clara and Don Luis. In fact the two resolution scenes evoke similar mannerist rhetoric to signal the various protagonists moments of recognition. In the contrived and carefully choreographed sequence in which each of the four young people first see one another, the rhetoric makes full use of a mannerist formalism. This "artificial" rhetoric becomes fully apparent when Dorotea faints:

> Acudió luego el cura a quitarle el embozo para echarle agua en el rostro, y así como la descubrió, la conoció don Fernando, que era él que estaba abrazado con la otra, y quedo como muerto en verla, pero no porque dejase, con todo esto, de tener a Luscinda, que era la que procuraba soltarse de sus brazos; la cual había conocido en el suspiro a Cardenio, y el la había conocido a ella. Oyó asimesmo Cardenio el ¡ay! que dio Dorotea cuando se cayó desmayada, y creyendo que era su Luscinda, salió del aposento despavorido, y lo primero que vio fue a don Fernando, que tenía abrazada a Luscinda También Fernando conoció luego a Cardenio, y todos tres, Luscinda, Cardenio y Dorotea, quedaron mudos y suspensos, casi sin saber lo que les había acontecido.

Callaban todos y miránbase todos: Dorotea a don Fernando, don
Fernando a Cardenio, Cardenio a Luscinda y Luscinda a Cardenio.
(pt. 1, ch. 36)

[The priest at once hastened to uncover her face and throw water
on it, and as he did so Don Fernando, for he it was who held the
other lady in his arms, recognized her and stood as if frozen by
the sight. Not for this, however, did he relax his grasp of Luscinda,
for it was she who was struggling to release herself from his
hold, having recognized Cardenio by his voice, as he had recognized her. Cardenio also heard Dorotea's cry as she fell, and
imagining that it came from his Luscinda, burst forth in terror
from the room The first thing he saw was Don Fernando with
Luscinda in his arms. Don Fernando, too, knew Cardenio at once,
and all three, Luscinda, Cardenio, and Dorotea, stood in silent
amazement, scarcely knowing what had happened to them.
      They gazed at one another without speaking Dorotea at Don
Fernando, Don Fernando at Cardenio, Cardenio at Luscinda, and
Luscinda at Cardenio.] (my translation)

This is not the language of verisimilitude. It is precisely the language of
Romance that has moved into the world of Don Quixote and Sancho.
Even if this *artificio* is seen an ironic gesture, the tone of the language
evokes other strata of literary discourse.
      The deliberateness of this strategy is further underscored in the reso-
lution of the story of Clara and Luis, even though the rhetoric of their
story and that of the captive is very different from the literary language
used by Cardenio and Dorotea:

Don Quijote puso mano a su espada y arremetió a los cuadrilleros.
Don Luis daba voces a sus criados, que le dejase a él y acorriesen
a don Quijote, y a Cardenio, y a don Fernando, que todos
favorecían a don Quijote. El cura daba voces, la ventero gritaba,
su hija se afligía. Maritornes lloraba, Dorotea estaba confusa,
Luscinda suspensa y doña Clara desmayada . . . de modo que
toda la venta era llantos, voces, gritos, confusiones, temores,
sobresaltos, desgacias, cuchilladas, mojicones, palos, coces y
efusión de sangre. (pt. 1, ch. 45)

Don Quixote drew his sword and charged the officers. Don Luis cried out to his servants to leave him alone and go and help Don Quixote and Cardenio and Don Fernando, who were supporting him. The priest was shouting at the top of his voice, the landlady was screaming, her daughter was wailing, Maritornes was weeping, Dorotea was aghast, Luscinda terror-stricken, and Doña Clara in a faint. (my translation)

The importance of this kind of narrative language in the Cide Hamete story confirms the existence of Romance energy in his text. As Thomas Mann observed, this is exactly the genre of romantic fiction that is supposedly under attack, and yet it exists in the "realistic" world of the inn of Juan Palomeque. In this environment everyone finds their salvation, since in fact the only stories that end happily find their resolution at the inn. All the other interpolations end either in tragedy, as in the case of Grisostomo, or in disillusionment, as in the case of Eugenio.

All these features, either of language or narrative pattern, mark the controlling force of Romance in the text. At the center of this energy we find the interpretive problem of Don Quixote's dream at the inn. There he achieves, whether asleep or awake, his most significant victory; and it is there that Dorotea finds the key to her dilemma with Fernando. The question of the knight's dream is related to other instances of Don Quixote's sleep. There are four times in the course of the entire book that he has significant sleep episodes, two in *Quixote*, part 1, and two in *Quixote*, part 2. In each of these instances of sleep there can be found radical shifts in the direction of either the operations of the text or in the development of the protagonist's story. The first occurs in the interstices between the first and second sallies. There, as Don Quixote sleeps in his bedroom, the priest examines and burns much of his library. This collection of books forms the "archive," in Foucault's sense, of the entire text. It signifies not only the unconscious content of the knight's imagination but also the linguistic, rhetorical, and narrative possibilites of the work as a whole. From a narrative point of view, the sealing off of the library also seals off the hero's access to his own unconscious, thus leaving the ego in an isolated state that marks the condition of his madness. This loss is never recovered but it is important that his last reported case of sleeping also occurs in his bedroom, and it is there that he awakens to announce his recovery from madness. Between these two episodes of deep sleep lies the trajectory of his two great sallies that form the bulk of the book. We are also told in the first paragraph that the hidalgo is a "gran madrugador" indicating that he survives on little sleep, a condition that coincides with his frequent all night vigils in the course of his adventures. This indicates that he, like people who suffer from prolonged sleeping deprivation, is more likely to experience visions in his waking state.

The other two sleep episodes are accompanied by a major dream world, the first at the inn of Juan Palomeque and the second in the cave of Montesinos. In the first he kills the giant Pandafilando, and in the second he is told that Merlin is the magus who holds Dulcinea enchanted in the cave. Both these situations constitute major challenges for the knight. In the first he will triumph over the power of the enemy enchanter, while in the second his quest for Dulcinea will gradually erode the fabric of his madness. Whether this release is a victory or a failure is a matter of the reader's interpretation, since the protagonist's return to La Mancha is something of a comedown after the intensity of an Otherworld. And as in the case of the Celtic stories, the return reduces the hero to a heap of ashes. After being preternaturally youthful in his old age, Don Quixote suddenly ages and dies. Such is the pattern of the *echtra* or adventure in the domain of the fairy gods. The Celtic tales themselves are ambivalent about the value of mortal involvement with the Otherworld. It would seem that the hero suffers a cursed condition in which he is not at home in either this world or the next. In the *Quixote* the Christianization of the hidalgo's death is a convention that dates back to the monkish scribes who preserved the pagan stories. As in other matters dealing with secular and sacred scriptures, it is all a question of a hermeneutics of belief or disbelief. Or, to revert to the language of Romance, the reader will find what he or she deserves to find in the challenge of the riddle. We each read what we deserve to read, and if we are dissatisfied with the results then we must return to ourselves and begin again.

Within the arc of these four sleep/dream episodes, the death of Pandafilando provides the key to the Romance hermeneutic of *Quixote*, part 1, and to the salvation of the lovers. This does not mean that after this episode the energy of Romance disappears from the text but only that in this particular component it finds its most complex articulation. In the same way Dorotea's reading of Don Quixote's dream provides both the resolution of her adventure and the climax of the Romance configuration of the text. Other features of Romance continue to operate in the novel but this particular *echtra* dissolves after Don Quixote leaves the inn of Juan Palomeque. He never again enjoys the full power of an Otherworld challenge, nor does the reader subsequently utilize the particular hermeneutic fix we have here examined. As in the shifting genres of Celtic tales and in the prolonged history of vulgate and post-vulgate Arthurian Romance, other hermeneutic strategies await the reader. It is the death of the reader that haunts the long and changing course of the two parts of *Don Quixote*. At the end it is our own death as a fictionally constituted reader—not merely for the death of the hero—for which we weep. We never again can reconstitute the pleasures of our reading experience, and so we too suffer loss of being. In Romance more than in other literary mode it is the reader's ontology that is at peril. That is why it is so addictive.

Just as the ancient Celts believed they received Otherworld benefits from listening to the story, so too the end of the story closes off the experience of those benefits. We can recollect the wisdom they impart as we pass forward in our life but the experience itself is evanescent and cannot be recaptured. It is with these expectations that re-reading the knight's dream becomes the core adventure not just for Dorotea but for the reader as well.

Reading beyond the Apocalypse: The Riddle of Dorotea

Any genre as a literary formula has the basic features of the riddle; it is all a question of hermeneutics. As in Borges' "Death and the Compass," the detective successfully reads the map and thereby discovers the time and location when the fourth murder will occur, but he fails to read the meaning relevant to the question of whose murder. He therefore remains blind to his own peril and goes to the place of his own murder. In this pattern we see that Borges has retold the Romance story of the hero who will fail or succeed depending on how he reads the riddle. It is essentially the same story as Conan Doyle's "The Musgrave Ritual" except that Borges has reconstituted the ancient feature of having the riddle's hidden message addressed directly to the detective's own fate. Holmes re-reads the directions for the location of the treasure in order to find the murderer. Borges takes the paradigm one step further and has the detective unknowingly predict his own demise. Nevertheless, give or take a few features both stories replicate an ancient story, and the reader's sense of completion at the end is due not just to adding the missing piece of information to the puzzle: it is also due to the unconscious sense that the story pattern is completed. There is nothing relevant left to say.

Dorotea's position in facing the Fernando enigma is very much like that of a detective or an ancient hero confronting the riddle. The paradigm of the ur-story lies buried somewhere between the two versions she has given to the Fernando/Pandafilando problem. The fact that the story already has a dual articulation makes it easier to recognize that the genre of the story possesses more features than those found in any single example. Fowler, we remember, stresses the fact that no single form of the story uses the full spectrum of possible features indigenous to the genre. Thus, as in a detective story, there is a missing clue, an absent sign that will allow the hero to solve the crime. This sign, in order to communicate effectively, has to be part of the language of the genre; that is, its meaning must be the product of the signifying system. Meaning is always generated, it does not pre-exist the linguistic formulation. In Dorotea's case this would indicate given the configuration of her two stories, that the missing clue belongs to the spectrum of Romance features. There exists, in what has already been articulated or read, another feature and another meaning beyond the one already presented. She has in effect to re-read her own story since the solution is always already there; she has merely misread the "facts" as Holmes would say. What meaning exists is to be found in what she has already said that can be re-interpreted. She has to sharpen her hermeneutic capabilities in order to find hidden or forgotten clues in one of the genre signs already presented. A review of the Romance features will help unpack this conglomeration of signs.

The double portrayal of her betrayer as Fernando/Pandafilando is itself a sign of shape shifting found in euhemerized gods as they "progress" to a more fully human ontology. We have also noted the Otherworld quality of Fernando's language which allows him to deceive, to make one thing appear as another. He also seems suddenly to appear to Dorotea like a vision in her bedroom as she broods over her partially repressed desires for a perfect lover. In his Pandafilando configuration he appears in her story as the fulfillment of her father's prophecy. This signals that his appearance is foretold in the story of her life. Armed with this knowledge and with the advice of her prophet father, Micomicona flees her kingdom and takes the high road to Spain, where it is again foretold that she will find the hero who will rescue her. In this narrative feature we find the role of Don Quixote, whom she thus places within the battleground of her conflict with Fernando. Now, with his dream, Don Quixote has brought into the confines of the inn/hostel his goal of beheading the giant, a gesture already inscribed by Don Quixote in his utilization of the Lancelot ballad for his own situation. The dream is so real that Sancho has scurried about trying to find the giant's missing head in Don Quixote's bedroom. These features re-present the problem of the riddle within the pattern of a well-known Romance motif. At this stage of action, however, Dorotea can still not recognize the meaning hidden in Don Quixote's dream, partially because the function or purpose of the beheading episode is still suppressed.

The fact that giants are commonly beheaded in chivalric Romance makes the suitability of this fate for Pandafilando seem all the more acceptable, and because it is a commonplace it remains unexamined. The next stage of the unpacking requires another look at the meaning of this feature within the generic system. Beheading or death by blows to the head is a very ancient feature of Celtic tales. We know that the Celts were head hunters, an aspect of their culture that their Roman conquerors emphasized, no doubt as a justification for their conquest of the barbarian Celts. Yet beheading as a form of execution survived legally well into modern times. In France, in addition to the orgies of the Revolution, the guillotine survived as a legal form of capital punishment until after the Second World War. Spanish garroting, a related practice, remained in practice during the Franco era. Likewise the execution of monarchs and aristocrats is widespread, as we know from stories of Mary, Queen of Scots; Anne Boleyn; Lady Jane Grey, Robert Devereaux, and so on. Burning was the other form of ritual death practiced by the Celts, and this too survived for heretics in Spain and elsewhere, as Giordano Bruno found out. Thus beheading in itself has a special if forgotten significance that is particularly relevant to Romance as a literary formula.

Don Quixote has repeatedly insisted that matters of chivalric adventure are intrinsically unstable. The shifting windmill/giant ontology is only the most famous of these kinds of transformations. In the same way, giants exist in Romance as symbolic representations of evil and constitute a challenge he must overcome. Dorotea has now entered that narrative formulation by performing the role of the princess beset by an amorous giant, a highly conventional arrangement. In fact it is the commonness of the story that blinds her to its meaning. Her figuration of Fernando as the giant signals that she is unconsciously aware of the challenge. She also would know that the unstable ontology of giant-like figures is another feature of their fictional ontology. In many Romance stories this factor is clearly seen. *Sir Gawain and the Green Knight* is a well-known example. In that story a number of features reveal a ritual source. The time factor is very clearly a residual feature in that Gawain, who is charged with beheading the green knight, must himself return in a year's time and submit himself to the same fate. In fact this beheading challenge is a fairly common feature in Arthurian stories.

The next step in this reading reminds us that in *Peredur*, the Welsh version of the grail story, the grail contains not a communion wafer but rather a much older component: a severed head. This gory detail was probably suppressed either by Chrétien or the earlier storyteller who provided him with the source "book" spoken of in his prologue. This version of the story then relates the beheading feature with two significant narrative patterns. Beheading relates to both the problem of enchantment and to the fact that it forms part of a test for the hero. In Dorotea's story both features form part of the riddle of Fernando. In this sense the solution to her problem is already at hand, but she has not recognized the meaning of her own story.

There is another clue at hand in the role Don Quixote has played in her story. In fact she played with this feature when she made puns on his name, relating it to *Gigote* and other unsuitable rhymes like *bigote*. However she overlooked the fundamental pun on his name, the one he himself created when he cited the ancient *Lanzarote* ballad. As noted he has repeatedly referred to that ballad since it contains a "message" relevant to his fate. Most importantly he seeks to experience a moment of reception into a castle similar to the one articulated in the ballad.

> Nunca fuera caballero
> de damas tan bien servido
> como fuera Lanzarote/don Quijote
> cuando de Bretaña vino . . .

> [Never was a knight
> so well served by ladies
> as was Lancelot/Don Quixote
> when he from Britain came . . .]

Although Don Quixote never recites the ballad to Dorotea it was extremely well known in Spain, a fact that he himself observes during his dialogue on chivalry with Vivaldo (pt. 1, ch. 13). Also the pun, given its repeated use in the text, hovers referentially even though unspoken in the linguistic environment, like a missing genre feature whose absence is noted.

Another relevant feature of the ballad, also unpronounced, anticipates Don Quixote's dream adventure at the inn. In the ballad Lancelot, after sleeping with Guinevere, beheads a proud competitor for her attention and presents the grizzly trophy to her. Thus the beheading of his opponent was written into his heroic scenario from the time Don Quixote cited the ballad at the inn in chapter 2. It was always and already a feature of his story.

Roger Sherman Loomis has pointed out that the beheading test, as in the Gawain tale, is a way of testing the hero's fidelity to his given word. The other knights who have challenged the green knight have all failed in not appearing at the appointed time to face their own beheading. The green knight, while not quite a giant, is nevertheless an Otherworld creature as is apparent when he re-constitutes himself after the beheading by either picking up his head, which is still talking, or by later appearing in his whole form. This reappearance of creatures who have been beheaded also occurs significantly to pigs that are eaten in ritual banquets but nevertheless present again the next day in the pig run. In either case what is at risk is the test of the hero's oath. For Dorotea the error has been that she read her own story as a test of Fernando's oath. She has not yet recognized the fact that she herself, as well as Fernando, is being tested.

As for the question of enchantment and its relation to shapeshifting, the story is also tied into the beheading feature. It is here that Don Quixote will play the pivotal role. As the scenario is constituted at the inn, the beheading is announced at a crucial moment. We remember that Don Quixote sleeps while the priest reads aloud the story of Camila/Anselmo/Lotario. In the same way, the Curioso story is an alter formulation of the dilemma faced by Dorotea. The story-reading episode is in fact introduced just after a discussion in the inn about the benefits received by the listeners, a Renaissance recapitulation of the ancient Celtic belief in the prayer-like efficacy of reciting a story. Don Quixote's interruption of the priest's reading, in which he announces the beheading of Pandafilando, occurs just as the deceptive power of Camila's *artificio* reaches its fullest dimension. Anselmo is now convinced, as he was not when she was chaste, of Camila's virtue. The deception has achieved what virtue itself could not. Camila, however, has betrayed herself in her effort to convince her husband that she is chaste. What she now expresses exists purely as a sign, as in Galileo's formula, with no relevance to her condition as an adulterous wife. The power of language is thus destructively reversed: Truth appears as deception and deception signifies truth. The meaning of that situation cannot be lost on the highly perceptive Dorotea. Fiction is more powerful than verisimilitude, and Romance is more truthful than history. It is at this moment that Don Quixote interrupts the reading and announces that he has beheaded Pandafilando, Sancho claims to have seen the head rolling on the floor, and the blood/wine floods the inn. The last image also evokes the Christian sacrament most at risk in the Counter Reformation's and the Church's insistence on the efficacy of the priest's language in the consecration of the bread and wine. Romance transformation becomes transubstantiation within the humdrum reality of the inn. Questions thus arise: Can Fernando change? Is he a prince or an ogre? Is his language efficacious? And is there a prince for the dreaming peasant princess to marry?

The answers can be found only in the forgotten meaning of ritual beheading. Loomis points out that in another variant of the Gawain tale, *Carl of Carlisle,* the giant is married to a beautiful woman whom he brutally abuses. Potential rescuers are frightened off by the conditions of the beheading test he proposes, until Gawain, the perfect knight, agrees to behead the giant and promises to return a year later for his own decapitation. When he fulfills his oath the resolution appears. The giant, transformed by the completion of the hero's oath, turns into an ideal knight of normal size. He then tells that he has been enchanted for centuries and could be released only by the completion of the beheading test. He now loves his wife and becomes a member of Arthur's Round Table company. The giant is redeemed by a hero.

Dorotea, who has already assumed male roles, now has to become the hero of her own tale. She has now re-read the story and discovered what to do. This means she must return to the frightening giant and submit herself to his power. Only in this way can she transform him back into the prince she had sought to marry. This interpretation then becomes the referential narrative pattern for her confrontation with Fernando in the inn. She must offer herself as his slave, figuratively placing her head under his foot. Only in this way will she disenchant him and free him from the power of his negative self. On a Romance level she performs the knight's role and validates her word to Fernando that she is his wife. Read on a psychological level, she performs the act that will convince

Fernando that he is loved or, better, that he is a man worthy of the love of a beautiful woman. Like his friend Cardenio, he has believed that women cannot really love him, and hence he goes from woman to woman, always escaping before anyone finds out who he really is. Since he has no ducal or paternal title, he has also believed that he had no substance. He has remained the unleavened bread before the ritual words were spoken. From a grail viewpoint Dorotea had to pronounce the magic words, which Camila could never find, to convince her husband that she really loved him, not just the disinherited son of a duke, but him, Fernando. In this way the title he lacked from his father is replaced by the power of Dorotea's ritual words as she places her head under his foot. "En fin, señor, lo que ultimamente te digo es que, quieras o no quieras, yo soy tu esposa; testigos son tus palabras, que no han de deben ser mentirosas, si ya es que te precias de aquello por que me desprecias, testigo será la firma que hiciste, y testigo el cielo, a quien tu llamaste por testigo de lo que me prometías." (pt. 1, ch. 36) [Finally sir, what I ultimately tell you is that, whether you wish it or not, I am your wife; your words are your witness, and they must not be untruthful if you really value yourself for that which you scorn me. A witness will be the oath you made, and witness will be the heaven called upon to validate the promise you made me]. These are the unspelling words that release him, and he responds with his ritualistic "Venciste, hermosa Dorotea, venciste" [You have conquered, beautiful Dorotea, you have conquered]. She has triumphed with the truth of her language where Camila had been vanquished by the deception of her artifice. In contrast, Dorotea's *artificio* is efficacious because it belongs to an ancient system of ritual signification deeply buried in the rhetoric of her Romance. The scenes at the inn have re-constituted this language in which the hero and heroine both escape their peril and find safety in one another's language.

This is the Romance that comes-to-be at the inn of Juan Palomeque, and with its conclusion we also have the resolution of Don Quixote's paradigmatic adventure. He has fulfilled the promise of his name and his original trajectory is completed. With the help of Dorotea and the language of women, he has disenchanted the inn. He is now ready for death. His return to the village in the cart is like that of his model Lancelot, whose original journey was a cart ride to his execution. The truth of the language of Romance will save the kingdom but the hero will die in the process.

So ends the adventure of Don Quixote, the knight of the mill, whose story saved the world of Romance.

Coda:
The Dark Night of the Word— A Sign of Trouble

Therefore, I think that tastes, odors, colors, and so on as regards the object in which they seem to reside are nothing but pure names . . .

Galileo, *Il Saggiatore* (The Assayer)

What is spoken is never, and in no Language, what is said.

Martin Heidegger

Our discussion of Romance began with a Celtic narrative frag ment describing the recovery of the *Táin*. The stories from the lost world of that culture, dating back at least to the Iron Age, provided the basis for a remarkably persistent tradition of narrative rhetoric that survived into the Renaissance (Jackson). In many ways *Don Quixote* marks a turning point in that tradition, one popularly recognized as the end of Romance and the birth of the novel. After the sixteenth century, Europe was no longer comfortable with Romance as a serious mode of discourse. It survived only in opera, a new generic mix of story and music, taking form just as *Don Quixote*, part 1, was published. Other less respectable formulations of Romance endured as stories for women or for children, as a de-privileged literature that in many cases never, at least until very recently, enjoyed the attention of the dominant critical establishment.

We likewise lost sight of the enduring importance of Romance. In the Middle Ages, even though under attack from Church and state, it had performed a crucial service for society in general. In an age in which all serious discourse excluded women, Romance alone included them and their matters. These concerns were in no way limited to their relationships to men, but incorporated problems of society, the cosmos, religion, and even women's involvement with the possibilities of human knowledge. In all these matters, Romance became the sole mode of education outside the halls of state and academe. It constituted the "other" discourse, the one that performed a civilizing task for both men and women. By the time of the Renaissance, works such as Jorge de Montemayor's *Diana*, Sydney's *Arcadia*, and even the defamed *Amadís de Gaula*, enjoyed the last brief period of society's attention.

It is appropriate that this inquiry conclude with another fragmentary and anonymous document, this one recently unearthed in the Archive of the Sacred Congregation for the Doctrine of the Faith in Rome. It dates probably from the 1620s, very shortly after the publication of *Don Quixote*, part 2, and reveals the troubled linguistic anxieties of the Counter Reformation, the world from which Dorotea had to carve out her survival. It tells us that the self-assured confidence of Renaissance humanism had run its course and that the new age was undercut with doubts in many areas of knowledge, language, religion, science, and philosophy.

The rise of an atomistic science was crowding out the old Platonic and Aristotelian verities and had begun re-writing the basis of European culture. Every aspect of belief was undergoing reformulations. Descartes was to re-write the nature of epistemology; the violence of the Thirty Years' War, begun three years after Cervantes' death, was re-ordering the cultural and political map of Europe; and in all the fields of knowledge the old beliefs were giving way to new insecurities. In Rome this disturbance was focused on the trial of Galileo. Along with his cosmology of worlds in motion, everything seemed to have come loose from its familiar fixed place. In art a sense of a floating universe, one with no fixed center, invaded human consciousness. Andrea Pozzi's spectacular and vertiginous ceiling for the new church of Saint Ignatius in Rome provided the visual rhetoric for this new de-centered universe. According to Pietro Redondi in his recent study *Galileo: Heretic* this aesthetic triumph "makes St. Ignatius into an allegorical representation of the Tridentine dogma of the Eucharist" (124). Within this context of displacement, confidence in the idea of language as an expression of a pre-existent Neoplatonic universe was to be profoundly shaken. In its place a battle line was drawn with the advent of new dictionaries, such as Covarrubias's *Tesoro* (1611), that in practice located all signifying power within the "atomistic" word itself. This attitude toward language was to persist until the twentieth century, when Saussure replaced it with the idea of signification as a product of the system rather than as a referential presence within the word.

This aspect of linguistic history is not usually addressed in a traditional philological studies, although Jonathan Culler's *Saussure* analyzes a similar linguistic reformation set into motion in our own century. His study reveals the general importance of how a culture at a given moment views the signifying power of its language. In practice, however, this problem is never voiced directly by the writers of an era, never brought out for open discussion. Nevertheless we do find this phenomenon implicitly written into the various discourses that appear upon the scene at such a moment. But it has not been much noted that *Don Quixote* as a text appears at just such a point in the history of Western literatures.

In the present study I have tried to address that problem by an extended examination of how the language works within that text, concen-

trating on certain key passages: the opening paragraphs, the hero's encounters at the inns, at the mills, and finally at the textual rupture in
chapter 23. This ushers in *entrelacement* as the organizing principle in its
narrative development and leads to Dorotea's triumph at the inn. In this
way Romance and the language of women emerge as the dominant force
in the creation of the novel as a generic discourse.

From this vortex the idea of a novel comes to be as a self-conscious
mode of discourse without any specific boundaries, as a text that lives off
the lexical, syntactic, and rhetorical environment that produced it. What
any language means at a given moment in time is, in this way, the nucleus
of the cultural and historical dynamic. For its readers a text can mean
only what this context allows it to mean. Only as the linguistic context
itself changes can new meaning, not necessarily a less important meaning, be created. A great text in this sense remains vital only by means of
its capacity to incorporate these signifying transformations.

Without pursuing the full value of such an assertion, it is still useful
to find other articulations of a text's possible meanings, ones situated
beyond the work itself and beyond what is normally considered literary
fictions. Pietro Redondi in his provocative re-examination of Galileo's
trial has uncovered such a document, one that compels a new reading of
the charges against Galileo. Based on an overlooked document, found by
Redondi in the Archives of the Holy Office in Rome, he has repostioned
that entire thrust of the trial.

His explanation of the nature of the trial, however, is not what concerns us here. Rather it is the curious document itself. This artifact is an
anonymous letter that brings to light a previously unknown reading of
Galileo's work *Il Saggiatore* (1623). Since the letter also cites earlier works
of Galileo, this challenge to the approved order of things deals with ideas
and attitudes contemporary with the both parts of *Quixote*. There is even
a strong Hispanic connection that places the arguments against Galileo
within the political and intellectual concerns of the Spanish party at the
Vatican. This faction was headed by no other than Cardinal Gaspare
Borgia, the Spanish ambassador, and the success of this endeavor almost
produced a collapse of the pontificate of Urban VIII. The unknown author of the document was clearly operating within the theological parameters of Spanish anxieties concerning the threat Galileo's writings
posed to the Tridentine dogma concerning the efficacy of the Eucharist.

Specifically cited among those concerns were the writings of Melchor
Cano, a Salamantine theologian, as they dealt with the definition of the

sacrament of the Eurcharist adopted by the Council of Trent. The author, following Cano, perceived that an atomistic re-organization of the physical sciences undermined the possibility of sacramental transubstantiation as it was then defined. Even more specifically, the performative efficacy of the liturgical language of the sacrament was at risk. In this perspective, the words themselves were deprived of referential value. The consequences were nothing less than apocalyptic in the judgment of the unknown author. According to Redondi, if Galileo had been tried on these charges instead of on his heliocentrism, he would have been burned at the stake as Giordano Bruno was. The actual trial, therefore, seems to have been a cover-up organized by Urban VIII to save his friend Galileo from such a sentence.

These conclusions, however well argued, are not what immediately concerns a reading of the *Quixote*, but the linguistic apprehensions of the unknown author of the letter are. He conceives the problem as a threat not only to the Church but to the more alarming problem of the possibility of meaning in human discourse.

It is in this kind of context that the writer raises the question of the language of the liturgy and the validity of the sacrament. In the claimant's attack we discern a heightened sense of cataclysmic fears operating just below the surface of public affairs. The writer senses a threat not only to the fabric of the political life of the time but to a comprehensive view of the meaning of human life. The heated struggle inside the Vatican was activated by the political interests of the Spanish monarchy in the Thirty Years' War. These concerns involved not only the divine order of things but also the more immediate threat of triumphant Protestant armies sweeping down upon Rome under the banner of the "King of the North," Gustavus Adolphus. The theoretical issues of the trial assume their place within these pressing and immediate threats to Spanish power in Italy and central Europe.

What concerns us is the question of the linguistic efficacy of sacraments. Are words effective enough to bring about divine changes in the substance of the *pane angelicus*? The specific issues of the debate seem rather remote today, and yet they clearly concern the problem of language as a transcendental force. Within the paranoid habitat of the Offices of the Inquisition such ideas were a matter of life and death for men and their institutions. This gives us a better idea of how Dorotea, a wild woman with her own de-stabilizing language, could have been read as a threat to the stability of the order of things. Romance as a mode of discourse had always posed this threat to "serious" matters, matters that concerned men and their cultural artifacts.

It is in this environment that the charges of the anonymous denouncement bring to the surface a sense of danger concerning the validity of language. The challenge has to do specifically with the terms *heat, color,* and *taste,* since these qualities had been expressly defined by the theology of Trent as existent within the bread. Even though Galileo's study never addressed the problem of the efficacy of the sacrament, his atomistic interpretation of the "qualities" of heat, color, and taste was revolutionary. He had argued that the quality of titillation in a feather rubbed beneath the nose resided not in the feather but in the nature of human perception. In this analysis heat, color, and taste were relocated outside the bread itself. For the author of the denouncement this is the red cape waved in the face of the Holy Office. The unknown author states:

> Therefore, the aforesaid Author [Galileo], in the book cited . . . , wishing to explain that proposition proffered by Aristotle in so many places—that motion is the cause of heat—and to adjust it to his intention, sets out to prove that these accidents which are commonly called colors, odors, tastes, etc., on the part of the subject, in which it is commonly believed that they are found, *are nothing but pure words* . . . thus these accidents which are apprehended by our senses and *are called tastes, smells, colors, etc.* are not, he says, subjects as one holds them generally to be, but only our senses, since the titillation is not in the hand or in the feather, which touches, for example, the sole of the foot, but *solely in the animal's sensitive organ.* (qtd. in Redondi 333, emphasis added)

A few pages later the document goes on to explain the relevance of these ideas to the Tridentine definition of the Eucharistic sacrament. The key instrument of transformation is *the power of language*:

> On this matter, judgment will fall to those who, teachers of a thought in conformity with truth and *scrupulous language,* watch over the safety of the faith in its integrity.
>
> Yet, I cannot avoid giving vent to certain scruples that preoccupy me. They come from what we have regarded as incontestable on the basis of the precepts of the Fathers, the Councils, and the entire Church.

> They are the qualities by virtue of which, although the sub-
> stance of the bread and wine disappear [as stated by the defini-
> tion of Trent], *thanks to omnipotent words* , nonetheless their *sensible
> species persist*; that is, their color, taste, warmth or coldness. Only
> by the *divine will are these species maintained, and in a miraculous
> fashion*, as they tell me. This is what they affirm.
>
> Instead, Galileo expressly declares that heat, color, taste, and
> everything else of this kind are outside of him who feels them,
> and therefore in the bread and wine, *just simple names*. Hence,
> when the substance of the bread and wine disappears [as taught
> by Trent], *only the names of the qualities will remain*.
>
> But would a perpetual miracle then be necessary to preserve
> *some simple names*? (336, emphasis added)

This would mean that the Godhead, in addition to performing the
miracle of transubstantiation, would also have to perform a miracle to
sustain the referential power of the language. The apocalyptic force of
this question for the writer appears a few lines later when he considers
the consequences of this problem:

> In the host, it is commonly affirmed, the sensible species (heat,
> taste, and so on) persist. Galileo, on the contrary, says that heat
> and taste, out of him who perceives them, and hence also in the
> host, *are simple names*; that is, *they are nothing*. One must therefore
> infer, from what Galileo says, that heat and taste do not subsist
> in the host. The soul experiences horror at the very thought.
> (emphasis added)

This kind of analysis indicates how, at certain levels of society, the question of the value of words was a matter of life and death. While the
unknown author is addressing theological problems relevant to atomistic
and field theory in physics, the nature of his arguments centers on the
question of a linguistic efficacy. Such hyper-sensitivity to language was
due to the theological battle lines of the Reformation and the Counter
Reformation, particularly as they concerned the validity of the sacrament
of the Eucharist, but such concerns did not differ from those effecting
biblical hermeneutics in general. The author lived in an age where "scru-
pulous" language, as he himself states, was still thought to be the fit
expression of a transcendental truth. Belief in the miracle of the mass was

in this way contingent on belief in the referential validity of language. He could not separate the belief in a divine event occurring at mass from the belief in the liturgical language itself as the cause of the miracle. A belief in an omnipotent God seems to translate in the infallibility of language. He does not recognize that such a deity would not be cirumscribed by the limits of human language. The author does not seemed to consider that if God could perform the miracle, He (not She) could also inform the language with the force needed for achieving transubstantiation. Why limit God to the defects of men's language? Yet the unknown author cannot conceive of a divine force operating outside the limitations of words, an obsession indicating the centrality of language as it was then understood. In the contentious atmosphere of Tridentine Rome, no force, divine or human, could transcend the restricted categories of the written word. There could be no trouble with the word.

The matter of the trial itself is secondary to the importance the denunciation placed upon the value of names. If they lacked referential presence, all human discourse was subverted and a sense of social chaos threatened civil order. Neither men nor words were reliable. This fear struck to his very soul.

Something of this concept of language is inherent in the problematics of Fernando's oath when he invokes the Virgin and a list of saints as his witnesses. At first sight this situation seems conventional enough in Dorotea's story. Such oaths were a common feature of everyday life. In fact within the *Quixote* Fernando's word is clearly of less value than that of the "puntualísima Maritones," who always honors her promise even if she gives it in the wilderness and without witnesses. The convention of the oath seems easily accommodated in the story only if one neglects to read the import of Dorotea's first words, which the priest overhears in the wilderness. There she places herself beyond the company of men because she can neither communicate her complaints to them nor seek remedy of her troubles from them. She is aware that she lives outside the possibilities of men's language, and their oaths are without meaning, whether witnessed by the saints or not.

But the more important question remains as to the validity of her own language during her story to the priest, where she cannot find words to express her own situation. It is only in her Micomicona story where she has recourse to the language of Romance that she can bring her story home to a good port and prepare herself for her confrontation with Fernando at the inn. After all an inn, like a wilderness, like an Otherworld locus, lacks the constraining forces of a fixed society. There she can fall back on the language of Romance, a language that takes its force from the language of women. This most ancient of languages, empowered with a pagan telluric force, allows for the expression of the truth of feelings of dismay and loneliness experienced in an alien world, whether that world be made up of rocks and trees or the affairs of men. In this situation she had to create a discourse that addressed her sense of self as a woman and at the same time, allowed her to speak to men in a meaningful way. Ultimately this language is much more threatening to the language of the patriarchs than is Galileo's atomism. Fortunately for Cervantes, this episode of Romance was read as a kind of story not relevant to serious matters, a tale for amusement only. Nonetheless, her language constitutes, as Romance always has, a power that irrevocably undermines the restrictive categories of men's affairs, but in so doing, it liberates the states of soul that define the human condition.

WORKS CITED

Adams, Alison, et al., eds. *The Changing Face of Arthurian Romance*. Cambridge: Boydell, 1986.

Amadís de Gaula. Garci Rodríguez de Montalvo. Juan Manuel Cacho Blecua, ed. 2 vols. Madrid: Catedra, 1988.

Auerbach, Erich. *Scenes from the Drama of European Literature*. Gloucester, MA.: Peter Smith, 1973.

Avalle Arce, Juan Bautista. *La novela pastoril española*. Madrid: Revista Occidente, 1959.

Bondanella, Peter. *The Eternal City: Roman Images in the Modern World*. Chapel Hill: U of North Carolina P, 1987.

Boyd-Bowman, Peter. *Léxico Hispanoamericano del siglo XVI*. London: Tamesis, 1971.

Brownlee, Kevin, and Marina Brownlee, eds. *Romance: Generic Transformation from Chrétien de Troyes to Cervantes*. Hanover: UP of New England, 1986.

Buckler, William E. *Novels in the Making*. New York: Houghton Mifflin, 1961.

Camurati, Mireya. *Poesía y Poética de Vicente Huidobro*. Buenos Aires: García Cambeiro, 1980.

Carilla, Emilio. *Manierismo y Barroco en las literaturas hispánicas*. Madrid: Gredos, 1983.

Casalduero, Joaquin. *Sentido y forma del "Quijote" (1605–1615)*. Madrid: Insula, 1970.

Cervantes, Miguel de. *Don Quijote*. Ed. John Jay Allen. 2 vols. Madrid: Catedra, 1989.

———. *Don Quijote de la Mancha*. Ed. Francisco Rodríguez Marín. 8 vols. 7th ed. Madrid: Espasa-Calpe, 1961.

———. *El ingenioso hidalgo don Quijote de la Mancha*. Ed. Rodriguez Marín. 8 vols. Madrid: Espasa-Calpe, 1964.

———. *Don Quixote*. The Ormsby Translation, Revised. Ed. Joseph R. Jones and Kenneth Douglas. New York: Norton, 1981.

Chadwick, Nora. *The Celts*. Harmondsworth: Penguin, 1984.

Chrétien de Troyes. *Le Roman de Perceval; ou, Le Conte du Gral.* Ed. William Roach. Genève: Droz, 1959.

———. *Perceval; or, The Story of the Grail.* Trans. Ruth Harwood Cline. Athens: U of Georgia P, 1985.

Close, Anthony. *The Romantic Approach to* Don Quixote. Cambridge: Cambridge UP, 1978.

Colie, Rosalie L. *The Resources of Kind: Genre Theory in the Renaissance.* Ed. Barbara K. Lewalski. Berkeley: U of California P, 1973.

Covarrubias, Sebastián de. *Tesoro de la Lengua Castellana o Española.* Ed. Martín de Riquer. Barcelona: Horta, 1943.

Culler, Jonathan. *Ferdinand de Saussure.* Rev. ed. Ithaca: Cornell UP, 1986.

Darrah, John. *The Real Camelot: Paganism and the Arthurian Romances.* London: Thames and Hudson, 1981.

DeMan, Paul. *The Rhetoric of Romanticism.* New York: Columbia UP, 1984.

Derrida, Jacques. *Of Grammatology.* Trans. Gayatri Chakravorty Spivak. Baltimore: Johns Hopkins UP, 1976.

De Santillana, Giorgio, and Hertha von Dechend. *Hamlet's Mill: An Essay on Myth and the Frame of Time.* 1977 Boston: Nonpareil-Godine, 1992.

Deyermond, Alan. "Problems of Language, Audience, and Arthurian Source in a Fifteenth-Century Castilian Sermon." *Josep María Solà-Solé: homage, homenaje, homenatge (miscelánea de estudios de amigos y discípulos).* Ed. Victorio Agüera and Nathaniel B. Smith. Barcelona: Puvill, 1984. 43–54.

Dillon, Myles. *Celts and Aryans.* Simla [India]: Indian Institute, 1975.

Dillon, Myles, and Nora K. Chadwick. *The Celtic Realms.* London: Weidenfeld, 1967.

Dudley, Edward. "Don Quijote as Magus: The Rhetoric of Interpolation." *Bulletin of Hispanic Studies,* 49.4 (1972): 355–68.

———. "Ring around the Hermeneutic Circle." *Cervantes* 6.1 (1986): 13–27.

Dudley, Edward, and Maximillian E. Novak, eds. *The Wild Man Within: An Image in Western Thought from the Renaissance to Romanticism.* Pittsburgh: U of Pittsburgh P, 1972.

Dundes, Alan, ed. *Sacred Narrative: Readings in the Theory of Myth.* Berkeley: U of California P, 1984.

Eisenberg, Daniel. *Romances of Chivalry in the Spanish Golden Age.* Newark, DE.: Cuesta, 1982.

———. *A Study of* Don Quixote. Newark, DE.: Juan de la Cuesta, 1987.

El Saffar, Ruth. *Beyond Fiction: The Recovery of the Feminine in the Novels of Cervantes.* Berkeley: U of California P, 1984.

Feal Deibe, Carlos. *En nombre de don Juan: Estructura de un mito literario.* Purdue University Monographs in Romance Languages 16. Ed. William M. Whitby. Amsterdam: Benjamins, 1984.

Fernández Gómez, Carlos. *Vocabulario de Cervantes.* Madrid: Real Academia Española, 1961.

Flores, R[obert] M. *The Compositors of the First and Second Editions of* Don Quixote *Part I*. London: Mod. Humanities Research Ass., 1975.

Forcione, Alban K. *Cervantes Aristotle and the "Persiles"*. Princeton: Princeton UP, 1970

Ford, Patrick. *The Mabinogi, and Other Medieval Welsh Tales*. Berkeley: U of California P, 1977.

Fowler, Alastair. *Kinds of Literature: An Introduction to the Theory of Genres and Modes*. Cambridge: Harvard UP, 1982.

Frappier, Jean. *Chrétien de Troyes: The Man and His Work*. Trans. Raymond J. Cormier. Athens: Ohio UP, 1982.

Freedberg, S[ydney] J[oseph]. *Circa 1600: A Revolution of Style in Italian Painting*. Cambridge: Belknap-Harvard UP, 1983.

Frye, Northrop. *The Secular Scripture: A Study of the Structure of Romance*. Cambridge: Harvard UP, 1982.

Gadamer, Hans-Georg. *Truth and Method*. Trans. and ed. Garrett Barden and John Cumming. New York: Crossroad, 1985.

Gantz, Jeffrey, trans. *The Mabinogion*. 1976. New York: Dorset, 1985.

———, trans. *Early Irish Myths and Sagas*. 1981. New York: Dorset, 1985.

Geoffrey of Monmouth. *History of the Kings of Britain*. Trans. Sebastian Evans. Rev. Charles W. Dunn. New York: Dutton, 1958.

Gimbutas, Marija. *The Language of the Goddess*. San Francisco: Harper, 1989.

———. *The Goddesses and Gods of Old Europe: 6500–3500 B.C..* Berkeley: U of California P, 1982.

Green, Miranda J. *Dictionary of Celtic Myth and Legend*. London: Thames and Hudson, 1992.

Guillén, Claudio. *Literature as System: Essays toward the Theory of Literary History*. Princeton: Princeton UP, 1971.

Heer, Friedrich. *The Medieval World*. Trans. Janet Sondheimer. New York: Mentor-NAL, 1963.

Heidegger, Martin. *Being and Time*. Trans. John Macquarrie and Edward Robinson. New York: Harper, 1962.

———. *An Introduction to Metaphysics*. Trans. Ralph Manheim. New Haven: Yale UP, 1959.

———. *On the Way to Language*. Trans. Peter D. Hertz. New York: Harper, 1982.

———. *Poetry, Language, Thought*. Trans. Albert Hofstadter. New York: Harper, 1971.

Hauser, Arnold. *Mannerism: The Crisis of the Renaissance and the Origin of Modern Art*. Vol. 1. London: Routledge, 1965.

Holmes, Urban Tigner, Jr. and M. Amelia Klenke. *Chrétien, Troyes, and the Grail*. Chapel Hill: U of North Carolina P, 1959.

Horney, Karen. *Neurosis and Human Growth*. New York: Norton, 1991.

Hubert, Henri. *The Rise of the Celts*. Trans. M. R. Dobie. New York: Dorset, 1988.

Jackson, K. H. *The Oldest Irish Tradition: A Window on the Iron Age*. Cambridge: Cambridge UP, 1964.

Jameson, Fredric. *The Prison House of Language: A Critical Account of Structuralism and Russian Formalism.* Princeton: Princeton UP, 1972.

Joyce, P. W. *Old Celtic Romances.* London: 1914.

Kennedy, William J. *Jacopo Sannazaro and the Uses of the Pastoral.* Hanover: UP of New England, 1983.

Kermode, Frank. *The Genesis of Secrecy: On the Interpretation of Narrative.* Cambridge: Harvard UP, 1979.

Keen, Maurice. *Chivalry.* New Haven. Yale UP, 1984.

Kinsella, Thomas, trans. *The Tain.* 1969. Oxford: Oxford UP, 1970.

Kruta, Venceslas. *The Celts of the West.* Trans. Alan Sheridan. London: Orbis. 1985.

Kuhn, Thomas S. *The Structure of Scientific Revolutions.* Chicago: U of Chicago P, 1970.

Lacy, Norris J., and Geoffrey Ashe. *The Arthurian Handbook.* New York: Garland, 1988.

Lacy, Norris J., et al. eds. *The Legacy of Chrétien de Troyes.* 2 vols. Amsterdam: Rodopi, 1987–88.

Lida de Malkiel, Maria Rosa. "Arthurian Literature in Spain and Portugal." *Arthurian Literature in the Middle Ages: A Collaborative History.* Ed. Roger S. Loomis. Oxford: Clarendon, 1959.

Lloyd-MOrgan, Ceridwen. "Perceval in Wales: Late Medieval Welsh Grail Traditions" *The Changing Face of Arthurian Romance* Ed. Adams, Alison et al. Cambridge: Boydell. (1986): 78–91.

Loomis, Roger Sherman. *Arthurian Tradition and Chrétien de Troyes.* New York: Columbia UP, 1962.

———. *Celtic Myth and Arthurian Romance.* New York: Columbia UP, 1927.

MacCana, Pronsias. *Celtic Mythology.* 1968. Library of the World's Myths and Legends. Feltham, Eng.: Newnes, 1983.

Malloy, J. P. *In Search of the Indo-Europeans: Language, Archaeology and Myth.* London: Thames and Hudson, 1989.

Markale, Jean. *Women of the Celts.* Trans. A. Mygind, C. Hauch, and P. Henry. Rochester, VT: Inner Traditions Int., 1986.

Meier, John P. "Jesus among the Historians." *New York Times Book Review* 21 Dec. 1986.

Munich, Adrienne. "Notorious Signs, Feminist Criticism, and Literary Traditions." *Making a Difference: Feminist Literary Criticism.* Ed. Gayle Greene and Coppelia Kahn. New York: Methuen, 1985.

Murillo, Luis. *The Golden Dial: Temporal Configuration in "Don Quijote."* Oxford: Dolphin, 1975.

Nelson, Lowry Jr.. *Cervantes.* Prentice Hall. Englewood Cliffs, N.J. 1969.

O'Driscoll, Robert. Ed. *The Celtic Consciousness.* New York: Braziller, 1982.

Owen, D. D. R., ed. *Arthurian Romance: Seven Essays.* Edinburgh: Scottish Academic P, 1975.

———. *The Evolution of the Grail Legend*. St. Andrews UP. 58. Edinburgh: Oliver, 1968.

Piggott, Stuart. *The Druids*. New York: Thames and Hudson, 1975.

Redondi, Pietro. *Galileo: Heretic*. Trans. Raymond Rosenthal. Princeton: Princeton UP, 1987.

Rees, Alwyn, and Brinley Rees. *Celtic Heritage: Ancient Tradition in Ireland and Wales*. 1961. London: Thames and Hudson, 1990.

Riquer, Martín de. *La leyenda del Graal y temas épicos medievales*. El Soto, 2nd ser. Madrid: Epañola, 1968.

———. *Aproximación al "Quijote."* Barcelona: Ed. Teide, 1967.

Rosenblat, Ángel. *La lengua del "Quijote."* Madrid: Gredos, 1971.

Russell, P. E. *Cervantes*. Oxford: Oxford UP, 1985.

Selig, Karl-Ludwig. "Cervantes: 'En un lugar de . . .' " *MLN*, 86 (1971): 266–68.

———. "Don Quixote I/22: The Exploration of Form in Mini-Form." *The Two Hesperides Studies in Honor of Joseph Fucilla*. Madrid: 1977.

———. "*Don Quixote* and the Game of Chess." *The Verbal and The Visual: Essays in Honor of William Sebastian Heekscher*. 203–11. Ed. Karl-Ludwig Selig and Elizabeth Sears. New York: Italica Press, 1990.

Sharrer, Harvey. "Malory and the Spanish and Italian Tristan Texts: The Search for the Missing Link." *Tristania*, 4.2. (1979).

Smith, Paul Julian. *Writing in the Margin: Spanish Literature of the Golden Age*. Oxford: Clarendon P, 1988.

Southern, R. W. *The Making of the Middle Ages*. New Haven: Yale UP, 1953.

Spitzer, Leo. *Linguistics and Literary History: Essays in Stylistics*. Princeton: Princeton U. Press, 1948.

Stagg, Geoffrey. "Revision in Don Quijote, Part I." *Hispanic Studies in Honour of Ignacio Gonzalez Llubera*. Oxford: Dolphin, 1959. 347–66.

———. "El sabio Hamete Venengeli." *Bulletin of Hispanic Studies* 33 (1956): 219–25.

White, Hayden. "The Forms of Wildness: Archaeology of an Idea." *The Wild Man Within: An Image in Western Thought from the Renaissance to Romanticism*. 3–38. Pittsburgh: U of Pittsburgh P, 1972.

Wilhelm, James J., and Laila Zameulis Gross, eds. *The Romance of Arthur*. New York: Garland, 1984.

Wilhelm, James J. *The Romance of Arthur II*. New York: Garland, 1986.

Williamson, Edwin. *The Half-Way House of Fiction: Don Quixote and Arthurian Romance*. Oxford: Clarendon, 1984.

Wilson, Diana de Armas. *Allegories of Love: "Persiles and Sigismunda"*. Princeton: Princeton UP, 1991.

INDEX